Cambridge English

EMPOWER

ADVANCED

Teacher's Book

C1

Wayne Rimmer
with Tim Foster and Julian Oakley

Welcome to *Cambridge English Empower*

A unique mix of learning and assessment

Cambridge English Empower is a new general English adult course that combines course content from Cambridge University Press with validated assessment from Cambridge English Language Assessment.

This unique mix of engaging classroom material and reliable assessment, with personalised online practice, enables learners to make consistent and measurable progress.

What could your students achieve with **Cambridge English Empower?**

Teacher's Book contents

For Students

Student's Book
with online access

**Online Assessment
Online Practice
Online Workbook**

Student's Book also available as Interactive eBook

Also available

- Student's Book (or eBook) without online access

- Print Workbook (with and without answers), with downloadable audio and video

For Teachers

Teacher's Book
with photocopiable activities and online access

Class Audio CDs

Class DVD

Presentation Plus

Student's Book with online access

- Comes complete with access to Online Assessment, Online Practice and Online Workbook – delivered via the Cambridge Learning Management System (CLMS)
- Syllabus informed by English Profile, the Cambridge English Corpus and benchmarked to the CEFR

Interactive eBook

- With the Interactive eBook, you can do the Student's Book activities in interactive form (specially designed for tablets), play all Class Audio and Video, check and display answers, control audio speed, create text and voice notes and more.
- The Interactive eBook can be accessed with the Cambridge Bookshelf iPad and Android apps, or using the Cambridge Bookshelf Web Reader on a desktop or laptop computer. With the iPad or Android app it can be used offline (after initial download).

Online Assessment

- Validated and reliable assessment throughout the course – developed by experts at Cambridge English Language Assessment
- A learning-oriented approach – assessment that regularly informs teaching and learning
- A Unit Progress Test for every unit (automatically marked) – covering grammar, vocabulary and functional language – plus a Unit Speaking Test
- Mid-course and end-of-course competency tests that cover all four skills and generate a CEFR report which reliably benchmarks learners to the target level

For more details about the **Cambridge English Empower** assessment package and Learning Oriented Assessment, please see pages 7–8.

Online Practice

- Personalised practice – automatically assigned according to each student's score in the Unit Progress Test, so their time is spent on what they need most
- Language presentations, practice activities and skills-based extension activities for every unit
- Automatically marked

Online Workbook

- Extra practice of all the grammar, vocabulary and functional language, plus extra writing
- Automatically marked

Teacher's Book

- Detailed teacher's notes for every lesson, including extra tips, ideas and support, and answer keys
- Photocopiable activities – a range of communicative extra practice activities for every unit, including grammar, vocabulary, pronunciation and Wordpower

Online access for teachers

To access **Cambridge English Empower**'s unique online assessment and practice package, please go to **cambridgelms.org/empower**, select 'Register' and follow the instructions.

Presentation Plus

- With Presentation Plus, you can display all Student's Book material, play all Class Audio and Video, show answer keys and more.
- Presentation Plus can be used with all types of interactive whiteboards, or with a computer and projector.

Class DVD

- All the video material for the Student's Book, plus Video Extra

Class Audio CDs

- All the listening material for the Student's Book

Print tests

- For print versions of the Unit Progress Tests and mid-course and end-of-course Competency Tests, please contact your local Cambridge representative: **cambridge.org/about-us/contact-us**

For more information and extra resources, go to:

cambridge.org/empower

Course methodology

A learner-centred approach

Cambridge English Empower, with its unique mix of learning and assessment, places the learner at the centre of the learning process. This learner-centred approach also applies to the course methodology – the Student's Book and additional resources provide a range of classroom materials that motivate learners, address their language needs and facilitate the development of their skills.

Supporting the teacher

Cambridge English Empower also supports the teacher through classroom methodology that is familiar and easy to use, and at the same time is flexible and creative. A number of key methodological principles underpin the course, enhancing the interface between learners and their learning, and between learners and teachers. **Cambridge English Empower:**

1 encourages learner engagement
2 delivers manageable learning
3 is rich in practice
4 provides a comprehensive approach to productive skills

Measurable progress

This leads to motivated learners, successful lessons and measurable progress. This progress is then measured by a uniquely reliable assessment package, developed by test experts at Cambridge English Language Assessment.

Key methodological principles

1   Learner engagement

Getting Started

Each unit begins with a Getting Started page, designed to engage learners from the very start of the unit – leading to greater motivation and more successful learning. It does this in the following ways:

- **Striking images** that take an unusual perspective on the unit theme – this raises curiosity, prompts ideas and questions in the mind of the learner, and stimulates them to want to communicate.
- **Speaking activities** that prompt a personal response – exploring beyond the surface of the image, providing a cognitive and linguistic challenge and a diagnostic opportunity for the teacher.

Remarkable texts and images

Throughout the C1 Student's book, learners encounter a range of **authentic reading texts** and a selection of **authentic broadcast audio** along with **specially recorded unscripted and scripted audio and video**. The texts have been carefully selected to appeal to advanced learners from a variety of cultural backgrounds. The topics will inform, amuse, surprise, entertain, raise questions, arouse curiosity and empathy, provoke an emotional response and prompt new insights and perspectives – this means that C1 learners are consistently motivated to deal with more complex language and engage with varied written and spoken styles.

Frequent opportunities for personal response

There are frequent opportunities to contribute personal views, experiences and knowledge to discussion of the themes in every lesson. Every lesson includes regular activities that encourage learners to respond personally to the content of texts and images. These include **personalisation** tasks which make the target language in every unit meaningful to the individual learner.

Independent learning

In order to progress, C1 learners must build their vocabulary and use a broad range of language appropriately. Reading and listening widely in English will help students to progress faster, as will good study skills. In Empower C1 the **Language in context** feature and **Learning Tips** support C1 learners both inside and outside the classroom. These features accompany the authentic texts and recorded audio and encourage learners to notice and systematically note topical sets, synonyms, collocations, idioms, metaphor, etc. The Teacher's Notes for each lesson include **Homework activities** which encourage learners to put the Learning Tips into practice in their independent learning and motivate further reading and listening outside the classroom.

2 Manageable learning

A second core principle that informs **Cambridge English Empower C1** is recognition of the importance of manageable learning. This offers learners (and their teachers) reassurance that the material is at the right level for advanced learners: the language syllabus avoids obscure language and the authentic reading and listening material is carefully chosen to be accessible whilst consistently acknowledging advanced learners' linguistic competencies and challenging them.
The **Cambridge English Empower C1** classroom material reflects the concept of manageable learning in three main ways:

Syllabus planning and the selection of language

A key element in making learning material appropriate for C1 concerns the selection of target language. In **Cambridge English Empower**, two powerful Cambridge English resources – the *Cambridge Corpus* and *English Profile* – have been used to inform the development of the course syllabus and the writing of the material. This means learners using **Cambridge English Empower C1** are presented with target language that includes:

Grammar

- a fresh approach to familiar language, accompanied by Cambridge Corpus-informed Tips, with notes on usage and typical errors, helping learners improve usage and tackle habitual mistakes
- lexical equivalents to grammatical structures – develop more precise and sophisticated language use
- structures likely to be new at C1 – for more sophisticated functions, e.g. emphasis or distancing, as well as more complex sentence structures, e.g. participle clauses and cleft sentences

Vocabulary

- lexical sets which build on existing knowledge and further develop the ability to use language precisely and flexibly – focusing on word-building, collocation and idiomatic use
- topical sets building learners' understanding of the precise meanings of closely related words and phrases
- topical sets encouraging appropriate use of rich descriptive language

The level is carefully designed to offer measurable progress through the core syllabus whilst they develop towards a C1 level of competency as independent individual learners.

Lesson flow

Teaching and learning is made manageable through the careful staging and sequencing of activities, ensuring that each individual learner at C1 will be challenged and engaged whilst working together as a class. Each lesson is comprised of several sections, each with a clear focus on language and/or skills. Each section builds towards the next, and activities within sections do likewise. Every section of language

input ends in an output task, offering learners the opportunity to personalise the target language. At the end of each lesson there is a substantial freer topical speaking and/or writing task motivating learners to use new language in a natural, functional context.

Task and activity design

Tasks and activities have been designed to give learners an appropriate balance between freedom and support. As an overall principle, the methodology throughout **Cambridge English Empower** anticipates and mitigates potential problems that learners might encounter with language and tasks. While this clearly supports learners, it also supports teachers because there are likely to be fewer unexpected challenges during the course of a lesson – this also means that necessary preparation time is reduced to a minimum.

How does Cambridge English Empower C1 meet the needs of Advanced Learners?

When learners join an advanced course they are already competent users of English, having achieved the B2 level. The Empower C1 level motivates advanced learners to further their skills and provides what they need to achieve C1 competency in the following ways:

- **Topics, tasks and texts with an appropriate level of cognitive and linguistic challenge** motivate learners by helping them to notice the gap between their current skills and those of a C1 user of English.
- As at all other levels, Empower C1 offers every learner **multiple communicative opportunities in every lesson**, helping them become fluent, natural and spontaneous speakers of English.
- **Regular focuses on register** help C1 learners to become flexible and effective users of English in a wide variety of spoken and written contexts.
- Learners improve their written style with extended controlled and semi-controlled practice in the **back of the book Writing Focus**. There is additional **writing practice in the A and B lessons**, when new language lends itself to written contexts.
- **Varied and stimulating texts** motivate learners to develop their reading and listening skills so that a wide range of texts become accessible.
- **Authentic reading texts** raise learners' awareness of style and register, and help build the broad vocabulary required of a C1 user of English.
- **A combination of authentic, semi-scripted and scripted listening material** exposes students to a wide variety of voices and natural, colloquial, idiomatic speech, whilst giving a strong focus on the language students need to produce themselves.
- The **Language in context** feature and **Learning Tips** support C1 learners to develop a broad vocabulary both inside and outside the classroom.

3 Rich in practice

It is essential that learners are offered frequent opportunities to practise the language they have been focusing on – they need to activate the language they have studied in a meaningful way within an appropriate context. **Cambridge English Empower** is rich in practice activities and provides learners and teachers with a wide variety of tasks that help learners to become confident users of new language.

Student's Book

Throughout each **Cambridge English Empower** Student's Book, learners are offered a wide variety of practice activities, appropriate to the stage of the lesson and real-world use of the language.

- There are frequent opportunities for spoken and written practice. Activities are clearly contextualised and carefully staged and scaffolded. Extended spoken and written practice is provided in the final activity in each of the lessons.
- In the 'Grammar Focus', 'Vocabulary Focus' and 'Writing Focus' pages at the back of the Student's Book, there are more opportunities for practice of grammar, vocabulary and writing skills, helping to consolidate learning.
- In the 'Review and Extension' page at the end of each unit, there are more opportunities for both written and spoken practice of target language.

Teacher's Book

- Many learners find practice activities that involve an element of fun to be particularly motivating. Many such activities – seven per unit – are provided in the photocopiable activities in the Teacher's Book, providing fun, communicative practice of grammar, vocabulary and pronunciation.
- The main teacher's notes also provide ideas for extra activities at various stages of the lesson.

Other components

Through the Cambridge LMS, **Cambridge English Empower** provides an extensive range of practice activities that learners can use to review and consolidate their learning outside the classroom:

- The Online Practice component offers interactive language presentations followed by practice and extension activities. Learners are automatically directed to the appropriate point in this practice cycle, according to their score in the Unit Progress Test (at the end of Student's Book lesson C).
- The Workbook (Online or Print) provides practice of the target input in each A, B, C and D lesson.
- The extension activities in the Online Practice component (via the Cambridge LMS) also offer further practice in reading and listening skills.

4 A comprehensive approach to productive skills

Most learners study English because they want to use the language in some way. This means that speaking and writing – the productive skills – are more often than not a priority for learners. **Cambridge English Empower** is systematic and comprehensive in its approach to developing both speaking and writing skills.

Speaking

The **C lesson** in each unit – 'Everyday English' – takes a comprehensive approach to speaking skills, and particularly in developing C1 learners to become flexible and effective users of language for social and professional purposes. The target language is clearly contextualised by means of engaging video (also available as audio-only via the Class CDs), filmed in the real world in contexts that will be relevant and familiar to adult learners. These 'Everyday English' lessons focus on three key elements of spoken language:

- Useful language – focusing on the discourse functions and speaking strategies that are most relevant to C1 learners' needs
- Pronunciation – focusing on intelligibility and the characteristics of natural speech, from individual sounds to extended utterances, developing C1 learners' ability to express finer shades of meaning by varying intonation and stress
- Idiomatic language (Language in context) – focusing on the use of high-frequency idiom in a variety of contexts and registers of social interaction

This comprehensive approach ensures that speaking skills are actively and appropriately developed, not just practised.

Writing

In the **Cambridge English Empower C1 Student's Book**, learners receive guidance and practice in writing a wide range of text types. The **D lesson** in each unit – 'Skills for Writing' – builds to a learning outcome in which learners produce a written text that is relevant to their real-life needs, appropriate to the C1 level, and related to the topic of the unit. However, these are not 'heads-down' writing lessons – instead, and in keeping with the overall course methodology, they are highly communicative mixed-skills lessons, with a special focus on writing. Each 'Skills for Writing' lesson follows a tried and tested formula:

1 Learners engage with the topic through activities that focus on speaking and listening skills.
2 They read a text which also provides a model for the later writing output task.
3 They then do a series of activities which explore the main features and structure of each genre of text as well as developing aspects of specific writing sub-skills that have been encountered in the model text.
4 They then go on to write their own text, in collaboration with other learners.
5 Process writing skills are embedded in the instructions for writing activities and encourage learners to self-correct and seek peer feedback.
6 The writing leads to a final communicative task, ensuring that learners are always writing for a purpose.

This means that writing is fully integrated with listening, reading and speaking – as it is in real life – and is not practised in isolation.

What is Learning Oriented Assessment (LOA)?

As a teacher, you'll naturally be interested in your learners' progress. Every time they step into your classroom, you'll note if a learner is struggling with a language concept, is unable to read at a natural rate, or can understand a new grammar point but still can't produce it in a practice activity. This is often an intuitive and spontaneous process. By the end of a course or a cycle of learning, you'll know far more about a learner's ability than an end-of-course test alone can show.

An LOA approach to teaching and learning brings together this ongoing informal evaluation with more formal or structured assessment such as end-of-unit or end-of-course tests. Ideally supported by a learner management system (LMS), LOA is an approach that allows you to pull together all this information and knowledge in order to understand learners' achievements and progress and to identify and address their needs in a targeted and informed way. A range of insights into learners and their progress feeds into **total assessment** of the learner. It also allows you to use all of this information not just to produce a report on a learner's level of competence but also to plan and inform future learning.

For more information about LOA, go to
cambridgeenglish.org/loa

How does Cambridge English Empower support LOA?

Cambridge English Empower supports LOA both informally and formally, and both inside and outside the classroom:

1 Assessment that informs teaching and learning
- Reliable tests for both formative and summative assessment (Unit Progress Tests, Unit Speaking Tests and skills-based Competency Tests)
- Targeted extra practice online via the Cambridge Learning Management System (CLMS) to address areas in which the tests show that learners need more support
- Opportunities to do the test again and improve performance
- Clear record of learner performance through the CLMS

2 LOA classroom support
- Clear learning objectives – and activities that clearly build towards those objectives
- Activities that offer opportunities for learner reflection and peer feedback
- A range of tips for teachers on how to incorporate LOA techniques, including informal assessment, into your lessons as part of normal classroom practice

1 Assessment that informs teaching and learning

Cambridge English Empower offers three types of tests written and developed by teams of Cambridge English exam writers. All tests in the course have been trialled on thousands of candidates to ensure that test items are appropriate to the level.

Cambridge English tests are underpinned by research and evaluation and by continuous monitoring and statistical analysis of performance of test questions.

Cambridge English Empower tests are designed around the following essential principles:

Validity – tests are authentic tests of real-life English and test the language covered in the coursebook

Reliability – tasks selected are consistent and fair

Impact – tests have a positive effect on teaching and learning in and outside the classroom

Practicality – tests are user-friendly and practical for teachers and students

Unit Progress Tests

The course provides an online Unit Progress Test at the end of every unit, testing the target grammar, vocabulary and functional language from the unit. The teacher and learner are provided with a score for each language area that has been tested, identifying the areas where the learner has either encountered difficulties and needs more support, or has mastered well. According to their score in each section of the test, the learner is directed either to extension activities or to a sequence of practice activities appropriate to their level, focusing on the language points where they need most support. This means that learners can focus their time and effort on activities that will really benefit them. They then have the opportunity to retake the Unit Progress Test – questions they got right first time will still be filled in, meaning that they can focus on those with which they had difficulty first time round.

Unit Speaking Tests

Cambridge English Empower provides a comprehensive approach to speaking skills. For every unit, there is an online Unit Speaking Test which offers learners the opportunity to test and practise a range of aspects of pronunciation and fluency. These tests use innovative voice-recognition software and allow the learner to listen to model utterances, record themselves, and re-record if they wish before submitting.

Competency Tests

Cambridge English Empower offers mid-course and end-of-course Competency Tests. These skills-based tests cover Reading, Writing, Listening and Speaking, and are calibrated to the Common European Framework of Reference (CEFR). They provide teachers and learners with a reliable indication of level, as well as a record of their progress – a CEFR report is generated for each learner, showing their performance within the relevant CEFR level (both overall and for each of the skills).

The **Cambridge Learning Management System** (CLMS) provides teachers and learners with a clear and comprehensive record of each learner's progress during the course, including all test results and also their scores relating to the online practice activities that follow the tests – helping teachers and learners to recognise achievement and identify further learning needs. Within the CLMS, a number of different web tools, including message boards, forums and e-portfolios, provide opportunities for teachers and learners to communicate outside of class, and for learners to do additional practice. These tools can also be used by teachers to give more specific feedback based on the teacher's informal evaluation during lessons. The CLMS helps teachers to systematically collect and record evidence of learning and performance and in doing so demonstrates to teachers and learners how much progress has been made over time.

2 LOA classroom support

Clear objectives

An LOA approach encourages learners to reflect and self-assess. In order to do this, learning objectives must be clear. In **Cambridge English Empower**, each unit begins with a clear set of 'can do' objectives so that learners feel an immediate sense of purpose. Each lesson starts with a clear 'Learn to ...' goal, and the activities all contribute towards this goal, leading to a significant practical outcome at the end of the lesson. At the end of each unit, there is a 'Review your progress' feature that encourages learners to reflect on their success, relative to the 'can do' objectives at the start of the unit. Within the lessons, there are also opportunities for reflection, collaborative learning and peer feedback.

LOA classroom tips for teachers

In a typical lesson you're likely to use some or perhaps all of the following teaching techniques:

- **monitor** learners during learner-centred stages of the lesson
- **elicit** information and language
- **concept check** new language
- **drill** new vocabulary or grammar
- encourage learners to **review and reflect** after they've worked on a task

The table below summarises core and LOA-specific aims for each of the above techniques. All these familiar teaching techniques are a natural fit for the kind of methodology that informally supports LOA. An LOA approach will emphasise those parts of your thinking that involve forming evaluations or judgements about learners' performance (and therefore what to do next to better assist the learner). The 'LOA teacher' is constantly thinking things like:

- *Have they understood that word?*
- *How well are they pronouncing that phrase?*
- *Were they able to use that language in a freer activity?*
- *How many answers did they get right?*
- *How well did they understand that listening text?*
- *How many errors did I hear?*
- *And what does that mean for the next step in the learning process?*

The **Cambridge English Empower** Teacher's Book provides tips on how to use a number of these techniques within each lesson. This will help teachers to consider their learners with more of an evaluative eye. Of course it also helps learners if teachers share their assessment with them and ensure they get plenty of feedback. It's important that teachers make sure feedback is well balanced, so it helps learners to know what they are doing well in addition to what needs a little more work.

Teaching techniques				
monitoring	**eliciting**	**concept checking**	**drilling**	**review and reflect**
Core aims • checking learners are on task • checking learners' progress • making yourself available to learners who are having problems	• checking what learners know about a topic in order to generate interest	• checking that learners understand the use and meaning of new language	• providing highly controlled practice of new language	• finding out what ideas learners generated when working on a task • praising learners' performance of a task • indicating where improvement can be made
LOA aims • listening to learners' oral language, and checking learners' written language, in order to: » diagnose potential needs » check if they can use new language correctly in context	• finding out if learners already know a vocabulary or grammar item • adapting the lesson to take into account students' individual starting points and interests	• checking what could be a potential problem with the use and meaning of new language for your learners • anticipating and preparing for challenges in understanding new language, both for the whole class and for individuals	• checking that learners have consolidated the form of new language • checking intelligible pronunciation of new language	• asking learners how well they feel they performed a task • giving feedback to learners on specific language strengths and needs • fostering 'learning how to learn' skills

Unit overview

Getting Started page
- clear learning objectives to give an immediate sense of purpose
- striking and unusual images to arouse curiosity
- activities that promote emotional engagement and a personal response

Lesson A and Lesson B
- input and practice of core grammar and vocabulary, plus a mix of skills

Lesson C
- functional language in common everyday situations
- language is presented through video filmed in the real world

Unit Progress Test
- covering grammar, vocabulary and functional language

Also available:
- Speaking Test for every unit
- mid-course and end-of-course competency tests

Lesson D
- highly communicative integrated skills lesson
- special focus on writing skills
- recycling of core language from the A, B and C lessons

Review and Extension
- extra practice of grammar and vocabulary
- Wordpower vocabulary extension
- 'Review your progress' to reflect on success

For extra input and practice, every unit includes illustrated Grammar Focus, Vocabulary Focus and Writing Focus sections at the back of the book.

Lessons A and B
Grammar and Vocabulary and a mix of skills

Authentic reading texts
Authentic texts raise learners'
awareness of style and register, and
help build the broad vocabulary
required of a C1 user of English.

Clear goals
Each lesson starts with a clear, practical
and achievable learning goal, creating an
immediate sense of purpose.

5A A place where you have to look over your shoulder

Learn to talk about crime and punishment
G Relative clauses
V Crime and justice

1 READING

a 💬 What do you think life in a typical prison is
like? Think of examples from your country or from
films and TV programmes.
1 What does it look like?
2 What are the conditions like? (cells, food, facilities,
activities for prisoners)

b 💬 Look at the photos of Halden prison in
Norway and answer the questions.
1 What do you think the conditions are like? (cells, food,
facilities, activities for prisoners)
2 What kinds of crimes do you think the prisoners here
might have committed?

Read the article and check.

c Read the article again and answer the questions.
1 On arrival, what two things does the writer notice?
2 How does Norway aim to deal with criminals?
3 Does the writer think the prison is like a hotel?
Why / Why not?
4 What are the aims of the design of the prison?
5 How are inmates motivated to do activities? Why?
6 What aspect of prison life does Kent find difficult?
7 What surprised the visiting prison governor?
8 What is the writer's impression of the atmosphere at
Halden?

d Work in pairs. Guess the meaning of the
highlighted words and phrases in the text. Then
check your ideas in a dictionary.

e 💬 Do you agree with Kent's statement in
italics in the text? Should prison be more about
punishment or rehabilitation? Why / Why not?

2 GRAMMAR Relative clauses

a Match the captions with the photos in the article.

1 ☐ Norwegian prison officers are tasked with rehabilitating the men in their
care, the result of which is a 20% reoffending rate, compared with 50%
in England.

2 ☐ Graffiti by Norwegian artist Dolk, from whom it was commissioned out
of the prison's 6m kroner (£640,000) art budget.

3 ☐ Welcome to Halden Prison, Norway, inside the walls of which prisoners
receive comforts often likened to those of boutique hotels.

4 ☐ The prisoners, some of whom have committed the most serious crimes
imaginable, are provided with plenty of opportunities for physical
exercise.

Can we have a swimming pool?
LIFE AT HALDEN PRISON
by Amelia Gentleman

H alden prison smells of freshly brewed coffee. It hits you
in the ¹communal apartment-style areas where prisoners
live together in groups of eight. The other remarkable
thing is how quiet the prison is. There isn't any of the
angry banging of doors you hear in British prisons, not least
because the prisoners are not locked up much during the day.

Halden is one of Norway's highest-security jails. Up to 252
criminals, many of whom have committed some of the most
serious offences, can be held there. Since it opened in 2010,
at a cost of 1.3bn Norwegian kroner (£138m), Halden has
acquired a reputation as the world's most ²humane prison. It is
the flagship of the Norwegian justice system, where the focus is
on rehabilitation rather than punishment.

Halden has attracted attention globally for its design and
comfort. Set in a forest, the prison blocks are a model of
³minimalist chic. At times, the environment feels more like
a Scandinavian boutique hotel than a class A prison. Every
Halden cell has a flatscreen television, its own toilet (which,
unlike standard UK prison cells, also has a door) and a shower,
which comes with large, soft, white towels. Prisoners have
their own fridges, cupboards and desks in bright new pine and
huge, ⁴unbarred windows overlooking mossy forest scenery.

Obviously the hotel comparison is a stupid one, since the
problem with being in prison, unlike staying in a hotel, is that
you cannot leave – hidden behind the silver birch trees is a
thick, tall, concrete wall, impossible to ⁵scale.

Given the constraints of needing to keep ⁶high-risk people
⁷incarcerated, creating an environment that was as unprisonlike
as possible was a priority for Are Høidal, the governor of
Halden, and the prison's architects. Høidal says, 'We felt it
shouldn't look like a prison. We wanted to create normality.
If you can't see the wall, this could be anything, anywhere.'

b Underline the relative clause in each caption
in 2a. Is it defining or non-defining? How can
you tell?

c Compare the clauses below with the examples
in 2a. What features of the clauses in 2a are
more formal?
1 which results in a 20% reoffending rate
2 who it was commissioned from out of the prison's
6m kroner art budget
3 where prisoners receive comforts often likened to
those of boutique hotels
4 who in some cases have committed the most
serious crimes imaginable

d ▶ Now go to Grammar Focus 5A on p.146

Regular speaking activities
Frequent speaking
stages to get
students talking
throughout the
lesson.

'Teach off the page'
Straightforward
approach and
clear lesson flow
for minimum
preparation time.

Regular focuses on register
Focuses on register
help C1 learners to
become flexible and
effective users of
English.

Rich in practice
Clear signposts to
Grammar Focus and
Vocabulary Focus
sections for extra
support and
practice.

56

Learner engagement
Engaging images and texts motivate learners to respond personally. This makes learning more memorable and gives learners ownership of the language.

Communicative outcome
Each input section is followed by a communicative outcome, so learners can use language immediately.

Manageable learning
The syllabus is informed by *English Profile* and the *Cambridge English Corpus*. Students will learn the most relevant and useful language, at the appropriate point in their learning journey. The target language is benchmarked to the CEFR.

Spoken outcome
Each A and B lesson ends with a practical spoken and/or written outcome where students can use language more freely.

HALDEN PRISON HAS BEEN COMPARED TO THE FINEST HOTEL

Prisoners are unlocked at 7.30am and locked up for the night at 8.30pm. During the day, they are encouraged to attend work and educational activities, with a daily payment of 53 kroner (£5.60) for those who leave their cell. 'If you have very few activities, your prisoners become more aggressive,' says Høidal. 'If they are sitting all day, I don't think that is so good for a person. If they are busy, then they are happier. We try not to let them get "institutionalised."'

Kent, a 45-year-old office manager serving a three-year sentence for a violent attack, is sitting in the prison's mixing studio. He admits he's enjoying being able to focus on his music, but says, 'Halden prison has been compared to the finest hotel. It is not true. The real issue is freedom, which is taken away from you. That is the worst thing that can happen to you. When the door slams at night, you're sat there in a small room. That's always a tough time.'

As we walk around the compound, an inmate comes up to ask Høidal, 'Can we have a swimming pool?' He laughs, and remembers the shock of a prison governor who visited recently and was horrified to see that the inmates didn't stand to attention when Høidal came past but instead 'clustered around him, seizing the chance to list their complaints.

The inmates tell Høidal they're annoyed by recent changes to the routine, but they are respectful when they 'address him. He listens politely, agrees that in prison 'minor irritations can become major frustrations, but remarks that people outside the building would laugh at the trivial nature of their complaints.

Maybe I'm not there long enough to sense hidden anger or deep despair, but Halden doesn't feel like a place where you have to look over your shoulder.

e What do you think prison life should be like? Complete the sentences with your own ideas.
1 Prisoners should *have their own / share* a cell, in which there should be:
_____ _____ _____ _____
2 Prisoners *should / shouldn't* have to do *some / any* kind of work, for which they should be paid '_____ per week.
3 The guards, _____ of whom should be trained in _____, should be paid _____ per week.
4 Prison meals, _____ of which should be _____, should be served _____ times a day.
5 The prison grounds …
6 Visitors …

f ⟲ Compare your ideas in 2e with other students. Whose prison is more like Halden?

A combination of authentic, semi-scripted and scripted listening material
The wide range of audio recordings exposes students to natural, colloquial, idiomatic speech, whilst giving a strong focus on the language students need to produce themselves.

The Language in context feature and **Learning Tips** support C1 learners to develop a broad vocabulary both inside and outside the classroom.

UNIT 5

3 VOCABULARY and SPEAKING
Crime and justice

a ▶2.34 Make the names of crimes by matching words and phrases from A with those in B. Then check the meanings in a dictionary. Listen and check.

A		B	
1	violent	a	corruption
2	tax	b	a controlled substance
3	possession of	c	assault
4	credit card	d	fraud
5	bribery and	e	evasion

b ▶2.35 Pronunciation Listen to the words below and notice the four different pronunciations of the letter *s*.
/s/ assault /ʒ/ evasion /z/ possession /ʃ/

c ▶2.36 Which sound in **bold** in the words below is different in each group? Listen and check.

1 assault   assassin   mission   dismiss
2 evasion   decision   explosion   impression
3 possession   cousin   comparison   reason
4 possession   permission   vision   Russian

d ⟲ Take turns giving definitions and examples of the crimes in 3a. Can your partner guess the crime?

e ▶ Now go to Vocabulary Focus 5A on p.162

4 LISTENING

a ⟲ What crime do you think is happening in the pictures?

b ⟲ Match the news headlines to the pictures.
☐ Cereal offender   ☐ Fake fan
☐ Would-bee burglar   ☐ The honest fraudster
☐ Dial a crime

c ▶2.37 Listen to the news stories and check. Then, in pairs, explain what's happening in each picture.

d ▶2.37 Listen again. In each story, how were the criminals caught or how do police hope to catch the criminals?

e Language in context *Crime*
Guess the meaning of the words in **bold**. Check your ideas in a dictionary.
1 … he **forged** the passport – it's a fake.
2 … he has been **detained** in a local facility …
3 They had this great plan to **pawn** them for cash …
4 … guess who was waiting? The police, of course, with the **handcuffs** ready!
5 Someone manages to **smuggle** in a mobile phone for him …
6 … the fraudster turns into an honest man – he **hands himself in**.

58

f ⟲ There are two puns in the headlines in 4b. What is a pun? Can you find and explain the puns in the headlines?

g ⟲ Discuss the questions.
1 Which crime do you think is the most serious?
2 Which criminal do you think is the least competent?
3 Do you find any of the stories funny? If so, which ones?

5 SPEAKING

a ⟲ Work in pairs. Discuss the criminals, 1–4. Decide on a fair form of punishment / rehabilitation for these crimes. Is there any further information you would need to make a judgment?
1 A 90-year-old man who is found guilty of income tax evasion over a period of 50 years.
2 A woman found guilty of causing death by dangerous driving. She swerved to avoid a pet cat and caused the death of a motorcyclist.
3 An airport employee who stole valuable items from suitcases that were left on carousels. She sold them for cash, or gave them away as presents.
4 A 17-year-old who has been caught shoplifting trainers. It's the first time he's been caught, but at home the police find a large collection of sportswear.

b ⟲ Work in groups of four. Are your suggestions for consequences similar? If not, can you agree on the consequences for each criminal?

Lesson C
Prepares learners for effective real-world spoken communication

Everyday English
Focusing on the functional language and speaking strategies that help learners to communicate effectively in the real world.

Spoken outcome
Each C lesson ends with a practical spoken outcome.

Real-world video
Language is showcased through high-quality video filmed in the real world, which shows language clearly and in context.

Comprehensive approach to speaking skills
A unique combination of language input, pronunciation and speaking strategies offers a comprehensive approach to speaking skills.

The **Language in context** feature in the C lessons broadens students' awareness of high-frequency idioms.

5C Everyday English
If I remember rightly

Learn to recall and speculate

S Deal with a situation without the facts
P Main stress

1 LISTENING

a Discuss the questions.

1 Do you find it easy to talk to people you've just met? Why / Why not?
2 Look at strategies a–e for talking to new people. Which of these do you use? Do you do anything else in particular?

a Open the conversation by commenting on something else that's happening around you.
b Pay them compliments where possible.
c Ask for personal information about where they live and what they do for a living.
d Try to be funny, but don't make jokes about other people. Always laugh at their jokes.
e Look for opportunities to empathise with them.

b ▶ 2.45 Watch or listen to Part 1. What strategies from 1a does Sara use? Note down some specific examples.

c What do you think the impact of Sara's conversation strategies will be on Max?

d ▶ 2.46 Language in context *Temporary states*

1 Match a–c with 1–3 to make phrases from Part 1. Listen and check.

a ☐ on a temporary   1 ups and downs
b ☐ hopefully, I'll snap   2 basis
c ☐ we all have our   3 out of it soon enough

2 Which phrases in 1 mean ... ?

a everybody experiences good times and bad times
b stop behaving in a negative way
c not permanently

e ▶ 2.47 Watch or listen to Part 2 and answer the questions.

1 What does Max think it's easier to write?
2 What had Sara assumed Max was doing?
3 What reason does Max give for his interview with Oscar being a disaster?

2 PRONUNCIATION Main stress

a ▶ 2.48 Listen to Max's lines below. Each pair of word groups ends with the same word, but it only receives the main stress in the first. Why?

1 a When your detective solves the <u>murder</u>,
  b you just invent <u>another</u> murder.
2 a He hadn't even read my <u>book</u>.
  b Hadn't even <u>opened</u> my book.

Choose the correct word to complete the rule.

The last word or phrase in a word group which gives *new / repeated* information is stressed.

b ▶ 2.49 <u>Underline</u> where you think the main stress in these pairs of word groups is. Listen and check.

1 a It's dangerous enough being a diver,
  b let alone a bomb disposal diver!
2 a I don't think wealth distribution in this country is fair –
  b quite the opposite of fair, in fact.
3 a I haven't got the right qualifications –
  b in fact, I've hardly got any qualifications!
4 a Halden is more than just a prison –
  b it's the world's most humane prison.

Practise saying the sentences.

62

Comprehensive approach to speaking skills
A unique combination of language input, pronunciation and speaking strategies offers a comprehensive approach to speaking skills.

3 LISTENING

a ▶2.50 Watch or listen to Part 3. How does Sara's meeting with Max nearly end in disaster?

b ▶2.50 Listen to Part 3 again and answer the questions.
1 What did Max think Sara's job was?
2 Why does Max say he wouldn't have agreed to meet a journalist?
3 What two reasons does Sara give for wanting to interview Max?

c 💬 Why do you think Max considers doing another interview?

Support for learners
Tasks are scaffolded to facilitate success.

4 USEFUL LANGUAGE Recalling and speculating

a ▶2.51 Complete the expressions from Parts 1, 2 and 3. Listen and check.
1 You're staying with Emma at the moment, **if my memory** _____ **me correctly**?
2 **I was** _____ **the impression that** you were writing another book?
3 **No** _____ you heard that from that guy from the radio interview.
4 **What** _____ **out in my mind** most **is** that that interview was a total disaster!
5 **I'd** _____ **a guess that** he hadn't even read my book.
6 _____, you're a technician, like Emma's boyfriend, right?
7 **I think I** _____ Emma saying that her boyfriend's a technician at *City FM*.
8 _____ you'd known, would you still have agreed to meet with me?

b Which expressions in 4a are used for recalling events? Which are used for speculating? Are there any which could be used for both?

c ▶2.52 Read this conversation. Find five mistakes and correct them. Listen and check.
A So when are you starting your new job? I was over the impression that you were starting next week.
B Oh, no. That would be too soon. I need a holiday first!
A But, if my mind serves me correctly – you went to Spain last month for a long weekend, didn't you?
B Who told you that?! I hazard a guess it was that sister of mine!
A Yeah, I think I remember she saying something along those lines.
B Well, you can't have too much of a good thing, can you? Presuming, you need a holiday too. Why don't you come with me?
A Well, I can't remember the last time I had a break. Why not?

d 💬 Practise the conversation in 4c with a partner.

e 💬 Recall your first day at school, or your first day in a job. Complete the sentences with your own ideas. Then tell a partner.
1 What stands out in my mind is …
2 I think I remember …
3 If my memory serves me correctly …

f 💬 Discuss the questions. Use expressions from 4a to speculate.
1 Why do you think writers sometimes suffer from writer's block?
2 Why do you think some famous writers avoid giving interviews?

Spoken outcome
Each C lesson ends with a practical spoken outcome.

Unit Progress Test
Learners are now ready to do the Unit Progress Test, developed by experts at Cambridge English Language Assessment.

5 SPEAKING

▶ Communication 5C Work in pairs.
Student A: Go to p.135. Student B: Go to p.137.

Unit Progress Test

CHECK YOUR PROGRESS

You can now do the Unit Progress Test.

Lesson D
Integrated skills with a special focus on writing

Skills for writing
The D lessons are highly communicative and cover all four skills, with a special focus on writing. They also recycle and consolidate the core language from the A, B and C lessons.

5D Skills for Writing
It's a way of making the application process more efficient

Learn to write an opinion essay

Ⓦ Essays; Linking: addition and reinforcement

1 LISTENING and SPEAKING

a 💬 Discuss the questions.
1 Do you use social media? If not, why not? If so, how often do you post comments about your work or study life? What kind of things do you say?
2 Do you think it's a good idea to post comments about work or study on social media? Why / Why not?

b 💬 You are an employer. You see these comments written by employees to their colleagues. How would you feel? What action (if any) would you take?

> Couldn't face it today – phoned in sick. Having a lovely day at the beach! ☺
>
> Our merger with Bookman & Associates looks imminent #superfirm #merger
>
> This year's pay offer – a miserable 1% increase. Do management live in our world or not?
>
> Things a bit slow at work today – spent all day online "doing research".

c 💬 Discuss the questions.
1 Have you ever heard of anyone losing a job because of something they did on social media? What did they post? Do you think that dismissal is fair punishment for work-related postings? Why / Why not?
2 What other types of posting on social media wouldn't employers approve of?

d ▶2.53 Listen to Mario and Laila talking about job applications and social media. What differences are there … ?
1 in the experiences they have had
2 in their attitudes and opinions

Receptive skills development
Challenging, motivating tasks practise and develop listening and reading skills while stimulating ideas for writing at C1.

e 💬 Read the opinions from Mario, Laila and their interviewers below. Tick (✓) the opinions you agree with and compare with a partner.
- ☐ It's essential that we project a positive image at all times – both in person and online.
- ☐ Demanding to see my social media is just a bit too Big Brother-ish for my liking.
- ☐ I don't really see a problem with employers having a look at my social media postings.
- ☐ I think that people tend to forget that just about anything you post online can be accessed in one way or another.
- ☐ If you don't want people to read it, then don't post it.

Personal response
Frequent opportunities for personal response make learning more memorable.

2 READING

a Read an essay about companies that research their job applicants on social media. Answer the questions.
1 Why do companies feel it's appropriate to use social media to find out about job applicants?
2 What are the reasons some job applicants are worried about this practice?
3 What position does the writer of the essay take on this topic?

b 💬 Do you agree with the writer's opinion? Why / Why not?

SOCIAL MEDIA AND
RECRUITMENT

① These days, an embarrassing photo on a person's social media profile might make all the difference when trying to land a top job. Increasingly, companies are examining applicants' social media profiles for information to use in the selection process.

② Young adults, many of whom have grown up with social media, are usually comfortable about sharing their lives online. Recently, however, some job applicants have voiced privacy concerns in relation to social media. They insist that their private life is private and is no business of any employer. In addition, they complain that companies go 'trawling' for negative information about applicants rather than getting a balanced general impression. They also express concern that they may be judged on the behaviour of their friends and family. What is more, some fear that employers may discriminate against them on factors such as their medical history or age.

1h ago

Comprehensive approach to writing skills
Clear focus on key aspects of writing helps
develop effective real-world writing skills.

Clear models for writing
Clear model texts are provided, on which
students can base their own writing.

3 WRITING SKILLS
Essays; Linking: addition and reinforcement

a What is the function of each paragraph in the essay?
  Match these descriptions with the paragraph
  numbers 1–4.

  ☐ to present ideas and opinions for one side of the
     argument
  ☐ to state the writer's final, balanced opinion of both
     arguments
  ☐ to present ideas and opinions for a second, contrasting
     side of the argument
  ☐ to outline the topic of the essay and get the reader's
     interest

b How does the writer create interest in the
  introduction?

  a ☐ state their opinion on the topic
  b ☐ refer to interesting facts and figures
  c ☐ make a surprising statement
  d ☐ clearly outline the issue to be discussed

  Which of the above are appropriate ways to begin an
  introduction to an essay? Why?

c How does the writer conclude the essay?

  a ☐ state their balanced opinion
  b ☐ briefly summarise key points
  c ☐ outline a possible course of action
  d ☐ introduce interesting new information

  Which of the above are appropriate ways to conclude
  an essay? Why?

d How many supporting arguments does the writer give
  for each side in paragraphs 2 and 3?

e Note the highlighted linker in paragraph 2. Underline
  more linking words and phrases in the essay that add
  information or reinforce an argument by adding a
  supporting idea.

f Write the words you underlined in 3e in the correct
  column of the table. Which linker highlights the most
  important argument?

Adds an idea in a new sentence	Adds two ideas in the same sentence
In addition	as well as

g Underline the linkers in these sentences and add them
  to the table in 3f.

  1 Beyond researching the applicant on social media,
    employers usually contact previous employers for
    references.
  2 It is standard to conduct a search of criminal records in
    addition to the methods mentioned above.
  3 It is often argued that a time-efficient process is best for all
    involved. Besides, time saved is money saved.

h ▶ Now go to Writing Focus 5D on p.172

Rich in practice
Clear signposts
to the **Writing
Focus** section for
extra support and
practice.

③ Employers argue that they are breaking no laws by
  researching their employees on social media – the
  information they are seeking is freely available. Moreover,
  as well as being a valuable tool for employers, social
  media provides information for the job applicant about
  the company they hope to work for. Above all, employers
  claim, their research makes the application process more
  efficient and allows them to filter out unsuitable applicants.

④ Whilst I agree that online research is a two-way process,
  I believe it is unfair for employers to judge an applicant's
  suitability solely on the basis of their social media postings.
  In particular, I understand applicants' concerns about
  'trawling'. Besides actively seeking negative information,
  the system clearly creates opportunities for employers
  to discriminate. I think the time has come for guidelines
  or laws to restrict the research employers can do.
  Furthermore, checks need to be made that their decisions
  are fair and transparent.

4 WRITING

a 💬 In some countries, employers are able to fire an
  employee without giving any reason for dismissal. Do
  you think this is fair? Discuss in small groups.

b Make notes of the ideas from the discussion in 4a.
  Organise your notes into opinions in favour of this idea
  and against it.

> 💡 **Writing Tip**
> When writing an essay on a controversial topic, it can help to
> talk to other people and note down opinions, even when these
> are not your own. Alternatively, brainstorm ideas from two
> different points of view. Your essay will be more interesting if you
> consider both sides of the issue and outline a range of opinions.

**Regular Writing
Tips**
Writing Tips in
every writing lesson
to help students
plan and improve
their writing.

c Write an essay on the fairness of employers dismissing
  employees without having to give a reason. Consider
  the points of view of both employers and employees
  and include your own opinion.

d Read another student's essay. Do you mention the
  same points? Is your opinion the same?

3h ago

65

Also in every unit:
- Review and
  Extension page
- Grammar Focus
- Vocabulary Focus
- Writing Focus
- Communication Plus

Syllabus

Lesson and objective		Grammar	Vocabulary	Pronunciation	Everyday English
Unit 1 Language (Teacher's Notes p.20)					
Getting started	Talk about animals learning language				
1A	Talk about second language learning	Adverbs and adverbial phrases	Language learning; Noun forms	Word stress: noun forms with -tion and -ity	
1B	Describe languages and how they change	The perfect aspect	Describing changes	Sentence stress	
1C	Express yourself in an inexact way			Sound and spelling: ea, ee and ie	Expressing yourself in an inexact way
1D	Write a web forum post				
Review and extension	More practice		**WORDPOWER** Idioms: Body parts		
Unit 2 Going to extremes (Teacher's Notes p.36)					
Getting started	Talk about tolerance of extreme conditions				
2A	Describe extreme sensory experiences	Comparison	Multi-word verbs: Social interaction	Consonant–vowel linking	
2B	Talk about plans, intentions and arrangements	Intentions and arrangements	Verbs of movement	Word groups and main stress	
2C	Give advice			Emphatic stress	Giving advice
2D	Write a report				
Review and extension	More practice		**WORDPOWER** Idioms: Movement		
Unit 3 Travel and adventure (Teacher's Notes p.52)					
Getting started	Talk about a mishap on a road trip				
3A	Emphasise positive and negative experiences	Inversion	Wealth and poverty	Tone in inversion structures; Word stress	
3B	Describe journeys and landscapes	Future in the past; Narrative tenses	Landscape features	Sound and spelling: the letter t	
3C	Paraphrase and summarise			Consonant groups across two words	Paraphrasing and summarising
3D	Write a travel review				
Review and extension	More practice		**WORDPOWER** Idioms: Landscapes		
Unit 4 Consciousness (Teacher's Notes p.66)					
Getting started	Talk about manipulating the senses				
4A	Talk about using instinct and reason	Noun phrases	Instinct and reason	Sound and spelling: /ʃəs/, /iəs/, /dʒəs/	
4B	Talk about memories and remembering	have / get passives	Memory	Sentence stress	
4C	Use tact in formal discussions			Homophones in words and connected speech	Being tactful in formal discussions
4D	Write a profile article				
Review and extension	More practice		**WORDPOWER** mind		
Unit 5 Fairness (Teacher's Notes p.81)					
Getting started	Talk about activities for prisoners				
5A	Talk about crime and punishment	Relative clauses	Crime and justice	Sound and spelling: s and ss	
5B	Talk about job requirements and fair pay	Willingness, obligation and necessity	Employment	Word stress: nouns and verbs	
5C	Recall and speculate			Main stress	Recalling and speculating
5D	Write an opinion essay				
Review and extension	More practice		**WORDPOWER** Idioms: Crime		

Listening and Video	Reading	Speaking	Writing
BBC interview: Second language learning	Quotes: four celebrities' language learning experiences	Describing experiences of language learning Discussing language learning factors	Five pieces of advice for language learners
Monologue: the origins of words Four monologues about how languages change	Article: *How quickly is the English language changing?* Fact file: *How languages are special*	Speculating when English words originated Discussing interesting facts about your language and others	Changes in your world
Friends and rivals		Sharing rough details of an experience	⟳ Unit Progress Test
Monologue: the dominance of English as a world language	Four discussion board posts	Predicting the main points of a talk and discussing your predictions	Web forum post Expressing opinions
Monologue: *My vow of silence*	Article: *I've been to the quietest place on Earth*	Questionnaire: *How sensitive are you to sound?* Discussing different views on communication	
Interview with a base jumper	Leaflet: *Itching for a good thrill?* Article: *Why some of us are thrill-seekers*	Giving opinions on extreme sports and dangerous activities Discussing a blog post	Blog post: a new experience
A guest overstays his welcome		Advising a friend on a tricky situation	⟳ Unit Progress Test
Four monologues about university social programme activities	Report: Review of a social programme and recommendations	Discussing the merits of activities for a social programme	Report Linking: contrast and concession
BBC talk: *The problem with volunteering,* Daniela Papi	Two reviews: *Thinking of volunteering abroad?*	Discussing volunteer work abroad Describing new experiences	Blog post: an unusual travel or tourism experience
BBC audio blog: *Journey of a lifetime,* Will Millard	Narrative article: *Survival on the Mano River*	Telling the story of an adventurous trip	Article: an adventurous journey
A disastrous interview		Paraphrasing and summarising in informal conversations	⟳ Unit Progress Test
Two monologues about Prague	Traveller's review: *Prague get-away weekend*	Describing the best and worst places you have been as a tourist Expressing an opinion about a place	Travel review Descriptive language; Writing briefly
BBC radio discussion: gut instinct in medical diagnosis	Article: *Learn to trust your gut!*	Quiz: *Do you have a sixth sense?* Dilemmas: would you go with your gut instinct?	
Four monologues about childhood memories	Article: *False childhood memories* Article: *How eyewitness evidence can be unreliable*	Talking about a childhood memory Giving an eyewitness account of a crime Discussing ways to improve memory	
Feedback and an unexpected opportunity		Giving opinions tactfully	⟳ Unit Progress Test
Interview: musician Nora Manning	Profile article: *Nora Manning: 'I come back from travelling with my head full of music'*	Asking and answering questions about being interviewed for a profile article Interviewing a classmate for a profile article	Profile article Organising information; Showing time relationships
Radio news: bizarre crimes	Article: *Can we have a swimming pool? Life at Halden Prison*	Giving definitions of crime vocabulary Discussing punishments for crimes	
Four monologues about employment	Four job descriptions: *Bomb disposal diver, Private butler, Ethical hacker* and *Social engineer*	Discussing employment terms and conditions Exchanging information about different jobs Negotiating salaries for a range of jobs	
Opening up		Dealing with a situation without the facts	⟳ Unit Progress Test
Two monologues about job applications and social media	Essay: *Social media and recruitment*	Discussing how an employer should respond to employee comments on social media	Opinion essay Essays; Linking: addition and reinforcement

Lesson and objective	Grammar	Vocabulary	Pronunciation	Everyday English
Unit 6 Perspectives (Teacher's Notes p.96)				
Getting started Talk about the impact of 3-D street art				
6A Describe photos and hobbies	Simple and continuous verbs	Adjectives: Describing images	Sentence stress	
6B Tell a descriptive narrative	Participle clauses	Emotions	Main stress and emphatic stress (adverbs and adjectives)	
6C Organise a presentation			Tone in comment phrases	Organising a presentation
6D Write a letter of application				
Review and extension More practice		**WORDPOWER** Idioms: Feelings		
Unit 7 Connections (Teacher's Notes p.110)				
Getting started Talk about technologies in the classroom				
7A Speculate about inventions and technology	Speculation and deduction	Compound adjectives	Main stress: compound adjectives	
7B Emphasise opinions about the digital age	Cleft sentences	Nouns with suffixes: Society and relationships	Tone in cleft structures	
7C Apologise and admit fault			Sound and spelling: *ou* and *ough*	Apologising and admitting fault
7D Write a proposal				
Review and extension More practice		**WORDPOWER** *self-*		
Unit 8 Body and health (Teacher's Notes p.126)				
Getting started Talk about physical activity in old age				
8A Describe sleeping habits and routines	Gerunds and infinitives	Sleep	Sentence stress	
8B Talk about lifestyles and life expectancy	Conditionals	Ageing and health	Pitch: extra information	
8C Negotiate			Intonation in implied questions	Negotiating
8D Write promotional material				
Review and extension More practice		**WORDPOWER** *and*		
Unit 9 Cities (Teacher's Notes p.142)				
Getting started Talk about obstacles to urban development				
9A Talk about city life and urban space	Reflexive and reciprocal pronouns	Verbs with *re-*	Sound and spelling: *re-*	
9B Describe architecture and buildings	Ellipsis and substitution	Describing buildings	Word stress	
9C Deal with conflict			Sound and spelling: foreign words in English	Dealing with conflict
9D Write a discussion essay				
Review and extension More practice		**WORDPOWER** *build*		
Unit 10 Occasions (Teacher's Notes p.158)				
Getting started Talk about an unusual wedding				
10A Give a presentation or a speech	Regret and criticism structures	Communication verbs	Word groups and main stress	
10B Talk about superstitions and rituals	Passive reporting verbs	Superstitions, customs and beliefs	Consonant groups	
10C Take turns in more formal conversations			Tone in question tags	Turn-taking
10D Write a film review				
Review and extension More practice		**WORDPOWER** *luck and chance*		
Communication Plus p.127	**Grammar Focus** p.138		**Vocabulary Focus** p.158	

Listening and Video	Reading	Speaking	Writing
Interview with an amateur photographer	Article: *Lessons Elliott Erwitt has taught me about street photography*	Discussing photography skills Talking about your favourite photos	
Narrative: the conclusion of *You are now entering the human heart*	Short story: *You are now entering the human heart*	Discussing the themes of a piece of fiction Reading a short story aloud	Creating an alternative ending to a short story
A big presentation		Presenting an application for a grant	**Unit Progress Test**
Five conversations about things to see and do in the local area	Advertisement: article writers required for local magazine	Talking about what's going on in your local area	Letter of application Formal letters; Giving a positive impression
Three monologues: inventions that would make the world a better place	Article: *I'm about to interview a robot.*	Discussing questions to ask a robot Presenting a new invention	
Radio programme: *From My Bookshelf*	Article: *Loneliness and temperature*	Talking about what you read online Explaining how you would overcome a hypothetical problem	
Unsolicited suggestions		Dealing with a situation where you are at fault	**Unit Progress Test**
Four monologues: people express their opinions of their colleagues	Proposal: a team-building programme for senior management	Ordering the personality attributes required to be an effective team member	Proposal Linking: highlighting and giving examples
Radio interview with a sleep researcher Radio phone-in programme about waking up at night	Article: *Top tips to help you sleep* Article: *The myth of the eight-hour sleep*	Discussing tips for a good night's sleep Planning a typical day for someone with a segmented sleep pattern	
BBC interview: living on a calorie restricted diet	Article: *Anti-ageing treatments* Interview: *We don't have to get sick as we get older*	Discussing anti-ageing treatments Presenting your views on health and ageing issues	
An exclusive story		Negotiating the price of a product or service	**Unit Progress Test**
Radio interview: *The Stone Age Diet*	Homepage: *Ancestors Restaurant*	Discussing what's important when you eat out	Promotional material Using persuasive language
Podcast: new ideas for 'smart cities'	Article: *Exhibition Road London's first example of 'shared space'* Fact files: four city initiatives	Sharing information about initiatives to improve cities Presenting ideas for 'smarter' cities	
BBC news report: *'Pants' skyscraper? China reacts against latest tall building*	Article: *Zaha Hadid 'I don't make nice little buildings'*	Describing buildings Presenting a proposal for the redevelopment of a derelict building Role play discussing the state of a town	
A leak and a fall out		Complaining and responding to complaints	**Unit Progress Test**
Conversation: life in a rural community in New Zealand compared to life in a city	Essay: urban migration	Discussing rural and urban living	Discussion essay Linking: reason and result
Three monologues about giving a presentation	Article: *How to give a killer presentation*	Discussing what makes a good presentation Giving a one-minute speech: *Learning from my mistakes*	
Radio interview: superstitions in the theatre	Article: *The game before the game*	Discussing superstitions, customs and beliefs Role play talking about plans and responding Explaining theatrical superstitions	The origins of the *Macbeth* superstitions in the theatre
A successful interview		Taking turns in an interview	**Unit Progress Test**
Four monologues about how people use reviews	Two film reviews: *Whiplash*	Discussing how much reviews influence your choices	Film review Concise description

| Writing focus p.169 | Audioscripts p.176 | Verb patterns p.190 | Irregular verbs p.191 |

UNIT 1

Language

UNIT CONTENTS

G GRAMMAR
- Adverbs and adverbial phrases (types and position)
- The perfect aspect (for complete and incomplete states and actions)

V VOCABULARY
- Language learning (Verb phrases): *acquire a (new/second) language, attain (a level/degree of competence), brush up (my Arabic), get accustomed to sth, get rusty, get to grips with sth, grasp new ideas, have an ear for (languages), hold a conversation, immerse yourself in sth, keep at sth, pick up (phrases), put sth into practice, struggle with sth*
- Noun forms: *acquisition, capability, competence, dedication, discipline, distraction, exposure, insight, interaction, interference, limitation, literacy, mentality, motivation, necessity, prestige, reluctance*
- Describing changes: *barely perceptible, clearly on the increase, grow substantially, (not) be noticeable, on a rapid rise, on the way out, ongoing, a steady shift over time, subtle, take hold*
- Language in context: Expressing meaning; Irony and understatement
- Wordpower: Idioms: Body parts: *be a safe pair of hands, be head and shoulders above sb, bite your tongue, fight tooth and nail, have a nose for, lose your head, stick your neck out*

P PRONUNCIATION
- Word stress: noun forms with *-tion* and *-ity*
- Sentence stress
- Sound and spelling: *ea, ee* and *ie*

GETTING STARTED

OPTIONAL LEAD-IN

Books closed. Ask students to write a sentence about one thing they did yesterday, e.g. *I downloaded a film for my sister*. Tell students to draw a maximum of three symbols or pictures to represent their sentence. Put students into pairs to look at each other's drawings and 'translate' them into a sentence. Ask the class how effective this system of communication is and how it could be improved.

a Ask students what animal this is (a bonobo /ˈbɒnəbəʊ/ – a small, intelligent African ape with black or brown fur, similar to a chimpanzee), and which country this is (the USA – *Center* is spelled the American English way on the woman's T-shirt). Give students one

 UNIT OBJECTIVES

At the end of this unit, students will be able to:
- understand and summarise details, attitudes and opinions in texts about language learning experiences and how the English language is changing
- follow broadcasts and lectures about language acquisition and English as a global language and note and summarise details and attitudes
- understand details, allusions and jokes in idiomatic conversations between colleagues
- use lexis accurately and appropriately to discuss and describe their own learning experiences, factors in language learning, changes and unique language features
- use a range of expressions in interaction and descriptions to express themselves in an inexact way when appropriate
- express opinions in a web forum post clearly and respond to the opinions of others with an awareness of register and the emotional impact of their choice of lexis

minute to think about their answers to the questions before talking about the photo as a class. If you wish, give students information from the Culture notes below.

CULTURE NOTES

This photo shows a scientist and a bonobo at the Language Research Center, Georgia State University, USA, communicating through a keyboard which has lexigrams instead of letters. Lexigrams are symbols which represent objects or ideas. Bonobos and chimpanzees have been trained to recognise and reproduce sequences of lexigrams to communicate with humans and others of their own species. There is some evidence that these apes can produce sounds, unrecognisable to humans, which correspond to lexigrams and are comprehensible to other bonobos/chimpanzees. Generally, the linguistic capabilities of animals is a controversial topic and while all animals can communicate, some scientists feel that language proper is restricted to humans.

b Pre-teach *converse* (have a conversation with someone). Put students into groups to discuss the questions. If students need encouragement, prompt them with ideas from the Suggested answers below. Take feedback as a class.

Suggested answers
1. sport, e.g. a jockey and horse; disabled people and service dogs; owners with pets
2. primates generally, dolphins and whales, dogs, parrots

EXTRA ACTIVITY

Play Pictionary. Whisper a word to one student. The student has to draw a picture representing that word on the board for the other students to guess. Students cannot speak, use gestures or write words on the board. Students take turns to draw the word you tell them. Start with easier words to illustrate, e.g. *furniture, run,* and then give more abstract words, e.g. *problem, law*.

1A I learned French entirely by ear

At the end of this lesson, students will be able to:

- read and understand a text about why and how different people learn languages
- use adverbs and adverbial phrases in their correct positions in a sentence
- use a lexical set related to language learning
- understand a BBC radio interview with a language expert about second language learning amongst native English speakers
- form nouns from adjectives and/or verbs in the same word family

💡 OPTIONAL LEAD-IN

Books closed. Use a 'live listening' to give students a chance to find out about you and introduce the topic of the lesson. Write or project the statements from 1a on the board and give students time to read them. Explain to students that you are going to tell them about your own language learning experience(s) and that you want them to decide which of the statements they think you might agree with. Talk for about three minutes about your experience(s), making sure you cover one or two of the areas in the statements, e.g. *I moved here to Italy four years ago and so I was able to immerse myself in the language every time I went out in the street. However, I really struggled with … .* Put students into small groups to compare what they understood and decide which statements you might agree with. Check answers as a class.

1 READING

a 💬 Ask students to read the statements and think about whether they agree with them. Put students into pairs or small groups to discuss their opinions before discussing their ideas as a class.

b Students read the texts and decide who might agree with each of the statements in 1a. Encourage students to guess the meaning of the words in the Vocabulary support box if they ask about them. Help with the meanings if necessary. They then compare their ideas in pairs. Take feedback as a class and ask students to share the reasons for their answers, e.g. *Chris Packham says, 'I want you to constantly correct me.' so I think he must agree with statement 1.*

Suggested answers

1 Chris Packham (I want you to constantly correct me.)
2 Thomasina Miers (The flavour and the language are linked because you know the taste and the memory and the words are all kind of caught up and bound into one,) Chris Packham (I bought some wildlife books … because I understood the context, I was able to read them cover to cover …)
3 Caroline Wyatt (She says she involuntarily uses her hands whilst talking in French, and in German becomes somewhat more direct.)
4 Nobody states or implies agreement with this statement. Ellen MacArthur might partially agree for a spoken second language (I'm now fluent, though having learnt the language almost entirely by ear… my written French is terrible.)
5 All: Thomasina Miers (I wanted to go and speak Spanish. I wanted to talk to everyone …); Ellen MacArthur (It opened up the warmth of a culture to me; a way into a world that I didn't at the time really understand, or even knew existed in my early teens.); Caroline Wyatt (Speaking the language makes a huge difference to how people relate to you … It enables you to relate to people in a different way …); Chris Packham (What's brilliant is that I can meet up with my neighbours now and have a laugh with them …)
6 Ellen MacArthur (I'm now fluent, though having learnt the language almost entirely by ear …)
7 Caroline Wyatt (Having another language from a very young age accustoms your mind to the idea that there are many different ways or words with which to express concepts and objects …)

📖 VOCABULARY SUPPORT

drink sth in – listen to, look at, or experience something with great interest and enjoyment

guttural – a sound produced at the back of the throat and therefore deep

earthy – basic, simple and natural

unpretentious – appearing simple and natural, not trying to be something else

resonating – connecting and evoking particular memories, feelings and emotions in your mind

draw sb in – attract somebody and make them become involved

be caught up / be bound into one – be joined together in a way that can't be separated

immersion – literally, to put something in a liquid until it is covered, here used figuratively to mean to be totally surrounded by something

nuance – a very small difference in something, which, although hardly noticeable, has an important effect

mannerism – specific characteristics a person has, particularly the way they speak or make small movements

shaky start – a beginning that is not firm, strong or confident

stint – a period of time, often short, spent doing something specific

shape (v.) (C2) – make something develop over time in a particular way

c 💬 Tell students to read the texts again in detail and encourage them to guess the meaning of any new words from the context. In pairs, students discuss the questions. Take feedback as a class and encourage students to justify their answers to questions 1–3 as far as possible using extracts from the texts. Finally, ask them which person they relate to most, and why.

2 GRAMMAR
Adverbs and adverbial phrases

a Individually, students add the highlighted adverbials from the texts to the lists. Check answers as a class.

Answers

2 absolutely, almost, entirely, somewhat, enormously, extraordinarily
3 by ear, properly, fluently, involuntarily
4 first, now
5 constantly

b Talk about the first adverbial with the class. Elicit that it can be used either at the front of the sentence or at the end, but not in the middle. Ask students: *Does the meaning of 'in the end' change depending on the position in the sentence?* (No, it doesn't.). In pairs, students then discuss the other adverbials. Check answers as a class, feeding in the additional information in the Language notes below as appropriate.

Answers

1 b 1, 2, 3
2 a 3 b 1, 2
3 a 1, 2, 3 b 3
4 a 3
  b 1, 3 See the Language notes below for changes in meaning (between position 1 and position 3).
5 a 1, 2, 3 See the Language notes below for changes in meaning (between position 1/2 and position 3).
  b 1 (used to indicate an explanation will follow), 3 (adverb of manner)

📖 LANGUAGE NOTES

Some adverbials have different meanings in different positions. In the examples in 2b, the following adverbials change meanings:

*   *clearly* used at the front or in the middle of a sentence indicates that you consider what you are about to say obvious, e.g. *Clearly, you need to learn French if you want to live in France.* It can also be used at the end to mean that something is (not) easy to understand, e.g. *The line's terrible, could you speak more clearly?*

*   *naturally* used at the front or in the middle of a sentence indicates that you consider what you are about to say totally normal and unsurprising, e.g. *Naturally, he failed the exam – he hadn't done any work!* It can also be used at the end to mean that something is done in a normal way, e.g. *Relax and try to behave naturally.*

c ▶ **1.2–1.5** Students read the information in Grammar Focus 1A on SB p.138. Play the recording where indicated and ask students to listen and repeat. Students then complete the exercises. Check answers as a class, making sure students are pronouncing the adverbs and adverbial phrases correctly. Tell students to go back to SB p.9.

Answers (Grammar Focus 1A SB p.138)

a 3 ✓
  4 … was utterly exhausted.
  5 ✓
  6 (Beforehand,) I had had a nasty feeling (beforehand).
  7 (Certainly,) That (certainly) was (certainly) the best game so far.
  8 ✓
  9 … have repeatedly ignored …
  10 ✓
  11 ✓
  12 We decided to go home by taxi.
b 2 … we still can't answer …
  3 … are simply ridiculous.
  4 It has even been said … / that we even copied
  5 No doubt language developed …
  6 … (dramatically) increased (dramatically) in size (dramatically) … became a great deal more …
  7 Also, unfortunately for other animals, we …
  8 (Undoubtedly,) group behaviour would (undoubtedly) have made … language absolutely essential.
  9 We probably won't ever know …
  10 … language will always fascinate …

⊙ CAREFUL!

The most common student mistake with adverbials is word order error, particularly after the verbs *be* and *have*, e.g. ~~The third day of our trip wasn't very good also.~~ (Correct form = … *our trip **also** wasn't very good.*). At C1 level, the most likely error is for students to place the adverbial too late in the sentence, e.g. ~~You can find easily an English-language newspaper to read at the library.~~ (Correct form = *You can **easily find** an …* with the adverb of manner placed before the correct verb).

💡 FAST FINISHERS

Ask fast finishers to look at the five categories of adverbials on SB p.9 (comment, degree, manner, time, frequency) and the sentences in Grammar Focus Exercises a and b and find at least one example for each category of adverbial, e.g.:

comment: ***Presumably**, your wife …*

degree: *Some of the theories are **simply** ridiculous.*

manner: *The secretary put the phone down **abruptly**.*

time: *I had had a nasty feeling **beforehand**.*

frequency: *… the origins of language will **always** fascinate us.*

d 💬 Books closed. Read out the first speech bubble in 2d and ask students to imagine what you might be talking about, e.g. *salsa dancing, playing tennis*, etc. Then read out the second speech bubble and ask students to refine their ideas, e.g. *Well, it can't be salsa dancing, but it could be playing tennis.* Finally, read the last speech bubble and elicit their ideas, e.g. *It must be playing golf!* Ask students: *Can you remember which adverbials I used?* (obviously, properly, extremely). Books open. Give students a few minutes to work individually and think of an experience to talk about. Help with vocabulary as necessary. Stress that students should not tell their partner what skill they are talking about. In pairs, students take turns to tell each other about their experience and try to guess what skill their partner is talking about.

🔄 LOA TIP MONITORING

*   Be careful not to interfere with pair or group work as you monitor. Students may want to ask you questions if you stand in front of them, which will stop their interaction.

*   Do not join in the discussion to prompt, give your personal reaction or correct errors. Let students speak and give feedback after the activity.

*   Discourage students from appealing to you during the activity by not making eye contact with them as you monitor.

*   It is worth explaining these 'rules' of pair/group work in your first lesson and repeating them when you set up tasks like this.

💡 EXTRA ACTIVITY

Choose an activity you do or a skill you have, but don't tell students what it is, e.g. *playing the piano*. Say a sentence about the activity using an adverbial, e.g. *This is something I do fairly well.* Elicit what type of adverbial you have used (manner) and ideas of what you might be talking about, but don't confirm the answer yet. Using a variety of adverbials from the lesson and Grammar Focus 1A, continue saying sentences until you have given students five in total, e.g. *Usually, I do this in the evenings and on Sunday mornings.* (frequency). *Every Thursday afternoon I have a 20-minute lesson to help me do this better.* (time). *The people in the flat below get very annoyed if I play late at night.* (degree). *Apparently, my great-grandmother was an excellent player and gave concerts.* (comment). After each sentence, students identify the type of adverbial used and guess what you are talking about. After five sentences, tell students what the activity or skill is if they haven't already guessed. In pairs or small groups, students then invent sentences of their own and repeat the activity.

3 VOCABULARY Language learning

a Individually, students match the underlined parts of the texts with the definitions. Check answers as a class.

Answers
1 c 2 d 3 a 4 b

b ▶ ⏵**1.6** Students complete the exercises in *Verb phrases* in Vocabulary Focus 1A on SB p158. Play the recording for students to check their answers to Exercise a. Monitor Exercise b and check answers as a class. Tell students to go back to SB p.9.

Answers (Vocabulary Focus 1A SB p.158)
a 1 acquire 2 struggle 3 attain 4 accustomed 5 brushed
   6 ear 7 hold 8 practice 9 keep 10 immersed
   11 pick 12 get 13 rusty
b 1 c 2 a 3 d 4 e 5 f 6 b

c Give students a few minutes to read the questions and think of two more questions. Monitor and point out errors for students to self-correct.

d 💬 Put students into pairs to ask and answer the questions. Take feedback as a class on any answers students gave which their partner found particularly interesting.

4 LISTENING

a 💬 Discuss the questions as a class and encourage students to justify their answers.

b ⏵**1.7** Draw students' attention to the photo and give them some basic information about Susanna from the Culture notes below. Then give students time to read through the sentences. Play the recording. Students listen to the conversation for general meaning and tick the points Susanna makes. Check answers as a class.

Answers
1 ✓ 2 ✓ 4 ✓

Audioscript

INTERVIEWER Let's hear now from Susanna Zaraysky. She speaks seven languages, and spent many years teaching English abroad and has even written a book called *Language is Music*. Um … Is this er … reluctance to learn foreign languages, um … just a feature of Britain or, do you think, all English-speaking peoples?

SUSANNA I think it's all over the English-speaking world and I think there are two main reasons: one, as I agree with your previous speaker that there's a lack of necessity. People don't see the necessity and, so, necessity breeds motivation, and for example we see that in Brazil there are English-language schools popping up everywhere because they need to learn English to be able to sell their products abroad. The other reason is, is that English speakers have little to no exposure to the sounds of foreign languages because almost all of our media is in English, so people in other countries will start to listen to music in English, watch programmes er … from the United States or from the UK or from other parts of the world in English. And so they get used to the sounds and prior er … exposure to the sounds of a language make it much easier for a student to learn a language and it's much more fun, when you have music and … and media.

I Is that what happened to you? I mean were you exposed to foreign languages from a young age?

S I was. I mean, I was born in the former Soviet Union and I came to the United States when I was three but I grew up in an area with a large Hispanic population and Vietnamese population, so I heard Spanish from a young age even though I didn't start formally studying it until I was 15 or 16. So I already knew a lot of songs in Spanish when I started learning. So, when I had to learn grammar and words, I … I had a context in which to reference to what I was learning in school. And because I already knew songs, I already knew some words and it was fun and I could pronounce things. So music is a huge aspect of language learning.

I So, you had a bit of a head start if you like, but um what would be your advice to other English speakers, perhaps averse to learning foreign languages?

S To find music that they like in the other language. Um … to find television programmes that they like in the language … To watch movies in the other language. Because your heart has to resonate with the language. You have to actually like it, because you live a language more than you study it. So you have to find something that you like about it. For example, if somebody likes watching soc … uh … football, they can watch football programmes in another language, so they're at least getting used to what it sounds like. Um … If they like a certain type of a movie, whether it's animation, they could look for those type of animation programmes in other languages.

I And er it's worth it, you reckon?

S Of course, of course. Because, you know, people … you get paid more money usually in government jobs if you speak another language. You have much more oppor … You have many more opportunities to do trade if you speak another language. And, I mean, in the United States we have 20 per cent of our population speaks another language at home, so even for domestic marketing reasons it's important.

I Susanna Zaraysky, who speaks seven languages.

📖 LANGUAGE NOTES

Highlight that the interview with Susanna Zaraysky is one of the many authentic recordings in *Empower*. Remind students that even native speakers frequently make mistakes when speaking and that there are a huge number of variations in the kinds of English used around the world. Point out that it is an important skill for higher-level learners to be able to deal with speakers who do not speak 'perfect' English. If students mention errors in recordings, e.g. speakers forming sentences which are grammatically incorrect, ask them to correct them.

CULTURE NOTES

Susanna Zaraysky was born in St Petersburg but moved to the USA when she was three. She is a polyglot and to date she has studied eleven languages, seven of which she can speak fluently. She has written two books, *Language is Music* and *Travel Happy, Budget Low*, and regularly speaks to teachers and students around the world about learning foreign languages.

c ⏵**1.7** Before students listen for specific details and answer the questions, use the Vocabulary support box to help with vocabulary if necessary. Play the recording again. Students compare answers in pairs. Check answers as a class.

Suggested answers

1 Because they want to be able to sell products abroad.
2 Hearing and getting used to the sounds of a language can make it much easier and much more fun to actively study a language.
3 Knowing a lot of songs in Spanish gave her a context for grammar and vocabulary, and helped her with pronunciation.
4 She means that you have to find real motivation to learn the language and find things you can enjoy doing in that language. She suggests finding something you enjoy doing in your own language, like watching certain types of TV programmes or films, and doing this in the language you are trying to learn.
5 She says that people who speak other languages usually get paid more money in government jobs. She also says that there are a lot more international business opportunities open to people who speak other languages. And it's also useful for business within the USA as 20 per cent of people speak another language at home.

📖 VOCABULARY SUPPORT

breed (C2) – cause something to happen

pop up – appear or happen, especially suddenly or unexpectedly

reference (v.) – if writing or information references someone or something, it relates to that person or thing

head start – an advantage that someone has over other people in something such as a competition or a race

🅦 FAST FINISHERS

Ask fast finishers to think about the English language music and media they currently engage with and discuss it with another fast finisher. Tell them to list their recommendations for other students in the class.

d 💬 Put students into small groups to discuss the questions. If students are interested and motivated by the topic, extend this to a full-class discussion.

5 SPEAKING and VOCABULARY

Noun forms

a ⏵**1.8** Books closed. Write sentence 1 from 5a on the board including the gap but without the word in brackets. Point to the gap and ask: *What kind of word do we need here?* (noun). Write *reluctant* on the board and ask: *What kind of word is this?* (adjective). Then ask students to change the adjective to the noun form and elicit the spelling. Books open. Students complete sentences 2–4 individually. Play the recording for students to check. Check spelling as a class.

Answers

1 reluctance 2 necessity 3 motivation 4 exposure

b ⏵**1.9** Students complete the exercises in *Noun forms* in Vocabulary Focus 1A on SB p.158. Check the answers to Exercise d as a class and play the recording for students to complete the Pronunciation activity. Read the Learning Tip with the class and monitor Exercise f. Tell students to go back to SB p.10.

Answers (Vocabulary Focus 1A SB p.158)

d 1 interaction 2 distraction 3 ded<u>ic</u>ation 4 lim<u>it</u>ation
   5 mot<u>iv</u>ation 6 ne<u>ces</u>sity 7 cap<u>ab</u>ility 8 men<u>tal</u>ity
   9 reluctance 10 interference 11 competence 12 literacy
   13 exposure 14 acquisition 15 insight 16 prestige
   17 discipline
e 1 limitation, capability, mentality
   2 See the underlining in Exercise d above.
   3 the syllable before the suffix

🅦 EXTRA ACTIVITY

Books closed. Play a 'last one standing' game with the class. Tell students to stand up and explain that you are going to give them a word from the table in Exercise d on SB p.158 and a part of speech. They have to change the word to the form you give them, spell the word correctly and use it in an example sentence. The first student who is ready to do that knocks on the table and has to answer immediately. Any student who does not answer immediately or makes any mistakes is eliminated and sits down. Give students an example, e.g. *necessary – noun*. Ask the first student who knocks on the table to give you the noun form (*necessity*), the correct spelling and an example sentence with the word, e.g. *Doing your homework is an absolute necessity if you want to learn a language.* When you are sure students have understood the activity, play the game. Continue the game using words from the table on SB p.158 until only one student is left standing and is declared the winner.

🅦 HOMEWORK ACTIVITY

⏵ Ask students to follow the advice given in the Learning Tip and record the vocabulary in Exercises d and f on SB p.158 according to their suffixes.

c 💬 Read through the factors with the class and elicit a few ideas for each item from the students. Then put students into pairs and give them time to discuss each of the factors in more detail. Take feedback as a class.

d Read about the first person together and ask students if they know anyone who matches the description. Then elicit some pieces of advice for that person from the class. Suggest students choose the person who they think they have the most advice for before they work individually and write their pieces of advice. Monitor and help as necessary.

e 💬 Put students into pairs or small groups. They then compare their ideas and make additional suggestions if appropriate. Finally, ask each pair to choose four suggestions to share with the class during feedback.

ADDITIONAL MATERIAL

⏵ Workbook 1A

⏵ Photocopiable activities: Grammar p.201, Vocabulary p.221

At the end of this lesson, students will be able to:

- talk about the meanings of words and how meanings evolve and change with time or distance
- understand a text about how the English language is changing and relate the content to specific examples
- describe changes, being precise in both the speed/ scale of the change and the register of the language
- use the perfect aspect correctly for completed actions and unfinished actions and states
- understand a fact file about unusual language features and suggest similar facts about their own language

⊗ OPTIONAL LEAD-IN

Books closed. Write *synonyms* in a circle in the centre of the board. Then draw five lines off it and five smaller circles with *good*, *bad*, *angry*, *nice* and *pretty*. Put students into five pairs or small groups and assign each pair/group one of the words. Give them two minutes to think of synonyms for their word, e.g. *fine*, *wicked*, *cross*, *pleasant*, *attractive*, etc. Regroup students so that the new groups have at least one person for each word on the board. Students copy and complete the word web, telling each other their words and suggesting any additional ones they can think of. In class feedback, ask five students to come up to the board and complete the word web for each of the five different words. Point out and correct any spelling mistakes. Elicit and add any additional words to the word web on the board. Ask students to correct and complete their word webs as necessary.

1 SPEAKING

a 💬 In small groups, students discuss the words and what they mean. Take feedback as a class but don't check the answers at this point.

b 💬 In their groups, students decide when each word was first used in English, giving reasons for their decisions. Again elicit students' ideas as a class but don't check answers.

c ▶**1.10** Students listen to the recording for specific details and check their answers to 1a and 1b. They then discuss the significance of the two pictures in their groups. Check answers as a class and use the Vocabulary support box to help with vocabulary if necessary.

Answers

1900s radio
1910s environmentalism
1920s spacecraft
1930s babysitter
1940s technophobe
1950s brainwash
1960s in-joke
1970s Bollywood
1980s ecotourism
1990s blog
2000s sudoku
2010s selfie
Photo 1 shows the first known selfie, taken by Robert Cornelius in 1839, around 170 years <u>before</u> the word *selfie* was first used.
Photo 2 shows the first real spacecraft, the Sputnik, launched in 1957, around 30 years <u>after</u> the word *spacecraft* was first used.

Audioscript

NARRATOR The word 'radio' was first used in the 1900s, although of course radios were invented long before that, in the 1820s, but they were originally called 'wirelesses'.
The word 'environmentalism' was first used in the 1910s. People began to be concerned about pollution and wildlife towards the end of the 19th century, and in 1916 a National Park Service was set up in the USA to help protect wildlife.
The word 'spacecraft', meaning any kind of spaceship or satellite, first appeared in the 1920s, at about the same time that science fiction stories became popular in films and magazines. However, the first real spacecraft, the Russian Sputnik, wasn't launched until 1957.

People started talking about 'babysitters' in the 1930s, and the word 'technophobe', meaning someone who has a fear of technology, was first used in the 1940s. This was about the time when people started using technology such as vacuum cleaners and washing machines in the home. 'Brainwashing' is making people believe an idea by constantly telling them it's true. This word was introduced in the 1950s. And an 'in-joke' – a joke that is only understood by a particular social group – was first used in the 1960s.
In the 1970s people first started talking about 'Bollywood' – the Indian film industry based in Bombay – in other words, the Bombay version of Hollywood.
The concept of 'ecotourism' came in in the 1980s when the tourism industry began to respond to the demand for tours which benefited, or at least did not harm, the local ecosystem.
The 1990s saw the invention of 'blogs' – originally called 'web logs' – as more and more people became connected by the Internet. And, in the 2000s, people all over the world started doing the Japanese puzzle, sudoku.
The word 'selfie' was introduced in 2013, to describe photos people take of themselves with their mobiles – although the first known selfie was taken 170 years earlier by Robert Cornelius, who took a photo of himself using a mirror in 1839.

📖 VOCABULARY SUPPORT

environmentalism – an interest in or the study of the environment, in order to protect it from damage by human activities

spacecraft – a vehicle used for travel in space

technophobe – someone who dislikes new technology, especially computers, and is not able to use it with confidence

brainwash – make someone believe something by repeatedly telling them that it is true and preventing any other information from reaching them

in-joke – a private joke that can only be understood by a limited group of people who have a special knowledge of something that is referred to in the joke

Bollywood – the centre of the Hindi film industry, based mainly in the Indian city of Mumbai, which used to be called Bombay

ecotourism – the business of organising holidays to places of natural beauty in a way that helps local people and does not damage the environment

sudoku – a number game in which you have to write a number between 1 and 9 in each small box of a 9x9 square

selfie – a photograph that you take of yourself, usually with a mobile phone. Selfies are often published using social media.

d 💬 Write a new word that has recently come into the English language on the board and elicit its meaning, e.g. *e-learning* (learning done by studying at home using computers and courses provided on the Internet). Give students two minutes to discuss the question in their groups and make a list. Ask groups to feed back to the class on any interesting new words and add them to the board.

💡 EXTRA ACTIVITY

Tell students that two new words that have recently come into the English language are *bikeable* and *hackable*. Elicit the meaning of the verb suffix *-able* (= can be) and ask students to think of words they know with this suffix, e.g. *breakable*, *loveable*. Ask students to make up five new words by adding *-able* to verbs and then check in a dictionary to see if they exist. Tell students that even if they don't exist, the meaning would be clear to native speakers as *-able* is used creatively in speech.

---

2 READING

a Students work individually, reading the text and identifying the points the writer makes. They compare answers in pairs before checking answers as a class. Use the Vocabulary support box to help with vocabulary if necessary.

Answers
Many changes to language take place gradually so we may not notice them.
Modern technology has helped us to see how language is changing.

📖 VOCABULARY SUPPORT

perceptible – that can be seen, heard or noticed

plague (C2) – cause worry, pain or difficulty to someone or something over a period of time

transcribe – record something written, spoken or played by writing it down

---

b Give students time to read the questions and think about their answers. They then discuss their ideas in pairs before sharing their answers and ideas with the class.

Answers
1 *far out*: strange and unusual, or excellent
   rad: extremely exciting or good
   wicked: excellent
   awesome: extremely good
2 Students' own answers

c ▶ Divide the class into pairs and assign A and B roles. Student As read about language changes 1 and 2 on SB p.127 and Student Bs read about language changes 3 and 4 on SB p.137. They answer the question and prepare to explain how each heading represents the change described. Monitor to check students understand what they have to do and clarify any problems before the pairwork stage. Tell students to go back to SB p.11.

Answers
Student A
The first heading is a famous quote from Shakespeare highlighting that *to* + infinitive is more old-fashioned, and the question *To be or not to be?* suggests that there is an alternative to using *to* + infinitive.
The second heading shows an example of the use of the continuous (or progressive) verb form with *be* which wouldn't have sounded correct 150 years ago.

Student B
The first heading uses *Do you want to* rather than the more formal *Would you like to*.
The second heading uses the *get* passive, which the text says is taking over from *to be* in passive structures.

d 💬 Put students into A/B pairs. Students look at the sentences, discuss which sentences show the changes they read about and explain these changes to their partner. Monitor and identify students who give good, clear explanations for each item and describe the change accurately. Allow time for class feedback and ask these students to share their explanations with the class.

Answers
1 yes (Student B, Text 3: Modal verbs are gradually giving way to other less formal expressions …)
2 yes (Student B, Text 4: … the use of *get* passives has grown substantially.)
3 yes (Student A, Text 1: … there was a steady shift toward more frequent use of the verb + *-ing* after verbs like *begin*, *start*, *like*, *love* and *hate* and these are still on the increase.)
4 yes, both students (Student A, Text 2: Constructions such as *I must be going now* … wouldn't have sounded correct 150 years ago, but nowadays are fairly high frequency.)
(Student B, Text 3: words like *shall* and *ought* are on the way out and words which cover the same ground, such as *going to*, *have to*, *need to* and *want to* are taking hold.)

---

3 VOCABULARY Describing changes

a Individually, students read the sentences and match the expressions in bold with the kinds of changes. Check answers as a class.

Answers
a 6, 10, 11
b 9
c 2, 4, 5, 8
d 11, 12
e 3, 8, 14
f 1
g 7, 10, 13, 14

b 💬 Give students a few minutes to write their sentences. Monitor and point out errors for students to self-correct. Then put students into small groups to compare their ideas. Take feedback as a class.

💡 FAST FINISHERS

Ask fast finishers to work together and change phrases 1, 2 and 5 in 3b to mean the opposite and then make suggestions for the category, i.e. 1 *something that is on the way in in your culture* (= something which is just about to start to become common or fashionable), 2 *a place that hasn't changed at all*, 5 *a major change to a popular product*.

4 LISTENING and GRAMMAR
The perfect aspect

a ▶**1.11** Tell students that they are going to hear four people commenting on the article in 2a. Play the recording. Students listen to the recording and answer the questions. Use the Vocabulary support box to help with vocabulary if necessary. Check answers as a class.

Answers
1 Paul: the influence of the Internet on the way language spreads and evolves and how words and expressions come in and out of fashion very fast
Rosa: the decline in the quality of written communications, particularly related to punctuation and spelling, and how spellcheckers and predictive text are partly to blame
Greg: the increasing speed at which language is changing and the progressive disappearance of regional variations in English and how people are speaking the same kind of English because of American TV and films and international communication
Claire: the changing nature of language and how this shows that English is alive, incorporating new words for things and assigning new meanings to existing words
2 Paul: LOL, BTW, Bluetooth, CD-ROM
Rosa: loose/lose, where/were
Greg: flat/apartment, movies / cinema, film
Claire: selfie, wireless/radio

Audioscript

PAUL Language has been changing much faster since people started using the Internet. Now, people pick up words and expressions from each other and new words spread much faster. This means though, a lot of new expressions probably won't last very long. LOL, BTW, Bluetooth, CD-ROM. I mean, 20 years ago these words didn't exist – no one used them. But, in a few years' time, they will have gone out of fashion and other new words will have come into the language.

ROSA Another thing that's changed is punctuation. Emailing has had an effect on the way people write. I mean, people have stopped using strict rules for punctuation, so people use commas much less than before. Spellcheckers and predictive text mean that people don't need to know how to spell. And people's spelling seems to just be getting worse: lose/loose; where/were – they don't show up on spell checkers. It's a pity. People are getting more information, but they're getting worse at expressing themselves.

GREG I agree with the article that language often changes slowly, but I think this process has been speeding up over the last few decades. A lot of American words have come into the language, probably because of TV and films. Um … for example, people used to use 'flat' but now more people have started saying 'apartment'. Because of international communication, dialects are disappearing and people are starting to speak the same kind of English. For example the word 'movies' which is originally used mostly in … in North America has now replaced 'cinema' and 'film' all around the world. In about 50 years, most dialects of English will have died out. And I think dialects are important because they're, they're part of people's identity. It's a pity they're disappearing and everything's just becoming more uniform.

CLAIRE Some people complain about new words, but it shows that the English language is alive … um … like the world is changing and languages need to change with them. And this is nothing new. Um … Older generations have always complained about language changing. They've always felt strongly about it, but … it's a natural process. New words come into the language because they enrich the language. For example, the word 'selfie' which people started using in around 2013. People had been taking photos of themselves before 2013, but they hadn't had a single word for it, so it caught on quite quickly. And some words also change their meaning. So for example 'wireless' these days is about internet connections. We talk about 'wireless LAN' and 'wi-fi'. The word 'wireless' had had a completely different meaning until computers came along – it meant 'radio'.

📖 VOCABULARY SUPPORT

LOL – written abbreviation for *laughing out loud*: used, for example in emails and text messages, when you think something is very funny

BTW – written abbreviation for *by the way*: used, for example in emails, when you are writing something that relates to the subject you are discussing, but is not the main point of the discussion

Bluetooth – a system for connecting electronic equipment such as mobile phones, computers and electronic organisers to each other and to the Internet using radio signals

predictive text – a feature of a mobile phone in which words are suggested automatically while you are writing a text message

dialect (C2) – a form of a language that people speak in a particular part of a country, containing some different words and grammar, etc.

LAN – abbreviation for *local area network*: a system for connecting the computers of people who work in the same building

b 💬 With a monolingual class, discuss the question as a class and encourage students to give examples. With a multilingual class, put students into groups of the same L1 to discuss the question and give examples before taking feedback as a class.

c ▶**1.12** Books closed. Write on the board: *1 Language _____ much faster since people started using the Internet. 2 In about 50 years, most dialects of English _____ .* Ask students: *Can you remember what the speakers said?* (1 has been changing 2 will have died out). Ask: *What do the two verb forms have in common?* (They are both perfect forms.) Then ask: *How are they different?* (They are in different tenses. Sentence 1 is the present perfect continuous and talks about a continuing action. Sentence 2 is the future perfect and talks about a completed action.) Books open. Individually, students do the exercise. Check answers as a class.

Answers
1 has been changing   2 will have gone   3 will have come
4 have stopped   5 will have died out   6 have always complained
7 have always felt   8 had been taking   9 had had

d Students work individually, answering the questions and choosing the best word to complete the rule. Check answers as a class.

Answers
1 a examples 1, 4, 6 and 7
   b examples 8 and 9
   c examples 2, 3 and 5
2 before

After discussing the questions and rule in 4d, check students understand some of the key areas relating to perfect verb forms by asking them: *Which perfect form (simple or continuous) do we use to focus on the fact that we have finished an activity?* (simple) and elicit an example from students. Then ask: *Which perfect form (simple or continuous) do we use to focus on the duration of an activity?* (continuous) and elicit an example. Finally, ask: *Which perfect form (simple or continuous) do we use to answer questions with 'How many'?* (simple)

e ▶ **1.12 Pronunciation** Play the recording again for students to listen and identify the kinds of words that are stressed and unstressed. Check answers as a class and drill the sentences.

Answers
The main verbs are stressed.
The auxiliary verbs are usually unstressed.

f ▶ **1.13–1.14** Students read the information in Grammar Focus 1B on SB p.139. Play the recording where indicated and ask students to listen and repeat, making sure students are stressing only the main verbs, not the auxiliaries, in the perfect tenses. Students then complete the exercises. Check answers as a class. Tell students to go back to SB p.12.

Answers (Grammar Focus 1B SB p.139)
a 2 a 3 g 4 e 5 b 6 h 7 c 8 f
b 2 died 3 tried 4 told 5 been painting 6 went 7 read
  8 had 9 had 10 done
c 2 (will) have noticed 3 have suggested 4 has accepted
  5 had been established 6 has become 7 will have invented

◉ CAREFUL!

Even at higher levels, there are still numerous common student mistakes with perfect tenses. When talking about the present, students frequently use the present simple or past simple when they should use the present perfect (and vice versa), e.g. ~~For the past six years, I live in Berlin.~~ (Correct form = *For the past six years, I've lived in Berlin.*). When talking about the past, students often use the past perfect instead of the past simple, e.g. ~~He got very angry when the teacher had been ill and cancelled the class.~~ (Correct form = *He got very angry when the teacher **was** ill and … *). They also often use the past simple when they should use the past perfect, e.g. ~~We should have taken an exam after that course to prove how much we learned.~~ (Correct form = *… to prove how much we **had learned**.*)

g 💬 Read through the bullet points with the class and give students some examples from your own experience. In small groups, students talk about words in their own language. With a multilingual class, if possible group students so that they all have a different L1 in order to give students more opportunities for authentic communication. Take feedback as a class.

5 READING and SPEAKING

a In pairs, students look at the pictures and answer the questions. Check their ideas as a class.

Suggested answers
1 The woman is using the points of the compass when we would expect her to use an expression like *Could you move up/along a bit?* instead.
2 The passenger is not using the colour but instead is using the shade. We would expect someone to use *red* rather than *dark* in this context.
3 The man is giving an extremely precise definition. In English, fruit would not be defined in such detail. Saying *A kilo of bananas, please.* would be sufficient.

b 💬 Students read the fact file and then discuss the questions in pairs. Use the Vocabulary support box to help with vocabulary if necessary. Take feedback as a class.

📖 VOCABULARY SUPPORT

downstream – in the direction a river or stream is flowing

inland – away from the sea

seaward – towards the sea

longing (C2) – a feeling of wanting something or someone very much

impermanence – the state of not lasting for ever or not lasting for a long time

c Language in context *Expressing meaning*
Remind students that learning to understand the meaning of words from their context is an essential language-learning skill and will allow them to become more independent learners. Individually, they complete the example sentences with the highlighted words in the correct form. Check answers as a class.

Answers
1 interpret 2 differentiate 3 distinguishes 4 illustrate
5 indicate 6 conveyed 7 embodies

💡 FAST FINISHERS

Ask fast finishers to list the noun forms of six of the highlighted words (*differentiation, conveyance, indication, interpretation, embodiment, illustration*). Tell them to use a dictionary if necessary to check which verb doesn't have a noun form (*distinguish*) and which noun form doesn't have the same meaning as the verb used in the fact file (*conveyance*).

d 💬 Give students time to think about the question and the three areas. Monitor and help as necessary. Students then work in pairs and explain their choices.

💡 EXTRA ACTIVITY

Remind students how important it is to be able to explain the meaning of words in order to be able to convey what they want to say even if they don't know the exact word in English. Ask them to choose five words from their language which they don't know the English for and to think about how they will explain the meaning of these in English to a partner. Put students into pairs to explain in as much detail as possible the meaning of the words they have chosen. With a monolingual class, their partner then guesses the word and suggests an English translation. With a multilingual class, if possible pair students with different L1s so that they can listen to each other's definitions and find out if they know the word their partner is describing in their own language and in English. Take class feedback on any words students think are untranslatable into English.

e 💬 Students read the opinion and discuss it in their pairs. If students are interested and motivated by the topic, extend this to a full class discussion. Alternatively, structure it as a more formal debate, dividing the class in half and telling each half whether they will be arguing for or against the opinion.

ADDITIONAL MATERIAL

▶ Workbook 1B

▶ Photocopiable activities: Grammar p.202, Vocabulary p.222, Pronunciation p.252

1C Everyday English
Something along those lines

At the end of this lesson, students will be able to:

- understand conversations between people in a work environment and infer details about the relationships between them
- use and recognise irony and understatement in conversations
- describe an experience using appropriate language for expressing details in an inexact way
- recognise the relationship between sound and spelling for *ea, ee* and *ie*

💡 OPTIONAL LEAD-IN

Books closed. Ask students if, why and how they listen to the radio, e.g. through podcasts to learn English. Put them into groups to discuss which of these radio programmes would be most interesting to them: news, interviews, talk shows, live sport events, music shows, documentaries. Take feedback as a class.

1 LISTENING

a 💬 Ask students if a colleague could be a friend or if work and personal life should be divided. Put students into groups to discuss the questions. Take feedback as a class.

b 💬 Ask students if the picture looks like a nice working environment. Put students into groups to discuss the questions. Take feedback as a class but don't check the answers at this point.

c ▶**1.15** Play Part 1 of the video or the audio recording for students to check their answers. If necessary, pre-teach *turn in* (submit a piece of work to an organisation or a person in authority). Ask how and why Alex thinks Sara can help him. Check answers as a class.

Answers
1 at a radio station called *City FM*
2 They're colleagues.
3 Sara isn't looking forward to a meeting she's got with her boss, Nadia, later that morning. Alex is going on holiday to Italy. Alex wants Sara to teach him some Italian because her father is Italian.

Videoscript/Audioscript (Part 1)

OSCAR Well, that's all from me today. Coming up after this short break is Katya with the *City FM* news …

ALEX Nice one, Oscar.

O Yeah, not bad. You've not broken the equipment again, have you, Alex?

A No. That's your job!

…

A Hi Sara! How are you this morning? Oh. Full of the joys of spring, I see!

SARA What? Oh, Alex, it's you …

A Well, don't sound so pleased to see me!

S Sorry, message from the boss.

A Right … ?

S She wants a meeting this morning.

A And … ?

S I've got a feeling it's not exactly good news.

A Oh, don't be so negative. Nadia probably just wants to thank you for all your hard work.

S Hm, that'd be something of a surprise. When's the last time I turned in anything decent?

A Oh come on!

S Anyway, what are you so cheerful about?

A I've just booked my holiday.

S Oh, good!

A Yeah, Italy!

S Lovely. You know, my Dad is Italian.

A No way! Hey, maybe you could teach me some bits and pieces, y'know, basic survival phrases, 'please' and 'thank you' and stuff like that?

S Survival phrases? I think I need a few of them myself!

A Hey, Sara! Ciao bella!

💡 FAST FINISHERS

Ask fast finishers to write down the five most important survival phrases, not single words, for learners of English from their country who are going abroad, e.g. *Where is the Argentinian Embassy?*.

d Language in context *Irony and understatement*

1 Say to students *1,000 euros is very cheap for a radio.* and *1,000 euros for a radio is rather expensive for most people.* Ask which sentence is an example of irony (the first) and which is an example of understatement (the second). Tell students to match the comments with the situations. (If necessary, you could play Part 1 of the video or the audio recording again and pause it after each comment.) Check answers as a class.

2 Ask students to discuss the questions in pairs. Take feedback as a class.

Answers / Suggested answers
1 a 3
  b 2
  c 4
  d 1
2 They want to use irony and understatement for humour in order to handle bad news or difficult topics in a lighter way. This is quite common between people who know each other well.

e ▶**1.16** Play Part 2 of the video or the audio recording for students to find the relationship between the characters. If necessary, pre-teach *get the hang of things* (C2) (learn how to do something, especially if it is not obvious or simple), *leave it out* (stop doing or saying that) and *touch base on sth* (to talk to someone for a short time to find out what they think about something). Check answers as a class.

Answers
Nadia and Sara: boss and (new) employee still in a probationary period
Sara and Oscar: colleagues in direct competition
Alex and Emma: boyfriend and girlfriend in a new relationship

Videoscript/Audioscript (Part 2)

NADIA Ah, Sara. Take a seat.
SARA Thanks, Nadia.
N Now, do you know why I've asked to see you?
S Um … Is it something to do with our long-running series of interviews with authors?
N Exactly. Look, Oscar has already booked six authors, give or take.
S Six?!
N He's even managed to persuade Max whatsisname to come in.
S Who?
N Max whatsisname – you know, author of *Solar Wind*? The guy who wrote the entire book sitting on a bench on the Palace Pier, here in Brighton.
S Max Redwood! Wow, that's great news!
N So, how far have you got?
S Well, um, I'm still sort of like in the research phase, y'know.
N I appreciate you're still finding your feet here at *City FM*.
S Well, I'm beginning to feel like I've got the hang of things.
N OK, but you must understand … For me to be able to offer you a permanent contract here, I need to see some evidence of your capabilities.
S I understand, Nadia. I'll get something to you soon, I promise.
N Ah Oscar, do come in. Let's touch base soon, Sara.
...
ALEX Scusami, signorina, parla inglese?
S Leave it out, Alex.
A Don't tell me – she's promoted you to editor-in-chief!
S Something along those lines, yeah.
A Go on, tell me all!
S Well, basically, she said if I don't get something big, like an interview with a best-selling author, I'm out of here, or words to that effect.
A Ah!
S You don't happen to know, like, a best-selling author or something, do you, Alex?
A No, 'fraid not.
S That's not your new girlfriend, again, is it?
A Yeah, it's Emma!
S She's keen, isn't she?
A Oh! Hang on, Em!

f ▶**1.16** See if students know any answers before they watch or listen again. Play Part 2 of the video or the audio recording again for students to check. Check as a class.

Answers
1 the long-running series of interviews with authors
2 Because he has already booked about six authors, and has even persuaded Max Redwood, the author of *Solar Wind*, to come in.
3 She wants some evidence of her capabilities.
4 He jokes that Nadia has promoted Sara to editor-in-chief.
5 finding a best-selling author for her to interview
6 She's keen on Alex and phones him (possibly too) frequently.

g 💬 Ask students if they think Nadia is being too hard on Sara as a newcomer to the station. Put students into groups to discuss the questions. Take feedback as a class.

Suggested answers
1 It's a radio station called *City FM* which features programmes with presenters, advertisements and the news. It seems to be a small company. Nadia is the boss. Sara (like Oscar) is a radio presenter, whereas Alex's job is more technical.
2 very worried, under pressure
3 Students' own answers

2 USEFUL LANGUAGE
Expressing yourself in an inexact way

a Ask the students what the difference between *Put it there* and *Put it somewhere there* is (*somewhere there* is more inexact). Tell students to match the expressions with the meanings. Check answers as a class.

Answers
1 d   2 c   3 a   4 b

b Ask students which three of the expressions in bold they could use in 2a. Check answers as a class and then ask students to rewrite the three ideas in 2a using these words. Check as a class. Ask students to do the matching task to show why they can't use the other two expressions in 2a.

Answers
2 Max thingy
3 somewhere in the region of six authors
4 I'm out of here, or something along those lines.
a 4
b 3

c Tell students to rewrite the sentences with the expressions for being inexact. Don't check answers until 2d.

Possible answers
1 William whatsisname/thingy, who wrote *A Midsummer Night's Dream* / thingy.
2 I went to the market and bought some bits and pieces / three items, give or take / somewhere in the region of three items.
3 She told me to go away, or words to that effect / something along those lines.
5 I know a little Polish – 'hello', 'goodbye', (the numbers one to ten) and stuff like that / some other bits and pieces.
6 I've been to somewhere in the region of 15 countries. / I've been to 15 countries, give or take.

d ▶**1.17** Play the recording for students to compare answers. Use the answer key in 2c to check any variations. Drill different ways of saying the sentences in 2c.

Audioscript
1 William whatsisname, you know, the guy who wrote *Romeo and Juliet*.
2 I went to the market and bought a few bits and pieces.
3 She told me to go away, or words to that effect.
4 I know a little Polish – you know, 'hello', 'goodbye', and stuff like that.
5 I've been to 15 countries, give or take a few.

3 PRONUNCIATION
Sound and spelling: *ea, ee* and *ie*

a ▶**1.18** Show students that the sound and spelling correspondence in English is not perfect by writing the non-word *ghoti* on the board and asking students to pronounce it. Then say it is pronounced *fish*: *gh* is pronounced as in *tough*, *o* as in *women*, *ti* as in *nation*. Play the recording and ask students to listen to the words. Then ask students what sound the letters in bold make (/iː/). Ask students if /iː/ is always spelt with two letters (no, *decent*) and elicit other examples of when /iː/ isn't spelt with two letters, e.g. *me*.

b ▶**1.19** Check that students know how to say the IPA sounds and highlight that *ea, ee* and *ie* aren't always pronounced /iː/. Then play the recording for students to listen and put the words in the correct columns. Check answers as a class. Drill the sounds and the words.

Answers

2 /e/	3 /eɪ/	4 /eə/	5 /ɪə/	6 /ɜː/
friend	great	bear	cheerful	research

c ▶**1.20** Tell students to put the words into the correct columns. If necessary, write *pierce* on the board and give its definition (to go into or through something, making a hole in it using a sharp point). Play the recording for students to check. Ask students which sound in 3b is the only short sound. Drill the words.

Answers
1 /iː/ Greek; meaning; increase; niece
2 /e/ meant; steadily; breakfast   3 /eɪ/ break   4 /eə/ pear
5 /ɪə/ hear; pierce; idea; career   6 /ɜː/ learn; heard; early
/e/ is the only short sound

LOA TIP ELICITING

- Students need to know how a sound is pronounced before you drill it in a word. With vowels and diphthongs, this means showing the shape of the lips and telling students whether the sound is long or short and whether the tongue is close to the roof or bottom of the mouth and at the front or back of the mouth. This is a complex combination so the most effective way to teach students the shape of the sound is to elicit the sound as they produce it and as they experience what they are doing with their tongue and lips.

- Ask students to put their tongue close to the front and roof of their mouth, spread their lips and blow out a steady stream of air through the middle of the tongue. Ask a student to point to the IPA symbol they are making (/iː/). Give students time to repeat the sound and then drill it with the words they have put in column 1 in 3b.

- With diphthongs you need to elicit the movement of the tongue between vowels. Once students know the shape for /e/ and /ɪ/ you can elicit the diphthong /eɪ/. Tell students to spread their lips and move their tongue slowly from the front and middle of the mouth (/e/) to nearer the higher /ɪ/ position, blowing out a stream of air through the centre of their tongue. Once students are comfortable with the movement, tell them to speed it up until they produce an /eɪ/ sound. Ask a student to point to the IPA symbol they are making (/eɪ/). Give students time to repeat the sound and then drill it with the words they have put in column 3 in 3b.

EXTRA ACTIVITY

Draw this 5x5 square on the board. Challenge individual students to pronounce all the words in the square correctly.

p	i	e	c	e
e	a	r	l	y
b	r	e	a	k
s	e	e	k	s
b	e	a	c	h

Put students into groups. Tell them to write a new 5x5 square in their notebooks. Tell them to fill it with new words containing *ea, ee* and *ie*. The first group to finish and pronounce all the words correctly wins.

4 SPEAKING

a ▶**1.21** Play the recording for students to listen and answer the questions. Check as a class. Ask students how they would have reacted if they had been the new flatmate.

Answers
1 meeting a new flatmate for the first time
2 the new flatmate arriving but her room being full of lots of the speaker's stuff

Audioscript

SPEAKER Well, I'd been renting accommodation, a room in a nice cottage in a village 60 miles from London, for four or five weeks, give or take. The landlord had told me at some point I'd be getting a flatmate, but to be honest, I'd kind of got used to being there on my own. To start with, I'd had all my stuff in my room, of course, but as the weeks went by, I kind of thought, 'Hmm, I could put some bits and pieces in the spare room.' And then, 'Oh! I'll put my drum kit in there too.' And so it went on. I was really making myself at home!
I'll always remember the morning I met Michelle for the first time: I had a cold, and I was still in bed feeling sorry for myself, when suddenly I heard a key turn in the lock of the front door. I raced down the stairs with the full horror of the situation dawning on me. Just as I got to the bottom step, she opened the door to see me in my pyjamas and a blind panic. She looked at me and said, 'Have I come at a bad time?', or something along those lines. That was roughly 13 years ago now, and we've been close friends ever since – after we moved all my stuff out of her room!

b ▶**1.21** Play the recording again for students to write down the expressions for being inexact from 2a and b.

Answers
give or take; stuff; bits and pieces; something along those lines

c Tell students to plan to talk about an experience they had, using the ideas given. Ask them to make notes and decide what exact details to give and what information to give in an inexact way. Give an example: *I want to tell you about missing a university deadline. Shall I tell you exactly how many words my essay was?*

d 💬 Put students into pairs to talk about and compare their experiences. Encourage students to use the expressions for being inexact. Take feedback as a class and ask pairs to retell particularly memorable experiences.

ADDITIONAL MATERIAL

▶ Workbook 1C
▶ Photocopiable activities: Pronunciation p.253
▶ Unit Progress Test
▶ Personalised online practice

At the end of this lesson, students will be able to:

- understand a person talking about the dominance of English as a world language and discuss the points made
- understand a web forum post and the opinions expressed in the comments and responses
- use phrases for agreement, disagreement, uncertainty and partial agreement/disagreement and soften these where necessary
- express their opinion in a web forum post and respond to and comment on the opinions of others appropriately

💡 OPTIONAL LEAD-IN

Books closed. Write *sudoku* on the board. Ask students if they remember this word from 1a in Lesson 1B. Ask them which language English has borrowed the word from (Japanese). Tell them that English borrows very heavily from other languages and that these words are often called *loanwords*. Write these loanwords and the languages they come from randomly on the board, and ask students to match them:

1 soprano – Italian

2 ski – Scandinavian

3 icon – Russian

4 tornado – Spanish

5 hamburger – German

6 garage – French

7 avatar – Sanskrit

8 giraffe – Arabic

9 ketchup – Malay

10 yacht – Dutch.

Check answers as a class. Then put students into groups and ask them to think of any other loanwords they know in English and the language they come from, e.g. *ballet – French, mosquito – Spanish*. Take feedback as a class.

1 SPEAKING and LISTENING

a 💬 Look at the photos and discuss the question as a class. Check students understand that *džús, lonche, janpa, gol, biznismyen* and *kampyutara* are phonetic approximations of *juice, lunch, jumper, goal, businessman* and *computer* in Slovakian, Mexican Spanish, Japanese, Spanish, Russian and Hindi respectively. In Brazilian Portuguese, the adjective *outdoor* has mutated dramatically to become a noun referring to a billboard.

Suggested answer

Because they convey a concept which may have originated in an English-speaking culture, or come from an area of language where common terminology is essential. Sometimes using English words might be seen as fashionable, even when there is a native-language equivalent.

b 💬 Give students a few examples of words from other languages that are often used in English, e.g. *paella* (from Spanish), etc. Then give them one minute to think of words that their language has borrowed from English. Put students into pairs or small groups to discuss the questions. Take feedback as a class.

c 💬 In their pairs or small groups, students make predictions about what they think Maxwell Kingsley will say about 1–6. Ask for suggestions and collate these on the board for the six areas.

d ▶ 1.22 Play the recording for students to listen and check their ideas from 1c and make notes. Use the Vocabulary support box to help with vocabulary if necessary. Make sure students know what you expect by making notes. Ask: *Should you write down full sentences?* (no). *Should you include all the information?* (no). *Which information should you include then?* (the main points). Emphasise that there's no need to write down phrases or sentences word for word and that there isn't time. Check answers and discuss the question as a class.

Suggested answers

1. Around a billion people worldwide speak English as a foreign or second language.
2. Some people say English is easy but it's no easier than other languages.
3. Latin played a similar role to English and was the international language for about 1,000 years.
4. English is the dominant, world language but doesn't have much effect on other languages.
5. Native speakers of English have less need to learn other languages, which is a disadvantage for them.
6. Speakers of other major languages might be resentful, but the dominance of English won't last.

Audioscript

MAXWELL KINGSLEY I think we're in a unique situation today with regard to language diversity and there is no precedent for it in history. The English language has become the world's dominant language, and although other languages such as Chinese and Spanish are more widespread, English is spoken by the largest number of non-native speakers. In fact, there are a vastly greater number of people who speak it as a non-native language than there are people who have English as their first language. There are probably around a billion people worldwide who speak English to some degree of proficiency as a foreign or second language – it's a huge number of people. It's been estimated for example that something like 80 per cent of all conversations in English between tourists are between non-native speakers, so a Russian talking to a Japanese, or a Spanish speaker talking to a German, but using English. The implications of this are, of course, enormous.

Naturally, this is quite unrelated to the nature of the English language itself. Some people say English is an easy language, but in fact English has the same degree of complexity or simplicity as other languages, and the reasons for its dominance are largely historical, and to some extent, accidental. It just so happened, for example, that the USA adopted English as its national language, rather than French or Spanish.

I mentioned earlier that the dominance of English is unique. It's true, of course, that Latin played a similar role as an international language for around a thousand years, starting with the Roman Empire and continuing until the 16th century. Latin was the language of science and of theology, and rather like English today, it was used in intercultural communication. But its use was limited to a few highly educated people, so it wasn't used nearly as widely as English is today. English is used by everyone, not just a small elite.

People often talk about how English is threatening other languages, but I don't personally believe that dominance of English as a world language is going to have much effect on the diversity of human languages. It's true that smaller languages have been dying out and they will continue to die out, but that's more as a result of improved communication, and not because of the spread of English. People are going to go on speaking their own language, whether it's Russian or Italian or Arabic or whatever it is. There's no sign at all that everyone is going to drop their own language or that there will be one single language spoken by everybody. It simply isn't going to happen, in my view. So the only real disadvantage of the dominance of English, as I see it, is for native speakers of English themselves, as it means that they have less need to learn other languages, so in a sense that's an impoverishment for them.

Also, of course it's quite understandable that speakers of other major languages might resent the rise of English as a global language, but the good news for them is that the dominance of English probably won't last. Before English, French was of course the international language, at least among educated people, for a couple of hundred years, and before that it was Latin and Arabic and Greek and so on. In other words, various languages have played this role and this has come and gone over time, and no doubt it will be the same with English. Take Sumerian for example, which was the main written language in most of the Middle East for centuries. The last records of Sumerian are from the third century, so it survived as an international language for over 3,000 years, but of course now most people haven't even heard of it, it's a dead language. Compare that with English – so far English as a truly global language has been going for about 50 years at the most, so who knows what's going to happen to it? One thing that's certain is that nothing lasts forever.

📖 VOCABULARY SUPPORT

there is no precedent for sth – there has never been a similar situation, so we have nothing to compare it with

widespread (C1) – existing or happening in many places and/ or among many people

elite (n.) (C1) – the richest, most powerful, best-educated or best-trained group in a society

threaten (C1) – be likely to cause harm or damage to something or someone

impoverishment – the process of making something weaker or worse in quality

resent (C2) – feel angry because you have been forced to accept someone or something that you do not like

💡 EXTRA ACTIVITY

Play the recording again for students to answer questions 1–4 about what Maxwell says. Check answers as a class and suggest students refer to the audioscript on SB p.177 if necessary.

1 *According to Maxwell Kingsley, what is the difference between Chinese and Spanish, and English?* (More people speak Chinese and Spanish than English as a first language, but English is spoken by a vast number of people as a second language.)

2 *Which country's choice of language does Kingsley suggest might have had an important role in English becoming an international language?* (the USA, which chose to adopt English rather than French or Spanish)

3 *In what way was the use of Latin as an international language fundamentally different from that of English?* (Latin was the language of both science and theology, but only the elite used it, unlike English, which is used by everyone.)

4 *Which languages had a similar role in the past to English today?* (French, Latin, Arabic, Greek, Sumerian)

② READING

a Books closed. Write on the board: *Maxwell Kingsley makes the point that … . Do you think he's right?*. Tell students they are going to read an internet web forum in which people comment on one of the points Kingsley made in his talk. In pairs, students predict what the point is. Students then read the post at the top of SB p.17 to check their ideas and read the four responses. Use the Vocabulary support box to help with vocabulary if necessary. Elicit which two writers agree with each other.

Answer
Neuling and Ariete agree with each other.

📖 VOCABULARY SUPPORT

interfere (C1) – prevent something from working effectively or from developing successfully

bombard sb with sth – direct so many things at someone that they find it difficult to deal with them

buzzword – a word or expression from a particular subject area that has become fashionable by being used a lot, especially on television and in the newspapers

fuss (n.) (C1) – a show of anger, worry or excitement that is unnecessary or greater than the situation deserves

isolate – put a person, country or organisation in a situation where they are seen as being separate

heritage (C2) – features belonging to the culture of a particular society, such as traditions, languages or buildings, that were created in the past and still have historical importance

b Give students one minute to reflect on the posts. Take feedback as a class.

3 WRITING SKILLS Expressing opinions

a Put students into pairs to identify the elements used by the writers. Check answers as a class and ask students to justify their answers using the relevant sections of the posts.

Answers
A Neuling, Ariete, ParsaUK   B All
C Flying D, Neuling   D Neuling, Ariete   E Flying D, Neuling, ParsaUK

b Individually, students complete the table. Check answers as a class.

Answers
1 … that's nonsense.   2 … there's no way …
3 … you are missing the point …   4 I'm in two minds about this.
5 … you're spot on.   6 I agree up to a point …

c Ask students to look again at the highlighted phrases for disagreement in the web forum. Discuss the questions as a class. Elicit the examples from the text and then any additional words and phrases students can think of for softening opinions. Tell students that another common technique for softening opinions is to avoid a negative adjective, e.g. *I'm not sure that's a very good idea.* rather than *That's a terrible idea.*

Answers
1 If you ask me …; as far as I'm concerned …; It seems to me …
2 Students' own answers, e.g. *I'm afraid that …*; *I do understand what you're saying, but …*; *Sorry, but …* , etc.

d Ask students to use a dictionary and identify which expressions are informal. Tell them to compare in pairs before checking answers as a class. Emphasise that students should take care when using the phrases for disagreement in spoken English as they could all be perceived as aggressive/rude depending on the intonation used.

Answers
That's a load of rubbish.; that's nonsense; there's no way …; you're spot on

e ▶ Students complete the exercises in Writing Focus 1D on SB p.169. They read the table and then cover it for Exercise a. Check answers to Exercise a and b before discussing the questions in Exercise c as a class. Tell students to go back to SB p.17.

Answers
a 1 possibly think; the point   2 to say; isn't true
3 spot on; go along; mixed feelings   4 nonsense / a load of rubbish   5 make a lot of sense   6 on the head
b Reply 3: I must say …; but I don't think …
You could add phrases like: *If you ask me …*; *It seems to me …*; etc.

🔆 FAST FINISHERS

Ask fast finishers to come up with a counter-argument for the six comments on Eva's post, e.g. *1 English isn't any more beautiful or richer than any other language. 2 You can create a language, Esperanto, for example.*, etc.

f Individually, students compare the two posts. Check answers as a class, discussing the different features.

Answers
more formal and abstract: Flying D – abstract nouns, e.g. *uniqueness*; sentence length and structure (longer sentences with more complex structures)
more informal and personal: Ariete – personal examples; questions and exclamation marks; colloquial expressions, e.g. *there's no way …*; first person

g Discuss the question as a class. Read through the Writing Tip with the class and remind students to bear these points in mind as they complete the final task.

4 WRITING

a Individually, students read the opinions and tick the ones they agree with. Check the meaning of *influx* (C2) if necessary (the fact of a large number of people or things arriving at the same time).

b Students write an initial post for a discussion forum about the opinion they chose in 4a. Check students understand the task by asking them to look at Eva's initial post on SB p.169 again. Monitor and point out errors for students to self-correct.

c Tell each student to pass their post to the person sitting on their left. They then read the post and respond to it or add a comment. Continue to monitor and help as necessary.

d Students repeat the process in 4c until each post has four comments.

e Return each discussion forum to the person who started it. Students read the four comments and decide which they found the most interesting. Take feedback as a class.

⟳ LOA TIP REVIEW AND REFLECT

- Draw three circles on the board. In the first write *This was useful for me.*, in the second *This was difficult for me.* and in the third *This was interesting for me.*

- Give students a few minutes to look back through the first unit of the course and choose two or three items from the course content for each category on the board. Take class feedback on what students found most useful/difficult/interesting and ask them to explain their choices.

- As well as allowing students to evaluate the course so far, this process also allows you to understand more about why your class are learning English, their strengths and weaknesses, and what they find interesting. It is also very valuable to help students understand that the course includes a wide range of topics and activities as all students have different expectations.

ADDITIONAL MATERIAL

▶ Workbook 1D

UNIT 1
Review and extension

1 GRAMMAR

a Correct the first mistake as an example with the class. Students then correct the other sentences, working individually. Remind them that some adverbials might be correct in more than one position. Check answers as a class.

Answers
1 Please try to speak slowly.
2 He will probably be late.
3 We do our washing by hand.
4 We will be living in London in June.
5 She made me laugh so loudly.
6 (In the end,) I managed to get in touch (in the end).
7 You can (easily) compare the different brands (easily).

b Students choose the correct form in each sentence. Check answers as a class. Drill the sentences, paying particular attention to the weak pronunciation of the auxiliary verbs.

Answers
1 have never visited
2 I've been learning
3 was crossing
4 wanted
5 has had
6 will have been studying

2 VOCABULARY

a Complete the first item with the class as an example. Individually, students replace the words in italics in the sentences with an expression in the box. Check answers as a class.

Answers
1 struggle with
2 immerse yourself in
3 hold a conversation
4 acquire
5 brush up
6 get to grips with
7 rusty

b Students work individually, completing the missing letters in each word. Check answers as a class.

Answers
1 rapid
2 subtle
3 shift
4 lasting
5 way
6 ongoing
7 perceptible

3 WORDPOWER Idioms: Body parts

a Ask students to cover the words in the box. Focus students on the title of the section *Idioms: Body parts* and the cartoon. Ask them to name as many of the different body parts shown in the cartoon as they can. Then tell students to look at the words in the box and complete the idioms. Play the recording for students to listen and check.

Answers
1 nose 2 head 3 hands 4 neck 5 shoulders 6 tongue
7 tooth

b Students match the idioms with the definitions. Check answers as a class.

Answers
a 4 b 7 c 1 d 6 e 2 f 3 g 5

> ### EXTRA ACTIVITY
>
> Ask students to change the sentences in 3a into more personal, memorable examples, e.g. *1 My uncle has absolutely no nose for business investment; he's tried three different businesses and they've all lost money. 7 I will fight tooth and nail to stop him being elected to the local council.*, etc. Monitor and point out errors for students to self-correct. Ask students to compare their sentences with a partner before asking them to share some of their sentences with the class.

c Individually, ask students to complete the idioms in the questions. Check answers as a class.

Answers
1 stick your neck   2 a nose   3 head and shoulders
4 their head   5 tooth and nail   6 bite their   7 safe pair of hands

d In pairs or small groups, students ask and answer the questions in 3c. Monitor and check that students are using the idioms correctly. Ask students to share some of their answers with the class.

> ### FAST FINISHERS
>
> Ask fast finishers to make a list of other idioms with body parts which they know, e.g. *pull sb's leg, head start, Achilles heel, a pain in the neck, put your foot in it*, etc. Ask them to tell another fast finisher what the idiom means and give an example sentence using it. Encourage them to say if there is a similar idiom in their own language or if they think the English idiom is untranslatable.

 Photocopiable activities: Wordpower p.241

> ### LOA REVIEW YOUR PROGRESS
>
> Students look back through the unit, think about what they've studied and decide how well they did. Students work on weak areas by using the appropriate sections of the Workbook, the Photocopiable worksheets and the Personalised online practice.

UNIT 2
Going to extremes

At the end of this unit, students will be able to:

- understand and summarise details, attitudes and opinions in texts about extreme sensory experiences and thrill-seeking activities
- understand, note and summarise details, opinions and attitudes in: extended speech and interviews describing physical and mental experiences; idiomatic conversations in which people discuss sensitive issues and give advice tactfully
- use a range of lexis and main stress accurately to discuss, describe and evaluate: extreme experiences; future plans; communication styles; suggestions for how to cope with noise; various extreme sports and leisure activities
- use a range of lexis to write descriptions of extreme experiences and future plans
- use a range of expressions to give advice in an appropriate register
- write a clearly structured, cohesive report, prioritising key issues, outlining problems and solutions and using linkers of contrast and concession appropriately

UNIT CONTENTS

G GRAMMAR
- Comparison (modifying comparisons with *than* and *as … as …*; comparative patterns; superlative patterns)
- Intentions and arrangements (*going to*; present continuous; future simple and continuous; present simple; expressions with *be*)
- Linking: contrast and concession: *alternatively* (offering alternatives), *by comparison* (comparing), *even though* (conceding), *on the contrary* (opposing), etc.

V VOCABULARY
- Multi-word verbs: Social interaction: *bombard (sb) with, bring out (the best/worst in sb), come across (to sb), cut (sb) off, fit in, go on about sth, hold (sb) back, relate to (sb), run (sb) down, slip out*
- Verbs of movement: *crawl, creep, drift, hurtle, leap, limp, march, plunge, roll, rush, slide, soar, stagger, stroll, whirl, whizz, whoosh, zoom*
- Language in context: Sounds; Synonyms; Being tactful or frank
- Wordpower: Idioms: Movement: *crawl, drift, plunge, soar, whirl, whizz*

P PRONUNCIATION
- Consonant–vowel linking
- Word groups and main stress
- Emphatic stress

GETTING STARTED

⚙ OPTIONAL LEAD-IN

Books closed. Put students into pairs to compare how long they could do these things and which would be the most challenging. As feedback, tell students the world records given in brackets for these extreme achievements:

- standing on one foot (76 hours)
- holding their breath (22 minutes)
- going without sleep (264 hours)
- running without stopping (80 hours / 560 km)
- staying in an ice bath (2 hours).

a Ask students what they notice about the man's hair (it has iced up). Give students one minute to think about their answers to the questions before talking about the photo as a class. If you wish, give students information from the Culture notes below.

🌐 CULTURE NOTES

This photo shows a man bathing in a hole in the ice in the sea. Cold-water swimming may be done as a challenge, for health reasons or even as a sport. The International Ice Swimming Association requires that the water is colder than 5°C (41°F) for ice swimming competitions. In 1987 Lynne Cox swam the freezing Bering Strait between Alaska and the then Soviet Union, braving waters of just 3.3°C (the water in a swimming pool is about 27°C). Ice swimming is most popular in Eastern Europe and Russia; for example, there is a tradition in Russia to jump into an icy pool after a *banya* (a type of dry sauna) because it is believed this hot/cold contrast helps the immune system. (Advise students that cold-water swimming, anything below 15°C, may be a risk for people with certain health conditions such as high blood pressure.)

b Put students into pairs to discuss the questions. Make sure that they make a list of at least six questions to ask the man. If students need encouragement, prompt them with ideas from the Suggested answers below. As feedback, find out the most interesting interview questions and who has had the coldest/hottest experience.

Suggested answers
1 How often do you do this? How long do you stay in the water for? How do you feel afterwards? Is it painful to be in such cold water? Why don't you wear a wetsuit? Do you think you'll keep doing this as you get older? Why / Why not?

⚙ EXTRA ACTIVITY

Put students into different pairs to take turns being an interviewer from the local newspaper and the man in the ice. Tell them to ask each other their questions from b1.

2A I would happily have stayed longer

At the end of this lesson, students will be able to:

- talk about their reactions to extreme physical and mental sensory experiences
- talk about the role and forms of social interaction
- read a text for detailed comprehension and work out the meaning of new words from context
- use a range of comparative forms to give different degrees of comparison
- listen and react to a personal narrative
- use multi-word verbs to describe social interaction

 OPTIONAL LEAD-IN

Books closed. Get students to write down three sounds that they find pleasant and three that annoy them. Give some examples, e.g. *a coffee machine working and the alarm clock in the morning*. Students then compare ideas as a class.

1 SPEAKING

a (▶) **1.24** Tell students to listen for one minute and then tell you what they heard around them, e.g. *a car parking nearby*. Play the recording for students to listen to the six sounds. Put students into pairs to identify the sounds and discuss the questions. Take feedback as a class and ask students which sound they have experienced most recently and how they felt.

Suggested answers
1 a market with lots of traffic 2 a beach with the sound of waves
3 a noisy nightclub heard through a wall
4 a forest with birdsong 5 a park with children playing
6 a restaurant with people talking

b ▶ Tell students to go to SB p.127 and do Communication Plus 2A. Put students into pairs to do the questionnaire. Discuss their answers as a class and see who is the most sensitive to sound. Students then discuss the questions in b. Check students understand *apprehensive* (feeling worried about something that you are going to do or that is going to happen). Take feedback as a class and tell students to go to SB p.133 and do Communication Plus 2A. Ask students to read and discuss each suggestion with their partner, answering the questions. Take feedback as a class. Tell students to go back to SB p.20.

2 READING

a 💬 Ask students where they go if they need to have some peace and quiet. Tell students to look at the picture and caption and say which country the 'quietest place on Earth' is in (the USA – Minneapolis is a city in the Midwest). Highlight that the pronunciation of *anechoic* is /ænɪˈkəʊɪk/. Tell students to discuss the questions. Check ideas as a class.

b Give students two minutes to read the text quickly and find out whether the experience was positive overall. Check the answer as a class.

Answer
Yes, it was. He says he felt rested and calm and would happily have stayed longer in there, despite some disappointment.

 LOA TIP REVIEW AND REFLECT

Get students to highlight the exact part of the text which told them that George had a positive experience. The key information can be found in the second from last paragraph, e.g. *began to enjoy it* in the first sentence. In the last paragraph George then makes a more general point about what the experience should teach us. Tell students that a final paragraph often summarises and evaluates a text.

c Do the first comprehension question with the class and ask students to identify the part of the text with the answer (the first paragraph). Give students time to read the text and answer the questions. To save time, students could underline the relevant parts of the text rather than writing out sentences. Encourage students to guess the meaning of the words and phrases in the Vocabulary support box if they ask about them. Help with the meanings if necessary.

Answers
1 He needed to get away from the constant noise in cities like New York and recapture a sense of peace.
2 It is insulated with layers of concrete and steel, internally lined with buffers and the floor is a suspended mesh.
3 No, they don't. Most people find its perfect quiet upsetting.
4 They can experience extreme symptoms, from claustrophobia and nausea to panic attacks and aural hallucinations.
5 He thought he might go mad or be disappointed.
6 He felt very peaceful.
7 No, he didn't. He was a little disappointed that he didn't experience total silence.
8 They should become master of their own sound environment.

📖 **VOCABULARY SUPPORT**

cower – to lower your head or body in fear

lined – with a thin layer of material covering the inside surface

buffer – a barrier which gives protection from something

sensory deprivation – a situation in which the senses (sight, hearing etc.) are not stimulated at all

business as usual – said when things are continuing as they always do

be plunged into darkness – suddenly be in the dark

jangle your nerves – make you feel annoyed or nervous

be going overtime – working much more/faster than usual

💡 **FAST FINISHERS**

Ask fast finishers to find the word in the text which means *a fear of closed places* (claustrophobia). Ask them to think of as many other phobias as they can while the other students finish, e.g. *technophobia* (fear of technology, which came up in Lesson 1B), *aquaphobia* (fear of water).

d Tell students to cover their text. Ask why George mentioned astronauts (NASA astronauts train in an anechoic chamber). In pairs, students try and remember the six things. In class feedback, try and get as much information from students as possible, e.g. question 1, elicit what exactly happened in the subway.

Answers

1 It's where the deafening noise made him want to find total silence.
2 They are very quiet places he went to in his search for absolute silence.
3 He could hear the blood rushing in his veins, so the anechoic chamber wasn't completely silent.
4 He became so aware of the sounds of his body that he heard the scraping sound of his scalp moving over his skull when he frowned.
5 Everyone was impressed that he'd beaten the record, but he was enjoying the experience and only came out because his time was up.
6 Turning off the TV is a way of becoming master of your sound environment.

e 💬 Ask students if they think George is eccentric (someone who behaves in a strange or unusual way). Then put students into small groups to discuss whether they could repeat his experience. Take feedback as a class.

f Language in context *Sounds*

1 Ask students to look at *whining*, the first highlighted word in the text on SB p.21 (note there is one highlighted word in the picture caption). Ask: *Is this a nice or not nice sound?* (not nice). *How do the children feel?* (unhappy). *What part of speech is it?* (verb). Ask students to go through the definitions and find the correct one (d). Students then match the rest of the highlighted words with the definitions. Check answers as a class.

2 Ask students to find the adjectives next to *roar, whisper* and *thump*. Tell them that *dull* and *soft* basically have the same meaning, *not loud*, but that *dull* collocates with *roar* and *thump*, while *soft* collocates with *whisper*.

3 Ask students to read the Learning Tip. Tell them that recording words as collocations increases your vocabulary and often makes words easier to remember. Then ask students to find the collocations for *noise* and *sound(s)* in the text and their part of speech, using a dictionary. Encourage students to look at the full information for words in the dictionary entry, e.g. *ambient* applies to both sound and light around you and is a technical word.

Answers

1 a eerie   b deafening   c hammered   d whining
 e gurgling   f roar   g thump   h whisper   i decibels
2 dull; soft; dull
3 *absorb* sound (v.); *ambient* sounds (adj.); a *scraping* noise (adj.); *background* noise (n., making a compound noun with *noise*)

💡 **HOMEWORK ACTIVITY**

▶ Highlight the sentence from the text *The experience was nowhere near as disturbing as I had been led to believe.* (at the end of the second to last paragraph) and ask which adjective collocates with *experience* (disturbing). Tell students to use several dictionaries to find as many collocations for *experience* as they can. Students then choose one of the collocations, e.g. *amazing experience*, and prepare and present a short anecdote about this in the next class, e.g. about a great holiday they had.

Suggested answers

adjective + *experience*: great; memorable; personal; terrible; unusual
compounds: hands-on experience; life experience; work experience
experience + preposition: experience as something; (no) experience of doing something; experience in something

---

3 GRAMMAR Comparison

a Write on the board *George stayed in the room __ anyone else*. Elicit comparative phrases to go in the gap, e.g. *a lot longer than*. Tell the students to cover the text and complete the sentences. Check answers as a class.

Answers

1 the   2 The   3 considerably   4 and   5 more
6 nowhere near   7 infinitely

b Tell students to look at sentence 1 and ask if you hear more things if it is quiet or loud (*quiet*). Tell students to look at sentence 6 and ask if the experience was more or less disturbing than George thought before he went in (*less*). Tell students to answer the questions in pairs, then check as a class.

Answers

1 sentences 1, 2 and 5. The degree of each is dependent on the other, for example as one increases so does the other.
2 sentences 2 and 4
3 sentence 3: slightly; a good deal; decidedly; significantly
 sentence 6: nothing like; not nearly

c ▶ ⏵ 1.25–1.29 Students read the information in Grammar Focus 2A on SB p.140. Play the recording where indicated and ask students to listen and repeat. Students then complete the exercises. Check answers as a class. Tell students to go back to SB p.21.

Answers (Grammar Focus 2A SB p.140)

a 2 The plant hasn't grown / didn't grow nearly as quickly/fast/ big/large/tall/high/much as she expected.
 3 He isn't/wasn't strong enough to control the horse.
 4 A kilogram of iron is no heavier than a kilogram of feathers.
 5 Sales have been marginally better since June.
 6 The harder the rain fell, the more difficult the game became.
b 1 and   2 the   3 so   4 than   5 far/miles   6 get   7 more
 8 not   9 nowhere   10 miles

◉ **CAREFUL!**

A typical error students make is with word order and *much more*. Highlight that when *much more* modifies a verb, it goes after the noun phrase: ~~Students will enjoy much more the film club than before.~~ (Correct form = *Students will enjoy the film club **much more** than before*.). Point out that when *much more* modifies an adjective or noun, it goes before the adjective or noun phrase: ~~They replaced the computers with new ones much more expensive.~~ (Correct form = *They replaced the computers with **much more** expensive new ones*.). Students also often make the mistake of adding *at* and/or *the* to the fixed phrase *last but not least*. ~~At last but not the least, the publicity for the club is boring.~~ (Correct form = ***Last but not least**, the publicity for the club is boring*.). Another typical error is to use either just *as* or *so … as* instead of *as … as*. ~~I'm surprised as you.~~ (Correct form = *I'm **as** surprised **as** you*.). ~~The candidates were not so experienced as I would like them to be.~~ (Correct form = *The candidates were not **as** experienced **as** I would like them to be*.).

d 💬 Give your own example (it doesn't need to be true!) of a place or an event using several comparative structures. Then ask students to think of a place or an event and discuss the questions in pairs.

4 LISTENING

a 🗨 Try and communicate something to the class using only gestures, e.g. what you did that morning. Stop after a few minutes and ask the class what they understood. Ask students if they have ever had a situation when they had to communicate in this way, e.g. they were in a foreign country and couldn't use English. Then put students into pairs to discuss the questions.

b ▶1.30 Ask students to look at the picture of Lena. Elicit what a *vow of silence* is (a promise not to speak for a period of time) and predict why a young woman would want to take one. Play the recording of the first part of Lena's story for students to listen and see if their prediction is correct. Check the answer as a class.

Answer

She was intrigued by the idea of a public vow of silence and wanted to see how it would affect her and other people.

Audioscript

LENA A few months ago, I went to a friend's place for dinner. It was a fun night – lots of lively company – y'know, one of those nights you feel you've talked about everything and solved the world's problems! Towards the end of the evening, I was feeling a bit tired and I just kind of sat back and watched and listened – did nothing. It was interesting. It struck me how what we say sort of defines who we are. Talking is a way of fitting in – y'know, a way of showing that we belong to a social group.

The next day I couldn't stop thinking about this and began to wonder what would happen if I just stopped talking altogether and was just … silent. What would happen to me? How would I come across to other people? I decided to read up on the topic of vows of silence. There were some really interesting stories online. Often a vow of silence is for spiritual purposes and people go into some kind of retreat to cut themselves off from the outside world. I guess you could say that's not about communicating at all – it's like taking time out to focus on yourself. But some of the other stories I read were about people taking what you'd call a more public vow of silence. What I mean is they continued to live in the real world and communicate with people – just they didn't speak. Some people did this as a protest – y'know, like against censorship or something like that.

I didn't have any kind of burning cause I wanted to protest against but, for my own reasons, I was still intrigued by the idea of a public vow of silence. So I decided to take one – just for a weekend. I knew I'd find it hard to last much longer than that. I looked on it as a kind of social experiment. I knew it was going to be a challenge!

📖 **VOCABULARY SUPPORT**

read up on sth – to learn about something by reading

take time out – spend time away from one's usual work or studies, for rest or leisure

a burning cause – a strong belief about something in society you want to change

c ▶1.30 Ask some questions before you play the recording again, e.g. *Did Lena enjoy the dinner party?* (yes). *How did she get information about vows of silence?* (through the Internet). Play the recording for students to summarise what Lena says about the four things.

Suggested answers

1 It was fun and everyone talked a lot.
2 She realised that what you say defines who you are and that by talking you show you belong to a social group.
3 A spiritual vow of silence means you retreat from the outside world, look inside yourself and don't communicate with other people.
4 A public vow of silence means you continue to live in the real world and communicate with people without speaking.

d 🗨 Tell students to discuss the questions in pairs. Ask some questions to get students thinking about what situations might be difficult, e.g. *What if she meets a friend? Will people who don't know about her vow think she's rude?*

e ▶1.31 Play the recording of part two of Lena's story for students to check their ideas.

Audioscript

LENA So … a whole weekend without speaking. The person I found hardest to deal with was … myself. When I'm alone I often talk to myself, or sing, or hum. But, no – I wasn't allowed to do any of that. I had to keep my vocal cords completely out of action. I managed OK, except for a couple of times – like when someone held a door open for me and a little 'thank you' slipped out.

Also when my phone rang, I couldn't answer. I was quite proud that I remembered, even when someone woke me up calling early on Saturday morning. But I did text back. So, you see, I still communicated – email, text – all that sort of thing. I just had to keep my mouth well and truly shut.

The first thing that amazed me was just how easy it is to communicate without words – like, buying a coffee. I just sort of pointed to what I wanted and nodded in agreement when the person in the café got it right. I even met a friend for a chat. I could react to what he had to say by means of a facial expression. Occasionally, I did have to write some things down on a notepad, but I was amazed how much information I could get across without trying too hard.

The most interesting thing was the way other people related to me. When I was queuing in the supermarket, a woman tried to have a conversation with me. She bombarded me with questions. When she eventually realised that I couldn't or wouldn't speak, she just made up her own answers to her own questions. She had a whole conversation with herself about why I couldn't speak! She thought I was unwell.

Also my landlord was interesting. I had to go and pay my rent on the Saturday. He always goes on about something when I go and see him – he usually likes to run down some politician or other. I don't always agree with him, and we often end up having a heated discussion. But this time, I just listened … And when I left he said, 'It was great to have a good chat.' This was interesting. I don't think he really noticed that I hadn't been saying anything. He was so caught up in what he was saying he wasn't very aware of me. And it made me think … well, aren't we all a bit like that? We're all so busy talking and expressing our ideas – it's like a kind of prison that doesn't allow us to communicate with each other and see what's going on around us. Most of the time people treated me kindly. I often felt that my silence brought out the best in people.

Being silent for two days really gave me a chance to see and feel things without feeling I needed to respond or react. I mean, I often wanted to, but I had to hold myself back. And this meant I just had to let things go – just let them be. And, you know, I felt more peaceful – more connected with everyone and everything. So it really was fascinating – my weekend of silence. I recommend giving it a go.

f ▶**1.31** You can treat this as a summarising exercise similar to 4c, playing the recording straight through, or you can pause after each person (this is helpful for weaker students who tend to get lost in a long listening). Check answers as a class.

Suggested answers
herself: she was the person she found hardest to deal with, she generally remembered not to speak but broke her own rules a couple of times, she still communicated by text and email
the person in the café: she could communicate by pointing and nodding
her friend: she could communicate by using facial expressions and writing some things down
the woman in the supermarket: she managed to have a conversation with herself while Lena said nothing; the woman thought Lena was ill
her landlord: they usually get into political arguments but this time he thought they'd had a good conversation even though Lena had said nothing
At the end of the experiment she felt more peaceful, and more connected with everyone and everything.

> 📖 **VOCABULARY SUPPORT**
>
> *out of action* (C1) – not in use
>
> *well and truly* – completely
>
> *a heated discussion* – a discussion in which people get excited/angry because they feel strongly
>
> *be caught up in sth* – so involved in an activity that you do not notice other things
>
> *let sth go* – not react to something annoying which somebody else says or does
>
> *let sth be* – not interfere or try to control a situation
>
> *give sth a go* – try something new

g 💬 Put students into small groups to discuss the questions. Then compare ideas as a class. Ask students if it would be easy for someone to do this in their country.

5 VOCABULARY
Multi-word verbs: Social interaction

a ▶**1.32** Write on the board:

I don't get __ well with my sister-in-law.

Ask students to complete the multi-word verb (*get on*) and give an equivalent phrase (*have a good relationship*). See if students can complete the sentences without listening again and then play the recording to check. Point out that *relate to* (to understand someone and be able to have a friendly relationship with them) can also mean *be connected to*: *This growth is **related to** the economic trends of those years.*

Answers
1 in 2 across 3 off 4 out 5 to 6 with 7 about
8 down 9 out 10 back

> 👁 **CAREFUL!**
>
> A typical error students make is to use *fit in* not *fit in with* when there is an object: ~~He doesn't fit in the rest of us.~~
> (Correct form = *He doesn't fit in **with** the rest of us.*)

b Get students to categorise the multi-word verbs according to their meaning by looking back at the sentences. Check answers as a class.

Answers

social interaction in general	spoken interaction
come across	bombard sb with questions
cut yourself off	go on about
relate to sb	run sb down
bring out the best in people	
hold (yourself) back	

c ▶**1.33** **Pronunciation** Write *I don't get on well with my sister-in-law* on the board again and ask students to repeat it. Ask whether *get on* sounds like one or two words (one) and why (there is linking between the final consonant and opening vowel). Tell students that identifying linking is very important for listening to connected speech and linking will help them sound more natural in many contexts, too. Play the recording for students to listen and identify the linking consonant sound. Check the answers as a class.

Answers
/m/; it's an example of consonant–vowel linking

d ▶**1.34** See if students can identify the linking before they listen and then play the recording for them to check. Check answers as a class. Drill the phrases concentrating on the consonant–vowel linking.

Answers
1 … cut themselves‿off from …; /z/
2 … a little 'thank you' slipped‿out …; /t/
3 … goes‿on about something …; /z/
4 … my silence brought‿out the best …; /t/

e 💬 Give your own examples of people you know and then ask the students to talk about people they know in pairs. Alternatively you could organise this as a *Find somebody who …* activity, with students going round the class and asking one another questions until they have a person for every multi-word verb in 5a. Take feedback as a class. Then elicit different ideas from the class for learning multi-word verbs before asking students to read the Learning Tip. Tell students that they also need to record grammatical information about multi-word verbs, e.g. separable verbs like *run (sb) down* or *run down (sb)* and non-separable verbs like *relate to (sb)*.

> 💡 **EXTRA ACTIVITY**
>
> Revise the multi-word verbs by saying sentences and getting students to rephrase them with a multi-word verb.
>
> *Do I belong here?* (fit in)
>
> *I asked him loads of questions.* (bombarded him with)
>
> *She gives the impression of being bored.* (comes across as)
>
> *Stop repeating it again and again.* (going on about it)
>
> *Our teacher does things so that we do as well as we can.* (brings out the best in us)
>
> *I wouldn't criticise people who do crazy sports.* (run down)

6 SPEAKING

💬 Write on the board *Humans are the only animals which can communicate in a meaningful way.* and get students to agree or disagree with you in a short class discussion. Put students into small groups first to read and then discuss statements 1–5, answering the questions.

ADDITIONAL MATERIAL

▶ Workbook 2A

▶ Photocopiable activities: Grammar p.203, Vocabulary p.223, Pronunciation p.254

2B I'll be jumping from 900 metres

At the end of this lesson, students will be able to:

- talk about experiencing extreme sports
- understand the main points and detail of a magazine-style article and identify synonyms
- divide connected speech into word groups and identify the main stress
- use a range of verbs of movement
- follow an interview and understand a detailed description
- use a range of future forms for intentions and arrangements

⚲ OPTIONAL LEAD-IN

Books closed. Ask students for examples of extreme sports and the risks involved. Give an example:

Cliff diving – jumping into the sea from a cliff – is very dangerous if you land badly in the water.

Then ask students to give you extreme sports vocabulary in three categories:

- types of sports (e.g. base jumping, skydiving)
- feelings (e.g. terror, stress)
- places (e.g. mountains, skyscrapers).

1 READING and SPEAKING

a 💬 Students rank the activities individually and then compare their ranking with other students. Take feedback as a class and ask students which of these activities they have actually done and what they were like.

b 💬 Ask students some questions about the four pictures, e.g.:

Is the ball on flat ground or on a hill? (a hill)
Are the two men snowboarding? (No, there isn't any snow.).

Put students into groups of four and allocate a different text to each person in the group. Students read and answer the questions about their text. They then report back to their group. Use the Vocabulary support box to help with vocabulary if necessary.

Answers

Zip-lining
1 Costa Rica, Hawaii and other places nearer home
2 a harness (attached to a wheel that dangles from a cable/line)
3 go very fast (100 mph) down a zip line
4 Suggested answer: quite safe because you wear a harness, although the speed and height would make a fall or a collision very dangerous
5 $100–$300

Indoor skydiving
1 at iFly facilities nationwide / inside a vertical wind tunnel
2 a flight suit and a helmet
3 do free-fall skydiving in a wind tunnel where winds of 160 miles per hour push you into the air
4 Suggested answer: quite safe because suitable for any age
5 $60–$250

Zorbing
1 anywhere in the world
2 –
3 roll downhill inside a clear plastic ball typically 10 feet in diameter at high speed
4 Suggested answer: quite safe because you're strapped in
5 –

Volcano-boarding
1 Cerro Negro volcano, Nicaragua
2 Suggested answer: In the picture the participants are wearing a safety helmet, elbow pads, knee pads and gloves
3 go very fast down a steep, 1,600-foot volcanic slope, on a plywood board reinforced with metal and Formica
4 Suggested answer: slightly dangerous because of the threat of another eruption although there hasn't been once since 1999
5 $28

c 💬 Check the meaning of *exhilarating* by asking *Does it mean very exciting or very dangerous?* (very exciting) and drill the pronunciation /ɪgˈzɪləreɪtɪŋ/. Students rate the sports individually and then compare with other students, giving reasons for their ratings.

2 READING

a 💬 Ask students to look at the picture of the people on the roller coaster and ask *How are the people feeling? How will they feel after their ride?* Then ask students to read the list of reasons for doing extreme sports. Put students into pairs to discuss the motivation for extreme sports. Encourage students to add more reasons to the list. Students then check which reasons from the list are mentioned in the text. Check answers as a class.

Answers
to feel more alive
to feel they are in control
to test their limits
to feel great afterwards

b Give students time to read the text in detail and answer the questions. Ask students to underline the sections of the text that give the answers. Check answers as a class and encourage students to paraphrase in their answers. Use the Vocabulary support box to help with vocabulary if necessary.

Suggested answers
1 skydiving
  zip-lining
  whitewater rafting
  going on a roller coaster
2 thrill-seekers: people who want variety, novelty, intensity and risk
3 Biology, from birth, is important, but it's not yet known how important. Neurochemicals like dopamine and testosterone, and the amount of white matter in the brain, appear to affect whether people are thrill-seekers or not.
4 They tend to be creative, energetic and self-confident. They feel in control and they don't like to be told what to do.
5 The relief of escaping death gives a rush of adrenaline, ecstasy and elation.

c **Language in context** Synonyms: *want, like, love*

1 Ask students if they know any synonyms of *want* (e.g. *desire, fancy, be desperate for*). Tell students to try and match the expressions with the sentences without looking at the text. They then check their answers in the text.

2 Tell students to look at their dictionaries and find how these expressions are different from *want*, *like* and *love*. They should look at both the explanations and the example sentences. Check answers as a class.

Answers
1 a crave; thrive on b long for c is inclined d are drawn to
2 *crave* and *long for* are very similar in meaning, the same as, but much stronger than *want*.
  thrive on and *love* have quite different meanings. If somebody thrives on something, it means that they feel at their best, for example happy, healthy and alive, when they experience that thing.
  be inclined to can mean *want*, but it also means *likely to*. If someone is inclined to be late, they are likely to be late.
  be drawn to means both *like* and *be attracted to* at the same time.

d 💬 Ask students: *Do Type T people play it safe or live on the wild side?* (live on the wild side). Then put students into pairs to discuss the questions. In class feedback, ask students what the advantages/disadvantages of being a Type T person in everyday life would be, e.g. they may get bored easily.

e ▶ 1.36 **Pronunciation** Write Helen Keller's quote from the end of paragraph 2 on the board and ask students how many word groups there are and where the main stress is in each word group: *Life is a daring adventure, | or it is nothing.* Play the recording for sentence 1 and tell students to mark the word groups and main stress as they listen. Tell students to look at the other sentences and try and mark the word groups and main stress. Play the recording for students to listen and check. Check answers as a class.

Answers
2 I need a <u>guide</u> | in new <u>cities</u> | in case I get <u>lost</u>.
3 I do feel <u>scared</u> | when I face <u>danger</u> | but I know that I'll be <u>OK</u>.
4 I'm paid to innovate at <u>work</u>, | so I spend half my time <u>daydreaming</u>!
5 I think people should dress <u>neatly</u> | and look <u>respectable</u>, | especially in <u>public</u>.

f Elicit the complete rule and then drill the comments in 2e.

Answer
last

g 💬 Put students into groups to discuss whether a Type T person would agree with the comments in 2e. You could make groups of all Type Ts and all non-Type Ts (based on the discussion in 2d) and see what consensus there is between the groups. Take feedback as a class.

3 VOCABULARY Verbs of movement

a Read out some verbs of movement and get students to say whether they are on land, through water or through air: *crawl* (land), *row* (water), *float* (water, air), *skip* (land), *paddle* (water), *dive* (land, water, air). Students look at the sentences and categorise them in the same way, using a dictionary. They should also check in the dictionary whether there is any sound suggested. Check answers and in class feedback, tell students that *whoosh* is a good example of an onomatopoeic word, based on the sound in real life.

Answers
1 a A b L; W; A c L d L; W; A e W; A f L; W; A
 g W; A h L; W; A
2 whizz; zoom; whoosh; whirl

💡 **FAST FINISHERS**

Ask fast finishers to list other onomatopoeic words that they know in English, e.g. *crash*, *babble*, *screech*, and find some new ones. The easiest way to do this is to find the English translation for words that describe a sound in their own language.

b ▶ ⏵**1.36** Students complete the exercises in Vocabulary Focus 2B on SB p.159. Play the recording for students to check their answers to Exercise a. Check answers to Exercise b, c and e. Monitor Exercise d and ask students to compare sentences in Exercise f. Tell students to go back to SB p.25.

Answers (Vocabulary Focus 2B SB p.159)
a 1 k 2 o 3 q 4 p 5 l 6 j 7 i 8 n 9 h 10 m
b 1 creep; crawl; drift; limp; stagger; stroll
 2 leap; march; rush; slide
 3 crawl, creep; drift
 4 limp; stagger
c creep, crept; slide, slid
e 2 She staggered/crawled down the road.
 3 He crept down the road.
 4 She hurtled/rushed/whizzed/zoomed down the road.
 5 He limped/crawled down the road.
 6 She drifted/strolled down the road.
 7 He hurtled/slid/whizzed/zoomed down the road.
 8 It hurtled/soared/whirled/whizzed/whooshed/zoomed down the road.
 9 He hurtled/rushed/whizzed/zoomed down the road.
 10 She drifted down the road.
 11 It crawled down the road.

4 LISTENING

a ⏵**1.37** If you have the technology, show a short YouTube video of base jumping and get the students to share their impressions. If you don't, tell students to look at the picture and ask: *How do the people watching feel? How does the person jumping feel? How high do you think they are?* Put students into pairs to say what base jumpers do and predict what Ada will say about base jumping. Then play the recording for students to check. Pre-teach *hit* (succeed in reaching or achieving a number) and *keyed up* (very excited or nervous, usually before an important event) if necessary.

Audioscript
PRESENTER Millions of visitors come to the Swiss Alps every summer. There's walking, climbing, swimming, cycling, paragliding – almost no limit to what you can do here. For some people these sports aren't exciting enough. Instead, they go base jumping. This means jumping off a cliff and free falling before opening your parachute and landing safely, they hope, in the valley below. The idea of jumping off a mountain may be a nightmare for some people. Base jumpers say it's an experience like no other. To find out, I watched 24-year-old Ada Hoffman go on her first jump.
So Ada, you're about to go base jumping and it's your first time.
ADA Yes. I'm due to jump in about 10 minutes.
P How are you feeling? Nervous?
A Yes nervous, but also excited, very excited. I'm keyed up – you know, I'm going to enjoy this. I've been parachute jumping quite a bit. I've had training in that, I jump maybe … about er … 300 jumps. Most people say, like, 200 is a minimum, other people say 5 … 500 is a minimum so … I feel ready for this base jumping, so …, yes it feels like a natural step.
P And what are you going to do exactly? You'll be jumping off the mountain, right?
A Yes. There is a platform which sticks out over the cliff. And um … yes, basically, I'm planning to jump off that one.
P And then?
A Then I'll be jumping from about 900 metres … So … I'm aiming to free fall for exactly 25 seconds. And um … then I'm going to fall for a further 30 seconds with er … the parachute completely open.
P And land safely in the valley?
A Yes – you'd hope so, yeah.
P And how will you know when it's time to open the parachute?
A I'm going to count the seconds – that's the only way of doing it. Um … when I reach 20 seconds, or count on 20, I'm going to pull this string hard and um … then the parachute will open in about 5 seconds.
P OK, well good luck. I'll talk to you again after the jump.
A Thank you.
...
A Hi.

P Hi, you made it.

A Yes.

P So how was it?

A Oh it was good, it was a good jump. Everything was fine.

P How did it feel?

A Amazing – there's nothing like it really – absolutely amazing! A bit scary at first – you know, you walk along this platform and then you just have to jump. And then, you feel really calm, completely in control. And after the parachute opens it's quite peaceful you know … it's just … you drift down, and it's … oh … it's just wonderful.

P So will you go base jumping again?

A Oh yes, definitely. I'm definitely going to do it again, maybe I'll go later today actually. I'm also thinking of trying a tandem jump some time. You know when you jump with somebody else, you jump together? I think that should be really fun, but er … you have to be very careful.

P With the number of jumps likely to hit 30,000 this year, it's clear that the sport is highly attractive. But there's no question that it is a very dangerous sport and not everyone survives. Many people say it should be better regulated, or even banned. But base jumpers disagree.

A Well it certainly is dangerous. Yes it's very dangerous and I think you need to be aware of the risks when you take a jump. So … if you don't … if you're not aware then you maybe shouldn't jump. But you know, you're not coming here thinking, 'Oh, I'm planning to have an accident.' That's … that's not what you're aiming to do. You come here with the intention of having a great experience and … and that's what you do.

b ▶ **1.37** See if students can remember what the numbers refer to before they listen again. Some numbers can be guessed quite easily, e.g. 900 metres, the height of the jump. Then play the recording to check.

Answers

1 a how long until Ada jumps
  b the number of parachute jumps Ada has done
  c the height she'll be jumping from
  d how long people free fall before opening their parachute
  e the number of seconds (you count) before you open your parachute
  f the number of jumps that will probably take place this year in the Swiss Alps
2 She says you need training and to be aware of the risks.

c 💬 Ask students to discuss the question in pairs. Then take feedback as a class.

5 GRAMMAR Intentions and arrangements

a ▶ **1.38** Write these sentences on the board:

1 Ada is going to fall off the mountain!

2 Ada is going to do another base jump.

3 Ada is going to jump next weekend.

Ask students how the meaning of *be going to* is different in each one. Elicit that sentence 1 is a prediction (Ada doesn't want to do this!), sentence 2 is her intention and sentence 3 is an arrangement. Ask students if they know any other ways of talking about intentions and arrangements. Students look at the pairs of sentences. Tell them to try and remember which one Ada said and explain why she said it. Then play the recording for them to check which sentence Ada used and then check students' explanations as a class.

Answers

1 a Ada's jump will happen very soon.
2 a She's expecting to jump at a certain, pre-arranged time.
3 b The jump height is fixed, therefore this will happen naturally, with no further decisions or arranging.
4 a She intends to do it again (but has not arranged it yet).

b ▶ **1.39** Students look at the sentences and try and remember what Ada said. Then play the recording for them to check.

Answers

1 thinking   2 planning   3 aiming   4 intention

c ▶ **1.40-1.43** Students read the information in Grammar Focus 2B on SB p.141. Play the recording where indicated and ask students to listen and repeat. Students then complete the exercises. Check answers as a class. Tell students to go back to SB p.25.

Answers (Grammar Focus 2B SB p.141)

a 2 going
  3 will you be
  4 going
  5 'll be standing
  6 about
  7 going
  8 'll be wearing
b 2 ~~'ll be doing~~
  3 ~~don't see~~
  4 ~~is looking~~
  5 ~~wears~~
  6 ~~'m not aiming to answer~~
  7 ~~repays~~
  8 ~~aims~~
  9 ~~due~~
  10 ~~are becoming~~
c 2 'll
  3 thinking
  4 due/going
  5 be
  6 due/going/about
  7 not
  8 won't
  9 'll
  10 is

⊚ CAREFUL!

Students often make mistakes with word order. A common error is to put adverbials like *as soon as* and *this morning/weekend* etc. between the verb and noun. ~~We're going to give as soon as possible the exact date.~~ (Correct form = *We're going to give **the exact date as soon as possible**.*) ~~We'll be organising this year transport.~~ (Correct form = *We'll be organising transport **this year**.*) Another problem students have is prepositions. Students sometimes use *in* in front of *this morning/weekend*, etc. ~~The report will be ready in this week.~~ (Correct form = *The report will be ready **this week**.*) Remind students to use *in* not *after* with measurements of future time. ~~I'm going to be back after two days.~~ (Correct form = *I'm going to be back **in** two days.*)

d Talk about your own plans using as much of the target language as you can. Then give students time to write down some ideas of their own. Give some more prompts if necessary (places they intend to visit, people they haven't seen for a long time that they want to meet up with, hobbies they want to take up, etc.).

e 💬 Put students into groups to compare their plans. Ask who has got the most unusual or challenging plan. Then find out if any students have the same or similar plans. Put them into groups made up of students who have the same or similar plans if possible. Ask them to talk about how they are going to achieve their plans, perhaps by helping each other.

6 SPEAKING and WRITING

a 💬 Ask students to look at the photo, guess where it is and say why someone would want to live there.

b ▶ Tell students to go to SB p.135, read the blog and answer the questions. Put students into pairs. Tell them to read the prompts and write a blog post about their plans. They could make a real blog post online if they have the technology or they could just write in their notebooks. Pairs swap blog posts. They read them, think of questions to ask and add comments. Students give back the blogs with the comments. Students imagine that a year has passed. They ask and answer questions, and respond to the comments. You could have an extra speaking stage where pairs compare their experiences, and say what the comments were and how they responded to them.

Answers
The photo shows the Rocky Mountains in Canada.
a He works in insurance. He's probably writing to the people he used to work with.

💡 **EXTRA ACTIVITY**

In groups, ask students to make a multiple-choice personality test to work out whether someone is a Type T person or not. Tell students to write questions testing the traits and attitudes, and ideally the vocabulary, covered in the reading and the lesson. Give an example:

If you won a thousand euros, how would you be inclined to spend it?

A go on holiday to somewhere new and exciting

B put it in the bank

C buy something I need for the house

Ask students to think of question types in their groups, divide them up and write them out of class. They then compile and check them in class, write a key to interpret the answers and give the test to another group to do.

ADDITIONAL MATERIAL

▶ Workbook 2B

▶ Photocopiable activities: Grammar p.204, Vocabulary p.224

2C Everyday English
Don't get so wound up about it

At the end of this lesson, students will be able to:

- **understand conversations between people in which they talk about their problems and concerns**
- **talk about problems and discuss solutions**
- **use a range of expressions to be tactful and frank**
- **recognise and use emphatic stress**
- **use a range of expressions for giving advice and warnings**

💡 **OPTIONAL LEAD-IN**

Books closed. Ask students to rank these typical aims for young people who have just finished school or university from 1 (easiest to achieve) to 6 (most difficult to achieve):

- finding a good job
- becoming financially independent from parents
- keeping in touch with friends from school/university
- finding new friends and interests
- understanding what they want to do with their life
- finding somewhere to live.

1 LISTENING

a 💬 Ask students where they live and how long they've lived there. Put students into small groups to discuss the questions. Take feedback as a class and ask students to justify their opinions on question 2.

💡 **EXTRA ACTIVITY**

Tell students that a shortage of housing in the UK is making it increasingly difficult for young people to buy their first property and that the cost of renting has increased. Have a short class debate on what governments could do to help young people buy or rent their own homes.

b 💬 Tell students to look at the pictures. Ask: *Does Emma look happy?* (no). *What book is Alex holding?* (*Solar Wind*). *Do you think Max would be a good guest?* (no). Students work in pairs and guess the connection between the pictures.

c ▶ **1.44** Check students understand the idiom *get on sb's nerves* (to annoy someone a lot) and pre-teach *volatile* (likely to suddenly become angry) and *boot sb out* (force somebody to leave). Play Part 1 of the video or the audio recording. Check answers to 1b as a class.

Answers
Emma's brother, Max Redwood, is the author of the book, *Solar Wind*. Alex is Emma's boyfriend and he is reading Max's book. He also knows that his colleague Oscar is interviewing Max on *City FM* the next day.

Videoscript/Audioscript (Part 1)

EMMA Uh-huh … yeah … uh-huh.

ALEX Right, so I'll pick you up about seven.

E Great!

A What else is going on today, then?

E Nothing much. Max is due back soon.

A Max? Who's Max?

E My brother. He's staying with me at the moment, remember?

A Oh, yeah, that's right.

E He's getting on my nerves, to be honest. There's just not enough space!

A Wait, he's not still sleeping on the sofa, is he?

E Yes! And his stuff's everywhere!

A Hmm …

E And he's just so volatile! It's like walking on eggshells half the time.

A Isn't it about time you asked him to leave?

E Well, I keep dropping hints, but he doesn't seem to notice.

A Why don't you just tell him straight, then? Don't beat around the bush. There's a lot to be said for being upfront about things.

E I can't just boot him out!

A Hang on, did you say his name is Max?

E Yeah.

A Max Redwood?

E Yes.

A The same as that guy who wrote *Solar Wind*?

E No, he is the guy who wrote *Solar Wind*.

A You mean it is him?! Your brother is **the** Max Redwood!

E It's no big deal.

A I don't believe it! Oscar is interviewing him tomorrow!

E I know. Look, I've really got to go. Max will no doubt be hungry when he gets in. See you tonight.

A Yeah, OK. Bye then … .

d ▶1.44 Play Part 1 of the video or the audio recording again and ask students to answer the questions. Check answers as a class.

Answers
1 Max is staying with her and he's very untidy and volatile.
2 She's kept dropping hints.
3 She should tell him what she thinks.
4 Emma isn't impressed. Alex is excited and impressed.

e Language in context *Being tactful or frank*

1 ▶1.45 Tell students to match the halves of the expressions from Part 1. Play the recording for students to listen and check.

2 Make sure that students understand what they are being asked by concept checking tactful and frank language. Say to students: *You're making too much noise. It's very annoying.* and then ask *Was that tactful?* (no) *Was it frank?* (yes). Then say: *It seems a bit noisy here.* Ask students: *Was that tactful?* (yes). Ask students which of the expressions describe being frank and which describe being tactful. Books closed. Read out half of the expression. Tell students to complete it and say whether it is frank or tactful, e.g. *drop …* (hints, tactful).

Answers
1 1 e
  2 c
  3 b
  4 a
  5 d
2 being tactful: walk on eggshells; drop hints
  being frank: tell someone straight; be upfront about something; don't beat around the bush

f 💬 Put students into groups to discuss the questions. Check that students understand *outstay your welcome*. Ask: *If your guests outstay their welcome, do you want them to stay longer?* (no). Check ideas as a class. Ask pairs to share interesting anecdotes about their experiences with the whole class.

2 PRONUNCIATION Emphatic stress

a ▶1.46 Ask students: *Would you like to write a book?* and elicit some answers from the class. Write the question on the board and ask students how many word groups there are (one) and where the main stress is (*book*). Play the recording for students to listen and underline the main stress in the word groups. Then ask them to say which word in a group has the main stress, and to refer to SB p.24 if necessary. Check answers as a class.

Answers
1 <u>Max</u> is due back soon.
2 He's getting on my <u>nerves</u>.
3 Isn't it about time you asked him to <u>leave</u>?
4 Did you say his name is <u>Max</u>?
The last word in a word group normally has the main stress.

b ▶1.47 Borrow a student's book and say *This isn't <u>my</u> book.* Ask students if the rule on SB p.24 applies here (no). Tell students to listen and underline the main stress in the word groups.

Answers
1 He's not <u>still</u> sleeping on the sofa, is he?
2 He <u>is</u> the guy who wrote *Solar Wind*.
3 You mean it <u>is</u> him?
4 Your brother is <u>the</u> Max Redwood!

c Put students into pairs to answer the questions. Check answers as a class. Ask students how *the* is pronounced differently in 4 (/ðiː/ not /ðə/).

Answers
1 Alex and Emma emphasise different words to communicate more precisely: 1 showing disapproval 2 correcting 3 checking / showing disbelief 4 (See answer to question 2 below.)
2 'the Max Redwood' means the famous person called Max Redwood, rather than another, non-famous person who has that name.

d Write *I know Max.* on the board. Say it three times, putting the main stress on a different word each time and asking students how the meaning changes.

I know <u>Max</u>. (normal main stress)

<u>I</u> know Max. (not everyone does)

I <u>know</u> Max. (but he's not really a friend)

Then tell students to match the sentences with their meanings. Students repeat the sentences with the main stress in the appropriate place.

Answers
1 d 2 b 3 a 4 e 5 c

e 💬 Read out the sentences and encourage students to think of an appropriate follow-up, e.g. *I'll give you a ring later.* (*You will? Why? Isn't Nino around today?*) Drill all three sentences. Put students into pairs to make and practise a conversation for each sentence. Stronger students can plan in their heads. Encourage other students to make notes rather than write out the conversations in full. Take feedback as a class and ask students to act out one of their conversations. The other students say which of the three sentences the conversation is based on.

3 LISTENING

a 💬 Tell students to look at the picture. Ask them to say what might be happening between Emma and Max and how each person might be feeling. Pre-teach *wound up* (very worried, nervous or angry), *be short of sth* (not having enough of something) and *desert island* (an island where no people live). Put students into pairs to look at the picture and guess who said the sentences.

b ▶ 1.48 Play Part 2 of the video or the audio recording and tell students to check their answers in 3a. Check answers as a class.

Answers
1 Max 2 Max 3 Emma 4 Emma 5 Max

Videoscript/Audioscript (Part 2)

EMMA So, Max, I was thinking – have you thought about the possibility of finding your own place to live?
MAX Hadn't really thought about it, to be honest.
E Well, I mean, it's not as if you're short of cash any more, is it?
M True.
E It might be in your interests to invest some of it into property.
M Invest? Property? What are you talking about?
E Well, it would be lovely to have your own workspace, wouldn't it? What do you think?
M Sure. Yeah. Yeah. But I can't think about any of that right now.
E Why not?
M Well, I've got that radio interview tomorrow.

E Uh-huh?
M I don't know what to say!
E Oh, don't worry about it. You might want to have a think about what you could say tonight.
M There's nothing else to say about *Solar Wind*! The book is the book.
E Oh Max, don't get so wound up about it. It's only an interview.
M Only an interview?! You're joking.
E Hey. I'll be able to listen to you.
M Don't you dare listen!
E Alright, alright. Calm down!
M Maybe I'll just go far, far away, take a vow of silence, live on a desert island somewhere …
E Yeah, you might as well!
M Emma!

---

c ▶ 1.48 Ask students to read the questions and note down any answers they remember. Play Part 2 of the video or the audio recording again for students to answer the questions or check their answers. Check answers.

Answers
1 Because he isn't short of cash any more.
2 It would be a good investment; it would be lovely for him to have his own workspace.
3 She suggests that he might want to have a think about what he could say that night.
4 He doesn't want her to listen.
5 He doesn't feel he has anything to say in the radio interview and he is being dramatic about how to avoid it.

d 💬 Put students into groups to discuss the questions. Take feedback as a class.

---

4 USEFUL LANGUAGE Giving advice

a Tell students to look at the picture and ask: *Who do you think the man with the map is?* Put students into groups to discuss the questions. Check answers as a class.

Suggested answers
1 It depends if there is a train coming or not; fine if there's no sense of urgency.
2 Look out! / Don't stand there – you're on a railway line! / Get off the line! / Move!, etc.
3 if someone was unintentionally in the way of somebody else and there is no urgency or danger involved / if there were plans to build an airport near your home / if your neighbours were very unpleasant, etc.

b ▶ 1.49 Tell students to match the sentence halves. Play the recording for students to listen and check. Check answers. You could point out that we use *it's (about) time* + past tense to say that it's past the time when something should have happened: *It's about time he got a job.* (See *It's time* used to express criticism in Grammar Focus 10A on SB p.156.)

Answers
1 b
2 e
3 d
4 g
5 c
6 f
7 a

c Put students into pairs to answer the question and check answers as a class. Ask students why the two expressions sound more polite and formal (the modal verb *might* is less strong than *must* or *should* so it implies a less bossy, more polite attitude from the speaker).

Answers
It might be in your interests to
You might want to

d Tell students to complete the sentences with expressions in 4b. Check answers.

Answers
1 might want to
2 thought about the possibility of
3 a lot to be said for
4 might as
5 your interests to

---

e 🗨 Put students into pairs to say which conversation is more formal and to think of possible contexts. Check which is more formal and compare ideas on context as a class.

Answers / Suggested answers
Conversation 2 is more formal.
Conversation 1 could involve one speaker trying to encourage the other to confront an issue/person they're finding it hard to deal with.
Conversation 2 could be two colleagues discussing a contract.

f 🗨 Tell students to plan and perform the two conversations in pairs. Tell them that the language in conversation 1 should be informal and formal in conversation 2.

🔄 LOA TIP MONITORING

During a freer speaking activity in groups (or pairs), do not interrupt students unless students make errors with the target language or conversation breaks down. Listen and make a note of other errors you notice which you feel would be useful for the students to focus on. At C1 it can be useful to correct for mismatched register as well as incorrect lexis. If you notice any particularly good language use, including consistent use of formal or informal register, note this too without making it clear who said them. Write up your notes on the board and point out good use of language and elicit corrections as feedback.

5 SPEAKING

▶ Divide the class into pairs and assign A and B roles. Student As go to SB p.137 and Student Bs go to SB p. 127. Tell students to read about their problem and think about what to say. Students take turns to tell their partner about it, paraphrasing rather than reading aloud. They should give each other advice including two suggestions, using the language for advice on SB p.27. Put students into groups to compare the advice they gave. Take feedback as a class.

💡 EXTRA ACTIVITY

▶ Put students into new pairs. Ask them to role-play a conversation between either the two flatmates or the boss and the employee. Tell them to discuss the situation and to try and find a solution. You could ask some pairs to act out their conversations for the class.

ADDITIONAL MATERIAL

▶ Workbook 2C
▶ Photocopiable activities: Pronunciation p.255
▶ Unit Progress Test
▶ Personalised online practice

2D Skills for Writing
Less adventurous students could try paintball

At the end of this lesson, students will be able to.
- discuss different sports activities
- make notes on a listening involving multiple speakers
- understand the structure and content of a formal report
- identify and use a range of linking devices in understanding and writing a report
- plan and write a report

💡 OPTIONAL LEAD-IN

Books closed. Give these examples of possible new sports: *underwater golf, synchronised bungee jumping, melon-and-spoon racing*. Ask students what kind of event could have these sports, e.g. an under-21 Olympics, and choose the most suitable event. Put students into groups to think of ideas for sports for this event. Compare ideas as a class and ask students to vote for the sport they'd like to include.

1 LISTENING and SPEAKING

a 🗨 Ask students what kind of activities their university or school have organised for them and if these include any of the activities shown in the photos. Put students into pairs to choose one activity based on the criteria given. Check ideas as a class.

b ▶1.50 Play the recording. Tell students to listen to the speakers and make notes on their feedback on the two activities they tried out. You may wish to pre-teach the words and phrases from the Vocabulary support box.

Answers

	Positives	**Negatives**
bungee jumping	very exciting, most incredible sensation, big rush, amazing sense of freedom	didn't understand the thrill, had thought there would be no cost but had to pay half the cost ($100)
whitewater rafting	a lot of fun, exciting, unpredictable	quite expensive (but worth it), slipped on wet rock and twisted ankle, not exciting enough, a bit risky for people who aren't such good swimmers
other feedback		no one from the social programme committee went with them to the river or to the jump site (airfield), doesn't like extreme sports

Audioscript

LUBA The social activity I liked most was the whitewater rafting excursion. I'd never done anything like that at all and it was a lot of fun. It was quite expensive to do, but I think it was worth it. We had to pay for the guide and hire of the wetsuits and everything like that. But the feeling of being swept along by the current of the water was a bit like being on a roller coaster – it was infinitely more exciting because everything was far less predictable. The only negative thing that happened to me was that when I got off the raft, I slipped on a wet rock, and sort of twisted my ankle. Still, it won't stop me from trying this again.

MEHMET I did both the social programme activities: whitewater rafting and the bungee jump. The rafting was nowhere near as exciting as the jump. I loved it – so much, in fact, I'm planning to do another jump before I go back home ... For me, there was one thing I found a bit strange about these activities. When we went to the river, and to the jump site, we were just picked up by a minivan driver – there was no one from the social programme who came with us. I mean, we had a good enough time just with ourselves, but it was a bit odd that no one from the committee was there. Not very friendly, I thought.

PAOLO Actually, I didn't do either of the sports activities. I like sports, but I'm not so keen on these extreme sports. The more dangerous they are, the less I want to do them. So, with the whitewater rafting – well, I'm not such a good swimmer, and I was told it'd be a bit risky. And then with the bungee jump – well, I've never really understood the thrill of throwing yourself off a bridge. I'm quite good at 'normal' sports – football, tennis, volleyball – and I like hiking. Why do sports have to be extreme all the time? Some people complained about the cost, but that didn't surprise me. These things cost money. I don't mind paying – it's just it needs to be something I really want to do.

CHANGYING For me, the highlight of the year was doing the bungee jump. To begin with, I really wasn't sure about it and I remember when we were in the minivan on the way there, the closer we got, the more nervous I became. I almost pulled out at the last minute, but everyone encouraged me to go ahead with the jump. It was truly amazing – the initial free fall is the most incredible sensation I've ever felt – just a big rush with this amazing sense of freedom. The only negative aspect of the experience was that we had to pay half the price. A hundred dollars is a lot of money. I'd been led to believe that all these activities would be paid for. I mean, I could afford it and it was worth it, but I thought these things were meant to be covered as part of the social programme.

📖 VOCABULARY SUPPORT

be swept along by sth – something powerful makes you move very fast and without control

twist your ankle (C1) – injure your ankle by suddenly turning it

pull out of sth – withdraw from something you had planned to take part in

a rush – a sudden strong emotion or other feeling

be led to believe sth – be caused to believe information which later is revealed as untrue

sth be covered by sb/sth – an expense is paid for by somebody else, or from a particular source of funds

---

c 💬 Put students into new pairs to think about the students' feedback in 1b. Then ask them to choose two different sports. Put pairs together into groups of four to explain their choices to one another. Check ideas as a class.

---

2 READING

a Ask students what the purpose of a report is (to analyse a situation and make recommendations). Tell students to read the report, compare the content with their notes on the four speakers' feedback and answer the questions. Check answers as a class.

Answers
1 safety, cost
2 No one from the social programme committee went with the students to the river or jump site (airfield).

b In pairs, students discuss if the recommendations in the report agree with their own. Take feedback as a class.

3 WRITING SKILLS
Reports; Linking: contrast and concession

a Ask students which order the headings should logically go in. Then tell the students to match the headings with the paragraphs. Highlight that report headings should be clear and brief. Check answers.

Answers
1 Introduction   2 Level of challenge   3 Safety concerns
4 Cost and budget   5 Recommendations

b Ask students to go through the report and find and underline the phrase which introduces the reason for the report and a phrase which introduces recommendations, noting whether the register is formal or informal. In class feedback, tell students that the register of reports is usually formal.

Answers
1 The purpose of this report
2 we would recommend (that) (we choose)
These phrases are formal.

c Tell students to cross out the word in italics in each sentence which is not possible and explain why. Check answers as a class.

Answers
1 agenda (this is about meetings)   2 establish (not a synonym of *recommend*)   3 resolution(s) (can mean the solution to a problem, but is not used in this type of text or context)

d Ask students to give three examples of linkers, e.g. *but, however, because of*. Elicit that linkers are either conjunctions, which connect ideas in sentences (*but*), adverbs, which give extra information (*however*), or prepositions, which go before noun phrases (*because of*). Students replace the words in the sentences with the linkers in the report. Check answers.

Answers
1 In contrast to   2 Nevertheless   3 However / On the other hand
4 Despite   5 Even though

LOA TIP ELICITING

When you elicit, give as much support as you can for students to give the correct answer. *What is a linker?* isn't an easy question to answer. *Could a conjunction be a linker?* is easier because it requires a *Yes/No* answer. *Could words like 'but' and 'so' be linkers?* is easier still because there are concrete examples.

e Write these two sentences on the board. Ask students to say which linker expresses a comparison where two different things are contrasted and which linker expresses a concession where two different ideas about the same subject are contrasted.

I'll try it, even though I'm scared. (concession)

Unlike football, rugby is quite dangerous. (comparison)

Explain that concession and contrast are not separate concepts; contrast means that two ideas are different in some way, which includes concession, some types of comparison and more. Some linkers, e.g. *however*, can be used flexibly for different types of contrast, but others only have one use, e.g. *even though* for concession, *unlike* for comparison. Students match the sentences and underline the linkers.

Answers

1 b For all that   2 f Despite the fact that   3 a On the contrary
4 e When compared to   5 d Regardless of   6 c While

💡 FAST FINISHERS

Ask fast finishers to choose three of sentences 1–6 and finish them in a different way, e.g. *1 … not everyone agrees that they belong on the social programme.*

---

f ▶ Students complete the exercises in Writing Focus 2D on SB p.170. Tell students to complete the sentences in Exercise a with linkers from the box and then, in Exercise b, to think of alternative answers from the table. Check answers as a class. Students rewrite the sentences in Exercise c using the linker in brackets. Check answers as a class. Then tell students to complete the sentences in Exercise d with their own ideas. Compare answers as a class. Tell students to go back to SB p.29.

Answers / Suggested answers

a 1 Regardless of   2 However   3 By comparison
   4 Even though   5 On the contrary   6 When compared to
b 1 In spite of; Despite   2 On the other hand; Alternatively
   3 However; On the other hand   4 Although   5 –
   6 In contrast to
c 1 Despite the large class, it was still possible to get individual attention.
   2 The teacher we had was very strict, unlike my old teacher, who was very easy-going.
   3 Although I was very disappointed with the lunches, the evening meals were great. / I was very disappointed with the lunches, although the evening meals were great.
   4 For all that it rained every single day, I enjoyed everything that we did. / It rained every single day. For all that, I enjoyed everything that we did.
   5 There were several injuries. Nevertheless, spirits were high among the groups.

---

4 WRITING

a 💬 Check students understand *itinerary* (a detailed plan or route of a journey). Put students into small groups. They should think of and discuss problems foreign students might have had during a three-day visit. Give some examples in addition to the prompts, e.g. local people not speaking much English.

b Tell students to plan the report in groups. Remind students that the first step is to decide on the headings as this gives the report structure. Students then make notes, based on their discussion in 4a, under each heading with possible linkers. Read through the Writing Tip with the class and remind students to bear these points in mind as they complete the final task.

c Ask students to write the report individually or in groups, with different students taking responsibility for a heading or paragraph. Encourage students to use the linkers covered in the lesson.

d Students read one another's reports and compare the structure and content. To save class time, students could post their reports and comments on a closed group of a social networking site.

💡 EXTRA ACTIVITY

Put students into small groups to act as a student committee. Tell students they have a budget of 12,000 euros and they need to choose how to spend the money. Write the budget on the board (add new categories if you like).

Cost	Categories
€4,000	Subsidising extreme sports
€5,000	Grants to students in financial hardship
€3,000	New sports equipment for the student sports hall
€2,000	Subsidising a late-night minibus service
€3,000	End-of-year party for all students
€6,000	Improving the quality of student accommodation
€4,000	Grants for students to study abroad

Students decide on their budget and explain it to the rest of the class.

ADDITIONAL MATERIAL

▶ Workbook 2D

UNIT 2
Review and extension

1 GRAMMAR

a Tell students to complete the sentences with one word only. Highlight the example and make sure students understand that the missing word is a grammar not a content word. Check answers as a class.

Answers
2 deal
3 far
4 the
5 more
6 like
7 near
8 as

💡 FAST FINISHERS

Ask fast finishers to write two more sentences each with a gap to test other fast finishers on comparative forms.

b Tell students to choose the best option for expressing intentions and arrangements. Check answers as a class.

Answers
1 are going to
2 begins
3 going to get
4 will you be
5 to
6 due to

2 VOCABULARY

a Tell students to match the sentence halves, remembering which preposition/adverb goes with each verb to make a multi-word verb. Check answers as a class.

Answers
1 d
2 a
3 e
4 c
5 b

b Tell students to answer the questions with one word only. Give an example: *Would a soldier or a base jumper march?* (soldier). Check answers as a class.

Answers
2 cat
3 no
4 truck
5 ill
6 child
7 stones
8 ice

3 WORDPOWER Idioms: Movement

a ▶ 1.51 Elicit the difference in meanings of the words in the box. *Which is faster, 'whizz' or 'crawl'?* (whizz). *If something plunges, does it go up or down?* (down). *If things are whirling around your head, do you feel calm?* (no). Ask *Are any of these verbs irregular?* (no). Tell students to look at the pictures and describe them. Then ask students to replace the word in italics in the sentences with the correct form of the verbs in the box. Play the recording for students to check their answers.

Answers
1 a soaring b plunged
2 a drift b whirling
3 a whizzing b crawl

b Give an oral example first and ask students to read out the definition which applies: *City will definitely win their next match, they're playing so well.* (on a roll). Students then match the expressions with the definitions. Check answers as a class.

Answers
1 do something you're afraid of
2 get a sudden strong feeling
3 accept something eagerly
4 having a series of successes
5 try something for the first time

c Write an example on the board and elicit the answer: *No one noticed that the boat had begun to ___ out to sea.* (drift). Students choose two words or expressions and write two sentences with a gap for the word/expression. They read out their sentences for other students to guess. Remind students that the word or expression should be in the correct form.

💡 EXTRA ACTIVITY

Dictate to students: *live in an English-speaking country for a year, go parachuting, be interviewed on TV, take part in a clinical trial for extra cash, travel back in time.* In pairs, ask students to discuss whether they would *jump at the chance* to do each one.

▶ Photocopiable activities: Wordpower p.242

LOA REVIEW YOUR PROGRESS

Students look back through the unit, think about what they've studied and decide how well they did. Students work on weak areas by using the appropriate sections of the Workbook, the Photocopiable worksheets and the Personalised online practice.

UNIT 3
Travel and adventure

UNIT CONTENTS

G GRAMMAR
- Inversion (adverbial + question word order for emphasis)
- Future in the past; Narrative tenses (review)
- Writing briefly: Informal ellipsis

V VOCABULARY
- Wealth and poverty: *affluent, deprived, destitute, disposable income, hardship, impoverished, live within your means, make ends meet, prosperity, well-off*
- Landscape features: *an arid desert, calm turquoise waters, dark pools of stagnant water, dense fog/vegetation/undergrowth, empty moorland, forest canopy, the heart of the rainforest/capital/jungle, huge sand dunes, a mosquito-infested swamp, the mouth of a cave, pristine beaches, a remote area/forest/village, a rich green meadow, rocky ground, rugged coastline, sheer cliffs, a tropical rainforest/storm/island/paradise, an untouched wilderness/forest/plate of food, wooded slopes*
- Language in context: Unusual experiences; Descriptive verbs; Exaggerating
- Word power: Idioms: Landscapes: *be a slippery slope, be on the rocks, be swamped, a drop in the ocean, get the lie of the land, out of the woods, an uphill struggle*

P PRONUNCIATION
- Tone in inversion structures
- Word stress
- Glottal stops
- Consonant groups across two words

GETTING STARTED

OPTIONAL LEAD-IN

Books closed. Write these sentences on the board:

1 Travel broadens the mind.

2 He's got itchy feet again.

Put students into pairs. Ask students to explain what the sayings mean and what their implications are. Ask students if they know any idioms or sayings in their language(s) connected with travelling. Tell them to translate and explain them to the rest of the class.

Suggested answers
1 Travelling makes you more tolerant.
2 He's bored and wants to go somewhere new.

UNIT OBJECTIVES

At the end of this unit, students will be able to:
- **understand and summarise details, attitudes and opinions in texts about various types of travel experiences**
- **follow broadcast material, including a speech and an audio blog, and extended speech about various types of travel experiences and note and summarise details and attitudes**
- **use a range of lexis to give clear, detailed descriptions and narratives of their own travel and tourism experiences and discuss and evaluate voluntary projects in other countries, using lexis and intonation accurately to emphasise particular events**
- **understand a radio interview and an emotional conversation and identify details and implicit opinions and attitudes of the speakers**
- **use a range of expressions which paraphrase and summarise information to clarify their remarks in social interaction**
- **write a descriptive narrative about a travel experience and a travel review of a tourist destination using appropriate lexis to express details precisely**

a Give students one minute to think about their answers to the questions before talking about the photo as a class. If you wish, give students information from the Culture notes below. Take feedback as a class.

🌍 CULTURE NOTES

This photo shows people trying to help a bus which has fallen off what has been called the world's most dangerous road, the North Yungas road from La Paz to Coroico in Bolivia. Most of the road is a narrow single-lane descent of over 3,000 metres with no barriers to stop vehicles falling off the cliffs. The rainy season from November to March is particularly dangerous and 200–300 travellers a year are killed on the road. Despite or perhaps because of the dangers, mountain bikers and other extreme sports enthusiasts come from all round the world to experience the road.

b Put students into pairs to retell the story of the day to each other. Tell them to take different perspectives, e.g. one student is the bus driver and the other is one of the people helping to get the bus back on the road. As feedback, ask some students to tell their story to the whole class.

c Put students into groups to discuss whether they would enjoy a trip on this road or something similarly extreme. Take feedback as a class.

EXTRA ACTIVITY

Ask students to imagine they are a passenger on the bus and to write a text message (maximum 160 letters) to a relative explaining the situation and asking for help. If students have mobile devices, they could send the text to a partner, compare their messages and write back answers.

3A Never have I had such a rewarding experience

At the end of this lesson, students will be able to:
- read personal experiences, interpret the perspectives of the writers and work out the meaning of vocabulary and expressions connected with the theme of experiences
- discuss unusual and challenging travel and volunteer experiences
- use a range of adverbials using inversion for emphasis
- signal inversion with the appropriate intonation
- write a paragraph for a blog using inversion for emphasis
- listen to a speech and summarise the topic areas covered
- use a range of words and expressions connected with wealth and poverty

OPTIONAL LEAD-IN

Books closed. Write the proverb *Charity begins at home.* on the board and ask students what it means (look after your own family/society before you help others). Put students into groups to discuss whether and how they have ever given their time or money to help people in their own country. Elicit ways in which students have helped and list them on the board.

1 READING and SPEAKING

a Ask students where Belize, Cambodia and Ghana are and what they know about these countries. Show them where these countries are on a map if you have one and also point out the Caribbean (/ˌkærɪˈbiːən/ or /kəˈrɪbiən/) Sea. Put students into different groups to discuss the different volunteer jobs. Take feedback as a class.

b Students discuss the questions in the same groups. Take feedback as a class.

c Ask students to look at the pictures and ask: *Why do you think the boy is wearing a hard hat? What are the children at the table doing?* Tell students to read the reviews quickly and say which of the jobs in 1a are described (1, 2). Then ask students to read the reviews in more detail and answer the questions. Encourage students to guess the meaning of the words and phrases in the Vocabulary support box if they ask about them. Check answers as a class.

Suggested answers

1 Similarities: Both reviews mention the relationships with the children, the types of work they did, the intense heat, and that the experience was rewarding.
Differences: Debbie focuses more on physical discomfort and relationships with children; Linda and Malcolm mention tourism as well as volunteering, they compare children at home with children in Belize and they mention gaining life skills through volunteering.
2 Debbie: sweating profusely, insects, missing home comforts, being frustrated, the intense heat saps a lot of your energy
Linda and Malcolm: not being prepared for the intensity of the heat, Malcolm being able to carry out more manual work than Linda

VOCABULARY SUPPORT

a fair few – (informal) a considerable number, several

chilling – (informal) spend time relaxing with other people

shortcomings – weaknesses/failings; ways in which something is not good enough

d Ask students which job seems the most interesting/ challenging. Then check students understand *prospective* by asking which review would be more helpful to people thinking about becoming volunteers. Elicit some reasons from the class.

LOA TIP REVIEW AND REFLECT

- Help students to reflect on the reading task more systematically. Elicit some criteria to evaluate the usefulness of each review, e.g. practical details; description of the responsibilities; objectivity; balance of positive and negative points; useful extra information.

- Ask students to evaluate the usefulness of each review according to these criteria. They could give a 1–5 rating for each criterion and/or make notes.

- Students then compare their evaluation in groups, e.g. Debbie's review is more practical because it gives a timetable for the day.

e **Language in context** *Unusual experiences*

1 Books closed. Write *feel __ by a fair few things* (frustrated), *to __ __ more manual work* (carry out) from the reviews on the board and tell students to fill in the missing words. Books open. Students check in the reviews. (The examples are in paragraph 1 of each review.) Students then do the matching exercise, using a dictionary if necessary. Check answers as a class.

2 Explain *comfort zone* (a situation in which you feel comfortable and in which your ability and determination are not being tested). Students complete the expressions with prepositions. They then check their answers in the reviews.

Answers

```
1 1 c  2 e  3 f  4 a  5 b  6 h  7 g  8 d
2 1 in  2 out  3 of
```

EXTRA ACTIVITY

Put students into groups of four. Each group chooses the volunteer job in either Ghana or Belize. Two students are candidates and prepare for an interview for the job. The other two students are interviewers and think of questions. Each interviewer interviews each applicant separately. The two interviewees then compare how their interviews went while the two interviewers compare notes and decide on one of the students for the job.

2 GRAMMAR Inversion

a Ask students to read the sentences and ask which sentences are about experiences (1 and 2) and which are about ideas or opinions (3 and 4). Ask students whether they think these particular experiences and opinions were important to the writers. Tell students to tick the reason for using these phrases. Check the answer as a class (for emphasis).

b Ask students if they notice anything unusual about the word order in the phrases in bold in 2a (the auxiliary verb comes before the subject). Tell them to complete the rule. Check answers.

Answers
1 negative   2 question

c Tell students to rewrite the sentences in 2a without an inverted word order. Check answers as a class.

Answers
1 As soon as I had woken up each morning, I would see a smiling face and hear a child's giggle that would melt my heart.
2 I have never had such a rewarding and truly enlightening experience.
3 We never regretted / We didn't regret for a moment the decision to go there.
4 Children back home (just) don't realise how the food they take for granted is a genuine treat for children here.

d ▶ ⏯ 1.52 Students read the information in Grammar Focus 3A on SB p.142. Make sure students read the tip about not overusing inversion. Play the recording where indicated and ask students to listen and repeat. Students then complete the exercises. Check answers as a class. Tell students to go back to SB p.33.

Answers (Grammar Focus 3A SB p.142)
a 2 a2 b1   3 a1 b2   4 a1 b2   5 a2 b1
b 2 Only in the evenings did we feel relaxed.
3 Barely had I got home when the phone rang.
4 Seldom does Rita take responsibility for her actions.
5 Not a single shop did we find.
6 On no account am I going to accept.
c 2 No sooner had I arrived   3 not in a million years did I think
4 Not until 21:00 did I find   5 not a single person did I see
6 Rarely have I been

3 SPEAKING and WRITING

a ⏯ 1.53 Say to the students: *Seldom can you find one when you need one* and ask what this could refer to (a taxi on a rainy day). Put students into pairs, play the recording and ask them to discuss what the context for each sentence could be. Take feedback as a class.

b ⏯ 1.53 **Pronunciation** So students can tune their ears, say *No* as a refusal in order to elicit that the tone falls and then *No* as a question in order to elicit that the tone rises. Play the recording for students to mark the intonation. Drill each sentence: first only the phrases in bold (fall then rise) and then the phrases in bold and the rest of the sentence (finishing with a fall). Check the answer as a class (fall then rise).

c 💬 Give your own short example of a travel story using inversion. Tell students to prepare their story individually and practise. Encourage them to use the adverbials in the box. Then put students into pairs to tell their stories. Ask students to share the most interesting experiences as a class.

d Students write a paragraph for a blog about the travel experience they have just spoken about. Make sure they use inversion in two sentences. Ask some students to read out their paragraphs and give feedback.

4 LISTENING

a 💬 If necessary, elicit the meaning of *developing country* (B2) (a developing country or area of the world is poorer and has less advanced industries). Put the students into groups to discuss the question and compare ideas as a class.

b ⏯ 1.54 Play the recording for students to compare the problems mentioned with their ideas in 4a. Check answers as a class.

Answers
Problems mentioned: lack of preparation/research; corruption; disillusionment; failure to understand local context; lack of criticism of volunteering

Audioscript

DANIELA PAPI I volunteered all over the world – building homes in Papua New Guinea, doing post-tsunami work in Sri Lanka, helping paint a school in Thailand. And I used to think it was the best way to travel. In 2005, I decided to organise my own volunteer trip – a bike ride across Cambodia with five friends. We were going to teach students we met along the way and raise funds to build a school. We spent months fund raising – through book sales, and bake sales, and speaking at community groups. We named the trip 'The PEPY Ride' – with PEPY being 'Protect the Earth, Protect Yourself' – because we were going to teach about the environment and health. The thing is, it turned out, there was more than one small problem with our plan. First of all, we didn't really know that much about the environment or health, or Cambodia for that matter. And the money that we raised for other small projects that we hadn't researched very much got wasted or landed in corrupt hands. And that school we helped to build, well, when I arrived to see it, I found a half-empty building and realised something I already should have known – schools don't teach kids, people do. I was pretty disappointed, as you can imagine, that we'd spent the better part of a year fund raising and planning and things hadn't turned out to be as simple as the celebrity volunteer trips I'd seen on TV. So, I decided to stay in Cambodia a bit longer and figure out how we could put that school building, and the rest of the funds we had raised, to better use. That 'little bit longer' turned into six years living in Cambodia. During which time, I founded an education NGO and to raise money for the non-profit work we were doing, I started a volunteer travel company – where I lead hundreds of volunteers on trips to Cambodia. At first, our tours looked a lot like that first bike ride, and I took people on trips where we'd teach English or yoga or paint a building. But I slowly began to see that I was part of a growing system that I no longer believed in. After a decade of joining and leading volunteer trips, and from interviewing volunteers from all around the world as part of a book I am now co-authoring, I now firmly believe that the growing practice of sending young people abroad to volunteer is often not only failing the communities they are meant to be serving, but also setting these travellers, and by extension our whole society, up for failure in the long run. More and more young people are going abroad to volunteer each year – as part of school requirements, to build their CVs, or part of gap-year trips. Much of this demand is fuelled by the opinion that because we come from financially wealthier countries, we have the right, or obligation to bestow our benevolence on people. Never mind if we don't speak the language, don't have the skills or experience to qualify for the jobs we are doing, or don't know anything about what life is like in that, quote-unquote, 'poor place'. Now, as a former serial-volunteer myself, I am in no way trying to criticise the good intentions of these volunteer travellers. I know from my former experience our desire to help is sincere. But I also now know that good intentions are not enough. Yet, good intentions are usually enough to get people to support your efforts. The praise and encouragement for international volunteering is almost blind to the details, the process, or the research for how these young volunteers are actually going to help. Throughout the time we were fundraising for that first bike trip, countless numbers of people praised our generosity and bravery – yet very few people questioned us at all about our plans. Perhaps instead of handing us a cheque someone should have asked us how we planned to learn all we needed to know to be of help to anybody. The local papers wrote articles about us that made it sound like part of our heroism was the fact that we didn't know very much. I believe that our lack of critical engagement when it comes to international volunteering is creating a double standard.

c (▶) **1.54** Go through the questions and see how much the students can already say about them. Play the recording again for students to summarise what Daniela says. You may wish to help students with the meaning of the phrases in the Vocabulary support box. Check as a class.

Suggested answers

1 to teach Cambodian students about the environment and health, and raise funds to build a school
2 Their knowledge of environmental and health issues, and of Cambodia, was insufficient. Lack of research meant that much of the money they raised was wasted or used dishonestly. Although a school was built, only half of the building was used as there wasn't enough money to staff it.
3 She founded an education NGO (non-governmental organisation) and started a travel company for volunteers going to Cambodia.
4 The increasing number of programmes for young volunteers abroad often fail the people they are designed to help and therefore also fail the volunteers and society as a whole, too.
5 Praising the efforts mean that they ignore the fact that young volunteers' efforts are often wasted. Instead of really helping people, the volunteers are the ones who benefit the most.

📖 VOCABULARY SUPPORT

meet along the way – meet without planning, during the time that you are doing something

land in sb's hands – unintentionally arrive in the possession of that person

the better part of – most of

set sb up for failure – create a situation which will cause somebody to fail

gap year – a year between leaving school and starting university that is usually spent travelling or working

be fuelled by sth – be caused / made stronger by something

quote-unquote – said to show that you are repeating someone else's words, especially if you do not agree

be blind to sth (C2) – not be conscious of or deliberately ignore something obvious

lack of engagement – the state of not considering something carefully/enough

double standard – a standard of good behaviour that is applied unfairly to different groups of people

d (💬) Ask students what they think Daniela means by *a double standard* at the end of the recording (the volunteers are not expected to be competent in their roles, yet benefit from the situation they are in) and what she will talk about next. Put students into pairs to discuss the questions. Compare ideas as a class.

5 VOCABULARY Wealth and poverty

a Tell students to make a table with *wealth* and *poverty* in their vocabulary notebooks and write down the words under each category by reading the words in context in the sentences. Point out that they need to find one word/phrase that applies to everybody. Check answers.

Answers

1 P 2 P 3 W 4 W 5 P 6 W 7 W 8 P
9 applies to people with any level of income 10 P

b Tell students to look back at the sentences and answer the questions. Check answers as a class.

Answers

1 prosperity 2 destitute 3 well-off 4 make ends meet 5 b

c (▶) **1.55** **Pronunciation** Play the first sentence of the recording. Ask: *How many syllables are there in the word in bold?* (two) *Which one is stressed?* (the first). Play the whole recording for students to work individually. Check as a class and then drill the words and phrases.

Answers

1 <u>hard</u>ship 2 im<u>pov</u>erished 3 <u>affl</u>uent 4 <u>pros</u>perity
5 <u>make</u> ends <u>meet</u> 6 well-<u>off</u> 7 dis<u>pos</u>able <u>in</u>come
8 de<u>prived</u> 9 <u>live</u> within our <u>means</u> 10 <u>des</u>titute

d (💬) Ask students to think of an example of each phrase in italics in 5a from knowledge/experience and compare their sentences in pairs. Take feedback as a class.

6 SPEAKING

a Tell students to look at the pictures and say what kind of volunteer work this is and how it might help the community. Pre-teach *cheetah* (a wild cat with black spots that can run faster than any other animal). Go through the four projects and ask students what would be interesting/challenging about them. Students think of someone they know and choose one of the projects for them or think of another project, perhaps a real one.

b Ask students for some more ideas about what to say to their volunteer about practical preparation, e.g. *speak to volunteers who have done this before, collect sports equipment,* etc. Tell students to make notes under the categories.

c (💬) Put students into pairs to tell each other about the project they have chosen, their volunteer and what they would say to them. Ask students to think of possible questions the volunteer might have, e.g. *How can I learn some of the local language quickly?* and how they can answer them.

ADDITIONAL MATERIAL

▶ Workbook 3A
▶ Photocopiable activities: Grammar p.205, Vocabulary p.225, Pronunciation p.256

3B I was expecting it to be tough

At the end of this lesson, students will be able to:

- **use the future in the past to talk about past intentions**
- **use a range of words and phrases to describe landscape features**
- **understand the informal conversational features of a spoken narrative**
- **read a travel narrative and work out the meaning of descriptive verbs**
- **understand when final /t/ sounds are not pronounced in connected speech**
- **consolidate their range of narrative tenses**
- **speak and write about an adventurous trip**

⊕ OPTIONAL LEAD-IN

Books closed. Ask students to choose one of these dream journeys:

- touring Australia, flying and staying in comfortable hotels
- trekking in northern Thailand, visiting local hill tribes
- cycling around the south coast of France, camping on beaches
- taking the Trans-Siberian railway across Russia.

Put students into groups according to their choices, e.g. all touring Australia, and ask them to talk about what they expect from their journey.

1 READING and GRAMMAR
Future in the past

a Ask students questions about the map: *Where are these two countries?* (West Africa). *Is this journey up or down the river?* (down). Put students into pairs to use the prompts and their own ideas to discuss the journey. Check ideas as a class.

b Ask students to look at the pictures of Will and say what kind of environment this looks like (tropical rainforest). Give students time to read the text and answer questions 1 and 2. Check answers as a class. Make sure students understand *paddle* (to push a pole with a wide end through the water in order to make a boat move). Although a demonstration is more effective, understanding complex explanations is a key skill for advanced students. Elicit why students think Will decided to paddle down the rivers rather than use some easier transport. Then put students into pairs to discuss question 3 and take feedback as a class.

Answers
1 It's unique. It's one of the last untouched wildernesses of the Upper Guinean forest belt and contains more than a quarter of Africa's total mammal species.
2 He wanted to find out what life in the heart of a tropical rainforest was really like. He paddled (went on a raft) down the rivers, as this was probably the only way to travel through such a wild environment.
3 Students' own answers

c Tell students to find and read the underlined sentence in the text and then complete the sentences with phrases in the box. Check answers as a class and explain that this form is an example of the future in the past.

Answers
1 in the future
2 in the past

🔄 LOA TIP ELICITING

- When you elicit grammar, use a simple personalised example before focusing students on the example in the SB. This is an easier and more engaging first stage. Tell students: *I felt bad this morning. I was going to have the day off, but then I felt better so I came to school.* Ask: *Am I telling you something about the past or future?* (past). *Did I intend to have the day off?* (yes). *Was I thinking about the future or past this morning?* (future).
- Elicit the form after the meaning. Write the sentence on the board and say: *Which verb form shows I was thinking about the future in the past?* (was going to).
- Now move on to the SB example.

d Tell students that there are different ways of expressing the future in the past. Adapt Will's example with *was planning to* rather than *was going to*, e.g. *I was planning to paddle down these rivers …* . Students underline six more examples in the article. Check answers.

Answers
was planning to start
would be in radio contact / on my own / separated
was expecting it to be
was to become
He uses: past continuous of certain verbs (+ indirect object) + *to* + infinitive (*was planning to start, was expecting it to be*); *be going to* + infinitive (*was going to paddle*); *would* + infinitive (*would + be*); past simple *be* + *to* + infinitive (*was to become*)

e Tell students to look at the examples and write five sentences using the future in the past about other things Will might have considered before his trip. Encourage students to use a variety of verb forms. Students compare their sentences in pairs. Take feedback as a class.

⊕ EXTRA ACTIVITY

Write these sentences on the board: *Last summer I was going to …, but … . When I was younger, I thought I would … and … . At the weekend I was planning to …, but … .* Students complete the sentences and compare them in pairs. Take feedback as a class.

f Put students into pairs and ask them to predict what will make Will's journey difficult and dangerous. Discuss ideas as a class but do not confirm or deny any ideas.

2 VOCABULARY Landscape features

a Ask students what the connection is between the highlighted words (they are all about landscape). Ask: *Which would have more vegetation – a jungle or a wilderness?* (jungle). Put students into pairs to give definitions for the words and find the differences, using a dictionary if necessary. Check answers as a class.

Answers

jungle: a tropical forest in which trees and plants grow very closely together
wilderness: an area of land that has not been used to grow crops or had towns and roads built on it, especially because it is difficult to live in as a result of its extremely cold or hot weather or bad earth
rainforest: a forest in a tropical area that receives a lot of rain
vegetation: plants in general, or plants that are found in a particular area

b Ask: *Would we say 'thick forest' or 'full forest'?* (thick). *Why?* (it's a collocation). Tell the students to complete the collocations and then check their answers in the text. Check answers as a class.

Answers

1 the heart of the   2 a tropical   3 dense
4 an untouched   5 a remote

> ### 💡 FAST FINISHERS
>
> Ask fast finishers to think of one more noun for each of the words and phrases in the box, e.g. *a tropical fruit, a remote beach*. Tell them to compare their answers with another fast finisher.

c ▶ ⏵**1.56** Students complete the exercises in Vocabulary Focus 3B on SB p.160. Monitor Exercise a and check answers as a class. Draw students' attention to the Tip. Play the recording for students to check their answers to Exercise b. Monitor Exercise c and take feedback as a class. Tell students to go back to SB p.36.

Answers (Vocabulary Focus 3B SB p.160)

a 1 d   2 c   3 f   4 g   5 b   6 a   7 e
b 1 pools   2 meadow   3 slopes   4 ground   5 moorland
6 cliffs   7 cave   8 face   9 dunes   10 undergrowth
11 canopy   12 beaches   13 waters

3 LISTENING

a ⏵**1.57** Ask students what kind of sounds they think Will will hear going down the river. Play the recording for students to compare the sounds with their predictions. Tell students to name the sound/activity and say what might be happening on the journey. Elicit students' ideas but don't check answers at this point.

b ⏵**1.58** Pre-teach *raft* (a small rubber or plastic boat that can be filled with air – see the picture on SB p.37). Play the whole recording for students to check their answers.

Answers

1 Will pumping up his raft
2 Will paddling and insect sounds
3 Will paddling and bird calls
4 Insect noises around Will's camp at night
5 Rapids on the river

Audioscript

WILL What do you think to my boat, Saqba?
SAQBA Oh the boat – it's nice … no problem.
w You think it's nice? No problem?
s Yeah, no problem.
w Cool … OK, I'm going to try and get inside. Ooh … This will be my home for the next few weeks. Here we go … Can you push me off, Saqba?
s Yeah, no problem.
w Thanks, buddy … OK, see you in a few days.
s Yeah. We shall see again. Safe journey.
w Thanks, mate! My first paddle strokes. Oh … First of thousands, probably. This is absolutely amazing. It's very shallow in parts. You might be able to hear the base of the boat just rubbing along the rocks, but it's so quiet out here. I've only been going about 20 minutes and already I've seen far more wildlife than I've seen in the last three days, just in the forest surrounded by jungle. There's dragonflies buzzing around, cattle egrets, large blue herons, kingfishers … There's a whole cloud of white butterflies just on the Sierra Leonean bank. I'm completely hemmed in on both sides by jungle. Ooh, a fish, a big fish swam straight past. The water is so clean here. I'm just silently drifting up to this enormous fish eagle. I can't be much more than eight feet away from it now. It's just staring straight at me. Big white-capped head, dark wings, burgundy-brown across the back. Just close enough now to see that it's got a massive catfish in its talons. I think I might leave him to it.
Managed to just get my camp sorted. So this is my first night alone in the forest. Er … I've got my mosquito net up. I'm actually in my hammock, but my hammock's on the floor because … I'm in a little stone island in the middle of the river. Just at the end of the day there was quite a large cataract and I didn't really fancy taking it on till tomorrow, so I've just camped in this little island, basically, but I'm kind of worried if it rains tonight though, that the rain might just run straight through the middle of my camp or something. I don't know though, I guess I'll find out.
I'm just trying to catch my breath. I think … I think the island last night marked the start of a series of rapids, just these rock-strewn whitewater passages, maybe 100 to 150 metres long. And then you get a short break, and then another, and then another, and another. I just took on this last one here and made a terrible mess of it, ended up sideways, hit this big rock in the middle of the river, which almost flipped the raft, just managed to get control of it again, and shot out of the bottom of this kind of small waterfall. So I'm just taking some shelter in this eddy right now and I'm going to have to unpack everything and tip out any water that I've taken on. And the thing is – just got to be so careful because if I lose the raft, I'm finished. It's got all my communication equipment on, it's got all my food on, it's got my shelter on it. Without it, I cannot survive and now I am so far from the next village.

c ⏵**1.58** Play the recording for students to listen again and summarise what Will says about each picture. Use the Vocabulary support box to help where necessary but also refer students to the Learning Tip and emphasise that they don't really need to know, for example, what an *egret* is to understand the text.

Answers

1 He's seeing lots of wildlife, including dragonflies buzzing around.
2 He's drifting close to a large fish eagle with a white head, dark-coloured wings and a red-brown back. The bird has caught a big catfish and is holding it in its talons/claws.
3 He's in his hammock but his hammock isn't hanging from anything. It's on the ground on a small stone island in the middle of the river.
4 He's sheltering in some quiet water in the middle of a series of rapids, each one about 100 to 150 metres long with white water and full of dangerous rocks.
5 He can't survive without his raft as it holds all his communication equipment, his food and his shelter.

VOCABULARY SUPPORT

egret – a white bird from the heron family

heron – a large bird with long legs, a long neck and grey or white feathers that lives near water

kingfisher – a small brightly coloured bird with a long pointed beak, that lives near rivers and lakes and eats fish

be hemmed in – be surrounded by barriers

leave sb to it – (informal) not interfere with somebody, so they can continue their activity

get sth sorted – (informal) complete the process of organising/setting up something

take sth on – attempt a particular task (especially a difficult one)

catch your breath – after being very active, rest for a moment, so that you can breathe more slowly

make a mess of sth – do something very badly

shoot – move very quickly in a straight line

be finished – (of a person, informal) not be able to continue with something / survive

HOMEWORK ACTIVITY

▶ Ask students to follow the advice given in the Learning Tip and find a short authentic text, less than one page, describing a journey or adventure. Students first read the text to understand the general meaning and only then underline any words and phrases they don't know. Tell them to look up these words and phrases in a dictionary just for interest. Ask students to bring their texts into class. Tell them to cross out all the words and phrases underlined and swap texts with a partner. They read their partner's text and tell each other what they have read. This activity is a very effective way of demonstrating the Learning Tip as students will find it motivating to be able to understand a text which is not even complete.

d Ask students if they can remember any examples of informal language from the listening, e.g. *buddy* = friend. Tell students to underline the examples in the sentences. Check as a class. Then ask students to say the sentences in more neutral language. Take feedback as a class.

Answers / Suggested answers

1 <u>Thanks</u>, <u>mate</u>. Thank you.
2 <u>Managed to just get</u> my camp <u>sorted</u>. I managed to set up my camp.
3 I didn't really <u>fancy taking it on till</u> tomorrow. I didn't really want to deal with it until tomorrow.
4 I <u>guess</u> I'll find out. I imagine/suppose I'll find out.
5 If I lose the raft, <u>I'm finished</u>. If I lose the raft, I won't be able to continue / I might die.

e ▶ **1.59** **Pronunciation** Play the recording and ask what is happening in this part of Will's journey (his raft with all his kit on it almost overturns). Play the recording again and ask how the words in bold are pronounced (without the /t/ sound at the end). Ask the students if the word following each word in bold starts with a consonant or vowel (consonant). Elicit the rule that when a /t/ sound is followed by a consonant it is not pronounced. Drill the phrases.

f ▶ Put students into pairs to discuss the question. Take feedback as a class.

4 READING

a ▶ Check students understand *malaria,* a disease you can get from the bite of a particular type of mosquito which causes periods of fever and makes you feel very cold and shake. Put students into groups to discuss the questions and then share ideas as a class.

b Give students time to read the text and check their answers.

Answers

1 Because malaria is a serious illness and he was alone in the forest.
2 a bad headache, a fever, pain in his joints
3 Make contact with someone (on the Sierra Leone bank) and get to the hospital for treatment.

c Remind students of the Learning Tip on SB p.36, which applies to reading as well as listening. Give students time to read the text again and answer the questions. Check answers as a class.

Suggested answers

1 It is almost silent so you can approach wildlife discreetly. Rivers are a very good place to see wildlife feeding, drinking and socialising.
2 He heard their sounds – a screaming call, a scuffle in the bushes, a warning shriek and saw a flash of fur. They were never quite close enough to see.
3 He was planning to have *fried and liquid-based treats,* i.e. more delicious food and drink than he had with him in the jungle, in the nearest village.
4 His symptoms got worse – his headache developed into a fever and he had heard of a woman who had ignored flu-like symptoms and died.
5 He was lucky that he was seen by a woman who called for help. He was rescued by local people. He had enough money to pay for hospital treatment.
6 An estimated half a million people in Africa die from malaria every year. They aren't as lucky as Will, because they don't have the money to pay for treatment.

VOCABULARY SUPPORT

unencumbered – without anything that makes it difficult to proceed

storybook (adj.) – (of real life) pleasant in the way of a children's picture book

a flash of sth – an occasion when you see something for a very short time

scuffle (n.) – the noise of hurried movement, or a short, sudden fight

put sth down to sth – decide that the cause of something is a particular thing

felt tip – a kind of pen, often used by children to colour with

be no stranger to sth – be familiar with something

FAST FINISHERS

Point out the gap in the text on SB p.37 marked by […]. Ask fast finishers to write two or three sentences to fill this gap. Tell them to compare their ideas with another fast finisher.

d ▶ Ask students if they think Will could have done anything to avoid getting sick. Put students into groups to discuss the questions. Take feedback as a class.

e **Language in context** *Descriptive verbs*
Tell students to read the definitions and then look at the first highlighted word, *teeming*. Ask: *What follows 'teeming'?* (with life); *Does that mean the jungle had a lot of living things or not many?* (a lot). Ask students to give the definition (b). Students work individually. Check answers as a class. Concept check some of the vocabulary, e.g. *If you have an important exam the next day, your friends might tell you not to … ?* (fret).

Answers
a grinding   b teeming   c hauled   d propped up
e crouched down   f peeled   g shrugged off   h fret
i summoned

5 GRAMMAR Narrative tenses

a 🗨 This is a review so students should already be familiar with the verb forms involved. The objective is to get students to use a range of narrative tenses more fluently and accurately. Books closed. Say sentences using these verb forms and tell students to name the tenses, e.g. *Will had always wanted* (past perfect simple) *to do this journey. He would dream* (would + infinitive) *about it back at home, but he didn't know whether he'd get the opportunity* (past simple, would + infinitive for future in the past). *He had been feeling bad* (past perfect continuous) *but he was hoping* (past continuous) *it wasn't serious. Will's family were told* (past simple passive) *he had been taken* (past perfect passive) *to hospital.* Books open. Put students into pairs. Students match the sentences with the verb forms and explain why that form is used. Check as a class.

Answers
1 past perfect continuous; a repeated action in the past happening over a period of time before a particular time in the past
2 *would* + infinitive; a repeated or habitual past action
3 past perfect simple; a complete action in the past with a past result (of completing the action)
4 past continuous; an action in progress at a particular time in the past
5 past perfect passive; a single past action happening before a particular time in the past, where we don't know the agent
6 past simple passive; a single past action where we are focusing on the object of the verb (Will)
7 past simple; a complete past action

b ▶ 🔵 **1.60** Students read the information in Grammar Focus 3B on SB p.143. Play the recording where indicated and ask students to listen and repeat. Students then complete the exercises. Check answers as a class. Exercise b could lead to a discussion of nightmare holidays students have had. Tell students to go back to SB p.37.

Answers (Grammar Focus 3B SB p.143)
a 2 would be getting   3 was to have paid
  4 had been planning to make   5 wondered   6 was driving
  7 had been crying   8 got   9 had been going to give
  10 would
b 2 hadn't been/gone   3 had told   4 turned / would turn
  5 were still preparing   6 had brought   7 was hoping / had been hoping   8 was planning / had been planning
  9 got   10 had lost   11 would give   12 was going to sue / would sue   13 (have) apologised
c 1 ✓   2 ~~are~~ were   3 ✓   4 ~~has sent~~ had sent / ~~was~~ am
  5 ✓   6 ~~she'll~~ she'd

⊙ CAREFUL!

A typical student error is to use the past perfect rather than the past simple, especially following time conjunctions like *when*: ~~I became very upset when the coach had broken down and the visit was cancelled.~~ (Correct form = *I became very upset when the coach **broke down** and the visit was cancelled.*).

c Put students into pairs to compare the verb forms. Check answers as a class.

Answers
1 *had heard* implies the action is now complete and finished, he has stopped hearing the primates; *had been hearing* implies he is still hearing this noise
2 *'d hear* implies it happened every day on his trip, as a routine; *heard* implies this happened once on his trip
3 *was being summoned* implies that the action was in progress and incomplete, he could hear or knew this was happening while he lay against the tree; *was summoned* describes a completed action, the next thing that happened in a series

6 WRITING and SPEAKING

a Ask students how many paragraphs there are in Will's article (six). Tell them to answer the questions. Check answers as a class.

Answers
1 with a time expression
2 opening paragraph: to set the scene
  closing paragraph: to summarise the experience

b Ask students if they have read *Around the world in 80 days* (Jules Verne), *The Beach* (written by Alex Garland, also a Danny Boyle film with Leonardo DiCaprio) or any other books about travel and adventure. Put students into groups to read the prompts and talk about an adventurous trip made by themselves or other people, real or imaginary. Take feedback as a class.

c Tell students to make a plan of the paragraphs of their article. Tell them that the first paragraph should set the scene, the last should summarise their experience and the middle paragraphs should start with time expressions to show the progress of events. Tell students to use the prompts as a guide as they write and to include a range of narrative tenses and descriptive verbs.

d 🗨 Put students into pairs to read out their story to each other and give feedback on the content and language of their partner's story. Remind students of the pronunciation point on SB p.36 and tell them not to pronounce the final /t/ sound before consonants.

e 🗨 Put students into groups to share their stories. Each group should decide on the most interesting story to tell to the whole class. As feedback, provide error correction on the use of narrative tenses and descriptive vocabulary.

ADDITIONAL MATERIAL

▶ Workbook 3B
▶ Photocopiable activities: Grammar p.206, Vocabulary p.226

3C Everyday English
To cut a long story short

At the end of this lesson, students will be able to:

- understand an interview in which an author promotes his work, and evaluate how successful the interviewer and interviewee were
- pronounce consonant groups over word boundaries
- learn phrases for exaggerating
- paraphrase and summarise ideas using a range of functional language

⚲ OPTIONAL LEAD-IN

Books closed. Ask students to think of a famous person, alive or dead, who they admire. Put students into pairs. They must interview each other and try and find out through the questions they ask who their mystery guest is (they can't ask *What's your name?* or *Who are you?!*). See which student can find out the mystery guest's identity in the fewest questions.

1 LISTENING

a ⚲ Ask students where they can watch or listen to live interviews, e.g. on a chat show. Put students into groups to discuss the questions. Take feedback as a class.

b ⚲ Ask students if they can remember why Max is famous (he wrote the bestseller science-fiction story *Solar Wind*). Tell students to look at the picture and then answer the questions. Check ideas as a class.

c ▶2.2 If you have the video, play it without the sound first. Ask who is doing most of the talking (Oscar) and why that might be. Play Part 1 of the video or the audio recording and ask students to check their answer in 1b2.

Answers
2 See the underlined questions in the audioscript below. Students can check their answers in the audioscript on SB p.179.

Videoscript/Audioscript (Part 1)

OSCAR OK! Max. So, I'll just talk for a minute to introduce you, and then we'll begin the interview, OK? Are you ready?

MAX Er, well, yeah, er, I think so …

O OK, when the light turns red, we're live. Hello, I'm Oscar Simmons from *City FM*, and I'm here to talk to Max Redwood, author of the bestseller *Solar Wind*. Thank you for coming in to talk to us, Max!

M Thanks.

O So, as many of you will already know, *Solar Wind* is a story about space travel. And basically, in a nutshell, a group of explorers are visiting a remote planet which is populated by people, that is to say, aliens! Now, these aliens look very similar to humans, but have a radically different culture. I'd like to begin by asking you <u>where you got the basic idea for *Solar Wind*</u>, Max?

M Well, the idea came to me when … it came to me when …

O I mean, <u>did you get the idea from your own travels and experiences of other cultures, for example</u>?

M I haven't really travelled much, actually. I was planning a trip across Asia once …

O Oh, right?

M But, well, to cut a long story short, I had to cancel it, so …

O Right. So in other words, <u>it all just came from your imagination, then</u>?

M Well, you could say that, yes.

O OK. So next I'd like to move on to your childhood. <u>Were you interested in science fiction growing up</u>?

M Er… … Well … Yeah.

…

O Right, so now for the question that all our listeners will be asking … <u>What happens next</u>? Or, to put it another way, <u>when will *Solar Wind 2* be published</u>?

M Um …

O Right, I see. <u>So it's top secret information, then</u>?

M Um, I'm sorry?

O What I meant by that was, <u>you're not allowed to give any dates yet</u>?

M Er …

O Right, so, to wrap things up now, I'd just like to thank Max Redwood for taking the time out of his busy writing schedule to come in and talk to us today. Thank you, Max, and looking forward to *Solar Wind 2*!

M Yeah, thanks. No problem.

ALEX Max. Hi. Alex. I'm, er, Emma's boyfriend.

M Emma's … Alex! Of course.

A Yeah, listen, um, I've read the book …

M Look, I'm really sorry. I've got to go.

A Nice to meet you too!

d ▶2.2 Play Part 1 of the video or the audio recording again. Tell students to choose the true ending for each sentence and say why the other endings are wrong. Check answers as a class.

Answers
1 b Oscar says 'these aliens look very similar to humans, but have a radically different culture'
2 a Oscar says 'I mean, did you get the idea from your own travels and experiences with other cultures, for example?'
3 b Oscar asks ' … when will *Solar Wind 2* be published?' and says 'looking forward to *Solar Wind 2*'

⚲ FAST FINISHERS

Ask fast finishers to make a list of interview tips for both the interviewer and the interviewee, e.g. *what to wear*, and to present them to the class when the other students have finished.

e ⚲ Put students into pairs to discuss the questions. Ask students to share interesting interview stories with the class.

⚲ EXTRA ACTIVITY

Ask students to work in pairs and rewrite the interview between Max and Oscar with Max confidently giving interesting and articulate answers to all the questions. Ask some pairs to act out their interview to the class.

2 PRONUNCIATION
Consonant groups across two words

a ▶2.3 Write these names of books on the board and ask students to underline the consonant groups (more than two consonants together): *The Great Gatsby, Frankenstein, Goldfinger, Uncle Tom's Cabin*. Point out that *Tom's Cabin* is an example of consonant groups going across words. Tell students to listen and underline the letters that match the transcription /kspl/, etc. Check answers as a class.

Answers
ex<u>pl</u>orers   spa<u>ce t</u>ravel   alie<u>ns l</u>ook   lo<u>ng st</u>ory   be<u>sts</u>eller

b ▶2.4 Books closed. Say the first three phrases and see if students can write the transcription for the consonant groups across two words themselves. Books open. Tell students to do the matching exercise. Check answers and drill the phrases.

Answers
1 f   2 e   3 c   4 d   5 a   6 g   7 b

💡 FAST FINISHERS

Ask fast finishers to think of another two-word phrase for each of the consonant groups, e.g. /kspl/ *takes place*; /lθkr/ *health cruise*; /ksr/ *likes rice*; /nsf/ *once for*; /nsdʒ/ *once jumped*; /psp/ *top speed*; /mst/ *optimism starts*.

---

c ▶2.5 Drill *bestseller* and ask students whether they can hear the /t/ clearly (no). Play the recording and ask students whether they can hear the letters in bold clearly in 1 or 2. Check the answer as a class.

Answer
2

d Ask students to complete the name of each group. Check answers as a class.

Answers
1 consonant   2 vowel

e 💬 Drill the phrases, concentrating on the pronunciation of /t/ and /d/.

↪ LOA TIP DRILLING

- Include a lot of variety and pace in drilling so that students don't get bored and switch off. First play the recording, pause and drill each phrase with the whole class. Then say each phrase yourself and drill. Repeat but go through the phrases more quickly. Next say pairs of phrases, *Westgate Street, Westgate Avenue*, and drill. Repeat at a quicker pace. Then choose individual students to repeat individual phrases and pairs of phrases after you.

- As a final stage, put students into pairs or groups (or both in separate stages) to drill amongst themselves. Monitor and make sure that all students are involved and pronouncing the /t/ and /d/ only where it's natural to do so.

📖 LANGUAGE NOTES

We usually pronounce /t/ and /d/ before /h/, e.g. *stopped him, called home*.

---

3 LISTENING

a 💬 Tell students to look at the picture and answer the questions in pairs. Check ideas as a class.

b ▶2.6 Ask students to predict how Emma is dishonest. Then play Part 2 of the video or the audio recording for students to check. Check the answer as a class.

Answer
She says that she didn't listen to the interview, but she did.

Videoscript/Audioscript (Part 2)

EMMA Oh, hello Max.
MAX You didn't listen, did you?
E Er, no. How did it go?
M It was an outright disaster! I came across as a blithering idiot!
E Calm down. I'm sure it wasn't that bad!
M OK, let me try and think about this calmly, shall I? All things considered, I think my first and last radio interview, listened to by the entire city, was, how shall I put this …? … A complete and utter embarrassment! And my career's totally ruined! And I'll never be able to show my face again! Yes, I think that just about sums it up.
E Calm down. I'll put the kettle on. You'll feel better after a cup of tea. And a biscuit? A chocolate one …

---

c ▶2.6 Tell students to complete the sentences. Then play Part 2 of the video or the audio recording again for students to watch or listen and check. Check as a class.

Answers
1 bad   2 face   3 the kettle

💡 EXTRA ACTIVITY

▶2.6 Put students into groups. Play Part 2 of the video or the audio recording again. Pause after *How did it go?* and ask students to write down as much as they can remember of Max's reply. Play the video or the audio recording again for students to check.

---

d **Language in context** *Exaggerating*

1 ▶2.7 Check students understand the meaning of *exaggerate*. Give a personal example, e.g., *My hair's getting so long. It'll be down to my knees soon.* Ask students if it is true that my hair is long. (yes) Ask students if it is true that it will grow to my knees soon. (no) Elicit that *exaggerate* means to state something is much more, better, longer, harder, etc. than it really is. Tell students to complete Max's words. Play the recording for students to check their answers.

Answers
1 outright   2 blithering   3 complete and utter   4 totally

2 💬 Put students into groups to discuss why they think Max exaggerated about his interview and in what situations people exaggerate. Give the example that old people may exaggerate about how hard life was when they were younger. Take feedback as a class.

📖 LANGUAGE NOTES

Point out that *blithering* /ˈblɪðərɪŋ/ is only found in the phrase *blithering idiot* (an extremely stupid person) and highlight that, like many *and* phrases (students will encounter more later, in Unit 8 Wordpower on SB p.102), you cannot reverse the order of *complete and utter* (NOT ~~utter and complete~~).

---

e 💬 Ask students to give an opinion on something you are wearing or something in the classroom, e.g. *Do you like my shirt?* When they answer, ask if they were being honest, and why (not). Put them into groups to discuss the questions. Take feedback as a class.

4 USEFUL LANGUAGE
Paraphrasing and summarising

a Ask students to paraphrase these expressions from the text on SB pp.36–7 (see 4e): *haul* (pull something heavy), *shrug off* (treat something worrying as if it is not important), *summon* (call someone to be present). Write this short paragraph on the board and ask students to summarise it in one sentence: *At the hotel we enjoyed the meal we ate in their restaurant. We thought the rooms were excellent, too. The prices were very reasonable.* (The hotel was great and good value for money.) Ask students to work individually and match the expressions with their uses. Check answers as a class.

> **Answers**
> 1 paraphrase   2 summarise

b ▶2.8 Students complete the extracts with the phrases. Play the recording for students to check their answers.

> **Answers**
> 1 in a nutshell   2 that is to say   3 to cut a long story short
> 4 in other words   5 what I meant by that was

c Students decide which phrases are paraphrasing and which are summarising and complete the table. Check answers and drill the phrases.

> **Answers**
> Paraphrasing: to put it another way; in other words; that is to say; what I meant by that was
> Summarising: all things considered; in a nutshell; to cut a long story short

---

🖤 FAST FINISHERS

Ask fast finishers to look at the audioscripts for Parts 1 and 2 on SB p.179 and to complete these sentences with the correct expressions: *Right, so, _____ now, I'd just like to thank Max Redwood …* (to wrap things up); *Yes, I think that just about _____ .* (sums it up). Tell them to think of more phrasal verbs with *up* and to list them in their vocabulary notebook with their meanings.

---

d Books closed. Read out each of the expressions in 4b with a mistake in it, e.g. *to cut a short story long*, and tell students to correct you. Then tell students to complete the sentences using their own ideas. Take feedback as a class.

5 SPEAKING

▶ Tell students to go to SB p.129. Tell students to read and complete the conversations using their own ideas. Students then think about how they will describe the situations. Divide the class into pairs and assign A and B roles. Tell Student As to use the pink bubbles and Student Bs the green bubbles and role play the four conversations. They then swap roles. Monitor and make sure students are paraphrasing and summarising where appropriate using the expressions in 4c.

ADDITIONAL MATERIAL

▶ Workbook 3C
▶ Photocopiable activities: Pronunciation p.257
▶ Unit Progress Test
▶ Personalised online practice

3D Skills for Writing
The view is stunning

At the end of this lesson, students will be able to:

- use descriptive language to talk and write about tourist destinations
- improve their writing style by using more concise language
- use adjectives and phrases with a positive or negative connotation

🖤 OPTIONAL LEAD-IN

Books closed. Write on the board (or show the students pictures of): *The Great Pyramid of Giza, Hanging Gardens of Babylon, The Lighthouse of Alexandria*. Ask students if they know what these places have in common (they are three of the Seven Wonders of the Ancient World – amazing ancient buildings/constructions which were listed by ancient Greek authors). Put students into groups. Ask them to make a list of seven wonders of the modern world and then compare their list with other groups.

1 SPEAKING

a 💬 Ask students what makes a rewarding place to visit, e.g. a long history, good infrastructure for tourists, etc. Put students into groups to discuss the questions. You could tell students to discuss this in two categories: places in their country and places abroad. Take feedback as a class.

b 💬 Ask students what they know about Prague. Tell them to describe the pictures and say what impression they make. Give students time to read the website and tell a partner what appeals to them about Prague and what doesn't. Take feedback as a class.

2 LISTENING

a ▶2.9 Tell students to read the questions. Ask: *Have Tony and Lola been to Prague?* (yes). You may wish to pre-teach *look beyond sth* (to ignore something superficial so you can see some more permanent/important quality). Play the recording. Tell students to answer the questions individually and then compare their answers in pairs. Check answers as a class.

Answers

1 **Old Town**
   Tony: exceptionally well preserved / full of beautiful buildings, all periods of history / Baroque buildings / skilfully restored and look stunning / friends who live there say don't go to the old city centre – too crowded, too expensive
   Lola: centre gets very crowded, especially in the summer / beautiful buildings / old-fashioned atmosphere
   View from Prague Castle
   Tony: doesn't mention this
   Lola: breathtaking view across the old city / maze of steep red tiled roofs spread out beneath you / like something out of a children's storybook
   The Charles Bridge
   Tony: very beautiful / teeming with people / impossible to stop and look at the view or take photos
   Lola: doesn't mention this
2 it's beautiful; there are crowds of tourists
3 Both Tony and Lola would probably go back. Tony has been there several times already and has friends who live there. Lola loved it and thought it was wonderful.

Audioscript

TONY I know Prague quite well – I've been there several times, I've got friends who live there. And, of course, it's one of the most beautiful cities in Europe. There's the old centre – exceptionally well preserved, it's full of beautiful buildings, all periods of history. And not to mention the Baroque buildings in the old city centre, that've been skilfully restored and look stunning. So, yeah, I'd say it's definitely a beautiful city, definitely worth visiting, no question. But, there are hordes of tourists. The last time I was there I went to the Charles IV Bridge which crosses the river. And don't get me wrong, it's a very beautiful bridge, but it was teeming with people. It was impossible to stop and look at the view or take photos. I'd recommend going outside the main tourist season, though there's not really any time when it isn't busy. I've got friends who live there and they say they don't go to the old city centre any more – it's too crowded and too expensive. They go to the other parts of the town. It is a real shame that tourism has made these historic places unaffordable to local residents.

LOLA I went to Prague last winter and I loved it. It's got such a romantic atmosphere. Beautiful old buildings, the cobbled streets, the squares with the fountains. People say that it's been spoilt by tourism and it's true in a way. The centre gets very crowded, especially in the summer. But, if you look beyond that, and appreciate the buildings and the old-fashioned atmosphere it's, it's still really a magical place. The thing I love most in Prague is going up the hill to the castle. I went up the twisty, narrow streets, and then, there's the breathtaking view across the old city. Looking down, there's a maze of steep red-tiled roofs spread out beneath you – it's like something out of a children's storybook. I took so many photos of Prague – every corner there's something to take a picture of. It was wonderful.

b Ask students which verb in box A was also used by Will when he was talking about how much wildlife there was (teeming). Tell students to match *teeming* with the correct phrase in B (with people). Then ask students to match the other phrases. Play the recording again for students to check.

Answers
well-preserved
skilfully restored
hordes of tourists
teeming with people
romantic atmosphere
cobbled streets
breathtaking view
tiled roofs

LOA TIP CONCEPT CHECKING

- At an advanced level, you need to check that students have a full understanding of new vocabulary and its meaning in extended contexts, e.g. *'Well-preserved' can be about a place but can it be about a person?* (Yes, someone who looks younger than their age.). *If you cobble something together, would it look nice?* (No, 'cobble something together' means to make something quickly and not very carefully.).

- It's important that students' vocabulary knowledge also includes grammatical information about the words. Books closed. Ask: *What preposition follows 'teeming'?* (with). *Do we usually use 'teem' in the simple or continuous?* (continuous). *Can we use 'hordes' in the singular?* (Yes, but it's less common.).

c 🗨 Put students into resident groups and tourist groups. Tell them to discuss the issues from their point of view. Then combine residents and tourists into new groups to present and defend their arguments. Take feedback on the issues as a class.

EXTRA ACTIVITY

Put students into groups to discuss how tourism might change in the future, e.g. *growth of ecotourism* (ecotourism = the business of organising holidays to places of natural beauty in a way that helps local people and does not damage the environment). Take feedback as a class.

3 READING

Tell students to read the review and find the extra information, using 2a and/or the audioscript on SB p.179 to help them. Check that students don't include information they already know by asking *There is Baroque architecture. Is this new?* (no). You may wish to pre-teach *be a better bet* (an action that is more likely to be successful). Check answers as a class.

Answers
Old Town: a mixture of architectural styles from every period, including Gothic and Art Nouveau; narrow streets, some less crowded little squares
Charles Bridge: 800 metres long; pedestrian only; lined with impressive statues; lots of music; very lively and laid-back; crowded with stalls selling souvenirs; great photo ops overlooking the river and city
the castle: isn't much to look at; dates from the 9th century but is restored so it doesn't look particularly old

4 WRITING SKILLS
Descriptive language; Writing briefly

a Ask if Tony thought *hordes of tourists* was a good or bad thing and why (bad, too many). Elicit that *hordes* has a negative meaning. Tell students to make two lists and write the words and phrases under the correct heading *Positive* or *Negative*. Pre-teach *much better bet* (something preferable). Do the first one together. *We know 'hospitable' is positive so is 'really put themselves out for us' positive or negative?* (positive). Check answers as a class.

Answers
1 Positive: really put themselves out for us; spotlessly clean; a must-see attraction; Great photo ops; authentic cuisine; reasonably priced
2 Negative: overrun with tourists; a bit of a nightmare; crowded with stalls; isn't much to look at; overpriced

b Tell students to replace the words in italics with highlighted words or phrases from the text. Do the first one as a class by asking the students to find the two phrases relating to money, *reasonably priced* and *overpriced* in the last paragraph, and to choose between them. Students then work individually. Check answers and read through the Writing Tip with the class.

Answers
1 reasonably priced
2 overrun with tourists
3 a bit of a nightmare
4 great photo ops
5 authentic cuisine
6 a must-see attraction
7 isn't much to look at
8 really put themselves out for us

c Ask students to read the sentences and say whether they look more like speaking or writing (speaking). Tell students to add words to make complete sentences. Check answers as a class.

Answers
1 **There's** lots of music and **it's** very lively and laid-back.
2 **I/We** took hundreds of photos.
3 Then **we went** back to the hotel for a quick shower.

d Tell students to read the paragraph and find examples of words that have been left out. Ask why the writer does this. Check answers.

Answers
We wrapped up our day in the city with a walk across the Charles Bridge, followed by a visit to the castle. The bridge is about 800 metres long; **it's** pedestrian only, and **it's** lined with impressive statues. **This is / It's** a must-see attraction if you visit Prague. **There's** lots of music and **it's** very lively and laid-back, but **it's** a bit crowded with stalls selling souvenirs. **There are** great photo ops from the bridge overlooking the river and city.
2 It seems less formal and more like a conversation.

Suggested answer
Sorry, can't meet at 8 because babysitter hasn't arrived yet

e ▶ Students complete the exercises in Writing Focus 3D on SB p.170. Ask students to read the description and say what kind of text it is and how they know. Students then say which words have been left out and complete the rest of the exercises. Check the answers to Exercise a–d as a class. In Exercise e and f, tell students to write a review of a tourist attraction, show a partner and ask each other questions. Tell students to go back to SB p.41.

Answers
a 1, 3 because the style is informal
b unimportant or repeated words that are clear from the context; linking words
c 1 **There** isn't much to do here in the evenings, and **the** food in most places **is** overpriced. **It's** quite a disappointing place to visit.
  2 **I/We have** been to most resorts in Mexico but there is nowhere as impressive as Tulum.
  3 **The** best time **to** visit **is** late autumn, **as there are** no tourists **and** great weather.
  4 **I/We** went to Budapest last year. **It's** much more interesting and **has** more reasonable prices.
d 1 Great place for a honeymoon, so romantic.
  2 So much to take photos of. Good thing I had my camera.
  3 Arrived late and couldn't find anywhere to eat. Not very impressed!
  4 Go early to beat the heat. Beautiful beach at foot of cliff. Great for cooling off.

5 WRITING

a Ask students to think about the local area and what these different kinds of people would enjoy seeing and doing: a student, a retired widower, a couple with young children, a middle-aged disabled person. Put students into pairs to make a list of things worth seeing locally and things not worth seeing. Combine pairs into groups to compare their lists. Take feedback as a class.

b Tell students to write a review of two or three attractions (or just one for weaker students). Remind students to look back at the Writing Tip and to include comments on accommodation and food.

c Put students into pairs to compare their work and suggest improvements using adjectives with a stronger positive or negative meaning and shorter sentences. Write an example on the board and ask students to improve it: *The views were nice* (Breathtaking views).

d Tell students to read out their reviews and see what other students think. If you have a large class or are short of time, tell students to pin their reviews around the classroom walls. Students then walk around and add their comments under each review.

ADDITIONAL MATERIAL
▶ Workbook 3D

UNIT 3
Review and extension

1 GRAMMAR

a Write these words on the board and tell students to reorder them beginning with the adverbial to make a sentence: *place / been / like / a / I / have / this / to / never* (Never have I been to a place like this.). Tell students to reorder the words into sentences. Check answers as a class.

Answers
1 John was about to get on a plane.
2 Very rarely did you see her at home.
3 Amelia thought that she was going to faint.
4 On no account must anyone be told.
5 We were set to leave early the next day.
6 No way would I go on a trip like that.

b Ask students why we can use the two forms in the example (both future in the past). Tell students to go through the sentences in pairs and say why one form is not correct. Check as a class.

Answers
2 Originally we *planned to take / had been going to take / ~~would be taking~~* the train.
3 As soon as we *arrived / had arrived / ~~had been arriving~~*, we checked in.
4 Our supplies *had ended / ~~had been ending~~ / ended* and we had to find more from somewhere.
5 Our room was terrible and I *had been complaining / ~~might complain~~ / complained* to the manager.
6 Travel *was / would be / ~~was to be~~* cheaper in those days.

> ### ⓦ EXTRA ACTIVITY
> Tell students to make sentences using the verb forms they crossed out in order to tell a story, e.g. *She **would leave** for work at 8:00 every morning. She knew that her friend **would be taking** the same train …*

2 VOCABULARY

a Ask *Is 'affluent' usually used to describe people or places?* (places). *Is 'disposable' about money you have spare or money you owe?* (spare money). Tell students to complete the sentences. Check answers as a class.

Answers
1 affluent 2 disposable 3 deprived 4 destitute 5 well-off
6 prosperity 7 hardship 8 means

b Do the first question as an example. *What part of speech is this?* (a noun). *Could it be talking about location?* (yes). *What word can mean 'centre'?* (heart). Students complete the sentences individually. Check as a class.

Answers
1 heart 2 vegetation 3 untouched 4 rugged 5 arid
6 pristine 7 swamp

3 WORDPOWER Idioms: Landscapes

a Ask the students *Is a swamp a nice place?* (no). Tell students to read the first conversation and then ask: *Does A need help?* (yes). Tell students to find the matching definition (f). Students do the rest of the exercise individually. Check as a class.

Answers
1 f
2 c
3 d
4 g
5 e
6 b
7 a

b **2.10** Read out this sentence with a gap for the expression and ask students to complete it: *It will be _____ to raise enough money for my trip* (an uphill struggle). Students complete the sentences. Play the recording for them to check.

Answers
1 a drop in the ocean
2 get the lie of the land
3 an uphill struggle
4 out of the woods
5 a slippery slope
6 get bogged down with
7 swamped

> ### ⓦ FAST FINISHERS
> Tell fast finishers to underline the /t/ and /d/ sounds in these phrases which would not be pronounced: *swamped this week, out of the woods, get the lie of the land, getting bogged down with, just a drop in the ocean.*

c 💬 Put students into pairs to imagine a context for each sentence. Take feedback as a class.

> ### ⓦ EXTRA ACTIVITY
> Put students into pairs to make a dialogue using one of the sentences in 3b. They act out their dialogue in front of the class without using that sentence. The other students guess the missing sentence.

▶ Photocopiable activities: Wordpower p.243

LOA REVIEW YOUR PROGRESS

Students look back through the unit, think about what they've studied and decide how well they did. Students work on weak areas by using the appropriate sections of the Workbook, the Photocopiable worksheets and the Personalised online practice.

UNIT 4
Consciousness

UNIT CONTENTS

G GRAMMAR
- Noun phrases (compound nouns, adverbs and adjectives, clauses and prepositional phrases, possessives)
- *have / get* passives (e.g. *have your bag searched, get sb thinking*)

V VOCABULARY
- Instinct and reason: *conscientious, conscious, consider, deep down, gut instinct, have a hunch, logically, objective, on a whim, on impulse, rational, reasonable, self-confident, self-conscious, sensible, sensitive, spontaneous, subconsciously, think it over, think twice, weigh up*
- Memory: *distant/lasting/painful/photographic/vague/vivid memory, cast your mind back to, come to mind, refresh your memory, slip your mind, treasure the memory of, trigger a memory, vaguely remember*
- Language in context: Doubt and uncertainty; Idioms 1/2
- Wordpower: mind: *bear in mind, cross your mind, put your mind to sth, read sb's mind, speak your mind*

P PRONUNCIATION
- Sound and spelling: /ʃəs/, /ɪəs/, /dʒəs/, e.g. *prestigious, outrageous*
- Sentence stress
- Homophones in words and connected speech, e.g. *due/ dew*

GETTING STARTED

a Give students one minute to think about their answers to the questions before talking about the photo as a class. If you wish, give students information from the Culture notes below.

At the end of this unit, students will be able to:
- understand and evaluate stated and implied opinions and summarise and relay the main details of popular science texts
- follow the main argument and respond to radio discussions on popular science topics; understand and compare accounts of versions of narratives and spoken and written interviews
- use a range of lexis accurately to discuss intuition and memory, and give clear detailed narratives about childhood experiences
- understand a formal discussion in which feedback is given and identify details and implicit opinions and attitudes of the speakers
- speak tactfully in formal discussions using a range of expressions to soften contradictory opinions and criticisms
- write an article based on an oral interview, creating coherence with effective use of time phrases and tenses and using appropriate devices to engage the reader

🌍 CULTURE NOTES

This photo shows a visitor to a conference in Singapore on wearable technology (clothing and accessories with computers and other devices), tasting food using Tasteworks technology. This technology, originally developed for older people with dementia who are losing their sense of taste, changes and improves the taste of food by giving people visual and auditory input that positively influences their eating experience. Scientists have long understood that the sense of taste does not just come from how food feels in your mouth. In a similar low-tech demonstration at the same conference scientists showed that making a fork heavier also changed the taste of the food.

b Put students into pairs to discuss the questions. Take feedback as a class.

ⓦ EXTRA ACTIVITY

Put students into groups. Tell them that they have to design a restaurant to stimulate the senses in innovative ways. Give some examples, e.g. tablecloths with designs of exotic fruits, edible plates, waiters trained to explain and emphasise how (wonderful) each dish tastes. Ask one student from each group to read out their list of design features for the class to choose the three most effective.

4A That little voice in your head

At the end of this lesson, students will be able to:

- talk about feelings, doubts and intuitions using a range of words and expressions for expressing instinct and reason, doubt and uncertainty
- read a text on gut instincts, work out the meaning of new expressions, and respond to the content
- pronounce *-ious*, *-eous* endings
- use complex noun phrases in speaking and writing
- listen to a discussion on a popular science topic and identify the stance of the speakers
- discuss dilemmas based on gut instinct and find solutions

OPTIONAL LEAD-IN

Books closed. Bring in some photographs of different people who the students won't know. Ask students what they think about each person based on their photograph. Ask specific questions, e.g. *What does she do? Do you think you could be friends with her? Where does she go on holiday?* Then ask students what they are basing their opinions on and how much they trust their judgement.

1 SPEAKING

a Ask students what they think the saying *You never get a second chance to make a first impression* means and what the consequences are if it is true (you can't change people's first impression of you; this first impression may not be logical or fair). Put students into pairs to discuss the questions and elicit that a 'sixth sense' is an ability that some people believe they have that seems to give them information without using the five senses of sight, hearing, touch, smell or taste. Take feedback as a class.

b Say to students: *If you suddenly felt very worried about someone in your family for no apparent reason, what would you do?* Discuss different reactions as a class. Put students into pairs. Tell students to do the quiz individually and make their own 'C' answer if they don't agree with A or B. Students then compare answers with their partner.

c Tell students to check their scores on SB p.137. Do they agree with the description of their behaviour? Tell students to go back to SB p.44. Go through some of the questions with the class and compare answers.

2 VOCABULARY Instinct and reason

a Say: *I took a chance and bought the bike.* Ask if you are A or B according to the quiz (A). Students categorise the statements. Check as a class.

Answers
1 B   2 A   3 A   4 B

b Tell students that *objective* in the box is an adjective. Ask students to replace the words in the sentences with words in the box and explain any differences in meaning to a partner. Check answers as a class.

Answers
1 *objective* means your work, behaviour, decisions, etc. are not biased or influenced by other people, feelings etc; *rational* means beliefs and decisions are based on reasons, not emotions.
2 *on a whim* and *on impulse* are very similar; however, *on a whim* implies that the feeling is temporary, and the decision is not serious. It would be strange or disrespectful to say this about a marriage.
3 *deep down* and *subconsciously* are the same in this sentence; however, *deep down* can also mean hidden only from other people.
4 *consider* and *weigh up* are the same in this sentence. However, *weigh up* specifically means evaluate and judge, whereas *consider* is more general and means think carefully about.

c ▶ 2.11-2.13 Students complete the exercises in Vocabulary Focus 4A on SB p.161. Play the recording where indicated and check answers to Exercise a–c. Take feedback as a class for Exercise d. Tell students to go back to SB p.45.

Answers (Vocabulary Focus 4A SB p.161)
a 1 f   2 d   3 e   4 a   5 c   6 a   7 b   8 c   9 c   10 d
b 1 Sound 2
2

1	2	3
subconscious ambitious precious conscientious	hilarious simultaneous curious	prestigious courageous outrageous

c 1 *reasonable*: using good judgement and therefore fair and practical; *rational*: showing clear thought or reason
2 *sensitive*: easily upset by the things people say or do, or causing people to be upset, embarrassed, or angry; *sensible*: based on or acting on good judgement and practical ideas or understanding
3 *conscious*: very aware of and concerned about something; *conscientious*: putting a lot of effort into your work
4 *self-conscious*: nervous or uncomfortable because you know what people think about you or your actions; *self-confident*: behaving calmly because you have no doubts about your ability or knowledge

CAREFUL!

Some students make the mistake of using *sensible* instead of *sensitive*: ~~This kind of life is depressing and can be difficult for sensible people.~~ (Correct form = *This kind of life is depressing and can be difficult for **sensitive** people.*) *Sensible* is about how you think and *sensitive* is about how you feel.

3 READING

a Make sure students understand *gut feeling/reaction* (a strong belief about someone or something that cannot completely be explained and does not have to be decided by reasoning). Ask students if there could be any biological or scientific reasons for gut instinct, e.g. a defence mechanism for early humans. Put students into groups to read the text and answer the questions. Use the Vocabulary support box to help with vocabulary as necessary. Check answers as a class.

UNIT 4 Consciousness   67

Answers

1 how to use intuition more effectively
2 The intuitive right brain is almost always 'reading' your surroundings, even when your conscious left brain is otherwise engaged in editing the world into a logical and coherent whole. The right brain registers spontaneous information while the conscious mind dismisses it as irrational.
3 Notice when intuition is operating and make an active choice over whether to follow this instinct or not.

📖 VOCABULARY SUPPORT

the big picture – the whole situation; all the facts/ information/factors and how they are connected

blissfully ignorant – completely and happily unknowing

tune into sth – become sensitive to something by paying attention to it

clammy palms – when the inside surface of the hands is slightly sweaty

tingle (n.) – a light pricking sensation in a part of the body

take the time to do sth – allow/make the necessary time for something to be done (well)

help sb on their way – help somebody to start doing something independently

---

b Students match the headings and advice. Remind students that we say *piece of advice* because *advice* is uncountable. Check answers as a class.

Answers

1 e   2 a   3 d   4 c   5 b

c Students work individually to look at the underlined parts of the article and think of an example of what the writer means. Tell them to use a dictionary if necessary. Ask students to compare their ideas in pairs. Then take feedback as a class.

Suggested answers

the left brain dismisses the urges of the right as irrational: the left brain automatically ignores messages from the right brain if they don't immediately make sense – e.g., ignoring a feeling that something is too good to be true
letting yourself in for trouble down the road: causing problems for yourself later – e.g., finding out you need an operation because you didn't see a doctor earlier
one of humanity's oldest survival mechanisms: an instinctive behaviour which helped us to survive before civilisation – e.g., running away from wild animals
Our urge to help others is often outbid by other priorities: we look after our own immediate needs rather than other people's – e.g., not stopping to help someone who is hurt because you are late for work
a decision that could affect the course of your future life: a life-changing decision – e.g., whether to accept a job offer

---

🔄 LOA TIP CONCEPT CHECKING

- When you are concept checking long expressions, it is often effective to give situations which fit one of them for students to supply the correct expression. For example, if you want to concept check the underlined parts of the article, say: *Your sister wants you to give her a lift to the station but you have to stay at home and wait for the electrician.* (our urge to help others is often outbid by other priorities).

- After students say the expression, check they have understood the full meaning: *Did I really want to help my sister?* (yes). *Was helping her more important for me than the electrician's visit?* (no).

d 💬 Ask students if they have ever had a *premonition* (a feeling that something, especially something unpleasant, is going to happen) or know any stories about premonitions. Put students into groups to discuss the questions. Take feedback as a class.

💡 EXTRA ACTIVITY

Give students this psychology test. Tell them that they must draw what you ask quickly based on their gut instinct. Say: *Draw a house.* and give students 30 seconds to draw it. Then give students this key:

- Conventional houses show you are fairly traditional.
- The larger the house, the more self-confident you are.
- The more floors, the more ambitious you are.
- The more windows, the more open you are.
- The more doors, the more opportunities you are looking for.
- Any people around means you are very sociable.
- A garden shows a love of nature.

Ask students to compare drawings and interpretations. Ask students if they think tests like this have any value.

---

4 GRAMMAR Noun phrases

a Tell students to underline *You feel an inexplicable certainty that you should not get on that plane.* from the first paragraph of the article. Explain that after *feel* the rest of the sentence is one long noun phrase. Make sure students understand the difference between nouns, parts of speech, and noun phrases. Point out that the function of the noun phrase in this sentence is to provide the object after *feel*. All nouns are parts of noun phrases and a noun phrase may be one word or several words. Break down this noun phrase on the board to show students how complex noun phrases can be:

article	adjective	noun	*that*-clause
an	inexplicable	certainty	that you should not get on that plane

Explain that noun phrases can be formed in many ways. Tell students to match the noun phrases with their type. Check as a class.

Answers

1 c   2 d   3 b   4 f   5 a   6 e

b Write this noun phrase on the board and ask students to improve it using the pattern article + adjective + noun: *a holiday that I won't forget* (an unforgettable holiday). Tell students to improve the noun phrases. Check as a class.

Answers
1 a chance meeting
2 my close friend's dreams
3 a day to remember
4 a disturbingly vivid dream
5 dark secret thoughts
6 the human capacity for imagination

c ▶ Students read the information in Grammar Focus 4A on SB p.144. Students then complete the exercises. Check answers as a class. Tell students to go back to SB p.46.

Answers (Grammar Focus 4A SB p.144)

a One memorable summer day I was coming home after an exhausting day at work when I met an old friend I hadn't seen for ages. I don't know why but I had the strong feeling that this was no mere coincidence. In fact, she had a proposition to make to me which was about to change my life. She said that she was looking for a reliable partner who she could trust to invest in a project started by a few friends of hers. I made a few phone calls to the bank and I had the money needed to get involved. My boring days of sitting behind a desk were behind me.

b 2 the tram stop
3 a brilliantly written book
4 an eagerly awaited moment
5 a one-hour meeting
6 a life-changing injury
7 Ed's bright idea
10 the aunt of the girl I introduced you to yesterday

c *Human resources experts* say that interviewers make *hiring decisions* within the first minute of an interview. Of course, *costly mistakes* can be made and sometimes the wrong people are hired. Nevertheless, companies have to rely on their managers' *decision-making skills*. Most of us have experienced at least *one nightmare interview*, perhaps conducted by a *relatively inexperienced manager*.

⊙ CAREFUL!

A common mistake made by students is to leave out articles in noun phrases, e.g. before ordinal numbers: ~~Second benefit is that there's less pollution.~~ (Correct form = **The** *second benefit is that there's less pollution.*). Students can also use the wrong article, e.g. *the* instead of *a* for something that has not been mentioned before: ~~Going to the new country and meeting new people is always scary.~~ (Correct form = *Going to **a** new country and meeting new people is always scary.*). Another typical mistake is to use the possessive 's instead of an *of* phrase when the possessor is an object not a person: ~~I read your advertisement in the last Fun World's edition.~~ (Correct form = *I read your advertisement in the last edition **of** Fun World*.). Students can also make mistakes by using an *of* phrase instead of the possessive 's, e.g. time expressions aren't usually used as part of an *of* phrase: ~~Most students felt fine about the programme of last year.~~ (Correct form = *Most students felt fine about **last year's programme***.).

5 LISTENING

a 💬 Tell students to look at the picture and ask how doctors deal with patients like children who can't explain or don't know what is wrong. Put students into pairs to discuss the question. Compare ideas as a class.

b ▶ **2.14** Ask students to say which statement they personally agree with. Pre-teach the abbreviation, *GP* (general practitioner: a doctor who provides general medical treatment). Play the recording for students to say what the three speakers agree on. Check as a class.

Answer
3

Audioscript

PORTER Now, you know that little voice in your head that questions if you've locked the car properly, or turned the iron off. That uneasy feeling that you get when you think there is something you should be doing, but you just can't remember what it is. More often than not these are groundless anxieties that simply reflect that many of us are born worriers, but sometimes that voice in your head – that gut feeling – warrants your attention. And many doctors, particularly GPs, do pay it attention when faced with a patient that doesn't quite fit the description in the textbook. All may appear well on the surface, but you're left with a nagging doubt that all is not quite as it seems. So are doctors right to heed their gut instincts? Ann Van den Bruel is a GP and research fellow at the University of Oxford.

VAN DEN BRUEL A lot of GPs especially, they recognise this feeling that they get sometimes, although not everybody admits or, or acknowledges that they sometimes act upon it – it's seen as something mysterious or maybe you should not talk about it. But it is real, and when you talk to GPs about it they're really happy to be able to share that experience of having this gut feeling and using it sometimes in their medical decision-making. So it is something real, but it's not always acknowledged as a valid, or a useful tool.

P Well, do we know if it's useful?

V Well we do, because er we've been doing studies in, for example, serious infections in children – so that's meningitis or pneumonia – and we have found that gut feeling is the most powerful predictor in general practice of a serious infection in a child.

P But how do you go about measuring the effect of something like gut feeling?

V Well, we asked doctors to record whether they felt something like gut feeling or an instinct that something was wrong in 4,000 children, and then we compared those recordings with what ultimately happened to those children and we were able to calculate the diagnostic accuracy, if you want, of gut feeling. And we found that it is very, very accurate – it's very useful. It's not a hundred per cent right, but the chance that something serious is going on is much higher when a doctor has a gut feeling.

P Well, Margaret McCartney's been listening in from our Glasgow studio. Margaret, I suspect that none of this will come as a surprise to you.

MCCARTNEY No … And I think gut instinct is one of those real rich seams of general practice that kind of goes under-explored, and I think, unacknowledged as well. When you talk to doctors over coffee, y'know, one of the things that we're always saying to each other is, y'know, 'I'm just not quite sure about that lady.' Or, 'I'm just not quite sure about that hanging together.' But, I think there's also a little bit of shame that goes along with it, y'know, I think sometimes it's seen as being a bit unscientific – y'know just having this kind of … gut instinct, this sort of feeling about someone and it's a kind of slightly romantic idea that kind of harks back to the kind of um old-style videos of pictures of doctors sort of just having a feeling about someone. And for me it's not unscientific at all, it's actually highly scientific, because what you're doing is you're saying actually, out of all the people that I've seen with similar symptoms, you're just a bit different from everyone else, so it's almost like recognising that this person just doesn't quite fit the pattern but you're not quite sure in what way they don't fit in with that pattern. So what you're doing is you're opening up to saying well I'm unsure, I'm uncertain and the possibilities here are potentially something quite serious and I'm not going to just let that go.

P And this isn't the only piece of evidence that suggests that it's a powerful tool …

M No … And what I find really fascinating is when you go and ask doctors around the world, as some researchers have done, 'Do you experience a similar kind of phenomena?', all doctors will say that they do. Some people will describe it as feeling something in their stomach – something just not quite right. Other doctors will say that they feel it in their bones that something's just not right. And it's just this idea that you get something that jars – something that just doesn't quite fit properly together – and you have a sense that you're not actually very certain about what's going on here at all.

V In general practice, we have to deal with a lot of uncertainty – we don't have all the tests and all the technology the hospital doctors do have … and … so, we're used to dealing with uncertainty and we're used to not having that much at our disposal, to make our decisions. So gut feeling for us is like our safety net, when we feel 'Hmm … I'm not really happy about this', then we may want to ask a second opinion, or we may want to schedule another appointment, or we may want to give the parents very detailed information on when to come back – that's how we want to deal with that uncertainty that is left at the end of the consultation.

c ⏯ **2.14** Tell students to read the statements. Then play the recording for students to listen again and choose the best answer. You may wish to help students with words from the Vocabulary support box. Check answers as a class.

Answers
1 often   2 having   3 how accurate gut instinct is   4 correct
5 important   6 less   7 similar   8 more

📖 **VOCABULARY SUPPORT**

heed – pay attention to something, especially advice / a warning

a research fellow – a member of a group of academics of high rank

act upon a feeling – do something as a direct result of a feeling

tool – something you use that helps you do a particular activity

a rich seam – an area full of good information/ideas/ material, etc.

hark back to (a time) – remind people of details of a time

open up to sth – become more willing to consider or accept something

have sth at your disposal (B2) – have something available for you to use

a safety net – a plan or system that will help you in a difficult situation

d 🗨 Ask students if they think advances in science and technology are reducing the significance of gut feeling in medicine. Put students into groups to discuss whether they've changed their mind about the role of gut feeling. Take feedback as a class.

e **Language in context** *Doubt and uncertainty*

1 ⏯ **2.15** Tell students to complete the sentences. Then play the recording for students to check their answers.

2 Ask students: *If you feel it in your bones, are you absolutely sure?* (no, it's just gut instinct). Ask students if this phrase is connected with a, b, c or d (d). Tell students to categorise the other words and phrases. Check as a class.

Answers
1 1 feeling   2 anxieties; worriers   3 doubt   4 pattern
    5 bones   6 jars; fit
2 a uneasy feeling; a nagging doubt; groundless anxieties
    b groundless anxieties; born worriers
    c doesn't quite fit the pattern; jars; doesn't quite fit together
    d feel it in their bones

💡 **FAST FINISHERS**

Explain to fast finishers that *jar* is a homonym (a word that sounds the same or is spelled the same as another word but has a different meaning): *jar* (n.) a container / *jar* (v.) used when something doesn't quite fit the pattern. Tell students to make a list of as many homonyms as they can, e.g. *fine* (adj.) good / (n.) penalty; *object* (n.) thing / (v.) complain.

6 SPEAKING

a 🗨 Pre-teach *can't put your finger on it* (not be able to understand exactly why a situation is the way it is) and *sterile* (having no imagination, new ideas, or energy). Put students into groups to read and discuss each dilemma. Take feedback as a class.

b 🗨 Ask students for examples of jobs where gut instinct may be important, e.g. customs officers. Check that students know that *CEO* is Chief Executive Officer. Put students into groups to go through each job and discuss the role of gut instinct. Take feedback as a class.

c 🗨 Students choose a job, write a dilemma and pass it to other students to discuss. Encourage students to use the language of doubt and uncertainty in 5e in their writing and discussion.

💡 **EXTRA ACTIVITY**

Put students into groups and ask them to use a dictionary and find as many expressions with *gut* as they can within a time period you set. Give groups one point for finding an expression, another for the definition, and another for a personalised example. See which group gets the most points and share the vocabulary information on the board.

Suggested answers
bust a gut (work very hard or make a big effort to achieve something): *I bust a gut to pass the last progress test.*
gut-wrenching (making you feel very upset or worried): *There was a gut-wrenching cry of agony.*
gutted (very disappointed and upset): *City were gutted to lose the final.*
have guts (B2) (have the bravery and determination that is needed to do something difficult or unpleasant): *You don't have the guts to climb to the top.*
slog your guts out (work extremely hard): *What's the point in slogging my guts out for this salary?*

ADDITIONAL MATERIAL

▶ Workbook 4A

▶ Photocopiable activities: Grammar p.207, Vocabulary p.227, Pronunciation p.258

4B He got himself locked in a shed

At the end of this lesson, students will be able to:

- speak, read and listen about the role and reliability of memories and respond using a range of words and expressions connected with memory
- use a range of *have/get* passive constructions in speaking and writing
- use sentence stress and rhythm to communicate more effectively

☿ OPTIONAL LEAD-IN

Books closed. Give students this memory test on Units 1–3.

1 *Who is Ellen MacArthur?* (a sailor, Unit 1)
2 *In which decade did people use the adjective* wicked *to describe their favourite music?* (1990s, Unit 1)
3 *Where is the quietest place in the world?* (the anechoic chamber in Orfield Laboratories, Minneapolis, Unit 2)
4 *What extreme sport did Ada do?* (base jumping, Unit 2)
5 *What disease did Will get?* (malaria, Unit 3)
6 *Who was the interviewer in what Max described as his 'first and last radio interview'?* (Oscar, Unit 3)

Ask the students who got the most answers right to say why they think they have a good memory.

1 LISTENING and GRAMMAR

have / get passives

a 💬 Ask students when childhood ends. Ask if there was a particular moment, like going on holiday without their parents, that signalled the end of childhood. Put students into groups to discuss the questions. Take feedback as a class.

b ▶ 2.16 Ask students what the wooden building is in photo C (a shed). Play the recording and ask students which photo is about which speaker (A Clara, B Tommy, C Marissa). Then tell them to answer the questions. Give students the information in the Culture notes if they don't know what Transformers are. Check answers and take feedback as a class.

Suggested answers

1 **Tommy**
Photo B shows a room after burglars have raided it. Their house was burgled and he was very upset because all his Transformer toys were stolen. The thieves were caught when the toys were found as a result of a security bag check at a football match. The toys were returned but Tommy never played with them again.

Marissa
Photo C shows a shed. Her brother went missing and people spent all night looking for him. He was found by a teacher the next morning in the garden shed at school and has liked gardening ever since.

Clara
Photo A shows a mother with her daughter on the daughter's first day at nursery school. Clara was so shocked by being left by her mother for the first time that she didn't react to anyone or anything at first. Eventually a boy asked her to play with him and she did. He became her best friend at nursery but then they didn't see each other for 15 years. Now he's her husband.

2 Students' own answers

📖 VOCABULARY SUPPORT

pick up on sth – understand something that is not communicated directly

blank (look) – showing no feeling or understanding

bump into sb – meet someone you know by chance

the rest is history – everything that happened since then is well-known or obvious

Audioscript

TOMMY We got burgled once … and believe it or not, they got the burglars. My parents were having their kitchen renovated – security wasn't very good and the burglars got in really easily. They took all the usual stuff – the TV, jewellery, but I also had all my toys stolen. That's strange! But I did have an impressive collection of Transformer toys. I felt really upset – my world had come to an end. Now the funny thing was, my toys were actually how they caught the thieves. One went to a football game and had his bag searched as part of security – the thief took the Transformer items to sell to a mate. Now, this particular security guard had a friend who was a policeman, and he'd told him about the strange theft of my toys, and he'd got in touch, and the thief got arrested as he was leaving that game! And the good thing was I got my toys back. I was happy on the day I got them back, but I lost interest in them almost immediately. I never played with them again.

MARISSA My brother got himself locked in the garden shed at school and he couldn't get out. What happened was, was my brother didn't come home from school so my mom and I, we started looking for him and … I mean, I was with my mother and she started getting more and more upset, and at first, I didn't completely understand what was going on, but I think I picked up on the general anxiety and that made me cry.
So his disappearance got everyone looking for him, in a small forest near our house. And people searched all night calling for him – I mean, I remember them shouting, 'Charlie! Charlie!' I mean, it was terrible and … there was this desperate sound in their voice – I was so afraid. Anyway, the next day, the teacher arrives early at school and heard my brother crying in the shed. No one knows how it happened I mean, maybe the door got locked from the outside. Anyway the funny thing is, is he's always loved gardening! I'm surprised it didn't put him off.

CLARA Er, so it was my first day at nursery, and I was left by my mother. This was the first time I'd been without her. Mum told me the nursery teacher was really worried. She said she was used to tearful upset children but, apparently, I was like an ice statue!
She didn't really know what to do with me. She had me sitting on my own and I think I remember her saying something like 'I'll get you set up with some paper and crayons' but … I just sat there looking at her. I'm sure I had some kind of blank look on my face. I guess it was a kind of a shock.
Er, eventually, a little boy asked me to join in a game. I'm not sure why – I went with him … and that literally broke the ice. He got me to play when no one else could. Guess who that little boy was … ? It was my husband Andrew! We ended up being best friends at nursery and, I actually didn't see him for 15 years. And then suddenly, we bumped into each other after university and the rest is history.

🌐 CULTURE NOTES

Transformers are action toys originally from Japan which you can change in shape from robots to vehicles. Transformers are incredibly popular and there are comics and films based on the concept.

c 💬 Ask students what toys were popular when they were children. Put students into groups to discuss the questions. Take feedback as a class.

d Ask students what happened to Clara and the boy she met and elicit *They got married.* Explain that we use *get* and *have* in different constructions. Tell students to look at the first pair of sentences and ask: *Is there a difference?* (yes); *Who is renovating in sentence 1a?* (workers); *Who is renovating in sentence 1b?* (the parents). Put students into pairs to go through the sentences and discuss whether there is a difference in meaning. Check as a class. Then ask the students which of the uses a–d sentence 1a should go with (b). Students match the other sentences. Check as a class.

Answers
1 yes 2 no 3 yes 4 yes 5 yes 6 yes
a 2 b 1 c 4; 5; 6 d 3

e Write 1 *Sandra got fired by Tim.* and 2 *Sandra got Tim fired.* on the board. Ask *Who lost their job in each sentence?* (1 Sandra, 2 Tim) Ask *What is Tim and Sandra's relationship in each sentence?* (1 Tim is Sandra's boss. 2 Sandra is not Tim's boss, she is probably a colleague. Ask *In sentence 2, why did Tim lose his job?* (Sandra caused him to lose it, for example she might have told the boss that he was stealing from the company, etc.) Ask if we can say *Sandra had Tim fired.* (yes). Tell students to complete the table and answer the questions. Check as a class.

Answers

Subject	Verb form 1	Object	Verb form 2
My parents	were having	the kitchen	renovated.
I	had	all my toys	stolen.
He	got	himself	locked in the garden shed.
His disappearance	got	everyone	looking for him.
She	had	me	sitting on my own.
He	got	me	to play when nobody else could.

1 yes; no, it doesn't, although *got all my toys stolen* could imply that it was in some way due to his own carelessness.
2 yes: *had himself locked in the shed* changes the meaning to mean he asked somebody to do this deliberately; *had everyone looking for him* no change in meaning; no: *had me to play* is not possible.

f ▶ ●**2.17–2.18** Students read the information in Grammar Focus 4B on SB p.145. Play the recording where indicated and ask students to listen and repeat. Students then complete the exercises. Check answers as a class. You could have a discussion about the generation gap after c. Ask: *Do children today live in a different world from their parents? Do children today grow up too quickly?* Tell students to go back to SB p.47.

◉ CAREFUL!

The difference in meaning between *have* and *get* can be confusing for many learners, especially those with Portuguese, Italian and Spanish L1s. With *have / get* passives learners may use *have* (meaning engage somebody else to do something) instead of *get* (meaning take an active role in completing something). ~~I'll help you have everything sorted out.~~ (Correct form = *I'll help you **get everything sorted out**.*) ~~The situation makes it harder to have deals closed.~~ (Correct form = *The situation makes it harder to **get deals closed**.*)

Answers (Grammar Focus 4B SB p.145)

a 2 get myself measured 3 had it checked 4 Getting
  5 to give 6 have 7 had everyone shouting 8 mended
b 2 Tina worked hard and got herself promoted.
  3 I got my bike stolen.
  4 Have your eyes checked.
  5 The news got everyone panicking.
  6 It wasn't easy to get the children to calm down / calmed down.
  7 Our teacher had us write an essay.
  8 Alex got me to go with him.
c 2 given 3 working 4 done 5 having
  6 to make 7 working

💡 EXTRA ACTIVITY

Put students into pairs to discuss these questions:

Would you like to get your hair cut really short?

Have you ever had your bag searched in customs at an airport?

What kinds of things get you worried?

Is it easy for you to get people to do what you want?

If you got yourself arrested but you'd done nothing wrong, what would you do?

Compare answers as a class.

---

2 SPEAKING

a ●**2.19 Pronunciation** Drill *He got himself <u>locked</u> in the <u>shed</u>.* and ask students which syllables are stressed (see underlining). Tell students to underline the stressed syllables in sentences 1–8. Play the recording for students to listen and check. Say: *Are content words stressed?* (yes). *What kinds of words are unstressed?* (grammar words). Drill all the sentences.

Answers
1 I <u>had</u> my <u>bike</u> <u>sto</u>len.
2 They <u>had</u> me <u>doing</u> <u>all</u> the <u>cleaning</u> for <u>weeks</u>.
3 I <u>had</u> my <u>arm</u> <u>broken</u> in a <u>football</u> <u>match</u>.
4 She had me <u>doing</u> all her <u>homework</u>.
5 It <u>got</u> me <u>thinking</u> about <u>what</u> I'd <u>done</u> <u>wrong</u>.
6 I <u>got</u> my<u>self</u> <u>locked</u> out of the <u>house</u>.
7 I <u>got</u> my <u>mum</u> to <u>say</u> I was <u>sick</u>.
8 My <u>brother</u> <u>got</u> me <u>punished</u> un<u>fairly</u>.

b 💬 Tell students the story about George Washington, the first president of the USA, and the cherry tree. When he was a young boy, George had an axe which he loved to use. One day, he cut down a cherry tree in his garden. The problem was it was his father's favourite tree. His father came home, saw the fallen tree and demanded to know who had done it. George was frightened and ashamed but he said to his father, 'I cannot lie. I cut the tree down.' George's father hugged him and said that telling the truth was more important than any tree. Give students time to read the questions and think of a childhood incident. Put them into pairs to tell each other about it. Encourage students to tell the class about particularly interesting incidents.

3 LISTENING and READING

a ●**2.20** Show some photos of people and places from your childhood and tell students what you remember about them. Students may be able to share similar photos on their mobile devices or have photos with them. Play the recording, which gives Marissa's story again, followed by Charlie's version of the same incident for students to make notes and compare.

Answers

Marissa: Charlie got locked in shed at school overnight, everyone searched for him all night in a forest, found by teacher arriving early at school the next morning

Charlie: was so interested in teacher showing him how to grow seeds in shed at school forgot about the time and didn't go home from school, Marissa and his mother came to school in the late afternoon and found him

Audioscript

MARISSA My brother got himself locked in the garden shed at school and he couldn't get out. What happened was, was my brother didn't come home from school so my mom and I, we started looking for him and … I mean, I was with my mother and she started getting more and more upset, and at first, I didn't completely understand what was going on, but I think I picked up on the general anxiety and that made me cry.

So his disappearance got everyone looking for him, in a small forest near our house. And people searched all night calling for him – I mean, I remember them shouting, 'Charlie! Charlie!' I mean, it was terrible and … there was this desperate sound in their voice – I was so afraid.

Anyway, the next day, the teacher arrives early at school and heard my brother crying in the shed. No one knows how it happened I mean, maybe the door got locked from the outside. Anyway the funny thing is, is he's always loved gardening! I'm surprised it didn't put him off.

CHARLIE So, my sister Marissa always tells this story of me getting myself locked in a garden shed. That's just … it's just not true … I mean, I wasn't locked in … I was in there with my science teacher, Mrs James. I mean, she was showing me how to grow things from seeds. Er, we were transferring seedlings from large containers to individual ones. We were like, just so concentrated on the job we forgot about the time. Marissa has a strange idea everyone searched through the night for me and Mrs James found me in the morning. That's just not true. I think my mom was just slightly concerned I wasn't home from school. Er … my mom came with Marissa to school late in the afternoon and found me and Mrs James at work. Mrs James was er … a bit embarrassed. Mo … Mom was pleased I'd, y'know, taken an interest. Marissa was right about one thing though … Thanks to Mrs James, I've always loved gardening.

b 💬 Tell students that most historians think the story about George Washington and the cherry tree is false. Ask how and why the story could have become popularised. Put students into groups to discuss the questions. Take feedback as a class.

c Divide the class into pairs and assign A and B roles. Student As read the text *False childhood memories* and Student Bs read the text *How eyewitness evidence can be unreliable*. Tell students to answer the questions about their text. If necessary, pre-teach to Student As *extraneous* (not directly connected with or related to something) and *neuron* (a nerve cell that carries messages between the brain and other parts of the body), and pre-teach to Student Bs *line-up* (a row of people for a witness to identify a suspect from, also called an *identity parade*) and *obliging* (willing or eager to help). Refer to the Culture notes as necessary. Check the two sets of answers as you monitor.

Answers

Student A

1 Memories are formed when neurons link together to form new connections, or circuits, actually changing the contact between the cells. Long-term memories, which include experiences that happened just a few minutes ago to information several decades old, are stored in mental 'drawers' somewhere in our brains. No one knows exactly where.

2 New information is added to the 'drawers', replacing older memories. He compares it to going through drawers, rearranging items.

3 The malleability of memory: our memory can be influenced by something that we have been told that is untrue, and we can be tricked into believing it really happened.

Student B

1 An eyewitness has enormous power as their testimony can convince a jury of someone's guilt or innocence.

2 They want to help to make sure that a criminal is caught and believe the police wouldn't conduct a line-up unless they had a good suspect.

3 By asking leading questions or by staring at a person in an identity parade. As a result, a witness might amend their visual image of the criminal they saw, by adding details of the person in front of them to an unclear memory.

🌐 CULTURE NOTES

Jean Piaget (1896–1980) was a pioneer of developmental psychology and contributed many theories to the field. He often reflected on his own development in his writings. This excerpt comes from one of his classic works.

He mentions that his nurse had been converted to the Salvation Army – this means she was converted to a religious way of life by a Christian charity.

---

d 💬 Tell students to compare texts and say what they found interesting or surprising. Share ideas as a class.

e Put students into pairs. Tell them to go through the two texts and guess the meaning of the words and expressions. Students then check in a dictionary. Do the first expression, *crumpled up*, as a class. Say *Look at the verbs around 'crumpled up'. Do the old memories become clearer?* (no). *What could this mean about the old memories?* (they fade or lose shape). Check answers as a class.

Answers

crumple up: of clothing or paper, to press carelessly into a small space, so it is folded in an irregular way, and possibly damaged

bear little resemblance to: be very different from

malleability: the quality of being easily influenced, or changed

fake (v.): make something look real or valuable in order to deceive people

carry weight: to be considered serious and important enough to influence other people

notify: tell someone officially about something

incentive: something that encourages a person to do something

conspicuously: in a way that is very noticeable

culprit: someone who is responsible for a crime / something bad

fuse (v.): join or become combined

4 VOCABULARY Memory

a Say to students: *I can remember my first day of school as if it were yesterday.* and ask them to tell you the collocation (a vivid memory). Tell students to match the adjectives with the definitions. Check answers as a class.

Answers
a 5
b 2
c 6
d 1
e 4
f 3

b Tell students to look at the collocations in 4a and see which one is different. Check as a class.

Answers

4 In collocation 4, *memory* describes the ability to remember. If you have a photographic memory, you are able to remember things in exact detail.
In the other collocations, *memory* describes the event remembered.

c ▶ ▶ **2.21–2.22** Students complete the exercises in Vocabulary Focus 4B on SB p.161. Play the recording for students to check their answers to Exercise a and b. Tell students to go back to SB p.49.

Answers (Vocabulary Focus 4B SB p.161)

a 1 vague 2 painful 3 distant 4 lasting 5 vivid
6 photographic
b 1 c
2 e
3 a
4 d
5 g
6 f
7 b

d ◯▶ Ask students to remember their first English class with you. Elicit how they felt and what they noticed. Give students time to read the questions, then put students into pairs to ask and answer them. Take feedback as a class.

- To avoid having to step in and interfere with the free speaking when the discussion breaks down or is not developed enough, write a framework for discussion of each point on the board which you can refer students to as you monitor.
- Write this framework and example on the board (elicit some of the content from students):

Question	How clearly do you remember the time before you went to school?
Response and example	Quite well, I mean, I'm still in touch with some of my friends from nursery.
Response	Really? I guess you talk about those times with them then.
Follow-up	What we can remember, yes. Anyway, what about you?

- As you monitor, notice when groups run out of things to say and point to the appropriate part of the framework, e.g. follow-up, to show students how they can expand the discussion.

5 SPEAKING

a ▶ Divide the class into pairs and assign A and B roles. Student As study the pictures on SB p.128 and Student Bs study the pictures on SB p.130 for one minute. Next tell students they have one minute to write down as many of the new words from the lesson as they remember. Tell students to check with each other and then look back at SB pp.47–49. Ask what kinds of words were easiest / most difficult to remember. Student As then go to SB p.130 and Student Bs to SB p.128. They test their partners on the pictures they studied and ask questions about details they have forgotten. Then ask the class how reliable their partners' memories were and whether they would make good witnesses.

b ◯▶ Ask students to name things which it is important to remember, e.g. people's names, vocabulary, passwords. Put students into groups to make a list of memory techniques. Take feedback as a class.

c ▶ Tell students to read the fact file about memory techniques on SB p.134 and find out if any of their ideas are listed. Tell students how *mnemonic* /nɪˈmɒnɪk/ is pronounced. Take feedback as a class.

d ◯▶ Ask: *Do you think men and women have better memories for different things?* Put students into groups to discuss the questions. Take feedback as a class.

 ADDITIONAL MATERIAL

▶ Workbook 4B

▶ Photocopiable activities: Grammar p.208, Vocabulary p.228

4C Everyday English
I see where you're coming from

At the end of this lesson, students will be able to:
- speak tactfully in formal discussions using a range of functional language to give opinions
- identify homophones in words and connected speech

💡 OPTIONAL LEAD-IN

Books closed. Tell students to choose one person from history and to think of three questions to ask them. Students compare interviewees and questions in pairs, and try to predict the answers the person would give to their partner's questions. Take feedback as a class and find out which of these people students think would be hardest to interview and why.

1 LISTENING

a 💬 Ask students how they would prepare for an interview with the famous person they talked about. Put students into groups to discuss the questions. Compare ideas as a class.

b ▶2.23 Ask students what they can remember about Max's interview with Oscar. Tell students to look at the picture and guess what Nadia, Sara and Oscar are discussing. Play Part 1 of the video or the audio recording. Check the answer with the class. Tell students the meaning of the informal use of *grand* here (very good).

Answer
the interviewer

Videoscript/Audioscript (Part 1)

NADIA So, Oscar, before you go, can we have a quick word about your interview with Max Redwood?

OSCAR Grand, yes!

N How do you think it went?

O Well, if you don't mind me saying so, it was like trying to get blood out of a stone.

N Right.

SARA Yeah, he wasn't an easy guy to talk to.

O Tell me about it! If you ask me, maybe he should stick to writing.

N I see where you're coming from, but guys, I think we're forgetting something here.

O What's that?

N We're the professionals.

O OK, but I thought I was being … professional.

N It's our job to get the best from our interviewees.

O Are you saying it was my fault?

N Look, don't take this personally, Oscar. I'm trying to be constructive.

O Really?!

N I think a good interviewer can get blood out of a stone.

O OK …

N I think we all need to learn from this.

O I do take your point, but I'm not sure there's anything more I could've done.

N I beg to differ. I agree Redwood wasn't particularly forthcoming, but my feeling is that there's always a way.

S No offence intended, Oscar, but … I couldn't understand why you were asking about a sequel.

O Well, he will be writing another book, surely?

S Well, anyway, Max clearly was a very hard nut to crack.

N With all due respect, Sara, I don't think you're in a position to tell us what does and doesn't make a good interviewer. We need to bear in mind that we're trying to run a business here. It's about getting results. We could lose a lot of listeners with an interview like that.

O OK, point taken.

N Let's pick this up again tomorrow.

c ▶2.23 See if students can name who mentioned the topics and any details about them. Then play Part 1 of the video or the audio recording again for students to check their answers.

Answers
1 Oscar: he suggests Max should stick to writing (rather than speaking in interviews) and assumes that Max will write another book
2 Nadia: being professional involves getting the best from interviewees; Oscar: he thought he was being professional during the interview with Max
3 Sara: she couldn't understand why Oscar was asking about a sequel; Oscar: he assumes Max will write another book
4 Nadia: they could lose a lot of listeners with an interview like Oscar's with Max

💡 EXTRA ACTIVITY

Give students examples of books and their sequels:
- *The Hobbit* and *The Lord of the Rings* by J R R Tolkien
- *The Adventures of Tom Sawyer* and *Adventures of Huckleberry Finn*, by Mark Twain.

Ask students to work in pairs and choose one book and its sequel they know. Tell them to discuss whether the sequel was better than the original. Take feedback from the class. You could ask students to research and write a comparison of the books.

d 💬 Put students into groups to discuss the questions. Take feedback as a class. Ask students if they agree with Nadia that it was Oscar's fault.

Suggested answers
1 Oscar is angry, hurt and defensive. Sara agrees with Nadia's feedback but is sympathetic towards Oscar and keen not to hurt his feelings.
2 Students' own answers

e Language in context *Idioms 1*

Check students know the meaning of *forthcoming* (friendly and helpful, willing to give information or to talk). Tell students to answer the questions. Play the recording for students to check their answers.

Answers
a like trying to get blood out of a stone
b a very hard nut to crack

💡 FAST FINISHERS

Ask fast finishers to use dictionaries to find out other idioms with *blood* and *nut*.

2 USEFUL LANGUAGE
Being tactful in formal discussions

a Ask students if they can remember any expressions describing tactful behaviour from Lesson 2C (*walk on eggshells, drop hints*). Tell students to match the expressions with their uses. Check as a class. Drill the expressions.

Answers
1 c 2 b 3 a 4 b 5 b 6 a 7 a

b ▶️ **2.24** Play the recording. Students match the expressions with the uses in 2a. Check as a class. Drill the expressions.

Answers
1 c   2 a   3 b

c 💬 Say some direct statements and ask students to make them more tactful, e.g. *You're wrong* (I can see where you're coming from, but I'm not sure I agree). Put students into pairs to make the discussions more tactful and expand them. Students then act out their discussions. Give feedback as a class.

Suggested answers
1 **A** My article was rather clever.
   B No offence intended, but I beg to differ. It was potentially offensive.
   A I see where you're coming from, but people shouldn't be so sensitive.
   B I do take your point, but you need to be more tactful.
2 **A** I think I handled that meeting quite well.
   B With all due respect, you allowed Leon to talk for too long.
   A I do take your point, but you could have interrupted him and helped me out.
   B If you don't mind me saying so, it was your job to chair the meeting.

LOA TIP REVIEW AND REFLECT

- Students will understand the purpose of new language and skills more if you show them how they are relevant to them. Personalise the expressions for being tactful and show their usefulness.

- Ask students to think of a time when they were not tactful or someone was not tactful with them. Give some example situations, e.g. giving advice to a friend who is quite sensitive; negative feedback at work.

- Put students into pairs to role-play the original untactful situation and then role-play the situation again, this time using tactful language. Ask students to compare the two role plays and how each one made them feel.

---

3 PRONUNCIATION

Homophones in words and connected speech

a ▶️ **2.25** Check students understand *homophone* (a word that is pronounced the same as another word but has a different meaning or spelling, or both) and ask students to give you more examples, e.g. *I/eye, here/hear*. Play the recording. Students find the incorrect words and write the correct homophones. Check answers as a class and check students understand *dew* (drops of water that form on the ground and other surfaces outside during the night), *grate* (to rub food against a grater in order to cut it into a lot of small pieces) and *knot* (C2) (a join made by tying together the ends of a piece or pieces of string, rope, cloth, etc.).

Answers
2 ~~weigh~~ way   3 ~~knot~~ not; ~~fare~~ fair   4 ~~sells~~ cells   5 ~~pear~~ pair
6 ~~hole~~ whole; ~~seen~~ scene   7 ~~grate~~ great; ~~wait~~ weight
8 ~~bare~~ bear

b Write *buyer nice cream* on the board and ask students to say it as a different phrase (buy an ice cream). Tell students to complete the homophone phrases. Read them aloud if students need help. Check as a class.

Answers
2 name   3 up   4 for/four cakes   5 locked inside

c ▶️ **2.26** Play the recording for students to listen to the sentences. Tell students to write out the phrases as they were said in the interview and then check in the audioscript on SB p.180. Use the information in the Language notes below to help students if necessary.

Answers
2 if you don't mind me saying so
3 I think we all need to learn from this
4 no offence intended
5 we need to bear in mind

📖 LANGUAGE NOTES

- When a word finishes in a consonant and the next word starts with a vowel, there is often linking, so *think it* sounds like one word.

- Remind students that the final /d/ or /t/ is often unpronounced before a word beginning with a consonant, so the *d* isn't pronounced in *nee(d) to* (see 3e on SB p.36).

- A final /n/ sound may become a /m/ sound if the following sound is /m/, as in *min(d) me*.

---

d Ask students why homophones might cause problems in listening (you may think it's one word/phrase when it is actually two). Tell students to complete the advice. Take feedback as a class.

Suggested answer
think about whether it could be a homophone or part of a homophone phrase.

---

4 LISTENING

a 💬 Tell students to look at the picture and say why Sara looks so happy. Discuss the question as a class.

b ▶️ **2.27** Play Part 2 of the video or the audio recording for students to check their answer in 4a.

Answer
get Max Redwood's phone number from Emma

Videoscript/Audioscript (Part 2)

SARA Phew, that was hard going!
ALEX What, Nadia? Yeah, she can be quite tough, can't she?
S You're telling me! It's the first time I've heard her criticise Oscar, though.
A Probably because of his interview with Max Redwood.
S You've hit the nail on the head!
A Speaking of which …
S Such a shame. I've read his book and it's fascinating. He must have loads to say about it.
A Yeah. Speaking of which, you'll never guess what I found out recently. Max Redwood is my girlfriend's brother!
S You're kidding! Emma's brother?!
A Yep.
S No way! Have you met him?
A Um, sort of. But he is staying with Emma at the moment.
S Hey, I wonder if …
A Yeah?
S Well, y'know – could you maybe, y'know … ?
A What? Get his number for you?
S Well, yeah.
A Yeah, sure, I'll call Emma.
S Brilliant! Thanks, Alex!
A I wouldn't mention that you're a journalist to start with though.
S Hm … Yeah, you're right. I'll say I'm a fan!
A Well you are a fan, aren't you?
S Well, yeah, I suppose I am!
A Hi Emma! Yeah, listen, I've got a favour to ask about your brother …

c ▶ **2.27** Ask students to read the questions. Then play Part 2 of the video or the audio recording again. Students answer the questions. Check answers as a class.

Answers
1 the same: she's very tough; different: she criticised Oscar for the first time
2 embarrassed; she's taking advantage of Alex's personal contacts
3 She shouldn't mention she's a journalist because Max's interview with Oscar didn't go well.

d 💬 Put students into pairs to discuss the question. Compare ideas as a class.

e **Language in context** *Idioms 2*

1 ▶ **2.28** Tell students to complete the idioms. Play the recording for students to check their answers. Concept check the meaning and ask which idiom means *I feel the same way* (Tell me about it!), *You are exactly right* (You've hit the nail on the head!), *I know this already* (You're telling me!).

2 ▶ **2.28** Tell students to underline the main stress. Play the recording again for students to listen and check. Check answers as a class. Drill the idioms.

Answers
1 1 Tell   2 telling   3 hit
2 1 <u>Tell</u> me about it!
  2 You're telling <u>me</u>!
  3 You've hit the <u>nail</u> on the <u>head</u>!

💡 **EXTRA ACTIVITY**
Put students into groups with the same L1. Ask half the groups to translate Part 2 from the start to *No way! Have you met him?* and the other groups to translate from *Not yet, no.* to the end. Put groups with the same L1 together to combine translations and check each other's work. Play Part 2 of the video recording again but without sound and tell a group to dub it with their combined translation by speaking in their L1 at the same time as the characters. This will take some practice and you will need to pause the video at points, but it is fun and challenging.

5 SPEAKING

▶ Divide the class into pairs and assign A and B roles. Tell students that A is an employee and B is a boss. Tell them to read their role play cards, Student As on SB p.127 and Student Bs on SB p.128. They then carry out the conversation, using the expressions for being tactful on SB p.50. Then tell them to swap roles, perhaps in new pairings. Monitor the role plays and give feedback to the class.

ADDITIONAL MATERIAL

▶ Workbook 4C
▶ Photocopiable activities: Pronunciation p.259
▶ Unit Progress Test
▶ Personalised online practice

4D **Skills for Writing**
Where does her talent come from?

At the end of this lesson, students will be able to:
• understand the effect of using direct quotes in writing
• use different tenses and time expressions to organise information more efficiently in writing
• write an article based on an interview

💡 **OPTIONAL LEAD-IN**
Books closed. Tell students to list as many different types of music as they can, e.g. rap, with – in their view – the best example of a modern-day performer of that genre from their country. Put students into groups to say what they think about each type of music and the performers they have listed.

1 SPEAKING and LISTENING

a 💬 Ask students to write down one interesting thing about themselves, e.g. *I was born on the same day of the week as my mother.*, and then tell other students. Tell students to read the questions and make notes about them. Then put students into groups to discuss the questions. Take feedback as a class.

b 💬 To introduce the subject of English folk music, play a clip of a song by the English folk singer/songwriter Roy Harper if you can and ask students what they think of it. Tell students to read the five things Nora says and then put them into groups to discuss how these things may have affected her. Take feedback as a class.

c ▶ **2.29** Tell students to listen and summarise what Nora says about the influences in 1b. You may wish to pre-teach the phrases in the Vocabulary support box. Check as a class.

Suggested answers
1 Her parents played a lot of music, but they weren't really musical and didn't play a musical instrument.
2 Her parents listened to music all the time, mostly rock music.
3 She thinks she's similar to her grandfather in many ways as he was very musical and travelled all over the world and she was inspired by him.
4 One day she picked up her brother's guitar and as soon as she started playing it she knew it was the right instrument for her.
5 She's travelled all over Eastern Europe and in North Africa. She listens to the local music and records it. She always comes back from travelling with her head full of music and gradually the music she's heard works its way into her songs.

INTERVIEWER So you've obviously got a talent for music. Where do you think that comes from? Is your family musical?

NORA Yes and no. My parents played a lot of music, but I wouldn't say they were really musical. They listened to music all the time.

I And so you did too?

N As a child yes, we had it played to us all the time – whether we wanted it or not. My parents grew up in the sixties. They had a huge record collection – mostly rock music. So, you could say I grew up with music in that way.

I But they didn't actually play a musical instrument?

N No, none of them played anything. But, my grandfather, he was very musical.

I Oh yes?

N Oh yes! He had an incredible musical ear. He was a violinist. He played the violin in an orchestra, and he also travelled all over the world – so I think I'm similar to him in many ways – like, a professional in an orchestra. They did international tours and everything like that. So, I think I probably take after him.

I Did you hear him play?

N Yes, when I was a kid – um … about five, I think. There was this day when I was at his place, with my parents, and he was rehearsing something in another room. And I remember being intrigued with this sound. I don't know – it was almost an emotional experience – I was very drawn to it. I think that's when I became aware of music and wanted to play. And it just dawned on me – I wanted to play like that … it was that feeling that got me interested in playing. It was a really formative experience.

I But you didn't start playing the violin?

N No. I started playing my brother's guitar, actually – my older brother. He had a guitar, but he couldn't really play it. So I picked it up one day and I started playing around on it. And like, the moment I started playing, I knew it was the right instrument for me. It was really weird actually, it just felt right.

I You've been very successful in a short space of time. Are you surprised by that?

N Well, I never set out to become famous or make money. Music was always something I just did for fun. It was only when someone asked me to play on the local radio station that I thought maybe I could make a living from it. That was about a year ago.

I And now you've released an album; it's called *Memory*.

N Yes.

I Is that about your grandfather, those memories of him playing the violin? I see you've had an elderly man put on the cover.

N No, it's not really, well, maybe partly. But it's really more to do with travelling.

I Travelling?

N Yes, it started in my teens, I've always travelled a lot.

I Like your grandfather.

N Yeah, that's right.

I So where did you travel?

N Oh, lots of places. All over Eastern Europe, um … Turkey, Morocco. I went for countries that had good music. And I always tried to listen to the local music and I recorded it. It's like most people take photos, well I do too, but I also recorded sounds I heard, music especially. I always come back from travelling with my head full of music, and gradually that works its way into my songs. So you could say they're my memories, I suppose.

I Musical ones.

N That's right, yeah. These are my musical memories.

📖 VOCABULARY SUPPORT

have a musical ear – be able to understand music just by listening to it

it dawns on sb – somebody realises something they had not been aware of previously

a formative experience – an influential event in a person's development

---

2 READING

Ask students how the article would be different from the audioscript in terms of language and content, e.g. fewer features of spoken language; an introduction to readers. Tell students to read the article and answer the questions, comparing the article with their answers in 1c. Compare answers as a class. Ask students whether they would rather listen to the live interview or read the article.

Answers

1 She's a folk musician. Over the last month she's had her songs played on local radio and she's about to embark on her first tour. She's studying biochemistry at Liverpool University. She was about seven when she started playing her brother's guitar. She started university two years ago and before long she was giving public performances. The rest of her family have never moved far from their home town of Manchester. She was 18 when she travelled through Eastern Europe.

2 Her parents had a huge record collection, mostly rock music. Her parents didn't play a musical instrument. Her brother is older than her. He couldn't really play his guitar. There's an elderly man on her album cover.

📖 VOCABULARY SUPPORT

not look back since – after an initial success, continue to be more and more successful

sth works its way into sth – something gradually influences or becomes part of something else

---

💡 FAST FINISHERS

Tell fast finishers to make a timeline of Nora's life, starting with her earliest memory (aged 5) and ending with her planning her first tour.

---

3 WRITING SKILLS

Organising information; Showing time relationships

a Write on the board:

'Where's the fun in being sensible?' she asked, smiling.

She asked me where the fun was in being sensible, and smiled.

Ask students whether they find the direct or the indirect speech more effective and why (the direct speech is probably more effective because it is a strong statement, a joke). Tell students to underline three direct quotes in the article and details of the setting. Put students into pairs to discuss what effect the quotes and the details of the setting have on the reader. Take feedback as a class. See SB pp.52–53, article, for examples of direct speech.

b Ask students why the verb in *She **tells** Saul Winthorpe about her musical memories.* (in the introductory piece of text) is in the present simple if the interview has already taken place (the present simple makes the interview seem immediate, as if it's taking place now). Tell students to find verb tenses and examples to match each category. Check answers as a class.

Answers

1 present perfect   2 present simple   3 past simple

- When you elicit patterns of usage, you need to make students aware of the context of the writing or the speaking.

- Highlight *Over the last month she's had her songs played on local radio and she's about to embark on her first tour* in the first paragraph of the article on SB p.52. Elicit the two verb forms, present perfect and *be about to*, and why they are used (present perfect for something continuing until now and *be about to* for something that will happen soon). Then elicit why it is effective to have two different forms in the same sentence (the interview is seen to be wide in scope, covering the past and the future).

- You can also use the audioscript. Tell students to highlight *Music was always something I just did for fun* in the audioscript on SB p.180–1. Elicit why Nora uses the past simple rather than the present perfect (Nora is now a professional so her attitude to music as fun has changed).

c Ask students if the sentences look like effective writing (no). Put students into groups to compare the sentences with the original and answer the questions. Check answers.

Answers
1 There is only one sentence in the article. The second and third sentences both begin with *She*, which sounds repetitive.
2 c

d Tell students to cover the text and then make the pieces of information in questions 1 and 2 into single sentences. Then ask students to compare their answers with the original sentences in the text and decide which are more effective. Take feedback as a class.

e Ask students what the highlighted phrases are (time expressions). Tell students to match the highlighted expressions with the functions. Check as a class.

Answers
1 The moment   2 It was only when … that; it wasn't until … that
3 before long; was closely followed by; subsequently

f Students underline the time expressions and match them with the functions in 3e. Check answers as a class.

Answers
1 No sooner had … than – 1
2 Not until (many years later) … (did) – 2
3 The instant – 1
4 In time – 2
5 Shortly after – 3

g Ask students what is unusual about 1 and 2 in 3f. Check as a class and refer students to the grammar section on inversion in lesson 3A if necessary.

Answer
The subject and verb are inverted.

h ▶ Students complete the exercises in Writing Focus 4D on SB p.171. They read the table with time expressions before completing the exercises. Check answers to Exercise a and then monitor Exercise b–e. Take feedback as a class. Tell students to go back to SB p.53.

Answers
a 1 The moment I saw her paintings, I knew she would be a famous artist.
2 Shortly after graduating / he graduated, he got a highly paid job in the City of London.
3 No sooner had I started asking questions than she got up and left the room.
4 It wasn't until we were both made redundant that we decided to form a business partnership.
5 It was only years later that I decided to take up horse riding again.

4 WRITING

a Ask students how these settings would affect an interview: an underground train, a cinema, a swimming pool, a roller coaster, the top of a mountain. Tell students to prepare for the interview by looking back at their notes, thinking of interesting questions and choosing a setting.

b Put students into pairs. It may be effective to pair up students who don't know much about each other so that there is more of an information gap. Students take turns to interview each other and take notes. Tell the stronger student in each pair to be the interviewee first as answering questions is more difficult and this will provide a model for the weaker student. Read through the Writing Tip with the class and remind students to bear these points in mind. If they have the technology, students may want to record the interview.

c Tell students to write their article using the Nora Manning article as a model. Encourage students to use direct quotes, and complex sentences with different tenses and time expressions. Tell students to show each other their writing and say how it is different in language and content from the oral interview with their partner.

EXTRA ACTIVITY
Repeat the interview procedure but tell students to imagine that 20 years have passed. Ask them to imagine what they have done in those 20 years and what plans they have realised. Tell students to put a copy of the final written text about them in an envelope addressed to themselves to open in 20 years' time. It is very unlikely students will still have the envelopes in 20 years, but they will like the idea of opening them then!

ADDITIONAL MATERIAL

▶ Workbook 4D

UNIT 4
Review and extension

1 GRAMMAR

a Write this sentence on the board and ask students to find the mistake: *Turn to your conference programme to find the timetable of Tuesday.* (Tuesday's timetable). Tell students to find the mistakes in the sentences. Check as a class.

Answers

1 A recently published published recently article has caused a political uproar.
2 For tea there were delicious strawberry tarts filled with cream tarts.
3 We need a new bed. Our old one one old is broken.
4 Every corner of the table table's corner was covered in papers and documents.
5 If you ever get a chance to see them in concert, I recommend it.
6 A friend of John's wife the wife of John is also interested.
7 The name of the recently elected leader of the council's name is Mr Singh.
8 I have to tell him a difficult something difficult this evening.

b Write this sentence on the board and ask students to choose the correct option: *I'll get / have the secretary make you an appointment.* (have). Tell students to choose the correct answers in the exercise. Check as a class.

Answers

1 got   2 get   3 the repairs done   4 Get   5 having
6 dressed   7 had

2 VOCABULARY

a Ask students to look at 1–7 and say which word could come next in each sentence half. Then tell students to match the sentence halves with the endings. Check as a class.

Answers

1 e 2 a 3 g 4 c 5 f 6 d 7 b

b Tell students to correct the vocabulary mistakes. Check as a class.

Answers

1 far distant
2 photographers photographic
3 freshen up refresh
4 foggily vaguely
5 in to
6 hurtful painful
7 leave slip
8 stimulate trigger

> **EXTRA ACTIVITY**
> Put students into pairs to discuss whether they agree or disagree with the sentences in 2b. Take feedback as a class.

3 WORDPOWER *mind*

a ▶ 2.30 Say to students: *Would you mind doing the next exercise?* Ask what *Would you mind … ?* indicates (a polite request). Tell students to complete the gaps and then play the recording for students to listen and check. Drill the phrases in bold.

Answers

1 speak   2 bear   3 read   4 put   5 cross

b Read aloud the first sentence from 3a. Ask students: *Does 'speak your mind' mean the same or the opposite of 'hold back'?* (opposite). *Which definition means 'don't hold back'?* (give your true opinion). Tell students to match the phrases with the definitions. Check answers as a class.

Answers

a 5 b 1 c 4 d 3 e 2

c ▶ 2.31 Tell students to match 1–5 with a–e. Play the recording for students to check their answers. Drill the phrases. Concept check the phrases: *when you feel calm and secure* (peace of mind), *when you have many things to think about* (a lot on your mind), *when you think objectively* (keep an open mind), *when something acts independently in a way you don't want it to* (a mind of its own), *when you can think sensibly* (in the right frame of mind).

Answers

1 c   2 a   3 b   4 e   5 d

> **FAST FINISHERS**
> Tell fast finishers to make new 1–5 beginnings for a–e in 3c, e.g. *a I still feel angry about it and I'm not in the right frame of mind*, and compare sentences with another fast finisher.

d 💬 Put students into pairs. Tell them to choose a sentence from 3a or 3c and make a conversation. When they have finished their conversation, tell them to choose a new sentence and make a new conversation. Monitor and ask students to change partners for variety. As feedback, ask some pairs to perform their conversation in front of the class.

> **EXTRA ACTIVITY**
> Put students into groups to discuss these statements:
> *Anyone can run a marathon if they put their mind to it.*
> *There may be life on other planets; we should keep an open mind.*
> *Famous people have a lot more on their minds than the rest of us.*
> *It's always better to speak your mind than say nothing.*
> Take feedback as a class.

▶ Photocopiable activities: Wordpower p.244

> **LOA REVIEW YOUR PROGRESS**
>
> Students look back through the unit, think about what they've studied and decide how well they did. Students work on weak areas by using the appropriate sections of the Workbook, the Photocopiable worksheets and the Personalised online practice.

UNIT 5

Fairness

UNIT CONTENTS

 GRAMMAR

- Relative clauses (defining and non-defining; use of relative pronouns and prepositional phrases)
- Willingness, obligation and necessity (modal verbs; phrases with *be*; idioms)
- Linkers: *above all, also, besides, furthermore, moreover, what is more*

V VOCABULARY

- Crime and justice: *arrest on suspicion of, ban from, be convicted of, be found guilty of, be held in custody, bring face-to-face with a victim, criminal, defence lawyer, do community service, fine, give testimony in court, judge, jury, make an allegation of, one-to-one / group counselling, plead guilty to, policeman, prosecution, receive a reduced sentence for good behaviour, receive psychiatric help, sentence to life imprisonment, serve the full ten years, show evidence in court, solitary confinement, trial, victim, witness*
- Areas of employment: *agricultural, construction, energy, financial, industrial, manufacturing, public, retail, transport*
- Language in context: Crime; Temporary states
- Wordpower: Idioms: Crime: *catch red-handed, get away with murder, get off lightly, give the benefit of the doubt, lay down the law, look over your shoulder, partners in crime, up to no good*

P PRONUNCIATION

- Sound and spelling: *s* and *ss*
- Word stress: nouns and verbs
- Main stress

GETTING STARTED

ⓦ OPTIONAL LEAD-IN

Books closed. Put students into groups. Ask students to discuss how fair these ideas are for the people involved and society in general:

- a higher tax rate for large salaries
- not allowing prisoners to vote
- raising the retirement age

a 💬 Give students one minute to think about their answers to the questions before talking about the photo as a class. If necessary elicit *barbed wire* (a type of strong wire with sharp points on it). If you wish, give students information from the Culture notes below. Take feedback as a class.

UNIT OBJECTIVES

At the end of this unit, students will be able to:

- understand and evaluate opinions and attitudes in texts about punishment and rehabilitation; understand, summarise and relay and respond to texts describing occupations
- follow and understand details of colloquial radio news stories, recognising usage of puns; understand details and opinions of speakers describing employment and recruitment experiences
- use a range of lexis accurately to: give descriptions of forms of punishment and rehabilitation; discuss crimes and their consequences; describe, evaluate and discuss employment conditions, job requirements and fair pay
- understand a conversation between people meeting for the first time and identify social strategies used by the speakers
- use a range of expressions for recalling and speculating in social interactions where they are uncertain of the facts
- write well-structured and coherent opinion essays using linkers effectively to add information and reinforce their argument

🌐 CULTURE NOTES

This photo shows a prisoner in Washington working with frogs as part of a state-wide Sustainability in Prisons Project. The aim of the project is to make the prison and general community more aware of and active in ecological concerns. Similar initiatives include a project in the US where prisoners train service dogs, and a restaurant open to the public in England where the prisoners only prepare dishes from sustainable products.

b Put students into groups to discuss the questions. If students need encouragement, prompt them with ideas from the Suggested answers below. Take feedback as a class.

Suggested answers
1 They may learn how to be responsible / care for others.
2 giving talks to teenagers about the mistakes they made; taking part in clinical trials
3 Reoffenders may not have had enough support in prison.

ⓦ EXTRA ACTIVITY

In groups, ask students to imagine they work at a prison, and to convince the prison governor to try one of their ideas in b2. Give students a few minutes to think of the advantages and then present them. The class votes for the most beneficial idea.

At the end of this lesson, students will be able to:

- read an article about a prison system and evaluate the claims made
- use defining and non-defining relative clauses with a range of constructions
- identify and use four pronunciations of the letter *s*
- discuss different forms of crime, punishment and rehabilitation using a range of vocabulary related to crime and justice

💡 OPTIONAL LEAD-IN

Books closed. Ask students to name famous prisons or prisoner camps throughout the world that have now been turned into museums, e.g. Solovki in Russia. Put students into groups to discuss why they think tourists want to visit these places. Take feedback as a class.

1 READING

a 💬 Ask students if they have seen any films or read any books about famous prisons throughout the world and what impression it gave them of prison, e.g. *The Count of Monte Cristo* about Château d'If, *The Birdman of Alcatraz* about Alcatraz, *Papillon* about Devil's Island, *Mandela: Long Walk to Freedom* about Robben Island. Put students into groups to discuss the questions. Take feedback as a class.

b 💬 Ask students if they think a prison in Norway would be different from a normal prison. Tell students to look at the photos, say what impression they give and then answer the questions. Take feedback as a class. Students then read the article. Check answers as a class.

Suggested answers

1 The conditions are very good. Every cell has a flatscreen TV, its own toilet, a shower with large, soft, white towels, fridges, cupboards and desks. There are no bars on the windows. Prisoners enjoy freshly brewed coffee, and they have their own fridges. They are encouraged to attend work and educational activities. The prison has its own studio for mixing music.
2 Many prisoners have committed very serious offences such as violent attacks, as Halden prison is one of Norway's highest-security jails.

c Tell students to answer the questions. Encourage students to guess the meaning of the words in the Vocabulary support box if they ask about them. Help with the meanings if necessary. Check answers as a class.

Answers

1 the smell of coffee; the quiet
2 through rehabilitation, not punishment
3 yes – because it looks like one; no – because you can't leave when you want
4 to make it look as if it isn't a prison; to make it seem normal
5 those who leave their cell to attend work and educational activities are paid; doing activities makes prisoners less aggressive and stops them getting institutionalised
6 being locked in his room at night
7 the prisoners didn't stand to attention when Halden's governor came past but clustered round him and listed their complaints
8 it feels like a place where you don't need to feel frightened

📖 VOCABULARY SUPPORT

flagship – the product or service which represents the best of an organisation

rehabilitation – the process of helping somebody return to a good/healthy/normal way of life

boutique hotel – small, stylish, independent hotel

stand to attention – (military) stand up very straight and still, with feet together and chest out

d Ask students to work in pairs and explain any of the highlighted words and phrases they already know to their partner. Tell students to work out any meanings they don't know from context. They can then check their ideas in a dictionary. Check answers as a class.

Answers

communal: belonging to or used by a group of people rather than one single person
humane: showing kindness, care and sympathy towards others, especially those who are suffering
minimalist chic: a fashionable style in art, design and theatre that uses the smallest range of materials and colours possible, and only very simple shapes or forms
unbarred: without metal bars, typical of cages or prisons
scale (v.): climb up a steep surface, such as a wall or the side of a mountain, often using special equipment
high-risk: involving a greater than usual amount of risk
incarcerated: put or kept in prison or in a place used as a prison
institutionalised: if someone becomes institutionalised, they gradually become less able to think and act independently, because of having lived for a long time under the rules of an institution
cluster around: when a group of people/things surround someone or something
address (v.): speak or write to someone (formal)
minor irritations: small problems

🔄 LOA TIP CONCEPT CHECKING

- If students understand the grammatical relationship between a word or phrase and the rest of the sentence, this can help them to work out the meaning.

- Tell students to look at *communal*. Ask students: *What part of speech is 'communal'?* (adjective). Tell students to underline the whole sentence, which is at the beginning of the text (*It hits you in the communal apartment-style areas where prisoners live together in groups of eight.*). Ask: *What does the compound adjective tell us?* (the cells are like apartments, or flats); *What does the relative clause tell us?* (one area has eight prisoners); *So could 'communal' be about being alone or being together?* (together).

- Show students how much the grammar helps unlock the meaning by rewriting the sentence as two separate sentences. *It hits you in the communal areas. These are apartment-style and prisoners live together in groups of eight.* Here it is harder to make the connection between *communal* and the other information.

e Ask students why Kent is in prison (a violent attack) and if they think his punishment is appropriate. Put students into groups to discuss the questions. Take feedback as a class.

2 GRAMMAR Relative clauses

a Tell students to match the captions with the photos. Check answers as a class.

Answers
1 d
2 a
3 b
4 c

b Write on the board:

1 The prisoners who escaped were punished.

2 The prisoners, who escaped, were punished.

Ask students in which sentence all the prisoners were punished (2). Ask students to rephrase sentence 1 to show the difference in meaning (*Only the prisoners who escaped were punished.*). Ask students what the difference in pronunciation is (1 is one word group; in 2, *who escaped* is a separate word group). Ask students which relative clause is defining (1) and which is non-defining (2). Elicit that non-defining relative clauses aren't essential and can be left out of the sentence. Tell students to underline the relative clauses in the captions, mark them as defining or non-defining, and say why. Check answers as a class.

Answers
1 Norwegian prison officers are tasked with rehabilitating the men in their care, <u>the result of which is a 20% reoffending rate,</u> <u>compared with 50% in England</u>.
2 Graffiti by Norwegian artist Dolk, <u>from whom it was commissioned out of the prison's 6m kroner (£640,000) art budget</u>.
3 Welcome to Halden prison, Norway, <u>inside the walls of which prisoners receive comforts often likened to those of boutique hotels</u>.
4 The prisoners, <u>some of whom have committed the most serious crimes imaginable</u>, are provided with plenty of opportunities for physical exercise.
all the relative clauses are non-defining; they aren't essential and are preceded by a comma

c Tell students to work individually to compare the alternative clauses with the clauses in 2a and say which features of the clauses in 2a are more formal. Take feedback as a class.

Answers
the clauses in 2a begin with prepositional phrases:
1 the result of which
2 from whom
3 inside the walls of which
4 some of whom

📖 LANGUAGE NOTES
You could point out to students that in caption 3, the participle clause, *comforts often likened to those of boutique hotels*, is similar to a reduced relative clause, *comforts (which are) often likened to those of boutique hotels.* In caption 1 the participle clause *a 20% reoffending rate, compared with 50% in England* is an adverbial, it does not post-modify the noun phrase before it. Tell students that they will learn more about participle clauses after nouns and participle clauses as adverbials in Lesson 6B.

d **2.32–2.33** Students read the information in Grammar Focus 5A on SB p.146. Play the recording where indicated and ask students to listen and repeat. Students then complete the exercises. Check answers as a class. Tell students to go back to SB p.57.

Answers (Grammar Focus 5A SB p.146)
a 2 c
3 e
4 h
5 a
6 d
7 b
8 f
b 2 whom
3 that
4 whose
5 by which time
6 few of whom
7 which
c 2 The criminals shared a prison cell, the floor of which was over the city drainage system.
3 The prisoners, who were desperate for freedom, built a tunnel through which they could escape / which they could escape through.
4 One night, when / on which there was a full moon, they went down the tunnel.
5 The two criminals came out into a street which / that looked familiar.
6 They had come up outside the local police station where / at which they had first been charged.
7 The local police, all of whom knew the criminals by sight, arrested them.
8 They took them back to the prison, from which they never tried to escape again.

👁 CAREFUL!
Students often make the mistake of leaving out a preposition in relative clauses, e.g. after quantifiers: ~~I would like to get some money back, at least 50% which will go to charity.~~ (Correct form = *I would like to get some money back, at least 50% **of which** will go to charity.*). Another common mistake is to use *which* + noun: ~~I am writing to participate in your competition, which advertisement I saw in a magazine recently.~~ (Correct form = *I am writing to participate in your competition, the advertisement **for which** I saw in a magazine recently.*).

e Tell students that in the UK there are open prisons where low-risk prisoners only need to spend the night in their cells and are free to do activities in the prison during the day. Some prisoners qualify for day release and work outside the prison in the community. Ask students if they think open prisons are a good idea. Then tell students to complete the sentences with their own ideas.

f Put students into groups to compare ideas. Take feedback as a class.

💡 EXTRA ACTIVITY
Put students into pairs and ask them to make a timetable of a prisoner's day in their ideal prison, e.g. 7:00 get up, 7:30 morning jog, etc. Put two pairs together to compare and use ideas from both to agree on the best timetable. Ask groups to present their timetable, explaining the reasoning behind it, to the rest of the class.

3 VOCABULARY and SPEAKING
Crime and justice

a ▶️ **2.34** Elicit the names of crimes students should know: *stealing from a house* (burglary), *stealing from a shop* (shoplifting), *using violence for political reasons* (terrorism). Tell students to match the crime collocations, using a dictionary if necessary. Play the recording for students to listen and check.

Answers

1 c
2 e
3 b
4 d
5 a

violent assault: an attack which hurts or seriously injures another person
tax evasion: when someone illegally pays less tax than they should
possession of a controlled substance: owning or carrying an illegal drug
credit card fraud: when someone pretends to be the owner of a credit card and uses false information to pay for goods and services or obtain money
bribery and corruption: giving money or a present that you give to someone so that they will do something for you, usually something dishonest, and illegal, bad or dishonest behaviour, especially by people in positions of power

b ▶️ **2.35** Play the recording for students to listen and repeat the pronunciation of the words. Drill the words.

c ▶️ **2.36** Write *base*, *case* and *vase* on the board and ask which one has a different *s* sound (*vase*, /z/). Students underline the words with a different sound. Play the recording to check. Drill the words.

Answers

1 mi**ss**ion – /ʃ/
2 impre**ss**ion – /ʃ/
3 compari**s**on – /s/
4 vi**s**ion – /ʒ/

d 💬 Put students into pairs to give definitions of the crimes for their partner to guess. Encourage students to use relative clauses.

> 💡 **EXTRA ACTIVITY**
>
> Tell students to solve this puzzle. A prisoner has escaped from prison and he runs towards two doors outside the walls. One door leads to safety and the other back to the prison but he doesn't know which is which. In front of the doors are two brothers who do know which door leads to safety. One brother always tells the truth, the other brother always lies. The prisoner knows this and has time to ask one question to one of the brothers before he chooses which door to go through. What would that question be?
>
> **Answer**
> The question would be *Which door would your brother say leads to safety?* and the prisoner would then go through the other door.

e ▶️ **2.37–2.38** Students complete the exercises in Vocabulary Focus 5A on SB p.162. Play the recording for students to listen to the sentences in Exercise a and c, and check answers as a class. Put students into groups to discuss Exercise b, d and e and compare ideas as a class. Ask students to read the Learning Tip. Tell students to go back to SB p.58.

Answers (Vocabulary Focus 5A SB p.162)

a 1 a *arrest on suspicion of*: when the police take somebody (by force if necessary) into the station to question them about a crime that they think they have committed
   b *make an allegation of*: make a statement, without giving proof, that someone has done something wrong or illegal
 2 a *be held in custody*: the state of being kept in prison, especially while waiting to go to court for trial (*court* = a place where trials and other legal cases happen, or the people present in such a place, especially the officials and those deciding if someone is guilty; *trial* = the hearing of statements and showing of objects, etc. in a law court to judge if a person is guilty of a crime or to decide a case or a legal matter)
   b *be convicted of*: to decide officially in a law court that someone is guilty of a crime
 3 a *show evidence in court*: lawyers show relevant documents, witness statements, scientific information, etc., in court, during a trial, which support the idea that something is or is not true
   b *give testimony in court*: give, in court, during a trial, (an example of) spoken or written statements that something is true
 4 a *plead guilty to*: to make a statement in a law court saying that you admit you are responsible for breaking a law (*sentence* = a punishment given by a judge in court to a person or organisation after they have been found guilty of doing something wrong)
   b *be found guilty of*: a court of law decides you are responsible for breaking a law

> 👁️ **CAREFUL!**
>
> Students can confuse *commit* with *convict*: ~~However, after the punishment finishes and the offender is released, that person can convict a crime again.~~ (Correct form = *However, after the punishment finishes and the offender is released, that person can **commit** a crime again.*).

> 💡 **HOMEWORK ACTIVITY**
>
> ▶ Ask students to follow the advice given in the Learning Tip and make a note of the difference between these words and expressions in their vocabulary notebooks: *bail/fine, commit/convict, evidence/proof, judge/jury, murder/manslaughter, persecution/prosecution, reduced sentence / suspended sentence*. Tell students to use a dictionary to find the differences in meaning and to give example sentences to show the different meanings.

4 LISTENING

a 💬 Ask students to tell you about a crime which has been in the news recently. Then tell students to describe the pictures and say what crime they think is happening.

b 💬 Pre-teach *fraudster* (someone who gets money by deceiving people). Tell students to match the headlines with the pictures.

c ▶️ **2.39** Play the recording for students to listen and check their answers to 4b. Check answers as a class. They then work in pairs and explain what is happening in each picture. If necessary, pre-teach *hive* (a structure where bees live, especially a beehive – a container like a box – or the group of bees living there), *truant* (a child who stays away from school without permission) and *pocket-dial* (phone someone by mistake and not realise you are making a call). Take feedback as a class.

Answers

1 Fake fan   2 Cereal offender   3 Dial a crime
4 The honest fraudster   5 Would-bee burglar

Audioscript

NEWSREADER 1 When it comes to football, I'm extremely patriotic. Who isn't? If I go to see England play anywhere in the world, there's only one football shirt you'll catch me wearing – I wouldn't be seen dead in anything else, particularly a French one. Same goes for any fan – only trouble is … the shirt can get you into trouble. So here's the thing … Man goes to Cyprus. Turns up to customs and hands over his French passport. The immigration officer looks at the passport and looks at the man. What's he wearing? An English football shirt. Just doesn't match, does it? A Frenchman wearing an English football shirt? C'mon! Turns out this guy – this not so clever guy – well, he forged the passport – it was a fake. And, by all accounts, he missed the game. The Cypriot police have locked him up.

NEWSREADER 2 Stealing things – it sure makes you hungry. Here's a story of a young man who brings new meaning to the term 'serial offender'. This 16-year-old was skipping class at high school and paying regular visits to a family home – not his family. The homeowner says he doesn't have a key to his own house so leaves it unlocked every day. So our 16-year-old truant gets into the habit of dropping in for some breakfast cereal and milk – not just once, but on a number of occasions. And it was all going well until he logged himself on to Facebook with the family's iPad … and forgot to log himself out! So our young 'cereal offender' got caught and has been detained in a local facility for young criminals.

NEWSREADER 3 Ever done the pocket-dial thing? It can be a bit embarrassing. It can also get you arrested! See, this couple thought they were being very smart. They allegedly went to a supermarket and stole a whole heap of video games and DVDs. They had this great plan to pawn them for cash at the local pawnshop. Trouble is, when they were making their getaway, they pocket-dialled emergency services. I mean, they thought they were pretty smart – boasting about how the operation had gone so smoothly and how much cleverer they were, compared to other thieves. They also talked about where they were going to sell their ill-gotten gains. Of course, what they didn't realise was that an emergency services operator could overhear the whole thing and noted down all the details. So when they got to the pawnshop, guess who was waiting? The police, of course, with the handcuffs ready!

NEWSREADER 4 Let me tell you about John Parsons – that very rare thing, an honest fraudster. And I have to say, Mr Parsons is extremely creative – ingenious, you could say. He was stuck in a high-security facility all nice and safe. Someone manages to smuggle in a mobile phone for him. Now, Mr Parsons gets busy and creates a fake web domain, and from this domain he emails a release form to officials – for his very own release! So out of jail he walks – a free man – and the officials don't discover his clever little scheme for another three days. But this is where the fraudster turns into an honest man – he hands himself in. Or maybe life was boring on the outside. Anyway, he's back inside serving his 15 years for numerous counts of fraud. But even lawyers and judges agree, John Parsons is nobody's fool!

NEWSREADER 5 Now here's a good story. You could say that it's un-bee-lievable! Police are on the hunt for a … I guess you could call him a 'would-bee burglar'. Last Thursday night he was having a go at stealing some bits and pieces from a shed in the Jesmond Dene area. So he was busy opening all these boxes, looking for some interesting items to steal. And one of the boxes contained something with a very interesting … buzz. Inside was a hive of bees! Police are pretty sure our burglar won't have got away without a whole host of bee stings. So police want to know if there are any medical professionals or chemists out there who've treated someone with bee stings. Not very common in these winter months.

CO-PRESENTER What you might call a … bumbling crook!

d ▶️ **2.39** Play the recording again. Students summarise how the criminals were caught or how the police hope to catch the criminals. They compare answers in pairs. Check answers as a class.

Suggested answers

1 An immigration officer noticed that a man with a French passport was wearing an English football shirt. The passport was a fake.
2 A 16-year-old regularly missed school to have breakfast in an empty house, but one morning he logged himself on to Facebook with the family's iPad and forgot to log himself out.
3 The criminals pocket-dialled the emergency services and the operator overheard their conversation. The police were waiting for them at the pawnshop where they were planning to sell the stolen goods.
4 Prisoner John Parsons managed to get somebody to bring him a mobile phone in prison and emailed a release form to officials and got himself released, but handed himself in after a few days.
5 A burglar opened a box containing bees. The police hope that medical professionals or chemists will let them know if they have treated someone for bee stings, which is very unusual in the winter.

📖 VOCABULARY SUPPORT

wouldn't be seen dead doing sth – (informal) would never do something because it is too embarrassing

a whole heap of – (informal) a lot of

ill-gotten gains – (literary / informal) money or goods obtained in a dishonest or illegal way

nobody's fool – a clever person who is not easily tricked

a whole host of – a large number of

bumbling – clumsy and disorganised, with no skill

---

e Language in context *Crime*

Ask students what *them* is in 3 (videos and DVDs). Ask what could be a synonym of *pawn* (sell). Say that *pawn* is a little different from *sell* and ask what an alternative to selling stolen goods could be. Ask students to go through the words and try to work out the meanings. Encourage them to look at the audioscript on SB p.181. Tell them to check their ideas in a dictionary.

Answers
forge: make an illegal copy of something in order to deceive
detained: be forced to stay in a place by officials
pawn (v.): leave a possession with a pawnbroker in return for money
handcuffs: two metal or plastic rings joined by a short chain that lock around a prisoner's wrists
smuggle: take things to or from a place illegally
hand yourself in: voluntarily go to a police station and admit to a crime

f Ask students: *How do prisoners communicate with one another?* (cell phones). Elicit the joke (*cell* = a room for a prisoner) and say that this kind of joke is a pun. Elicit that a pun is a humorous use of a word or phrase that has several meanings or that sounds like another word. Ask students to find the two puns in the headlines in 4b. Tell students to work in pairs, each choose a different one of the puns and explain it to their partner. Check answers as a class.

Answers
The two puns are in these headlines:
Cereal offender: *cereal* sounds like *serial*. *Serial* is used to refer to a person who repeatedly commits crimes. The offender regularly went into an unlocked house and ate breakfast cereal.
Would-bee burglar: *bee* sounds like *be*. *Would-be* means wanting or trying unsuccessfully to be. The burglar wanted to steal things from a shed but was attacked by bees when he opened a hive he thought was a box.

g 💬 Ask students if they have ever had an embarrassing pocket-dial situation. Put students into groups to discuss the questions. Take feedback as a class.

5 SPEAKING

a 💬 Elicit the different types of punishment and rehabilitation students studied in Vocabulary Focus 5A on SB p.162, e.g. *to charge someone an amount of money as a punishment for not obeying a rule or law* (fine).

Tell students to work in pairs and decide on a suitable consequence for each person, discussing whether there is any further information they would need in order to make a judgement.

b 💬 Ask pairs from 5a to work in groups of four to compare and agree on consequences for each person. Take feedback as a class.

ADDITIONAL MATERIAL

▶ Workbook 5A

▶ Photocopiable activities: Grammar p.209, Vocabulary p.229, Pronunciation p.260

5B It's essential to have the right qualifications

At the end of this lesson, students will be able to:

- Listen and relate to people discussing employment issues
- Use word stress accurately and distinguish between words which have a different stress according to their part of speech
- Read and discuss employment terms and conditions using a range of words and expressions connected with employment
- Use a range of forms for willingness, necessity and obligation
- Discuss the advantages and disadvantages of different job opportunities

1 LISTENING and VOCABULARY

Employment

a 💬 Say: *Most people want to earn as much money as possible while doing as little as possible.* and ask students if they agree. Put students into groups to discuss the questions. Take feedback as a class.

b ▶ 2.40 Ask students to speculate about what kind of work the people in the pictures might be doing. Play the recording. Tell students to listen and answer the question. Check answers as a class.

Answers

Mike works in a café but wants to work in conservation.
Olivia wants to work in sustainable tourism.
Andrew works in investment banking, in the financial sector.
Karen works in retail.

Audioscript

MIKE Well I actually studied biology at university and er ... I've always wanted to get into conservation work. Er ... And I've been trying to get work on nature reserves, in order to gain practical experience. And the trouble is I can't find a job with a paid salary – there's too many people these days who are willing to work on a voluntary basis so, er ... so at the moment what's happening is I'm volunteering at weekends and I'm working in a café during the week, in order to make ends meet and pay the bills.

OLIVIA I left college in June and have a degree in tourism. Since then I've been applying for many jobs in sustainable tourism, for example, y'know, ecotourism. That's what really interests me and I'm very passionate about. But unfortunately in this current climate, it's very difficult to get a job. Unfortunately, the last job I applied for had 200 applicants, and I got on a shortlist of 10 but, er ... in the end I didn't get it. The only way to gain experience nowadays seems to be to do an internship – but instead of them paying us, we have to end up paying them for this privilege!

ANDREW I applied for a job in investment banking straight after I left university. Er ... my background is economics and business. I was lucky because I was immediately offered jobs by three different companies and I decided that I would go for the job that I deemed to be most interesting. Um ... I managed to negotiate a higher salary than they were offering and since then I've been working very hard indeed, in order to prove myself – as there have been a lot of redundancies in the financial sector recently. And I certainly want to make as much money as possible while I can.

KAREN I left school um ... at 16, and I went straight to do an apprenticeship in retail. Um ... unfortunately, by the time I finished my apprenticeship a lot of people were made redundant and they couldn't keep me on. So I was unemployed for probably about two years ... But, er, eventually I found a job in this large store selling sports equipment, which I'm still there, I'm working shifts. I work morning shifts, afternoon, and evening shifts. Um ... I get paid by the hour so I try to get as many shifts as possible – so if I'm lucky I can get a double shift and work er ... around 40 hours a week, maybe. But more often it's only around 10–15 hours a week ... and that's hardly enough to live on.

c ▶ **2.40** Tell students to try and match the statements with the speakers before they listen. Then play the recording again for students to check their answers. Check answers as a class.

Answers
1 Andrew   2 Mike, Olivia, Karen   3 Mike, Olivia   4 Mike, Olivia
5 Karen

📖 VOCABULARY SUPPORT

shortlist – a list of candidates competing for a job, chosen from a longer list

the current climate (C2) – the general (economic/political) situation at present

prove yourself – show that you are good at sth

keep sb on – (informal) continue to employ somebody

d 💬 Ask if recent graduates like Mike and Olivia are often unrealistic about what to expect from the job market. Put students into groups to discuss the questions. Take feedback as a class.

💡 EXTRA ACTIVITY

Put students into groups to discuss what kind of problems these people face in the job market and what can be done to help them: immigrants, women, disabled people, ex-prisoners, people near retirement age. Take feedback as a class.

e Put students into groups to discuss the questions. Take feedback as a class.

Answers
1 *sector*: one of the areas into which the economic activity of a country is divided
2 Students' own answers
3 Suggested answers: educational, entertainment, private, service

💡 FAST FINISHERS

Ask fast finishers to list the sectors in order of their contribution to their country's economy.

f Go through the words in the box with students to find the verb forms and adjectives. Check answers as a class.

Answers
verb forms: finance; construct; publicise; manufacture; transport; energise; industrialise; retail
adjectives: financial; agricultural; public; manufacturing; industrial

👁 CAREFUL!

A common mistake students make is to use the wrong form of these words in the box in 1e: ~~concentrate our finance resources on this challenge.~~ (Correct form = *concentrate our **financial** resources on this challenge*.); ~~the constructing of the metro.~~ (Correct form = *the **construction** of the metro*.). Some students also mistakenly use *public* when *audience* and *state* are correct: ~~Italian soap operas have gained a wide public.~~ (Correct form = *Italian soap operas have gained a wide **audience**.*); ~~a substantial gap between public and private education.~~ (Correct form = *a substantial gap between **state** and private education*).

g ▶ **2.41** **Pronunciation** Play the recording for students to match the words with the stress patterns. Play the recording again. Pause after each sentence and ask students to say whether the word in bold is a noun or verb. Then drill the words according to whether they are a noun or verb. Elicit the answer to the question and ask students what other noun/verb pairs they can think of, e.g. *finance*.

Answers
b trans<u>port</u>   a <u>Trans</u>port
The stress is on the first syllable in the noun and on the second syllable in the verb.

h ▶ **2.42** Play the recording. Tell students to write a or b in the tick boxes according to whether the sentence contains the word used as a noun or as a verb. Check answers as a class.

Answers
1 a noun   b verb   2 b noun   a verb   3 a noun   b verb
4 b noun   a verb   5 a noun   b verb

Audioscript
1 a There's been an increase in employers offering apprenticeships.
1 b The number of employers offering apprenticeships has increased.
2 a We import most of our stock from China.
2 b The majority of our products are Chinese imports.
3 a Her attendance record is spotless.
3 b Line managers have to record any absences.
4 a We don't export anything at present.
4 b Exports are lower than expected this year.
5 a When are you getting a new contract?
5 b We need to contract a number of short-term staff.

- A stressed syllable is louder, longer and higher in pitch. A good way to demonstrate this is for students to hum the word because then they are focusing purely on pronunciation.
- Hum *transport* as a noun, *HUMhum*, for students to repeat. Do the same with *transport* as a verb, *humHUM*. Repeat with more words from 1g and 1h. Put students into pairs to hum the words as nouns and verbs. Monitor and check students are stressing the correct syllable, using all three features: loudness, length and pitch.
- Then drill the words with sounds rather than humming, e.g. *finance* and *finance*, and check students maintain the distinction in stress.

💡 EXTRA ACTIVITY

Put students into groups to think of more words where the word is written the same but the different parts of speech change the pronunciation, e.g. *read* /riːd/ infinitive and /red/ past tense; *house* /haʊs/ noun and /haʊz/ verb; *aged* /eɪdʒɪd/ adjective and /eɪdʒd/ verb. See which group has the most words and write all the words with their pronunciations on the board.

---

i 💬 Give examples of your own family and friends first. Put students into groups to discuss the questions. Take feedback as a class.

2 SPEAKING

a 💬 Ask students to tell you some of the terms and conditions in their jobs or in jobs they would like to do, e.g. *holiday arrangements*. Tell them to read the list and tick the ones they actually have in their job. Pre-teach *sabbatical* (a period of time when college or university teachers are allowed to stop their usual work in order to study or travel, usually while continuing to be paid). Put students into groups to discuss the questions. Take feedback as a class.

💡 FAST FINISHERS

Point out *paternity* and *maternity* and ask fast finishers to write down as many male/female word pairs, e.g. *waiter/waitress*, as they can while the others are finishing.

> **Suggested answers**
> bridegroom/bride, hero/heroine, lion/lioness, nephew/niece

---

b 💬 Ask students how performance-related pay could work in a café. Put students into groups to discuss terms and conditions for the two businesses. Take feedback as a class.

3 READING and SPEAKING

a 💬 Books closed. Ask students to make a list of very well-paid jobs and compare with a partner. Books open. Students see if bomb disposal diver and butler are on their lists. Ask students to read the headings and look at the photos. Put students into groups to discuss what they think each job involves. Take feedback as a class. Students then read to check. If necessary, pre-teach *ordnance* (military supplies, especially weapons and

bombs), *run errands* (go out to buy or do something) and *scout out* (try to find something by looking in different places). Check answers as a class.

> **Suggested answers**
> Bomb disposal diver: safely recovering or disposing of unexploded bombs on the seabed
> Private butler: providing a personal service for a very wealthy individual by doing anything the employer wants done at any time

b 💬 Ask students for obvious differences, e.g. there is personal risk as a bomb disposal diver. Put students into groups to discuss the similarities. Take feedback as a class.

> **Suggested answers**
> lack of privacy: a diver has to live with five to ten people in close proximity for a month or longer and a butler has to live in someone else's home most of the time
> risks and danger: physical risks and danger for the diver, though the long hours and the danger of suffering from isolation could adversely affect the butler's health
> working hours: unpredictable for both. A diver works to a narrow timescale and only works two months out of three but a butler works long hours and can be asked to do anything at any time.
> qualifications and training: essential for a diver, but only advisable for a butler
> getting on with other people: essential for both. A diver has to live in close proximity with lots of other people and a butler has to enjoy looking after others and be able to deal with all sorts of people.
> impact on family life: negative for both. A diver is away from home for at least six months of the year and it's difficult for a butler to have their own family life.

c 💬 Ask students whether they think these jobs are more suitable for men than women, vice versa or it doesn't matter. Put students into groups to discuss the questions. Take feedback as a class.

💡 EXTRA ACTIVITY

Put students into groups. Half the groups should think of five job interview questions to ask potential bomb disposal divers; the other groups should think of five interview questions to ask potential private butlers. Students from different groups pair up and answer each other's questions as if they were candidates.

---

4 GRAMMAR
Willingness, obligation and necessity

a Tell students to read the examples from the texts and tell you the different implications of *must* and *should*, and *must* and *have to*.

> **Answers**
> a yes – *should* means desirable but not obligatory
> b no – both are obligations
> *must* describes a rule
> *have to* describes a necessary part of the job (not a rule but living conditions, which are a necessary part of the job)

b Tell students to complete the sentences and then check in the texts.

> **Answers**
> 1 expect you   2 a mandatory requirement   3 be required
> 4 be called on   5 It's advisable   6 It's essential   7 be obliged

c 💬 Put students into groups to discuss the questions. Check answers as a class.

Suggested answers

1 1 You will have to have diving qualifications.
   2 You must / have to have these qualifications.
   3 You must / have to have an explosive ordnance disposal qualification.
   4 A private butler must / has to be ready to do anything.
   5 You should do a course at a training college.
   6 You must / have to have an eye for detail.
   7 They may have to work for people who aren't always nice.
2 The expressions are more precise and allow a variety of subjects and structures.

d ▶ ⏵ **2.43–2.44** Students read the information in Grammar Focus 5B on SB p.147. Play the recording where indicated and ask students to listen and repeat. Students then complete the exercises. Check answers as a class. Tell students to go back to SB p.61.

Answers (Grammar Focus 5B SB p.147)

a 2 against   3 obliged   4 had to   5 ought
   6 was supposed to
b 2 I have no objection to waiting until the end.
   3 I'm afraid I/we have no choice but to cancel the trip.
   4 It is forbidden (for members of the public) to go beyond this point.
   5 It is up to you when you leave.
   6 Gerald has got to attend the meeting.
c 1 have no choice but to   2 have nothing against
   3 be willing to   4 be prepared   5 be under no obligation to
   6 be up to   7 ought to

💡 EXTRA ACTIVITY

Put students into pairs, A and B. Student A thinks of a job, e.g. *night nurse*, and makes a statement about it using the grammar for obligation and necessity, e.g. *You are required to work at nights.*, and Student B has to guess the job. If Student B doesn't guess, Student A says another statement about the job, e.g. *A university degree is a mandatory requirement*. They continue keeping a score of the number of statements until Student B guesses the job. They then swap roles. The student who guesses the job after the fewest statements wins.

5 READING and SPEAKING

a ▶ Divide the class into pairs and assign A and B roles. Student As read the text on SB p.129 and Student Bs read the text on SB p.130. They prepare to tell their partner about the main points in each section. Monitor to check students understand what they have to do, and look out for any problems and clarify these before the pairwork stage. Encourage student to guess the meaning of unfamiliar words and then check in a dictionary. Use the Vocabulary support box to help with more idiomatic phrases. Tell students to go back to SB p.61.

📖 VOCABULARY SUPPORT

stand up to sth – not be damaged by something, e.g. an attack

not come the traditional route – reach a position of employment without the typical qualifications/background of people in that position

stay on top of sth – remain in control or up-to-date with e.g. work, developments, etc.

out of place – not fit your surroundings

read people – know, by observing them, what people are thinking or will do next

label sb – categorise somebody in a simple, negative way, usually unfairly

---

b 💬 Put students into Student A and Student B pairs to exchange information about the jobs they read about.

c 💬 Put students into groups to discuss the questions. Take feedback as a class.

d 💬 Ask students to use these phrases to talk about teaching, e.g. *It's essential to be able to communicate well.* Put students into groups to describe the requirements of their own job or a job they would like to do and to answer the question. Take feedback as a class.

💡 EXTRA ACTIVITY

Tell students to write a job description for their job or job they would like to do, using the ideas they have just talked about. Tell them to divide the description into categories like working hours, holiday, dress code, etc. and write ideas in each category.

---

6 SPEAKING

a 💬 Ask students if they personally know anyone who does any of these jobs and what that person thinks about the job. Put students into pairs to choose a job, say what its value is and give a salary based on the criteria suggested.

b 💬 Put students into groups of five, ideally made up of students who chose different jobs in 6a. Students discuss how to divide the fund between the four jobs. Groups then present their decision to the rest of the class and answer any questions other students may have.

c ▶ Tell students to go to SB p.137 to find the average salaries in the UK for the jobs in 6a. Students compare the figures with the salaries they suggested in 6b.

💡 EXTRA ACTIVITY

Put students into groups and ask them to think of cynical interpretations of typical requirements given in job adverts, e.g. *a driving licence is an advantage* (you will be expected to drive all over the place and not get paid for it). Ask groups to tell the class their requirements and interpretations.

ADDITIONAL MATERIAL

▶ Workbook 5B
▶ Photocopiable activities: Grammar p.210, Vocabulary p.230

5C Everyday English
If I remember rightly

At the end of this lesson, students will be able to:
- use conversation strategies for talking to new people
- use contrastive stress to highlight meaning
- recount a story of injustice using functional language for recalling and speculating

OPTIONAL LEAD-IN

Books closed. Ask students how successful these opening lines would be when you want to get to know a complete stranger in a café:

Do you come here often?

Haven't we met before?

What's a nice person like you doing in a place like this?

It's a nice day, isn't it?

Could you pass me the sugar, please?

Put students into (mixed-nationality) groups to discuss the question: *In your country and culture, in what circumstances, if any, would it be acceptable to approach a stranger and start a conversation?*

1 LISTENING

a Ask students which of these people they would find it hardest to have small talk with: their boss, someone sitting next to them on the train, an ex-boyfriend/ex-girlfriend, a distant relative, their bank manager. Put students into groups to discuss the questions and read the strategies. Take feedback as a class.

b (▶) **2.45** Ask students how Sara managed to organise a meeting with Max (Alex gave her Max's phone number). If you have the video, play it without sound and see if students can see which strategies Sara uses based on her body language. Play Part 1 of the video or the audio recording. Students name strategies from 1a and give specific examples using the audioscript on SB p.181. Check answers as a class.

Answers

b I'm such a fan of your work!
c You're staying with Emma at the moment, if my memory serves me correctly?
e I know how busy you must be. Oh no! That must be tough. Yeah, I suppose.

Videoscript/Audioscript (Part 1)

SARA Hi, Mr Redwood? I'm Sara Neroni.

MAX Hello. Just call me Max. Nice to meet you!

S Nice to meet you, too. Coffee?

M Oh, yes, please.

WAITRESS Two coffees.

M Thanks.

S I am such a fan of your work! Thank you for agreeing to meet me like this.

M Well, I try to find time for my fans. I'm just sorry we couldn't meet up sooner.

S That's fine. I know how busy you must be.

M Yeah. So, er, you work with my sister's boyfriend Alex?

S Yes, that's right. You're staying with Emma at the moment, if my memory serves me correctly?

M Just on a temporary basis, till I get my own place.

S It must be a bit hard to write, stuck in her flat?

M Well, I'm not actually doing any writing at the moment.

S No?

M No. To be honest, I think I've got writer's block. But hopefully, I'll snap out of it soon enough.

S Oh no! That must be tough.

M Well, we all have our ups and downs, I guess.

S Yeah, I suppose.

FAST FINISHERS

Ask fast finishers to find these phrases in the audioscript on SB p.181 and say if they are formal (F) or informal (I): *Just call me Max.* (I); *Thank you for agreeing to meet me like this.* (F); *I guess* (I). Then ask students to make the formal phrases more informal and vice versa (You can call me Max; It's great you can meet me; I imagine).

c Ask students which strategies Sara doesn't use (a, d), and why. Put students into pairs to discuss what they think the impact of the ones she does use will be. Take feedback as a class.

d Language in context *Temporary states*

1 (▶) **2.46** Tell students to match the beginnings and endings to make phrases. Play the recording for students to check their answers.

2 Ask students to match the phrases with their meanings. Check answers as a class.

Answers

1 a 2 b 3 c 1
2 a ups and downs b snap out of it c on a temporary basis

EXTRA ACTIVITY

Tell students that *ups and downs* is an idiom that uses a metaphor of life as a journey. Ask students to use a dictionary to find other idioms which use the same metaphor of life as a journey, e.g. *go off the rails* (start behaving in a way that is not generally acceptable, especially dishonestly or illegally); *the end of the road* (the point at which it is no longer possible to continue with a process or activity).

e (▶) **2.47** Ask students to predict the answers to questions 1–3 before they listen. Play Part 2 of the video or the audio recording for students to check. Check answers as a class.

Answers

1 crime fiction
2 writing another book / a sequel
3 Oscar hadn't even opened Max's book

Videoscript/Audioscript (Part 2)

SARA It must be really difficult writing science fiction.

MAX I suppose so. I reckon I should've been a crime writer.

S Yeah?

M When your detective solves the murder, you just invent another murder, and then away you go.

S I never thought of it like that!

M Not so easy with science fiction. I think I've said everything I wanted to say in my first book.

S Oh? I was under the impression that you were writing another book?

M No. No doubt you heard that from that guy from the radio interview.

S Oscar.

M Yeah. Him. What stands out in my mind most is that that interview was a total disaster! I'd hazard a guess that he hadn't even read my book. Hadn't even opened my book. Otherwise he wouldn't have asked about a sequel!

S Hm …

---

2 PRONUNCIATION Main stress

a ▶ **2.48** Say to students: *Max is a writer. He's a science-fiction writer.* Write the two sentences on the board. Ask students which words have the main stress in each sentence. Ask students why *writer* does not have the main stress in the second sentence (we already know this information). Play the recording. Tell students to listen to Max's lines and say why the main stress changes to a different word.

Answer
Because the information stressed in the first line is no longer new in the second line, the stress switches to what is new.

b 💬 Ask students to choose the correct word to complete the rule. Check the answer.

Answer
new

c ▶ **2.49** Students underline the main stress. Play the recording for students to listen and check. Then drill the sentences and ask students to practise saying them.

Answers
1 a It's dangerous enough being a <u>diver</u>,
   b let alone a <u>bomb disposal</u> diver!
2 a I don't think wealth distribution in this country is <u>fair</u> –
   b quite the <u>opposite</u> of fair, in fact.
3 a I haven't got the right <u>qualifications</u> –
   b in fact, I've hardly got <u>any</u> qualifications!
4 a Halden is more than just a <u>prison</u> –
   b it's the world's most <u>humane</u> prison.

3 LISTENING

a ▶ **2.50** Ask students to predict what could go wrong with Sara's meeting with Max. Play Part 3 of the video or the audio recording. Students answer the question. Check as a class.

Answer
She tells him she's a journalist and mentions the possibility of another interview.

Videoscript/Audioscript (Part 3)

MAX Still, enough about me. What about you? Presumably, you're a technician, like Emma's boyfriend, right?
SARA Well, I'm not actually …
M Oh. I think I remember Emma saying that her boyfriend's a technician at *City FM*.
S Yes, he is. But I'm a journalist, myself. Sorry.
M Oh. I see. Emma didn't mention that. I thought you were just a fan. I didn't know you were a journalist.
S Suppose you'd known, would you still have agreed to meet with me?
M Well, not after that interview with Oscar whatsisname!

S So, I suppose another interview would be out of the question.
M Time to go!
S I'm sorry! It's just that I'm a really big fan, and I really need this break. I just didn't know how else to … Look, I've read your book and I absolutely love it. And I get that there simply can't be a sequel – after all, time does stand still at the end, doesn't it?
M Right.
M Look, I might consider doing another interview.
S You would?
M But I need to have a think about it. Let's meet up again soon to talk some more?
S Oh, fantastic! Thank you so much! When are you free?

b ▶ **2.50** Play Part 3 of the video or the audio recording again. Students answer the questions. Check answers as a class.

Answers
1 a technician
2 because of his interview with Oscar
3 she's a really big fan; she needs this break

c 💬 Put students into pairs to discuss the question. Take feedback as a class.

Suggested answer
Because Sara shows she's read his book and understands that there can't be a sequel.

4 USEFUL LANGUAGE
Recalling and speculating

a ▶ **2.51** Tell students to complete the expressions. Then play the recording for students to check their answers.

Answers
1 serves
2 under
3 doubt
4 stands
5 hazard
6 Presumably
7 remember
8 Suppose

b Before students categorise the expressions, make sure they understand *recalling* and *speculating*. Ask: *What is a synonym of 'remember'?* (recall) *What is a synonym of 'guess'?* (speculate). Students answer the questions. Check answers as a class.

Answers
recalling events: 1, 4, 7
speculating: 3, 5, 6, 8
both recalling events and speculating: 2

c ▶ **2.52** Ask students to read the conversation and find out what the speakers decide to do (go on holiday together). Tell students to find the five mistakes. Then play the recording for students to check their answers.

Answers and audioscript
A So when are you starting your new job? I was <u>under</u> the impression that you were starting next week.
B Oh, no. That would be too soon. I need a holiday first!
A But, if my <u>memory</u> serves me correctly – you went to Spain last month for a long weekend, didn't you?
B Who told you that?! I<u>'d</u> hazard a guess it was that sister of mine!
A Yeah, I think I remember <u>her</u> saying something along those lines.
B Well, you can't have too much of a good thing, can you? <u>Presumably</u> you need a holiday too. Why don't you come with me?
A Well, I can't remember the last time I had a break. Why not?

d 💬 Put students into pairs to act out the corrected conversation. Then ask them to swap roles and practise the conversation again. Books closed. Ask students to see if they can act out the conversation from memory.

- Regular informal tests of new language allow students to see how much they've learned and how they can make more progress.

- A week after this class, dictate the conversation in 4c to students, leaving gaps for students to complete the expressions: *I was _____ that you were starting next week* (under the impression); *if _____ correctly* (my memory serves me); *I'd _____ it was that sister of mine* (hazard a guess); *I think I _____ something along those lines* (remember her saying); *_____, you need a holiday too* (Presumably). Students write out the complete conversation and check with a partner.

- Then check answers as a class and ask students which expressions they couldn't fill in or filled in incorrectly. Ask students how they could learn these expressions better, e.g. write each expression on a sticky note and stick it on their fridge.

e 💬 Tell students to complete the sentences individually. Then put them into pairs to tell their partner about their first day at school or their first day in a job. Take feedback as a class.

f 💬 Put students into groups to discuss the questions. Encourage them to use the new expressions in 4a. Take feedback as a class.

5 SPEAKING

▶ Divide the class into pairs and assign A and B roles. Student As read their first card on SB p.135 and Student Bs read their first card on SB p.137. Tell Student As to start the conversation. Students then read their second cards. If necessary, pre-teach *bump into sb* (C1) (meet someone you know when you have not planned to meet them). Tell Student Bs to start the conversation. Monitor and make sure students are using the language for recalling and speculating.

ADDITIONAL MATERIAL

▶ Workbook 5C

▶ Photocopiable activities: Pronunciation p.261

▶ Unit Progress Test

▶ Personalised online practice

5D Skills for Writing
It's a way of making the application process more efficient

At the end of this lesson, students will be able to:

- **listen to and discuss the relationship between job applications and social media**
- **write more coherent paragraphs using linking words and phrases**
- **write an opinion essay on an employment issue**

💡 OPTIONAL LEAD-IN

Books closed. Ask the class which of these would be valid reasons for firing someone: their partner works for a major competitor; they are looking for another job; they won't do overtime; they have been prosecuted for tax evasion; they have a lot of sick days.

1 LISTENING and SPEAKING

a 💬 Ask students if employers/teachers should care what employees/students do in their personal life. Then put students into groups to discuss the questions. Take feedback as a class.

b 💬 Ask students to read the posts and say which one would concern an employer the most. Put students into groups to discuss their reactions. Take feedback as a class.

c 💬 Put students into groups to discuss the questions. Take feedback as a class.

d ▶2.53 Ask students if employers would be suspicious of anyone who doesn't use social media today. Then play the recording. Tell students to listen and compare the speakers' experiences. Check answers as a class. Use the Vocabulary support box to help with vocabulary as necessary.

Answers

1 Mario's interviewer asked for log-ins to all his social media (not just professional). He refused them the information and decided that he didn't want to work for the company.
Laila's interviewer asked to friend her so that he could have access to all her personal information and postings. Her interviewer was impressed by her profile and she got the job.

2 Mario thinks that there are privacy concerns if a company accesses an applicant or employee's private social media, and he doesn't think employers should do this.
Laila thinks that employers should be able to access private social media, and is relaxed about sharing information. She thinks you should present yourself in a good light on social media, and that it works to your advantage if an employer sees positive things about your life.

Audioscript

MARIO I saw this really interesting job ad online – working in marketing for an IT company. It's a bit like my current job, but there were opportunities in the new job for more travel and I thought, 'Why not give it a go and apply?' I sent in my CV and got offered an interview immediately. I thought, 'Great!' So I had this interview with an HR person. To start off with, it went really well. She told me she was impressed by my CV, and I could feel that I was giving her the answers she wanted to hear. Y'know, you just get a sense of whether a job interview is going well or not. Then, after about half an hour, this HR woman said, 'Oh, and of course we'll need log-ins for all the social media you use.' And I replied, 'Oh, you mean the professional one?' And this kind of suspicious look crept across her face and she said, 'No, I mean all social media.' I was truly shocked – I was completely lost for words. For a minute I just sat there and didn't say anything. Eventually she asked, 'Is there a problem?' At which point I said that I didn't really think it was appropriate for a company to access private social media. Then there was this stony look in her eyes and she said, 'All staff are required to provide access to the social media they use.' I'm afraid I couldn't help myself and I said that I felt they were overstepping a boundary by asking me for this, and there were really privacy concerns. But she didn't back down. She said that the company expects access to social media, particularly of marketing staff. She said that it's essential that we project a positive image at all times – both in person and online. Well, I don't want my private life to be controlled in this way. And besides, I've heard of people getting sacked for making 'inappropriate comments' about work – but of course, it's always the company that decides what's inappropriate or not. So, in the end, I politely told this woman that I wouldn't feel comfortable working for her company and quickly left. I mean, I know everyone's life is more out there and online these days, but, demanding to see my social media – that's just a bit too Big Brother-ish for my liking.

LAILA I read this article the other day about people being surprised or shocked because prospective employers expect access to applicants' social media. I was a bit surprised by this article myself – surprised, because I thought, 'What do people expect in this day and age?' We live so much of our lives online and it's such a public thing so, I don't really see a problem with employers having a look at my social media postings. In fact, this happened to me a couple of months ago. I applied for a job as an account manager at an advertising agency. During the first interview, the guy who's now my boss asked if he could friend me and I agreed immediately – in fact, we sorted this out during the interview. This meant he could read through all my personal information and postings. He called a couple of days later to say I'd got the job. And, do you know what swung it in my favour? He really liked my way of presenting myself online, and he was impressed by the sports training and charity work that I do in my free time. He also thought my pet cockatoo was very cool! So really, why wouldn't you want to give a prospective employer this kind of access? I really think it's advisable to do so. Of course, if you've posted material that puts you in a bad light, then I can see why you wouldn't. But in that case, the real issue is the way you use social media. I think that people tend to forget that just about anything you post online can be accessed in one way or another – so if you don't want people to read it, then don't post it. Social media are so much a part of my life and I feel completely relaxed about sharing information. I do think carefully about the way I present myself, but no more carefully than I would if I walked into a room full of people I don't know. It's the same thing – what's the difference?

📖 VOCABULARY SUPPORT

creep across – gradually start to appear

be lost for words – so shocked you cannot speak

stony – unfriendly, hostile

overstep a boundary – behave in an unacceptable way

back down – withdraw from an argument, admit defeat

Big-Brother-ish – referring to authorities that use surveillance and censorship to control people

friend sb – become somebody's friend on social media

swing it in sb's favour – successfully influence a positive outcome for somebody

put you in a bad light – make you look bad in some way

---

e 💬 Tell students to tick the opinions they agree with and then compare with a partner. Take feedback as a class.

2 READING

a Ask students if they know any recruitment websites and how effective they are for employers and/or employees. Tell students to read the essay and answer the questions. If necessary, pre-teach *trawl* (search among a large number or many different places in order to find people or information you want). Check answers as a class.

> **Answers**
> 1 It makes the application process more efficient and allows them to filter out unsuitable applicants. (They aren't breaking any laws and the information is freely available.)
> 2 Companies look for negative information about applicants rather than getting a balanced general impression; they may be judged on the behaviour of their friends and family; employers may discriminate against them on factors such as their medical history or age.
> 3 The writer thinks it is unfair for employers to judge an applicant's suitability solely on the basis of their social media postings; employers shouldn't actively seek negative information; the system creates opportunities for employers to discriminate; there should be guidelines or laws to restrict the research employers can do, and checks need to be made that their decisions are fair and transparent.

b 💬 Put students into groups to discuss the questions. Take feedback as a class.

3 WRITING SKILLS Essays; Linking: addition and reinforcement

a Ask students to look at the descriptions and say what the logical order would be. Then tell students to match the descriptions with the paragraphs in the essay. Check answers as a class.

> **Answers**
> 2, 4, 3, 1

b Write these opening sentences on the board and ask how effective they are: *Social media sites began to get popular in the 2000s.* (ineffective, historical perspective is irrelevant); *Everybody knows that social media is bad news for applicants.* (ineffective, too early to give an opinion and too informal). Ask students to read the strategies and say which are effective, and why. Check answers as a class.

> **Answers**
> c, d
> b, c, d because it's good to create interest (b, c) and introduce an issue objectively (d), but not stating an opinion before presenting the arguments isn't logical

---

💡 EXTRA ACTIVITY

Ask students to write an alternative first sentence to start the essay, using strategies b, c or d. Put students into groups to compare their sentences and choose the best one to read out to the rest of the class.

---

c Ask students to read the strategies and say which are used in this conclusion, which are generally appropriate and why. Check answers as a class.

d Elicit the purpose of a supporting argument (to back up the main argument and give concrete examples). Ask students to read paragraphs 2 and 3 again, compare their functions and say how many supporting arguments there are in each paragraph. Check answers as a class.

e Refer students to the highlighted linker and then ask what linkers they can remember from Lesson 2D on SB p.29, e.g. *regardless of, when compared to*. Tell students to underline linkers in the text that add information or strengthen an argument with a supporting idea. Check answers as a class.

f Tell students that the expressions in the first column will be adverbials and the expressions in the second column will be either conjunctions or prepositional phrases. Ask students to add linkers to the table and find the one that introduces the key supporting argument. Check answers as a class.

g Tell students to underline the linkers in the sentences and add them to the table in 3f. Check answers as a class.

📖 **LANGUAGE NOTES**

You could point out that *Besides* is a conjunction in the essay and an adverb in 3g question 3. *In addition to* is a prepositional phrase and is followed by a noun phrase. *In addition* is an adverb which usually goes first in a sentence and is followed by a clause.

---

h ▶ Students complete the exercises in Writing Focus 5D on SB p.172. They read the table and then cover it for Exercise a. Check answers to Exercise a and b and take feedback as a class for Exercise c. Tell students to go back to SB p.65.

4 WRITING

a 💬 Ask students if they know anyone who they think was unfairly dismissed. Put students into small groups to discuss the questions. Take feedback as a class.

b Read through the Writing Tip with the class and remind students to bear these points in mind as they organise their notes.

c Tell students to write an essay using their notes. A good structure would be to have four paragraphs matching the functions in 3a. Encourage students to use linkers.

🔄 LOA TIP MONITORING

- Teachers usually monitor speaking more than writing tasks but students need help in writing too. Teachers may feel reluctant to disturb students when they are in the process of writing so they need strategies to help without interfering.

- Look out for signs that students are struggling. Typical signs are not writing anything, talking with other students, and behaviour showing their boredom and frustration. Go to these students, explain the task again and refer them to the model essay.

- Have a system where students can show when they need help and when they are all right on their own, e.g. SB closed and SB open. Go round in turn to the students who need help and let the others work.

- Check the work of students who finish much earlier than other students as often they have not done the task properly. If the structure of the essay is incomplete, refer them to 3a.

d Put students into pairs to compare essays. Ask students to read out any points that are particularly interesting.

💡 **EXTRA ACTIVITY**

Tell students to name the famous people who were fired: *He was sacked as captain in the military because he wasn't considered a natural leader.* (Abraham Lincoln); *She only lasted one day in a doughnut shop because she squirted cream over a customer.* (Madonna); *The bosses got sick of this secretary wasting work time writing stories.* (J K Rowling); *He founded a company but the same company fired him.* (Steve Jobs).

ADDITIONAL MATERIAL

▶ Workbook 5D

UNIT 5
Review and extension

1 GRAMMAR

a Write on the board: *She committed a crime. It was serious.* Ask students to make this into one sentence (She committed a crime that/which was serious.). Students then compare the sentence with question 1 and add the correct pronoun. Tell students to complete the rest of the sentences. Check as a class.

Answers
1 that/which 2 why 3 which 4 whose 5 wherever 6 in

b Tell students to cross out the wrong words or phrases. Point out that the mistakes in the sentences could be mistakes in form or meaning. Check as a class.

Answers
2 Bill *doesn't mind / has no objection to / ~~is expected~~* going on the training course.
3 You are not *allowed / permitted / ~~obliged~~* to throw litter outside.
4 *It's up to you whether you / ~~You have no choice but~~ / You are under no obligation to* sign up for the course.
5 Module 2 is optional and you *~~mustn't~~ / don't have to / are not obliged to* do it.
6 Once I *had to / ~~must have~~ / was required to* do a four-hour practical exam.
7 Students *should / ought to / ~~have to~~* make a study timetable.
8 I *was supposed to / ~~had better~~ / had to* be at the office at 9:00 but I overslept.

> **FAST FINISHERS**
>
> Ask fast finishers to make sentences using the words/phrases they crossed out and compare their sentences with another fast finisher.

2 VOCABULARY

a Give short definitions of crime and punishment vocabulary and the first letter for students to guess, e.g. *violent attack = a__?* (assault); *financial punishment = f__?* (fine). Tell students to complete the sentences. Check as a class.

Answers
2 Community 3 banned 4 fraud 5 evasion
6 confinement 7 counselling 8 serve

> **EXTRA ACTIVITY**
>
> Ask students to mark whether they agree or disagree with the statements in 2a by writing a tick or a cross next to each sentence. Then put students into groups to discuss the statements they had different opinions on.

b Ask students what sector they work or would like to work in. Students identify the sector for each job. Check as a class.

Answers
1 public 2 retail 3 energy 4 construction 5 agricultural
6 manufacturing 7 financial

c Put students into groups to discuss the jobs in 2b. Share ideas as a class.

3 WORDPOWER Idioms: Crime

a ▶ **2.54** Ask students if they can remember what the writer said she didn't need to do in Halden prison because she felt safe (look over her shoulder). Tell students to complete the idioms, using a dictionary if necessary. Then play the recording for students to listen and check. Drill the idioms.

Answers
1 shoulder 2 good 3 murder 4 doubt 5 red-handed
6 in crime 7 lightly 8 the law

b ▶ **2.55** Concept check some of the idioms: *when your punishment is less than you deserve* (get off lightly), *when you see somebody committing a crime* (catch somebody red-handed). Tell students to complete the exchanges. Then play the recording for students to listen and check.

Answers and audioscript
1 **A** I can always tell when my children are up to no good. They have a guilty look on their face.
  B I never can. Unless I catch them red-handed, I can never work out if they've been naughty or not.
2 **A** He may have made up his story about feeling sick, but I'm going to give him the benefit of the doubt.
  B OK, but if you trust him too much, he'll try and get away with murder.
3 **A** He's found himself a partner in crime in a boy called Jim from school, and now he never comes home at a reasonable time any more.
  B You should lay down the law. He's only a teenager.
4 **A** You really got off lightly at work after messing up that big order. I can't believe they didn't take it more seriously.
  B I know, I can't stop looking over my shoulder now. I'm sure that can't have been the end of it.

c Put students into pairs to tell each other their stories. Take feedback as a class.

> **EXTRA ACTIVITY**
>
> Put students into pairs. Tell them they need to tell a crime story using all the idioms. Students plan their story, making notes, practise it and then each read out half of the story to the class. The class votes on which story is the most interesting.

 Photocopiable activities: Wordpower p.245

> **LOA REVIEW YOUR PROGRESS**
>
> Students look back through the unit, think about what they've studied and decide how well they did. Students work on weak areas by using the appropriate sections of the Workbook, the Photocopiable worksheets and the Personalised online practice.

UNIT 6
Perspectives

UNIT CONTENTS

G   GRAMMAR
- Simple and continuous verbs: uses, verbs not usually used in the continuous, verbs with different meanings in the simple and continuous
- Participle clauses: post-modifying nouns, adverbial use

V   VOCABULARY
- Adjectives: *Describing images: bleak, cluttered, elaborate, evocative, exotic, flawless, gritty, humorous, iconic, ironic, meaningful, nonsensical, playful, powerful, raw, repetitive, sensational, well-composed*
- Emotions: *ashamed, devastated, disillusioned, frustrated, gleeful, helpless, insecure, jealous, over-excited, petrified, protective, restless, satisfied, speechless*
- Language in context: Descriptive language; Idioms 1/2
- Wordpower: Idioms: Feelings: *at the end of sb's tether, can't believe my eyes, get sb's back up, get on sb's nerves, grin and bear it, over the moon*

P   PRONUNCIATION
- Sentence stress
- Main stress and emphatic stress (adverbs and adjectives)
- Tone in comment phrases

GETTING STARTED

💡 OPTIONAL LEAD-IN

Books closed. Tell students this anecdote: *A famous modern artist wanted an extension to his house. He called a builder and drew a quick sketch of what he wanted. The builder agreed to the work and the artist asked him how much it would cost. 'Nothing,' said the builder, 'just sign the sketch.'* Put students into pairs to discuss what this anecdote says about our attitude to modern art and artists. Take feedback as a class and elicit whether students think that modern art can be created very quickly without much thought and that the public will buy anything from anyone famous.

🔄 UNIT OBJECTIVES

At the end of this unit, students will be able to:
- understand attitudes and opinions in an instructional article about a creative activity and relate these to an artist's work
- follow an interview with a speaker describing a creative pursuit in detail using some technical language and infer the speaker's attitudes
- understand a detailed descriptive narrative including the relationships and attitudes of the characters in an authentic work of fiction; follow the narrative in an audio recording of an authentic work of fiction
- use a range of lexis appropriately to: describe and evaluate visual arts; describe and discuss creative activities; write and tell fictional narratives, adding details and describing emotions precisely
- understand a presentation and analyse its effectiveness and coherence
- use a range of expressions to organise and give a presentation
- use formal and positive language to write a letter of application creating a positive impact

a Ask students which country this photo was taken in (the letter Φ on the right is a clue). Give students one minute to think about their answers to the questions before talking about the photo as a class. If necessary, pre-teach *passer-by* (someone who is going past a particular place, especially when something unusual happens). If you wish, give students information from the Culture notes below. Take feedback as a class and ask students why they think the artist drew a dragon, e.g. it is a symbol of the East.

🌍 CULTURE NOTES

This photo shows the American artist Strum and assistants making the 'Singing Dragon' interactive 3D street painting as part of a music festival in Krasnoyarsk, Russia in 2014: the *ATΦ* on the right stands for *Asian Pacific Festival* in Russian. In a sense, this is an unusual example of street art because it has been commissioned. Most street art is unauthorised, sometimes even illegal, and is often created as a deliberate challenge to mainstream artistic activity and institutions.

b Ask students to give you examples of street art, e.g. graffiti, pavement drawings, posters, stickers, ice sculptures, sand sculptures. Put students into groups to discuss the questions. Take feedback as a class.

💡 EXTRA ACTIVITY

Put students into groups and ask them to design a piece of street art for a public place where they live. Tell them to discuss where the art will be, what type of street art it is, and what it will look like and represent. If they have time, ask them to draw a rough sketch of their plan. Each group then presents their street art and ideas to the rest of the class.

6A We all seem to be using digital cameras

⚲ OPTIONAL LEAD-IN

If the technology is available, ask students to show one another photos on their mobile devices and say what impression they give. If not, ask students to go through the SB and choose three pictures which particularly impress them. Tell them to show one another and explain their choice.

1 SPEAKING and READING

a Ask students how digital cameras and phones have changed photography. Put students into groups to discuss the questions. Take feedback as a class.

b Ask students if they have heard of Erwitt. Before they read the fact file, ask students what kind of pictures they think Erwitt takes based on his own photograph on SB p.69. Check the answer as a class.

Answer

advertising and street photography (especially ironic black and white photos of everyday life)

c Ask students if they think anybody could be a good photographer. Put students into groups to discuss the skills. Take feedback as a class.

d Tell students to check their ideas from 1c with the article. Take feedback as a class.

e Ask students if they were surprised by anything they read. Give them time to read the article again and answer the questions. Use the Vocabulary support box to help with vocabulary as necessary. Check answers as a class.

📖 VOCABULARY SUPPORT

fall into a trap of doing sth – make a mistake which other people often make

(have) sth in mind – have a particular plan or intention

take away from sth – detract from something (make something less good than it should be)

stumble upon sth (C2) – discover something by chance

balance sth out – create a state where things are (more) equal

garbage – (US English) rubbish; something that you think is wrong, or very bad quality

frame – (technical) everything that you can see through the camera, which will become the image

composition (C2) – the way that people or things are arranged in a painting or photograph

hone (your skills) – develop your skills to a high level

lens – the curved, clear glass or plastic part of the camera that affects light, focuses, zooms, etc.

cultivate sth – develop or improve an ability, public image, relationship, etc.

an opportunity presents itself – get a chance to do something

Answers

1 Suggested answer: it takes away the element of luck and enjoyment from street photography
2 The most important thing is content, and its relevance to the human condition.
3 Suggested answer: photos which don't have real meaning/ emotion, such as advertising or paparazzi photography
4 Suggested answer: humour, observation, curiosity
5 keeping the ability to view things as an outsider

⚲ FAST FINISHERS

Ask fast finishers to remember something interesting they saw on the street recently which would have made a great photo. Tell them to sketch it and then show and describe it to another fast finisher.

f Ask students if they agree that you don't need an expensive camera to take good photos. Put students into groups to discuss the questions. Take feedback as a class.

↻ LOA TIP MONITORING

- Monitoring is more efficient if you set up the room properly.
- When the students are reading the text in 1d/e, they can sit in a traditional row formation. However, when they are discussing in groups in 1f, rearrange chairs in a circle so that students in the same group are facing one another. It is then easier for all students to contribute and they are focused on one another rather than you. You can quietly monitor, collecting errors, etc., and move around the class in the space between groups.
- If arranging the seats in a circle isn't possible in your classroom, consider asking students to stand up and talk in their groups. This arrangement is even easier to monitor as you are now the same height as everyone and stand out less.

2 VOCABULARY
Adjectives: Describing images

a Ask students if *iconic* means something positive or negative (positive). Elicit that the photo on SB p.68 is described as *iconic* in the article. Ask in what way it could be *iconic* and try to elicit the meaning of the word (see Answers below). Students work out the meanings of the other highlighted words, using a dictionary if necessary. Highlight the difference between *iconic* and *ironic*.

Answers

ironic (C2): interesting, strange or funny because of being very different from what you would usually expect
iconic: very famous or popular, especially being considered to represent particular opinions or a particular time
well-composed: where the people or things have been arranged well, to look good in a painting or photograph
powerful (B2): having a very great effect
meaningful (B2): intended to show (serious/important) meaning
gritty: showing all the unpleasant but true details of a situation
raw: art, writing, etc. that is raw shows something unpleasant / very strong emotions in a realistic way, and does not try to hide anything about the subject
playful: funny and not serious
humorous (C1): funny, or making you laugh
evocative: making you remember or imagine something pleasant
exotic (B2): unusual and exciting because of coming (or seeming to come) from far away, especially a tropical country
observant (C2): good or quick at noticing things
nonsensical: silly or stupid

b ▶ **3.2–3.3** Students complete the exercises in Vocabulary Focus 6A on SB p.163. Play the recording for students to listen and check their answers to Exercise a and c. Monitor and check answers to Exercise b, d and e, and refer students to the Tip on collocations. Tell students to do the Communication Plus activity on SB p.132. Students work in pairs and talk about the photos using collocations made from the adverbs and adjectives in the boxes and their own ideas. They then agree on which photo should win the competition and justify their choice. Take feedback as a class. Tell students to go back to SB p.70.

Answers (Vocabulary Focus 6A SB p.163)

a 1 powerful 2 nonsensical 3 playful 4 gritty
5 well-composed 6 meaningful 7 humorous 8 exotic
9 evocative 10 raw 11 iconic 12 ironic
b 1 power*ful* 2 nonsens*ical* 3 play*ful* 4 grit*ty*
5 well-compos*ed* 6 meaning*ful* 7 humor*ous* 8 exot*ic*
9 evoca*tive* 10 raw – no suffix 11 icon*ic* 12 iron*ic*
Students' own answers
c 1 b 2 c 3 a 4 f 5 d 6 e
d 1 truly powerful 2 completely nonsensical
3 extremely playful 5 very well-composed
7 gently humorous 8 wonderfully exotic
9 very evocative 11 truly iconic 12 rather ironic
e a cluttered: incredibly, pretty, a little, extremely, rather
b sensational: pretty, utterly, truly
c bleak: incredibly, pretty, a little, extremely, rather
d repetitive: incredibly, pretty, a little, extremely, rather
e flawless: utterly, truly
f elaborate: all

3 LISTENING

a 💬 Ask students about hobbies they have or used to have. Put students into groups to talk about the person they know who is passionate about their hobby. Take feedback as a class.

b ▶ **3.4** Ask students what they think of the photo of Monika and the photo that Monika has taken. Play the recording and ask students if they think she is passionate about photography and why. If necessary, pre-teach *jargon* (C1) (specialist words and phrases associated with a particular activity). You may also wish to review this vocabulary from SB p.69: *composition, frame, lens* and tell students Monika will use the following technical words: *auto-mode* (an option on a device to have certain functions controlled automatically); *panning effects* (effects of carefully moving the camera while shooting); *settings* (the position(s) on the controls on a device).

Suggested answers

Yes, she is. She sounds very enthusiastic and wants to learn, and practise, as much as possible.

Audioscript

INTERVIEWER So Monika, I understand you're an amateur photographer?
MONIKA Well, I wouldn't go that far, um …, I'm definitely amateur but I'm not a photographer yet, perhaps in the future.
I But you've been studying photography?
M Um … yes that's correct. I've been doing this course about photography and it's for complete beginners.
I Why did you decide to do the course?
M Um … I think I could blame my husband for it! Um, because he got um … he got me this fantastic DSLR um … camera and er, it is a, quite a complicated um … object really. If you don't know how to use it, it can be really complicated to take some photos. So I was wondering what I could do to … to improve, and to know how to use it. And I was um … I started with those um … kind of tutorials on YouTube that you can watch, um … but it wasn't, it wasn't good enough because they were using quite a lot of jargon and I wasn't really sure what they were referring to. Um … so I decided to do a course, to learn a little bit more about it so that I can use the tutorials in my own time.
I Have they taught you anything useful?
M The tutorials um … not really, but then when I went to the course, and I started my course, I've been doing this course now for a few weeks um … and I'm learning all the time something new so it's really, really good.
I So, do you feel more confident with your camera now?
M Um, a little bit, um, it depends on the types of photo that I want to take. Um … let's say that it's more kind of um … documentary-type photos then I would still use my auto-mode, um, but I would still be quite um … perhaps … I would be thinking more about the frame and, and the composition of the photo because these are the things that I would normally learn during the course. So um, our tutor would be giving us some specific tasks on for example composition or … panning effects or different techniques and, so after that I would go outside the classroom – I would go and for example take some photos and focus on either one technique and then practise it, um, or I would just take as many shots as I can, 'cause sometimes it's … um, improvisation is also very good.
I Have you discovered any bad habits since you started your course?
M Um … I think I was taking too many photos. And … potentially I was taking photos of everything and I wasn't really following any rules. But now I know that I have to be more careful with my um settings of the camera and what exactly I want to take a photo of. Um … so when I'm taking my photos now, I'm more cautious and kind of careful how I do it and what I really want to um … take photos of.
I What's your favourite photograph that you've taken?
M I think I've got um, two pictures that are my favourite pictures. Um … the first one is … it's, it's a static photo of a building um … so when I was um … doing my course, there was this project. We were meant to take photos of an object, or of a static object. So I chose this building that is meant to be demolished. Actually, it is being demolished now. So, every single day you could kind of take a different photo of a different part of the building. So one day I was standing there and I was really lucky because they were actually taking a part of the window down, and there was this massive hole in the building. So I was able to take a few interesting photos of the whole process as well as the, just, just the hole in the building, but there was this chair just in front of the hole and it made the whole picture quite realistic like there was still life in it, but actually the building is being demolished, so that's one of my favourites. And then the second one was a completely different project when I was trying to take photos of moving objects and er, my subject was um … a three-year-old girl, and she was playing in a garden, and she had this yoga mat that her mum was using, and she was just rolling into this er … yoga mat and um, luckily for me, um, I was able to take a few interesting photos of her playing in the garden.

c ▶**3.4** See if students can answer the questions before you play the recording again for them to check. Check answers as a class.

Answers
1 Her husband gave her a fantastic but complicated camera; the tutorials on YouTube showing how to use the camera weren't good enough.
2 She's more selective about the photos she takes and thinks about the techniques she needs to use.
3 Although the building was being demolished, the chair gives the impression that life was still going on in it.
4 It's a photo of a three-year-old girl rolling herself up in a yoga mat in the garden.

d 💬 Ask students if they think Monika would follow Elliot's advice and be spontaneous when taking pictures (yes, she talks about *improvisation*). Put students into groups to discuss what else Monika might agree with. Take feedback as a class.

4 GRAMMAR
Simple and continuous verbs

a ▶**3.5** Ask students to work individually to decide whether Monika used a simple or continuous verb form in each example, 1–8. Students then compare answers in pairs. Play the recording for students to listen and check.

Answers
1 do you feel
2 depends
3 discovered
4 started
5 was taking
6 'm taking
7 think
8 is being demolished

b Dictate sentences 1 and 2 and ask students how *hear* is used differently in each sentence:

1 *I've heard that Simon has started a photography course.*
2 *I've been hearing good things from Simon about his photography course.*

Elicit that sentence 1 is about one piece of news and sentence 2 is about regular feedback. Ask students to tell you more differences between the simple and continuous. Then tell students to match the verb forms in the sentences in 4a with one or more of the descriptions.

Answers
2 simple for a verb not usually used in the continuous
3, 4 simple for a completed action
1, 2, 7 simple for general truth or attitude
5 continuous to describe a repeated action
6 continuous to focus on the duration of an action
8 continuous for an action in progress at a particular time
7 a verb with different meanings in the simple and continuous

c Ask students to decide if the alternative verb forms are possible and if the meaning would change.

Answers
1 Both possible: the present continuous makes the question more focused on a change in how she feels
5 Both possible: the present continuous stresses repetition
6 Both possible: the present continuous stresses the duration of the process of taking a photo

d ▶**3.5** **Pronunciation** Ask students to look back at the two sentences about Simon you dictated in 4b and underline the stressed syllables:

1 *I've <u>heard</u> that <u>Si</u>mon has <u>star</u>ted a pho<u>tog</u>raphy <u>course</u>.*
2 *I've been <u>hear</u>ing <u>good</u> <u>things</u> from <u>Si</u>mon about his pho<u>tog</u>raphy <u>course</u>.*

Then tell students to look at the sentences that Monika said in 4a again. Ask them to listen and underline the stressed syllables in the sentences. Play the recording and check answers. Drill the sentences.

Answers
So, do you <u>feel</u> more <u>con</u>fident with your <u>ca</u>mera <u>now</u>?
It de<u>pends</u> on the <u>types</u> of <u>pho</u>to that I <u>want</u> to <u>take</u>.
Have you dis<u>cov</u>ered any <u>bad</u> <u>hab</u>its since you <u>star</u>ted your <u>course</u>?
I was <u>tak</u>ing <u>pho</u>tos of <u>eve</u>rything and I <u>wasn't</u> <u>real</u>ly <u>fol</u>lowing any <u>rules</u>.
When I'm <u>tak</u>ing my <u>pho</u>tos <u>now</u> I'm more <u>cau</u>tious and <u>care</u>ful of <u>how</u> I <u>do</u> it.
I <u>think</u> I've <u>got</u> <u>two</u> <u>pic</u>tures that are my <u>fa</u>vourite <u>pic</u>tures.
I <u>chose</u> this <u>build</u>ing that is <u>meant</u> to be de<u>mol</u>ished. <u>Act</u>ually it <u>is</u> being de<u>mol</u>ished <u>now</u>.

e ▶ ▶**3.6–3.7** Students read the information in Grammar Focus 6A on SB p.148. Play the recording where indicated and ask students to listen and repeat. Students then complete the exercises. Check answers as a class. Tell students to go back to SB p.70.

Answers (Grammar Focus 6A SB p.148)
a 1 b left   a right   2 a left   b right   3 b left   a right
   4 a left   b right
b 2 be learning   3 Are you being   4 left   5 's thinking
   6 Do you realise   7 been gossiping   8 is increasing
   9 opened   10 suppose
c 2 had   3 been complaining   4 see   5 decided
   6 belongs   7 been watching   8 changed   9 wanted
   10 are you saying

> 👁 **CAREFUL!**
>
> A typical mistake is for students to overuse the continuous tense for verbs showing increase and decrease: ~~The second half of December started with a score of 97%, which was increasing to 100% by the end of January.~~ (Correct form = *The second half of December started with a score of 97%, which* **increased** *to 100% by the end of January.*). Another common mistake is to use *do* in the continuous to talk about routine things: ~~First of all, I should tell you how I'm doing that.~~ (Correct form = *First of all, I should tell you how I* **do** *that.*).

f Say to students: *I've waited for you for an hour* and ask if the grammar is correct (yes). Ask students to put the sentence into the continuous, *I've been waiting for you for an hour,* and ask if it is an improvement (yes, it emphasises impatience). Ask students to improve each sentence by putting one verb into the continuous and say how it changes the meaning. Check answers as a class.

Answers
1 asks – is (always) asking (annoying habit)
2 have played – have been playing (emphasises duration)
3 use – be using (emphasises the activity)
4 'm not – 'm not being (shows that the speaker is usually careful)
5 've looked – 've been looking (emphasises duration)

g 💬 Tell students to change the sentences to make them true for them and then compare their ideas with a partner.

5 SPEAKING

a Ask students if they find selfies embarrassing or good fun. See if any students have got good or terrible examples on their mobile devices, if they have them. Put students into groups to discuss the questions. Take feedback as a class.

b Elicit from students other kinds of visual art, e.g. posters, graffiti, and tell them to compare them with the ones listed. Ask students to decide which visual art interests them most, and why.

c Put students into pairs to discuss the visual art that interests them most, using the prompts to help them. Take feedback as a class.

d Ask the class to share ideas about the visual arts they like. Is there one kind that is more popular than the others?

ADDITIONAL MATERIAL

▶ Workbook 6A

▶ Photocopiable activities: Grammar p.211, Vocabulary p.231, Pronunciation p.262

6B Waiting for the drama to begin

At the end of this lesson, students will be able to:

- use a range of adjectives and collocations to describe emotions
- use main stress on adverbs for emphasis
- read a story in several parts and understand the descriptive language in context
- use participle clauses in noun phrases and as adverbial
- speculate about a story, discuss an alternative ending and write a continuation

OPTIONAL LEAD-IN

Books closed. Write some emoticons on the board or show them on a mobile device if you have the technology to do so. Tell students to interpret them, e.g. 😃 (happiness), 😋 (playfulness), 😨 (fear), 😕 (uncertainty). Ask students why people use emoticons rather than just say how they are feeling.

1 VOCABULARY Emotions

a Concept check the meaning of some of the adjectives, e.g. *when you are disappointed with something and stop believing in it* (disillusioned). *The opposite of 'calm'* (over-excited). Put students into pairs to discuss which adjectives apply to which age group. Check answers as a class and ask students to justify their answers.

b ▶3.8 Tell students to match the adjective in the first sentence with the correct continuation in the second sentence. Play the recording for students to listen and check.

Answers

1 d 2 b 3 g 4 f 5 e 6 a 7 c 8 h

LANGUAGE NOTES

You could point out the difference in meaning between these words at C1 and at C2:

insecure (C1): no confidence; (C2): not safe

restless (C1): unable to relax; (C2): wanting something new.

c Tell students to make new sentences for the emotions in 1a. Put students into pairs. Ask them to take turns to read their sentences for their partner to guess the feeling.

d ▶3.9 **Pronunciation** Ask students to listen and say how the stress is different in the a and b sentences and which show stronger feelings. Check answers and drill the sentences.

Answers

1 a I'm absolutely <u>devastated</u>.   b I'm <u>absolutely</u> devastated.
2 a I felt extremely <u>jealous</u>.   b I felt <u>extremely</u> jealous.
3 a I feel so <u>ashamed</u>.   b I feel <u>so</u> ashamed.
a sentences: the main stress is on the adjective
b sentences: the main stress is on the adverb
The b sentences show stronger feelings.

- Using gestures to model stress or intonation patterns during drilling is particularly effective for kinaesthetic learners. Repeat *I'm absolutely <u>devastated</u>.* and then use a gesture, such as punching the air in front of you, on the main stress. Encourage students to copy you, first just the movements and then the movements and the pronunciation. Repeat the procedure with the alternate stress pattern (*I'm <u>absolutely</u> devastated.*). You can also use sweeping gestures upward for rising intonation, and downwards for falling.

e 💬 Put students into pairs to take turns reading out their sentences to show strong feelings. Students then ask questions to continue the conversation with their partner.

ⓦ EXTRA ACTIVITY

Put students into groups. Tell them to use adverbs and adjectives, using stress appropriately, to say how they would feel in these situations: in the dentist's chair, in a chauffeur-driven Rolls-Royce, about to take a penalty at the World Cup, diving 50m under the sea, stuck in a lift.

2 READING

a 💬 Ask students to name situations where their hearts would beat quickly, e.g. running for a train. Ask students to describe the photograph and say how the words are connected with the picture. Check answers.

Suggested answers

large museum installation of a human heart, which people can walk through, with adults and children exploring it
1 The blood vessels take the blood to and from the heart.
2 Beat is the sound or the action of a heart.
3 The heart is divided into four chambers.
4 The heart pumps blood around the body.

b Ask students to read the first part of the short story and answer the questions. Check answers as a class.

Answers

1 the heart exhibit, being popular, the children, the blood vessels
2 the ceiling, one corner of the exhibition hall, the entrance to the heart being roped off, the worn and dusty floor of the blood vessels, the marks on the chamber walls, the notice

c Students read the first part of the story again. Ask students the questions and check the answers.

Suggested answers

1 She: doesn't live locally; only has an hour before her train; is interested in biology and natural history; is observant.
2 It must be late afternoon because the exhibit is looking dirty from use by visitors.
3 The narrator plans to visit another exhibition, and if there is time, return to the heart.

d Ask students what they think will happen in the Hall of North America. Give students time to read the next part of the story and then tell them to discuss the questions. Take feedback as a class.

Suggested answers

1 a The attendant is experienced with snakes and feels safe around them. He is protective of them.
   b Miss Aitcheson is scared of the snake and snakes in general. As a city woman she probably thinks they should be killed and she should be protected from them.
   c One or two of the children are afraid of the snake but most are curious, they are probably afraid of snakes in general as they aren't accustomed to them.
2 a She's unmarried, nearing retirement age, and a city woman. She's fearful and timid but determined.
   b Their opinion of her is important to her.
   c He's brisk, forceful, encouraging, persistent and insensitive.
   d She's polite, thoughtful, sympathetic and observant.

📖 VOCABULARY SUPPORT

get them (children) *young* – introduce children to an idea or activity while they are young enough to be easily influenced

get through to sb (C1) – succeed in making someone understand or believe something

born and bred – used to say that someone has the typical character of the people from a particular place, because they grew up there

e Language in context *Descriptive language*

See if students can remember the original words and then tell them to check in the text. Ask students to discuss how the original words used in the text add to the meaning. Then tell students to read the Learning Tip and use dictionaries to check how the descriptive language is effective. Students find three more examples of descriptive language in the text, find out their common synonyms and say why they are effective.

Suggested answers

1 1 *drag* means move something heavy by pulling it along with difficulty, implying that the fear in her eyes is difficult to hide.
   2 *lurk* means that something unpleasant is waiting, perhaps threateningly, so it implies that her fear is alive, unpleasant and a threat.
   3 *hushed* implies that somebody has told the children to be quiet / the intense situation has caused this.
   4 *drape* tells us about the way somebody hangs something; the museum attendant puts the snake around her neck like a piece of clothing, like a salesperson in a clothes shop.
   5 *stand still* could be quite relaxed, whereas *stand rigid* gives the impression of every muscle being tense.
2 *gaze* (v. = look) adds the idea that the children are fascinated
   brisk (adj. = efficient) tells us that the attendant's manner is business-like rather than friendly or caring
   blink (v. = flash, in this context), used metaphorically to make the light seem like an eye, watching her because it knows she wants to leave
   hooded (adj. = covered), used metaphorically to make the light seem like an eye with large eyelids – hooded eyes are hidden, secretive – she cannot leave, so the exit is not open to her
   swift (adj. = quick, fast), adds the idea that the movement is smooth and efficient as well as fast
   persist (v. = ask), adds the idea that the attendant is continuing with an unwanted behaviour
   jerk (v. = move, pull away), tells us that the action is very sudden and slightly uncontrolled
   whisper (v. = say quietly) tells us that she spoke using the breath and not the voice, because she was so scared

3 LISTENING and SPEAKING

a ▶ **3.10** Ask students to predict the end of the story. Before you play the recording, remind students that they do not need to understand every word. Encourage them to listen past any words they do not understand the first time they listen. Play the recording for students to listen and check (Miss Aitcheson will panic.).

Audioscript

I could see her defeat and helplessness. The attendant seemed unaware, [1]as if his perception had grown a reptilian covering. What did she care for the campaign for the preservation and welfare of copperheads and rattlers and common grass snakes? What did she care about someday walking through the woods or the desert and deciding between killing a snake or setting it free, as if there would be time to decide, when her journey to and from school in Philadelphia held enough danger to occupy her? In two years or so, she'd retire and be in that apartment by herself with no doorman, and everyone knew what happened then, and how she'd be afraid to answer the door and to walk after dark and carry her pocketbook in the street. There was enough to think about without learning to handle and love the snakes, harmless and otherwise, by having them draped around her neck for everyone, including the children – most of all the children – [2]to witness the outbreak of her fear.

'See, Miss Aitcheson's touching the snake. She's not afraid of it at all.' As everyone watched, she touched the snake. Her fingers recoiled. She touched it again.

'See, she's not afraid. Miss Aitcheson can stand there with a beautiful snake around her neck and touch it and stroke it and not be afraid.' The faces of the children were full of admiration for the teacher's bravery, and yet there was [3]a cruelly persistent tension; they were waiting, waiting.

'We have to learn to love snakes,' the attendant said. 'Would someone like to come out and stroke teacher's snake?'

Silence.

One shamefaced boy came forward. He stood petrified in front of the teacher.

'Touch it,' the attendant urged. 'It's a friendly snake. Teacher's wearing it around her neck and she's not afraid.'

The boy darted his hand forward, rested it lightly on the snake, and immediately withdrew his hand. Then he ran back to his seat. The children shrieked with glee.

'He's afraid.' someone said. 'He's afraid of the snake.'

The attendant soothed. 'We have to get used to them, you know. Grownups are not afraid of them, but we can understand that when you're small you might be afraid, and that's why we want you to learn to love them. Isn't that right, Miss Aitcheson? Isn't that right? Now who else is going to be brave enough to touch teacher's snake?'

Two girls came out. They stood hand in hand side by side and stared at the snake and then at Miss Aitcheson.

I wondered when the torture would end. The two little girls did not touch the snake, but they smiled at it and spoke to it and Miss Aitcheson smiled and whispered how brave they were.

'Just a minute,' the attendant said. 'There's really no need to be brave. It's not a question of bravery. The snake is harmless, absolutely harmless. Where's the bravery when the snake is harmless?'

Suddenly the snake moved round to face Miss Aitcheson and thrust its flat head towards her cheek. She gave a scream, flung up her hands, and tore the snake from her throat and threw it on the floor, and, rushing across the room, she collapsed into a small canvas chair beside the Bear Cabinet and started to cry.

I didn't feel I should watch any longer. Some of the children began to laugh, some to cry. The attendant picked up the snake and nursed it. Miss Aitcheson, recovering, sat [4]helplessly exposed by the small piece of useless torture. It was not her fault that she was city-bred, her eyes tried to tell us. She looked at the children, trying in some way to force their admiration and respect; [5]they were shut against her.

She was evicted from them and from herself and even from her own fear-infested tomorrow, because she could not promise to love and preserve what she feared. She had nowhere, at that moment, but the small canvas chair by the Bear Cabinet of the Natural Science Museum.

I looked at my watch. If I hurried, I would catch the train from Thirtieth Street. There would be no time to make the journey through the human heart. I hurried out of the museum. It was freezing cold. The icebreakers would be at work on the Delaware and the Susquehanna; the mist would have risen by the time I arrived home. Yes, I would just catch the train from Thirtieth Street. The journey through the human heart would have to wait until some other time.

Support on meaning

1 The attendant was so insensitive to Miss Aitcheson's fear he was more like a reptile than a human.
2 to see her fail to control her fear
3 a continuing atmosphere which is cruel because everyone is waiting for Miss Aitcheson to publicly fail
4 unable to change the fact that the children have seen what she was trying to hide, because of this relatively unimportant and cruel act
5 the children have rejected Miss Aitcheson, her own self-image has been damaged and she feels absolutely hopeless, as if there is no future

b ▶ **3.10** Tell students to work individually to answer the questions. They then compare answers in pairs. Ask students to note any words they don't understand which relate to each question in 3b whilst they are checking their answers. Play the recording for students to listen again and check. Check answers and take feedback as a class. Ask students to check the unfamiliar vocabulary they noted against the script and then in a dictionary.

Answers

1 being attacked on her journey to work, being alone in old age, being attacked in her home
2 They admire her.
3 Because the snake is absolutely harmless.
4 The snake's suddenly moving its head towards her cheek.
5 Some of them laugh, some of them cry.
6 She finds Miss Aitcheson's public humiliation too painful to watch.
7 a Miss Aitcheson – because she's lost the children's respect
  b the narrator – because she understands Miss Aitcheson
  c the children – because they don't know how to react
  d the attendant – because he seems to be completely unaware of, and even takes pleasure in, Miss Aitcheson's fear

---

💡 EXTRA ACTIVITY

Write sentences 1–5 from the story on the board. Ask students to work out a simpler synonymic paraphrase for each underlined part. Check answers as a class, using the key below, and ask students what the infinitives of the irregular verbs are.

1 *Her fingers recoiled (from the snake).* (move back/away from something because of disgust)

2 *The boy darted his hand forward.* (move suddenly and quickly)

3 *The children shrieked with glee.* (scream loudly and excitedly)

4 *The snake … thrust its flat head towards her cheek.* (push something towards somebody suddenly, infinitive: *thrust*)

5 *She gave a scream, flung up her hands, and tore the snake from her throat.* (raise suddenly, hard, infinitive: *fling*; pull off, using force, infinitive: *tear*)

Now ask students to compare the correct paraphrase with a dictionary definition of the verb. What are the differences? (The paraphrases above are likely to be more precise for this context.) Explain that dictionaries cannot cover every possible use of a word.

c 🗨 Ask students if they feel sorry for Miss Aitcheson. Put students into groups to discuss the questions. Check answers and take feedback as a class.

Suggested answers

1 Our secret fears and our need for pride and respect, as these are what drive Miss Aitcheson and lead to her humiliation.
2 The narrator feels she has already journeyed through the full range of human emotions: protectiveness, need, fear, respect, pride, glee, cruelty, etc., i.e. a journey through the metaphoric human heart. So the last line is ironic – there is no need to journey through the model of the human heart in the exhibition.

💡 **HOMEWORK ACTIVITY**

▶ Tell students to find an authentic short story in English and note down 8–10 new descriptive words. Tell them to use a dictionary to find synonyms for the descriptive words, example sentences and notes about their usage. In the next class, put students into groups to tell one another about their story and present the new words.

---

4 GRAMMAR Participle clauses

a Write this opening of a novel on the board: *The strangers, having no alternative, fell into each other's arms.* Ask students if they would like to read the rest of the novel based on this opening. Ask students how many verbs there are (two), which one is a participle (*having*) and how the participle clause could be rephrased (because they had no alternative). Ask students if they think the participle clause is more effective (yes, it is more concise). Ask students to compare the participle clauses from the story with alternative clauses and say if there is a difference in meaning and form. Check answers and explain to students that participle clauses are more common in writing than in speaking.

Answers
Yes, the meaning is exactly the same.
The participle clauses don't have subjects or auxiliary verbs and the verb in these examples is verb + *-ing* (present participle).

b Tell students to read the example, and say which clause would give the same meaning and what the form is.

Answers
1 with the *-ing* form of *touch*
2 with the *-ing* form of *have* + past participle

c Tell students to complete the sentences. Check and ask students what kind of fiction these sentences come from and what could be happening in the stories.

Answers
1 approaching the house   2 crying her eyes out
3 Wanting to reassure him   4 Having finished her breakfast
Students' own answers

d Tell students participle clauses have different functions and ask students to match the clauses with the functions.

Answers
a 4   b 1,3   c 2,3

e Say *Breathing in the sea breeze* and ask students which extract in 4c this would complete (extract 4 is probably the best fit, but 2 and 3 are also possible). Tell students to think of other clauses to complete the extracts and to read them out for other students to name the extract.

f ▶ Students read the information in Grammar Focus 6B on SB p.149. Students then complete the exercises. Check answers as a class, providing explanations for Exercise a if students are finding the exercise challenging. After Exercise c, students could continue the story, using participle clauses. Tell students to go back to SB p.73.

Answers (Grammar Focus 6B SB p.149)

a 2 ✓
  3 I will find the person <u>who</u> committed this crime. (not a continuous or a passive verb so no participle clause)
  4 ✓
  5 Having caused the accident, he offered to pay for the damage. (the accident happened before he offered to pay for the damage, because he caused it, he offered to pay)
  6 As I <u>read</u> the letter, my hands were shaking in excitement. (the subject of the clause is *I*, so no participle clause is possible)
  7 ✓
  8 Paddy is the kind of man <u>who never arrives</u> anywhere on time. (not a continuous or a passive verb so no participle clause)

b 2 coming outside, 3 wearing orange, 4 being realistic, 5 being overworked and underpaid, 6 getting stressed out, 7 waiting to strike

c A cake ~~which was~~ covered in chocolate was quickly brought over to my table. ~~I noticed~~ Noticing something ~~which was~~ sticking out from under the cake ~~so~~ I lifted it up. I found underneath a note ~~which was~~ written in red <u>saying</u>, 'Get into the car ~~which is~~ <u>waiting</u> across the road'. ~~I was frightened by the tone and I feared the worst so~~ Frightened by the tone and fearing the worst, I did what the note said. A thousand negative thoughts were crowding my head when I got to the car. The familiar figure ~~who was~~ dressed in orange was in the front seat, with a sinister smile on his face. 'We meet at last,' he said.

g Read out the story and ask students if it is interesting writing (no). Tell students to rewrite it with three or more participle clauses and to compare their stories with one another. Take feedback as a class.

5 SPEAKING and WRITING

a 🗨 Put students into pairs to discuss an alternative way the story about the snake could continue from the end of the Reading text.

b Give pairs a time limit to write one or two paragraphs, using descriptive language and participle clauses.

c Set the same time limit for pairs to swap stories, read them, correct any mistakes and add one or two more paragraphs.

d Swap stories with a different pair. Again, give students time to read the stories, correct any errors and finish them.

e 🗨 Ask each pair to give back their story to the pair that started it. Tell students to correct any mistakes in the endings and then read out their stories to the class for students to vote on.

ADDITIONAL MATERIAL

▶ Workbook 6B

▶ Photocopiable activities: Grammar p.212, Vocabulary p.232, Pronunciation p.263

At the end of this lesson, students will be able to:

- organise and give a presentation using a range of functional language
- use a range of idioms to make points in discussions
- use tone in comment phrases according to their position in the sentence

💡 OPTIONAL LEAD-IN

Books closed. Ask students to think of a novel which they would like to read a sequel to and say what would happen in the sequel. Give an example: *Animal Farm 2* by George Orwell, where the animals throw out the corrupt pigs and create a happier, more balanced society.

1 LISTENING

a 💬 Ask students if they have ever seen or met anyone famous in real life. Put students into groups to discuss the questions. Take feedback as a class.

b ▶ **3.11** Tell students to look at the picture of Sara giving her presentation. Ask what kind of information they expect Sara to present about Max. Tell students to guess what the numbers relate to. Play Part 1 of the video or the audio recording for them to find out how the numbers are relevant. Use the Vocabulary support box to help with vocabulary if necessary. Check answers as a class.

Answers

half a million: sales of nearly half a million copies of Max's novel
8: number of languages his novel has been translated into
300,000: Max's Twitter followers

Videoscript/Audioscript (Part 1)

SARA Er, Nadia?

NADIA Yes?

S I've got some great news! I met up with Max Redwood the other day, and he says he's going to consider doing another interview with us!

N What?

S Max Redwood? He says he'll think about doing another interview with us.

N Oh, I don't know about that, Sara. You know, after last time.

S I know, but he's really hot stuff at the moment!

N That's true, but would he actually have something to say?

S Well, if I do the proper preparation …

N To be honest, it won't even be my decision, Sara. I'd need to get Paul to sign off on this.

S Paul?

N It would need someone more senior than me to give the go-ahead for this. There's a lot of risk involved. It was a disaster last time. We need some really compelling reasons to go down this route again.

S I see. Well, I could come up with those! Look, I really think this is worth a shot.

N Well look, why don't I invite Paul to our next team meeting and we can raise it then?

S OK, great!

…

N OK, the next item on the agenda is the author interview series. And, as I mentioned earlier, I've invited Paul today to get his take on it. OK, so over to you, Sara.

S Thank you.

P That's not a picture of Max Redwood, is it?

S Yes, that's right – an up-and-coming author, but not a forthcoming one, as poor Oscar discovered!

O You can say that again!

N Oscar!

S … And there were many questions left unanswered. Now, as luck would have it, I bumped into Max the other day and I've got him to consider doing another interview. My focus today is on this second interview. Let me talk you through why our listeners want to hear more from Max Redwood. Well, first and foremost – he wrote his book from a bench on the Palace Pier right here in Brighton. However,

he's not just a local celebrity – he's becoming famous on a national level. Let me take you through some facts and figures.

O This is a bit over the top, is it not, Sara?!

S I think these facts speak for themselves: sales of nearly half a million; rumours of a huge advance offered for a second novel; translations into eight languages; 300,000 Twitter followers … I don't want to labour the point, but one thing is clear – Max Redwood is on the road to becoming an international best-selling author.

Turning now to the focus of the interview itself, I've decided to talk about the creative process behind his work.

More specifically, I propose to find out how science fiction writers like Redwood can imagine in such detail places and events that they can't possibly have experienced in real life.

So to recap on what I've been saying, I'm proposing to re-interview Max Redwood, due to his imminent stardom, and focus on what inspired him to write *Solar Wind*. Now, if you'd like me to elaborate on anything I've just said, go right ahead.

O What will you do if Max won't reveal any interesting information?

S Well, I'll just have to cross that bridge when I come to it. But, I'm planning to work quite closely with him in the run-up to the interview, so there shouldn't be any nasty surprises on the day.

P That's absolutely the way to go. And you've clearly put a lot of effort into this, Sara. Thank you. But I'm going to have to give it some thought.

S OK.

P Nadia, can we touch base again on this later?

N Sure. That's fine. OK, moving on to the next item …

📖 VOCABULARY SUPPORT

be hot stuff – be very popular

sign off on sth – approve something officially

over the top (C2) – too extreme

touch base on sth – talk to someone for a short time to find out what they think about something

c ▶ **3.11** Ask students what Sara says that isn't true (she didn't just bump into Max, their meeting was arranged). Tell students to answer the questions. Then play Part 1 of the video or the audio recording again for them to listen and check. Ask students how important social networking is for promoting the work and image of famous people.

Answers

1 b
2 c
3 b
4 c

💡 FAST FINISHERS

Ask fast finishers to write two tweets from Max's Twitter feed an hour after his meeting with Sara.

d **Language in context** *Idioms 1*

1 Ask students what the idioms mean, referring them to the audioscript on SB p.183 if necessary.

2 💬 Ask students to personalise the idioms from their own experience. Give an example yourself: *I've sent my entry off for a crossword competition. I think I've got all the answers right so it's worth a shot.*

Answers
1 a having potential rewards that make something worth trying, even if it's not likely to succeed
    b an expression that means you will not worry about a possible future problem but will deal with it if it happens

2 USEFUL LANGUAGE
Organising a presentation

a ▶3.12 Ask students what kind of opening to a presentation is effective. Tell students to complete Sara's opening. Play the recording for students to listen and check. Then check answers as a class. Ask students to paraphrase *an up-and-coming author* and *not a forthcoming one* and explain the wordplay (*up-and-coming* and *forthcoming – forth* and *up* both have movement meanings and the expressions sound similar which gives the phrase Sara uses an interesting rhythm; despite the similar form, the expressions have very different meanings, which Sara has used together cleverly to describe Max.). Students then discuss whether Sara's opening is successful. Check ideas as a class.

Answers / Suggested answers
up-and-coming; forthcoming
an up-and-coming author is likely to achieve success soon or in the near future
not a forthcoming one is an author who isn't very willing to give information or talk (*forthcoming* = friendly and helpful, willing to give information and talk)
It is successful because the wordplay is amusing and puts everyone at their ease. The reference to the previous interview (and the photo of Max) gets everyone's attention, particularly Oscar's.

b ▶3.13 Tell students to complete the expressions. Play the recording for students to check their answers. Drill the expressions and then the full sentences.

Answers
1 on
2 through
3 First
4 thing
5 to
6 More
7 on
8 elaborate

c Put students into pairs to answer the questions. Check answers. For 3, write all the suggestions on the board.

Answers / Suggested answers
1 *talk* in *Let me talk you through* can be replaced with *take*
   Turning in *Turning now to* can be replaced with *Moving on*
2 to introduce a presentation: My focus today is on; Let me talk you through
   to highlight ideas: One thing is clear; More specifically
   to sequence ideas: First and foremost; Turning now to
   at the end of a presentation: So to recap on; If you'd like me to elaborate
3 Students' own answers

🔅 **EXTRA ACTIVITY**

If you have the video, ask students to watch the scene showing the team meeting and Sara's presentation again. Tell them to evaluate Sara's body language, e.g. how she stands, gestures, eye contact with the audience. If you don't have the video, or after watching the video, put students into groups of four. Ask them to look at the audioscript on SB p.183 and act out the team meeting, taking turns to play Sara's role. Tell the other students to evaluate 'Sara's' body language each time.

3 LISTENING

a ▶3.14 Ask students how Alex is connected to Max (his girlfriend Emma is Max's sister). Play Part 2 of the video or the audio recording for students to answer the question. If necessary, pre-teach *be on to sth* (know or discover something useful or important). Check that students know that a *prequel* is set before the original book.

Answer
for Max to write a prequel to *Solar Wind*

Videoscript/Audioscript (Part 2)

ALEX Atishoo! Sorry …
SARA Oh, you're back!
ALEX Yeah.
S How are you feeling?
A Well, not a hundred per cent to be honest, but, y'know …
S Well, anyway … I've been dying to tell you about my meeting with Max the other day!
A Of course! How was it?
S Pretty good, on the whole. But he thought I was a technician like you, and he was a bit angry when he found out I was a journalist.
A Oh sorry. I told you not to mention that you were a journalist.
S Not to worry. He didn't seem to mind too much in the end.
A Well, that's good.
S Anyway, more to the point, he's agreed to think about doing another interview!
A Great!
S Yeah, I've just been presenting some ideas on it to the team.

A Hm. Have you got any further with the famous sequel that Oscar was talking about?
S Actually, no.
A No?
S No, there can't be a sequel because his first book was the end of the story.
A Oh?
S Because at the end time …
S and A … stands still!
A Oh, I see what you mean …
S Yeah, it's a bit of a sore point with him, actually …
A Hmm. So he's reached the end of his story, but has he done the beginning?
S What?
A Well, if he can't do a sequel, he could do a prequel, y'know, what happens before the events in *Solar Wind*.
S Hmm, I wonder. You might be on to something there, Alex …

b ▶3.14 Ask students what the sentences are responses to. Then play Part 2 of the video or the audio recording again for students to check.

Answers
2 Alex apologises for the fact that Max was a bit angry when he found out Sara is a journalist.
3 Sara tells Alex that Max has agreed to think about doing another interview.
4 Alex asks Sara if she has got any further with the famous sequel Oscar was talking about.
5 Alex suggests that Max could write a prequel to *Solar Wind*.

c 💬 Ask students why people make sequels to films (giving one or two examples which will be relevant to your learners) instead of new concepts. Put students into groups to discuss the questions. Take feedback as a class.

d Language in context *Idioms 2*

Tell students to match the idioms with their meanings. Ask them to look at the audioscript on SB p.183 if necessary. Check answers.

Answers
a 2
b 3
c 1

4 PRONUNCIATION

Tone in comment phrases

a Ask students what grammatical function the phrase in bold has (adverbial). Ask students if the sentence would make sense without it.

Answer
yes

b ▶ **3.15** Play the recording and ask students to listen to the tone. If necessary, read the sentence yourself and exaggerate the intonation.

Answer
fall then rise

c ▶ **3.16** Ask students if adverbials can go at the start or end of sentences (usually both). Play the recording and ask students to tick the sentences where the comment phrase also has rising intonation. Check answers as a class.

Answers
1 b
2 b
3 a

d Tell students to complete the rule. Check answers.

Answers
fall–rise; rising

e 💬 Drill all the sentences. Then tell students to practise in pairs. Monitor and make sure students are using the appropriate intonation.

5 SPEAKING

a 💬 Ask students what the place where they are studying English needs to make it even better. Encourage them to think big! Put students into pairs to choose a reason for the grant, describe exactly what they need and make a strong case for getting it. Students then plan their presentation. They could use technology like PowerPoint™ when they come to do their presentations or just stand up and speak.

b 💬 Students practise their presentation. Encourage them to use the functional language studied in the lesson and tell them to be ready to give the presentation by themselves in the next stage.

c 💬 Put students with different proposals into pairs. They give their presentation to each other and decide whether their partner deserves the grant. Take feedback as a class.

> ### ⟳ LOA TIP REVIEW AND REFLECT
>
> - Encourage metacognition, learning about learning, by using the same task and asking students to reflect on the task type.
> - Put students into groups and tell them to make a presentation about how to give successful presentations. Tell students to cover the functional language from the unit in their presentation and use language from Sara's presentation.
> - Students plan and practise their presentation. Then ask two groups to give their presentations to each other and provide feedback on the other group's content and structure.

ADDITIONAL MATERIAL

▶ Workbook 6C
▶ Unit Progress Test
▶ Personalised online practice

6D Skills for Writing
I played an active role

At the end of this lesson, students will be able to:
- read and talk about news and activities in your area
- use a range of phrases to create a more positive impression on readers
- write a formal letter of application based on a model letter

☺ OPTIONAL LEAD-IN

Books closed. Ask students how they think the way people spend their free time in their local area has changed in the last 20 years, e.g. you can now watch films on a mobile device anywhere and at any time. Tell students to predict trends and changes in the next 20 years.

1 SPEAKING and LISTENING

a 💬 Ask students to tell you about an interesting local event they went to recently, e.g. a film festival. Tell students to rate their knowledge of the things on the list and then compare their rating with a partner.

b ▶ **3.17** Tell students to read the reviews in *Local View* and ask some comprehension questions, e.g. *Can you still see the film?* (yes); *What is the artist's name?* (Roxanne Delaney). If necessary, pre-teach *cram* (force a lot of things into a small space), *gag* (a joke or funny story) and *foreboding* (a feeling that something very bad is going to happen soon). Play the recording. Ask students to match the conversations with the reviews and note down the words which helped them. Check answers as a class.

Answers / Suggested answers
A 4   B 3   C 1   D 5   E 2
1 sang, productions (*singers, performance*)
2 gloomy colours, depressing, landscapes (*dark greens, blacks and browns, watercolours, melancholy, foreboding*)
3 relaxing, tables, order (*Café, relaxing*)
4 special effects, helicopter (*blockbuster, spectacular*)
5 worked out, equipment, trainers (*Leisure Centre, workout*)

Audioscript

1 **SPEAKER 1** Well I thought she sang wonderfully. What an amazing voice! I don't know how she does it.
SPEAKER 2 Yes, she really is great.
S1 I think it's one of the best productions I've seen here.
S2 So it should be for that price!
S1 Well, she is quite a big name.
S2 Mm.
2 **SPEAKER 3** Hmm, interesting. But, why all those gloomy colours?
SPEAKER 4 Yeah, a bit depressing, weren't they? I thought the early landscapes were the best. They were more colourful.
S3 Yeah, I liked those – they were quite lively.
3 **SPEAKER 5** Mm, nice here, isn't it.
SPEAKER 6 Yeah, it's one of my favourite places. I often come here after work. It's so relaxing.
S5 Yes, I hate those places where all the tables are crammed together, and you can't hear yourself speak.

S6 Yeah, me too. So … um, what shall we order?
4 **SPEAKER 7** Wow, amazing!
SPEAKER 8 Yeah! Great special effects … Pity it wasn't 3D though.
S7 Yeah, it was cool, that bit where he jumped out of the helicopter.
S8 Yeah, and landed safely! Don't know how he did that.
5 **S1** Ooh, I really needed that. I haven't worked out for over a week. I've just been sitting in front of the computer every day – I've been getting so unfit … Nice place …
SPEAKER 9 Yeah, they've got a good range of equipment. Good trainers, too.
S1 Have you been a member long?
S9 Yeah, let me see, next month, I will have been coming here for exactly a year, I think. So about a year, yes. I come here most afternoons. It's not so full then.
S1 Oh well, maybe I'll join.

c 💬 Ask students if cinemas are still popular where they live, given that films can now be downloaded. Put students into pairs to discuss the questions. Take feedback as a class.

d 💬 Ask students if they have ever been to something because of a good review. Put students into groups to discuss the questions. Take feedback as a class.

☺ EXTRA ACTIVITY

Ask students to make one of the reviews negative, saying how poor the place/event is or was. Give an example: *This film is massively overrated, especially considering the famous names involved and the money spent – wasted rather – on special effects. Spend your ticket money on ice cream instead.*

2 READING

a Ask students if they've ever written anything for a print or online magazine or newspaper. Tell students to read the advertisement. Elicit the requirements of the job (in touch with arts and music in the area; a strong interest in what is going on locally) and ask students to suggest any other qualities the publishers would be looking for. Find out if students think they'd be good at the job. Take feedback as a class.

b Ask students what kind of person would be ideal for the job. Tell students to read Helen's application letter and discuss in pairs how suitable she is. Take feedback as a class.

Suggested answers
She seems very suitable for the job. She has the right academic background, is doing a degree in History of Art and wrote a dissertation on art and music in the community, takes a keen interest in local arts, has written about local artists and includes a sample article of her work. She isn't unsuitable in any way.

☺ EXTRA ACTIVITY

Ask students to write a short (imaginary) review of one of these events for *Local View*:
- a poetry evening with translations of a new Iraqi poet
- a concert of traditional Turkish folk music
- a new version of *Romeo and Juliet* set in the year 2050
- an exhibition by an up-and-coming young photographer from Brazil.

Tell students to work alone, or in pairs, and set a time limit of ten minutes. After ten minutes, ask students to display their reviews around the classroom. Students mingle and read each other's reviews. Take feedback on which review was most engaging and why.

3 WRITING SKILLS

Formal letters; Giving a positive impression

a Ask students what purpose would logically come first (to state the reason for writing). Tell students to read the application letter again and match each paragraph with its purpose. Check answers as a class.

Answers

4, 5 to give examples of relevant experience
3 to state her qualifications
2 to demonstrate enthusiasm for their company
6 to summarise her strengths
1 to state the reason for writing

 LOA TIP ELICITING

- When eliciting language to match the purpose of parts of a text, make sure students are very clear about what the purpose is before you ask them to supply the language. Give simple examples which match the purpose before the main task.

- Ask students what purposes these sentences match: *I've done a course in journalism.* (to state qualifications); *I once wrote an article for a student magazine.* (to give examples of experience); *You can trust me.* (to show strengths).

- Then encourage students to think about register and purpose by asking them to rephrase the three sentences in a more formal way for a positive impact: *I've completed a course in journalism*; *I have experience of writing for a student publication*; *I am considered to be responsible.*

- Students can now deal with matching the language in the application and they are also prepared for the register task in 3b.

b Ask students if they can remember the original phrases used in Helen's application letter instead of the underlined phrases. Then tell them to check in the text.

Answers

1 I would like to express my interest in
2 extremely well-written and informative
3 I especially admire your policy of providing a platform for
4 on the topic of
5 producing; deserve to be more widely recognised

c Ask students how writers create a positive impression, e.g. use effective collocations about themselves. Ask students to look through the text and underline the phrases Helen uses to describe herself and her experience. Take feedback as a class.

Answers

I am very much in touch with
I enthusiastically maintain my knowledge of
I played an active role in
I have been able to establish contact with
I have also taken a keen interest in
I feel that, with my combination of academic knowledge and local involvement in the arts, I would be very well qualified to

FAST FINISHERS

Ask fast finishers to express the phrases Helen uses to describe herself and her experience informally, e.g. ~~I am very much in touch with~~ *I keep up to date with.*

d Students complete the exercises in Writing Focus 6D on SB p.172. They read the table of expressions and then complete the exercises. Check answers to Exercise a and b as a class. After Exercise c, students compare their application letters and say which gives the most positive impression. Take feedback as a class. Tell students to go back to SB p.77.

Answers

a 1 guess; do   2 answering; was   3 in a bit   4 a real fan
5 Here are   6 loads of   7 am free any time   8 picked up;
priceless

b

Formal letters	Giving a positive impression
I am replying to … which appeared / was published in … I look forward to hearing from you soon / in due course I am attaching … I can offer … with regard to …	I believe / am certain that my knowledge … will enable me to … I have close contact with … I'm an enthusiastic supporter / a keen follower of … I have considerable/extensive experience of … I acquired/developed some relevant/valuable skills …

c Students' own answers

4 WRITING

a Put students into pairs to say which of the areas listed interests them most and how they could sell themselves as writers for that area. Students then work individually. Tell them to choose an area, make a paragraph plan and then write an application letter using the formal and positive language introduced in the lesson. Weaker students could rewrite Helen's letter, changing phrases and introducing their own ideas and language from Writing Focus 6D or other expressions they know.

b Put students into pairs. Tell them to read each other's applications and say whether they would be interested in using their reviews, justifying their decision.

EXTRA ACTIVITY

Ask students to take turns to interview their partner based on their application letter. As part of the interview, they could ask the applicant to give a presentation on their ideas for writing about their chosen area, using the language and techniques learned earlier in the unit.

ADDITIONAL MATERIAL

▶ Workbook 6D

UNIT 6
Review and extension

1 GRAMMAR

a Say some sentences and tell students to say an appropriate follow-up, e.g. *Thank you for your application letter.* (We would like to offer you an interview.); *First of all, I'd like to go through the advantages.* (Then we will move on to disadvantages.). Tell students to choose the correct follow-up for the sentences in the exercise.

Answers
1 b   2 a   3 a   4 b   5 b   6 a   7 b   8 a

> ### 💡 FAST FINISHERS
> Ask fast finishers to write some other follow-ups for sentences 1–8. Tell them to read them to other fast finishers for them to say which sentence prompts it, e.g. *So I'm surprised she hasn't this time.* (3 Emily always consults me on everything.).

b Write on the board *She saw a rat in the fridge and she shrieked in terror.* Tell students to rewrite the underlined phrase using a participle clause: *Seeing a rat in the fridge, she shrieked in terror.* Students rewrite the underlined phrases. Check as a class.

Answers
1 involved
2 Not wanting to seem rude
3 approaching platform 5
4 Not understanding Spanish
5 Waiting; displayed
6 Using just my hands

2 VOCABULARY

a Ask students which words they often spell wrong. Tell students to correct the spelling mistakes in the sentences. Check answers as a class.

Answers
1 iconic   2 humorous   3 playful   4 flawless   5 evocative
6 meaningful   7 exotic

> ### 💡 EXTRA ACTIVITY
> Put students into groups to discuss and write down a list of tips to improve spelling, e.g. use the spellcheck function on the computer to see what kind of words you regularly spell incorrectly. Ask each group to present their tips to the class (tell groups not to repeat a tip given by a previous group) and ask the class to give feedback on how useful they think each tip is.

b Write this sentence on the board and ask students to complete it:

The documentary is a g __ portrayal of inner-city poverty. (gritty)

Tell students to complete the sentences in the exercise. Check as a class.

Answers
1 protective
2 petrified
3 ashamed
4 helpless
5 devastated
6 restless
7 over-excited

3 WORDPOWER Idioms: Feelings

a Ask students if each idiom in bold is a positive or negative emotion, e.g. *grin and bear it* (negative). Then ask them which pictures have negative images, e.g. 1. Tell students to match the pictures with the comments, using a dictionary if necessary. Ask them where the people are and why they are making the comment. Check answers as a class.

Answers / Suggested answers
a 1 Watching TV. The babysitter didn't want to watch the programme the three boys were watching.
b 4 At a swimming pool. The swimmer is being interviewed by a journalist after winning a race.
c 6 In bed. The woman can't sleep because her neighbours are playing loud music.
d 2 Approaching the city he used to live in. The man is surprised by how much the city has changed since he last saw it ten years ago.
e 5 At a party. The man is annoyed with another man who thinks himself really wonderful.
f 3 In the kitchen. The mother is trying to work and cook, and her two children are arguing.

b Tell students to match the idioms with the definitions. Check answers as a class.

Answers
1 f   2 a   3 b   4 c,e   5 d

c 💬 Tell students to complete the questions using the correct words or phrases from the idioms. Check answers as a class. Students then ask and answer the questions in small groups. Take feedback as a class.

Answers
1 gets; back   2 end; tether   3 grin; bear   4 over the moon
5 believe; eyes   6 get; nerves

▶ Photocopiable activities: Wordpower p.246

> ### 🔄 LOA REVIEW YOUR PROGRESS
> Students look back through the unit, think about what they've studied and decide how well they did. Students work on weak areas by using the appropriate sections of the Workbook, the Photocopiable worksheets and the Personalised online practice.

UNIT 7
Connections

GETTING STARTED

💡 OPTIONAL LEAD-IN

Books closed. Put students into pairs to say or guess what these words connected with technology mean:

bit coin (digital currency)

clickbait (attractive hyperlinks that encourage you to click to another website)

permadeath (when a computer game character cannot reappear after it is killed)

selfie stick (a device for holding a smartphone or camera so you can take a photo of yourself)

silver surfer (an older person who uses the Internet)

wikiality (information that is assumed to be true because it appears in a web-based encyclopedia)

a Give students one minute to think about their answers to the questions before talking about the photo as a class.

🔵 UNIT OBJECTIVES

At the end of this unit, students will be able to:

- understand opinion and attitudes and follow complex discussions and descriptions in articles and broadcast material about the social implications of technological advances and scientific findings, responding to the ideas raised
- use a range of lexis to describe, speculate and make deductions about technological advances and hypothetical inventions including their origins and implications
- use a range of lexis to describe qualities of society and social relationships and situations, giving emphatic opinions on life in the digital age
- understand the attitudes and opinions of speakers using idiomatic language in arguments and strategies they use to resolve conflict
- use a range of expressions to apologise and admit fault in social and professional contexts
- write a clearly structured, cohesive proposal using linkers to highlight and give evidence appropriately

🌍 CULTURE NOTES

This photo shows pupils watching a robot which is helping their classmate, Jonas, in hospital to keep up with school. Jonas uses a tablet from his hospital bed to control the robot's eyes and follow the lesson. This is part of the *Avatar Kids* project by a French company, Aldebran Robotics, to allow sick children to continue in school and even go on school trips. As well as being Jonas's 'eyes', the robot can put his hand up in class for Jonas, set maths questions, give feedback, read different languages and demonstrate gym class activities. Jonas's classmates look after the robot.

b Put students into groups to discuss the questions. If students need encouragement, prompt them with ideas from the Suggested answers below. Take feedback as a class. If you wish, give students information from the Culture notes above.

Suggested answers
1. advantages: allows sick children to keep up with school; makes them feel less isolated
   disadvantages: technology not available to everybody; could be broken or misused by younger pupils
2. An internet connection is static and can't move with the lesson. The robot gives the boy a physical body in the classroom. The children feel curious.
3. social activities like parties; speaking with family and friends

💡 EXTRA ACTIVITY

Ask students to think about how far they do/don't like to adopt new technologies into their life and mark their position on a line from 'always the last to get one' to 'always the first to get one'. Put students into pairs to explain their position with examples and then talk about the position of other people in their family with examples.

At the end of this lesson, students will be able to:

- read an article about technology and speculate about the ideas and opinions stated using a range of grammatical forms for speculation and deduction
- use a range of compound adjectives and pronounce them with the appropriate stress
- listen to different ideas for innovation from a range of speakers and present their own idea in a one-minute time frame

⚲ OPTIONAL LEAD-IN

Books closed. Put students into groups to discuss which of these inventions would be the most useful:

- an alarm clock which wakes you up when you've had the exact amount of sleep needed
- a tablet which contains all the calories and vitamins needed for one day's nutrition
- an instrument which tells you what kind of mood someone is in on a scale of 1 (terrible) to 5 (fantastic).

1 READING and SPEAKING

a 🗩 Ask students to name and describe the capabilities of any well-known robots, real or fictional, e.g. *RoboCop* (from the film). Put students into pairs to look at the photos and discuss the questions. If necessary, pre-teach *state-of-the-art* (C1) (using the newest ideas, designs, and materials); *humanoid* (a machine or creature with the appearance and qualities of a human); *come close to doing sth* (C1) (almost achieve or do sth). Take feedback as a class.

b 🗩 Tell students to read the short text and think of four questions to ask these robots. Ask some students to read out their questions and ask other students to predict how a robot might answer them.

c Tell students to read the article and answer the questions. Use the Vocabulary support box to help as necessary. Check answers as a class.

Answers

1 Students' own answers
2 (a) face, skin, facial expressions, can interact, witty, profound responses to questions (b) nothing from the neck down, not all of her responses to questions make sense
3 He said he would be satisfied with a semi-coherent chat, and so he is probably satisfied.
4 Students' own answers
5 Robots will come to life one day as self-determined, fully conscious beings who will match or be superior to human beings intellectually. It will be reached by filling the robot with more and more information.

⚲ EXTRA ACTIVITY

Put students into pairs. Ask them to take it in turns to be Bina48 and answer their partner's questions from 1b in a similar way to the robot.

d Tell students to work out the meaning of the words in bold, using a dictionary if necessary. Check answers as a class.

Answers

1 *disconcerted*: worried by something and uncertain
2 *reassuringly* (C1): in a way that makes you feel less worried
3 *be something of a sth* (C2): used to describe a person or thing in a way that is partly true but not completely or exactly; *recluse*: a person who lives alone and avoids going outside or talking to other people
4 *hidden depths*: serious qualities that you do not see immediately

📖 VOCABULARY SUPPORT

off-the-shelf – if a product can be bought off the shelf, it does not need to be specially made or asked for

or so sb claims – this phrase implies the speaker does not believe what has been said

an array of sth (C1) – an admirable variety of something on display

settle for sth – accept something, although it is not exactly what you want

heart-to-heart – a serious conversation between two people, in which they talk honestly about their feelings

semi-coherent (C2) – almost but not completely logical / possible to understand

tipping point – the moment at which a series of small events builds up enough to cause a larger more important development

counterpart (C1) – a person or thing that has the same purpose as another one in a different place or organisation

e 🗩 Ask students if they think robots could replace them in their (future) job. Put students into groups to discuss the questions. Take feedback as a class.

Suggested answers

It is improving all the time, and the stage where robots become really like humans may not be far off.
Students' own answers

2 VOCABULARY Compound adjectives

a Ask students what you would call somebody who works for themselves (self-employed). Say that *self-employed* is a compound adjective, refer students to *lifelike* and *self-conscious* and their meanings and ask students to match the compound adjectives in the text with their meanings. Check as a class.

Answers

1 clear-headed 2 human-like 3 absent-minded
4 glassy-eyed 5 self-determined

⚲ FAST FINISHERS

Write *cyber* on the board and ask fast finishers what it is related to (computers, especially the Internet). Ask what these words (might) mean and which are real: *cyberdate* (a romantic meeting on the Internet, not real); *cyberpet* (a device acting like a pet, real); *cyberspeak* (computer jargon, real); *cyberteacher* (a robot teacher, not real).

b Put students into pairs to think of as many compound adjectives with *self-*, *-like*, *-eyed* and *-minded* as they can in a time limit. Ask the pair with the most compound adjectives to write them on the board and explain them.

Suggested answers
1 self-aware; self-centred; self-catering; self-motivated; self-obsessed; self-taught
2 birdlike; catlike; childlike; model-like; warlike
3 blue-eyed; dry-eyed; pop-eyed; wide-eyed; big-eyed; one-eyed
4 high-minded; like-minded; open-minded; strong-minded

c ▶ ⏵**3.18–3.20** Students complete the exercises in Vocabulary Focus 7A on SB p.164. Ask students to read both Tips. Play the recording for students to listen and check their answers to Exercises a and b. Play the recording for Exercise c. Check answers and elicit the pronunciation rule. Drill the compound adjectives. Tell students to go round the class and ask questions for each prompt in Exercise d so that they find at least one student for each prompt. Tell students to go back to SB p.81.

Answers (Vocabulary Focus 7A SB p.164)
a 5 left-handed
6 hard-hearted
7 clear-headed
8 mouth-watering
9 jaw-dropping.
b 1 narrow-minded
2 half-hearted
3 absent-minded
4 short-sighted
5 light-headed
6 light-hearted
7 hair-raising
8 mind-boggling
c 1 <u>mind</u>-boggling; <u>heart</u>warming; open-<u>minded</u>; short-<u>sighted</u>
2 adjective + <u>body part</u> + -ed; <u>body part</u> + present participle

---

⊙ CAREFUL!

A typical error students make with compound adjectives is punctuation: ~~It should be mentioned that only an efficient, well-qualified and openminded assistant would give the support we need.~~ (Correct usage = *It should be mentioned that only an efficient, well-qualified and **open-minded** assistant would give the support we need.*). Another mistake students sometimes make is to hyphenate compounds with *well* when they come after nouns: ~~The area was well-known for its high environmental standards.~~ (Correct usage = *The area was **well known** for its high environmental standards.*).

---

d Put students into groups. Tell them each to think of a compound adjective, e.g. *self-conscious*, but not say what it is. One student starts and the other students tell him or her to do things in a way that will show the word, e.g. *Brush your teeth* – the student will brush their teeth in a self-conscious way. The students keep giving instructions to do things until they find out the word. Then it is another student's turn to listen to instructions and demonstrate their word.

3 SPEAKING and GRAMMAR
Speculation and deduction

a ⬚ Put students into pairs to read the opinions and discuss how far they agree with them. Take feedback as a class.

---

b Ask students to look at *may well have been* in opinion 1 and elicit how sure the speaker is (quite sure but not certain) and whether it refers to the past, present or future (past). Do the same with the other phrases in bold.

Answers
a 1 quite sure   2 very sure   3 certain   4 very sure; quite sure
5 quite sure   6 certain; very sure
b 1 past   2 past and present   3 present/future
4 future; future   5 future   6 past; present

c ⏵**3.21** Tell students to rewrite the opinions in 3a using the expressions. Play the recording for students to check.

Answers and audioscript
1 It's likely that was because the interviewer asked difficult questions.
2 I bet they've been developing this technology for decades, to get this far.
3 There's no way robots can ever replace human beings.
4 It's quite possible that robot nurses will soon be looking after patients in hospitals. Although it's highly unlikely they'll be doing skilled jobs.
5 There's a good chance robots that can respond to feelings will be developed in the next 50 years.
6 Scientists are bound to have made progress since the article was written. I'm sure they're getting closer and closer to creating conscious machines.

d ▶ ⏵**3.22–3.27** Students read the information in Grammar Focus 7A on SB p.150. Play the recording where indicated and ask students to listen and repeat. Students then complete the exercises. Check answers as a class. Exercise c could lead to a discussion about whether time travel might be possible one day and if it were, what the consequences would be. Tell students to go back to SB p.81.

Answers (Grammar Focus 7A SB p.150)
a 2 's going to   3 highly   4 could   5 will   6 slim   7 can
8 must   9 can't   10 can
b 2 Customers are bound to complain.
3 I may well see/be seeing Ian tomorrow.
4 Barbara must have broken the window – she was playing round here.
5 The referee can't have seen the incident.
6 Damien should know the answer.
7 I/You can tell that Greta is dissatisfied.
8 The lights are on so Karen has got to be at home.
c 2 ✓   3 might/could/would   4 no way
5 ✓   6 ✓   7 could   8 should/will/could
9 unlikely   10 won't

⊙ CAREFUL!

A mistake students sometimes make is to use *bound to* rather than *likely/obliged/forced to*: ~~Also, music is not bound to be of use to a scientist.~~ (Correct form = *Also, music is not likely to be of use to a scientist.*).

---

e Ask students to rewrite the sentences using the verbs in brackets to speculate or make deductions. If necessary, pre-teach *foresee* (C1) (expect a future situation or event) and *pose* (C1) (cause a problem/threat). Monitor to make sure students are using the expressions accurately.

f ⬚ Put students into pairs to compare their sentences and discuss their opinions. Take feedback as a class.

4 LISTENING

a 💬 Put students into groups to discuss what issues the pictures show. Take feedback as a class.

b ▶️ **3.28** Play the recording for students to listen and check their ideas in 4a. If necessary, pre-teach some of the words from the Vocabulary support box. Ask students to write a one-sentence summary of each solution. Check answers.

Answers
1 People get away with telling lies and misleading others; the invention is a fact-checker app that would alert us when someone tells lies or mistruths
2 There is too much noise and visual stimulation in the modern environment; the invention is a remote control that would modulate, tone down and filter sensory information
3 Being good-looking gives some people an unfair advantage in life; the invention is a mask that would conceal people's appearance when they are interviewed so that they wouldn't be judged on how they look

Audioscript
SPEAKER 1 Politicians, media pundits, writers and students get away with claims that are not based on fact.
If I was ruler of the world for a day, I would install fact-checker apps into our smartphones, into our computers, so that when facts were broken, when people told lies, or told mistruths, our phones went 'Brrrrrrr!', or the lines on our computer screen popped up in red. That way, we'd know what was fact and what was fiction.
Of course, I wouldn't apply it to everyone. I wouldn't apply it to poets, to novelists and others who specialise in imaginary ideas. My aim would be to ensure that we benefit from the age of the Internet of things to have an Internet of facts and ideas, and through this we would hopefully get away from the infuriating falsehoods that are being widely disseminated.
Over time, good ideas would be spread far and wide, and bad ideas would be seen as a joke, rather than being the source of misinformation and perpetuating ignorance.
SPEAKER 2 The invention I would like to propose is a remote control that can modulate the amount of sensory information you get – the amount of sound, or smell, visual information, etc.
I came up with this idea because I cycle around London quite a lot, and every day I notice how much I am bombarded with the sounds of traffic and the smells of the city and visual advertising and media. I think this is something that in general people deal with in a number of different ways. Often it relies on putting more information or stimulus into your body, like wearing headphones or looking in your phone.
A remote control would allow you to tone down what's there. I imagine it would work like a force field you can set at your ideal level, because everyone is different, and everyone has different ideal levels, and it just filters everything that comes in and out.
SPEAKER 3 Well, my idea for changing the world is quite simple, and it can be justified on the grounds of justice and fairness. It is simply that when someone is interviewed, for a job, for example, that they should have to conceal their appearance.
They would have to wear a mask. They would not be able to exploit their, let's say, personal or their social, visual capital. They would have to be judged according to their merit. It would create a level playing field. It would ensure that the best person was recruited to a company – irrespective of whether that person was good-looking or ugly, as conventionally determined.
It would serve the interest both of fairness in respect of that person's rights, and it would ensure a level playing field therefore for that reason. But it would also ensure the most meritocratic outcome – the best person would be chosen for the job.

c ▶️ **3.28** Play the recording again, pause after each speaker and ask students what impact the idea is intended to have.

Suggested answers
1 Good ideas would reach more people and bad ideas would be exposed. People would be better informed.
2 Everyone could receive their ideal level of stimuli from the outside world.
3 It would ensure employers hired the best possible candidates and create a fairer employment market.

📖 VOCABULARY SUPPORT

pop up – suddenly appear

apply a rule/standard to sb/sth (C1) – make somebody or something obey a rule or judge them by a standard

far and wide – to/from/in, etc. many different places in the country/world

perpetuate sth – make something continue to happen / be the situation

ignorance (C2) – lack of knowledge, understanding or information

modulate sth – change the amount of something to make it more suitable

stimulus (C2) – something which stimulates the senses

tone sth down – reduce something such as noise, colour, strong language etc. to an acceptable level

on the grounds of (C1) – (formal) because of a particular reason

a level playing field – used to describe a competitive situation which is fair because everyone has the same chance of success

irrespective of sth (C2) – (formal) without considering something, often because it is irrelevant

determine sth (C1) – (formal, often passive) make a decision or judgement

serve the interests of sth/sb (C1) – (formal) help achieve something which is an advantage (for sth/sb)

meritocratic – of a system/society/organisation in which people have power because of their abilities, not because of money, social position, etc.

d 💬 Put students into pairs to discuss the questions. Take feedback as a class.

💡 EXTRA ACTIVITY

Put students into groups to discuss whether these statements are fact or fiction:

You use more calories sleeping than watching TV. (fact)

There are more English native speakers than Spanish. (fiction)

Mount Everest would fit into the deepest area of the sea. (fact)

You could live without water if you ate enough fruit. (fact).

Tell students to write five of their own fact/fiction statements to test other groups.

e ▶️ **3.29** Put students into groups to predict the experts' reactions to the ideas. Then play the recording to check. If necessary, pre-teach *close to home* (relevant and familiar, possibly because it is uncomfortably close to the truth).

Suggested answer
They all think the ideas are good, but they have reservations about them.

Audioscript

SPEAKER 1 It's hard to argue with the idea that we want truth over falsehood. I think the trickiest part of this is actually knowing what the truth is and what facts are and aren't correct. And so, my biggest concern would be that the fact app might itself be full of falsehoods that we haven't found out yet, or could be used to deceive us.

SPEAKER 2 I was intrigued though by the idea that you want to filter out these noises or smells or whatever it is when you're cycling. Isn't there a danger you could miss out something that's rather important for your safety? For example, you might just miss that taxi that was coming round the corner that you didn't know about. So turned down, you go straight into it. So I think you'd need a smart filter which would be able to recognise what was essential for you to see and hear, red traffic lights, for example, and what could safely be filtered out, like advertisements or noise from building sites.

SPEAKER 3 It's a fascinating idea, and it's very close to home for me because I've hired hundreds of people and done hundreds of job interviews, many of which have been over Skype or telephone. And I think I like the values and the spirit behind the suggestion. My hesitation about it is that you know they say 80 per cent of communication is non-verbal, and I think a lot comes across in expressions and bearing. Some of it is unfortunate and shouldn't influence your decision. Some of it is actually essential, I think – to assess someone's characteristics for a job. So I'm not sure what I think.

f ▶ **3.29** Tell students to choose the point each expert makes. Play the recording again for students to check their answers.

Answers
1 b
2 b
3 a

g ▶ **3.30** **Language in context** *Information*

1 Elicit the meaning of some of the words, e.g. *If you filter information, do you let all of it in?* (no) *Do you let none of it in?* (no) *So what do you do?* (only let some of it in). Ask students to complete the sentences. Play the recording for students to listen and check.

2 Students answer the questions. Check answers.

Answers
1 a claims; fact
   b falsehoods; disseminated
   c misinformation
   d filters
   e conceal
2 1 fact
   2 claims
   3 falsehoods, misinformation
   4 disseminated, conceal, filters

h 💬 Put students into groups to discuss the questions. Take feedback as a class.

5 SPEAKING

a 💬 Encourage students to think of as many inventions or new ideas as possible, using the prompts to help them, and write them on the board. Put students into small groups to choose an invention or idea, make notes, then plan and practise a 60-second presentation (it may be useful to remind students of the presentation language in 6C on SB p.74). Students choose one person from each group to present their idea to the rest of the class. Tell students to make notes of each idea as they listen as they will need them for the next stage.

b 💬 Put students back into their groups to discuss how necessary, interesting and practical the other ideas were. Groups then ask each other to clarify any points or get extra information. Finally, ask students to vote for the best idea (they can't vote for their own!).

ADDITIONAL MATERIAL

▶ Workbook 7A

▶ Photocopiable activities: Grammar p.213, Vocabulary p.233, Pronunciation p.264

7B What I enjoy is a heart-to-heart chat

At the end of this lesson, students will be able to:

- listen to and read about research-based opinions on how people relate to one another in society and react to the views expressed
- use cleft structures with the appropriate intonation to emphasise information
- use a range of noun suffixes to express their opinions, including abstract ideas

OPTIONAL LEAD-IN

Books closed. Put students into pairs and ask them to have an SMS conversation: they cannot speak and can only send messages on their mobile devices. If they don't have the technology, ask them to pass each other messages on a piece of paper. After about five minutes, ask students how it felt compared to speaking to each other.

1 SPEAKING and LISTENING

a Ask students to compare online and print newspapers and say whether print news still has a future. Put students into groups to discuss reading habits and choose a headline they might read. Take feedback as a class.

EXTRA ACTIVITY

Put students into groups and tell them to choose one of the headlines. Ask students to discuss what story might be behind the headline: what happened and why it is news. Groups then take it in turns to present their story, briefly, to the rest of the class, each student saying part of the story.

b Ask students where you would find a blurb (on the back cover of a book). Tell students to read the blurb and say whether the writer thinks the Internet makes us more or less connected. Check as a class.

Answer
not necessarily more

c Ask students: *What is the subject of 'accelerated'?* (one). *What does 'one' refer to?* (the age of connection). *What does 'age of connection' mean?* (everyone being in communication). *What could be happening to communication?* (it is increasing). Ask students to work out the meanings of the other highlighted words from the context. Tell them to check in a dictionary if necessary. Check answers as a class.

Answers
accelerate (C1): happen or make something happen sooner or faster
ubiquitous: seeming to be everywhere
immensely (C1): extremely
inevitably (C1): in a way that cannot be avoided
cosmopolitan (C1): containing or having experience of people and things from many different parts of the world
engage (with something/somebody): become closer to something/somebody so that you can understand it/them

d Ask students why they think the author uses water as an example of shipping goods (water is a strange product to ship such a long way given that it falls free from the sky). Ask students to discuss the comparison in pairs. Take feedback as a class.

e ▶ 3.31 Ask students why they think the book is called *Rewire*. Ask students to summarise the main point the book makes, according to Zelda, in one sentence. Tell three or four students to give you their answers and ask the rest of the class to comment on how accurate and complete they are.

Suggested answer
We need to change our online behaviour so that we can connect more with different people and cultures.

Audioscript

PRESENTER Welcome to *From My Bookshelf* – the weekly programme where guests talk about a book that they think everyone should read. This week's guest is media expert and commentator Zelda Freeman. Welcome Zelda, thank you very much for being here today. Tell us about your book.

ZELDA Well um … the most intriguing book I've read in the past few years – *Rewire* by Ethan Zuckerman – er, he's an academic, um, and he thinks deeply about the role of media in our society.

P Zuckerman. The main thing about his book, I hear, is that he's challenging the myth about the Internet, is that true?

Z Yes, er … the myth. And what's interesting is that we only think we're more connected … But, the point he's making is, that we're actually wrong. Er, in some ways, the Net manages to isolate us.

P So we're all connected together but we're isolating ourselves? That sounds like a contradiction – how is that possible?

Z Well, use myself as an example. I use the Internet to find out news. I read a lot of newspapers online, but it's only British ones that I read. There's nothing stopping me from reading an English-language newspaper in China – it's just a click away. But, I don't. What Zuckerman is saying is that the Internet is a very powerful tool, but very few of us exploit it to its full potential.

P I have to ask – does it matter?

Z Well, yes … The reason why it matters is that we're living in an age of economic and physical connection. Um, our economies are connected. So, if the share market in the US sneezes, then we all feel the effects. Um, a dangerous virus breaks out somewhere in the world and it can travel around the globe very quickly. And more people are moving around. What we really need to understand is how other countries and cultures work. We're more linked into each other than we used to be, so we need to be a lot more cosmopolitan.

P But in the 21st century, I'm sure a lot of people already know this. Does it actually matter if we don't do anything about it?

Z Well, good point … I mean, Zuckerman makes a very good point about that. We tend to think we know more than we actually do. It's a kind of false cosmopolitanism. And he uses this example because we know we could in theory read *The Times of India* online, but we almost begin to imagine that we actually do that, although in reality we don't. It's the possibility of connection that means we begin to think of ourselves as being cosmopolitan.

P So we begin to think that a possibility is a reality?

Z Exactly, I mean that's fine for many things, but as far as the Internet is concerned, I really think we need to think about it a bit more.

P So why do you think that we don't connect more?

Z Well Zuckerman suggests that our online behaviour is not that different from our offline behaviour. Um, so for example we form social groups according to the people we meet as we grow up, and we get together with people with similar attitudes and interests.

P So like we do in social media, we only friend people we want to actually be friends with?

Z Yes, that's right. What we don't do is explore much beyond that. But the thing is, we can – we actually have the potential to do that.

P So does Zuckerman himself, does he have any suggestions?

z Well, he says that all we need to do is 'disconnect' from our current way of thinking and 'rewire'. We all have to learn to behave in a very different way.

P How?

z That's the problem. It's a challenge. You need to identify what he calls 'bridge figures'. These are people who are able to translate ideas from one culture to another. They can explain it, give it context, and they help us to understand it.

P So like in some kind of magazine or journal?

z No not really. He means being much freer than that. So, for instance, bloggers. These are people who have a passion for this kind of thing. Um … their information needs to be open and accessible and therefore it's free for everyone.

P Won't this just be more information online that people don't read?

z So, as I mentioned before, business and politics are more and more connected. Um, um, business and political leaders need to be genuinely cosmopolitan in this day and age. So people who are 'bridge figures' are likely to assume more and more important roles in business, and also in politics. They've rewired already. So, if we want to do well in the world, we need to rewire as well.

f ▶ **3.31** Ask students if they would read *Rewire*. Play the recording again. Tell students to note down examples. Check answers as a class. Use the Vocabulary support box to help with vocabulary as necessary.

Suggested answers

1 we read a lot of newspapers online (but not necessarily those from other cultures, although they're widely available); we form social groups (but only with people similar to ourselves)
2 economically: we're affected by changes in the US share market; physically: dangerous viruses can spread quickly round the world and more people are moving around
3 we know we could read *The Times of India*, so we almost begin to think that we do
4 bloggers, business and political leaders; they translate ideas from one culture to another

---

📖 VOCABULARY SUPPORT

myth (C1) – a commonly believed, but false, idea

isolate (C1) – separate one, or a group, from the main group so that it has no contact

contradiction (C2) – the state in which two statements, ideas, etc., cannot both be true because they contain opposing ideas

sneeze (B2) – used figuratively to mean change slightly/ suddenly/briefly

assume (*a role*) (C2) – (formal) to start to take responsibility for a particular thing/job

---

g 💬 Ask students if any of them see themselves as 'bridge figures'. Put students into groups to discuss the questions. Take feedback as a class.

💡 EXTRA ACTIVITY

Tell students that they are 'bridge figures' and need to share ideas from their culture(s) with others. Put students into groups, mixed nationalities if possible, to think of three things that other countries/cultures would find interesting and informative and to decide how to share that information, e.g. upload a video onto YouTube about wedding traditions in their region. If time and resources are available, ask students to put their suggestions into practice.

---

2 GRAMMAR Cleft sentences

a ▶ **3.32** Ask students to match the sentence halves. Play the recording for students to listen and check.

Answers

1 c   2 e   3 a   4 d   5 b

b Write this sentence on the board: *What's important is people care about each other.* Ask students: *What is important?* (People care about each other.) Write this sentence on the board: *All I want is to live in a fair world.* Underline *What's important is …* and *All I want is …* and ask students: *What does this part of the sentence do? Make the sentence more polite, or emphasise the information that follows?* (emphasise) Ask students to answer the question in pairs.

Answer

the information (a–e) that follows each cleft structure (1–5)

c Ask students how many verbs there are in the cleft part of the sentences (two or three). Ask students which verb joins the cleft to the complement to elicit the answer.

Answer

be (is)

d ▶ **3.32** **Pronunciation** Ask students what tone comment phrases take at the start of sentences (fall– rise). If necessary, refer students back to SB p.75. Ask students to predict what tone the cleft part of the sentence takes. Play the recording for students to listen and check their prediction. Check the answer.

Answer

fall–rise

e ▶ **3.33–3.34** Students read the information in Grammar Focus 7B on SB p.151. Play the recording where indicated and ask students to listen and repeat. Students then complete the exercises. Check answers as a class. Tell students to go back to SB p.83.

Answers (Grammar Focus 7B SB p.151)

a 2a   3d   4f   5h   6b   7c   8e
b 2 ~~The captain of the ship was she~~ It was the captain of the ship
  3 ~~what~~ (that)   4 ~~taking~~ (to) take   5 ~~to~~ (that) you
  6 ~~which~~ (that)   7 ~~What~~ It   8 ~~Is~~ It is
c 2 All I need is ten euros.
  3 It is a job (that/which) nobody wants to do.
  4 What you are asking for is unreasonable.
  5 The reason (why) we chose Portugal was the friendly people.
  6 What happened was (that) our car ran into a tree.
  7 It was her cousin who/that was causing all the trouble.
  8 The thing that bothers me is (that) I don't know Jason so well.

👁 CAREFUL!

A mistake students sometimes make is to forget *be* in the cleft: ~~What is special about soap operas that they attract attention more than any other TV programme.~~ (Correct form = *What is special about soap operas **is** that they attract attention more than any other TV programme.*).

---

f ▶ **3.35** Say: *Zelda wants more awareness of the problems.* and ask students to change it into a cleft sentence beginning with *What* (What Zelda wants is more awareness of the problems.). Tell students to change the sentences. Then play the recording for students to listen and check.

1 What we don't need is wi-fi all over town.
2 It's only at work that I use the Internet.
3 All we have to do is unsubscribe from social media to help us reconnect.
4 What's incredible is just how liberating it is to go digital.
5 The reason it worries me is (because/that) people end up living in virtual worlds and losing touch with reality.

g 💬 Ask students to complete the cleft sentences individually. Put students into pairs and tell them to take turns to say their sentences and comment on their partner's sentences. Take feedback as a class and ask some students to say their sentences.

3 READING

a 💬 Ask students if they regularly communicate with anyone who they have never met face-to-face and if so whether they could call these people friends. Put students into pairs to discuss the difference between face-to-face and online friendships. Take feedback as a class.

b 💬 Put students into pairs to say whether they think the statements are true or false, and why. Take feedback as a class.

c Ask students to read the article and check their answers in 3b. Use the Vocabulary support box to help with the idiomatic expressions if necessary. Check answers as a class. If students have struggled with the scientific language in the article, do the Extra activity.

Answers

1 T (those exposed to cold temperatures find it easier to grasp viewpoints other than their own)
2 F (to take the heat out of a disagreement, you should decrease the heat of the room)
3 F (the writer says he wants to draw this conclusion, but it's not proven)
4 T (cold makes us lonely and loneliness makes us feel cold; warmth makes us feel the opposite)
5 T (loneliness has been found to make numerous serious diseases worse)

📖 VOCABULARY SUPPORT

take the heat out of (an argument) – reduce the level of anger/ excitement

be music to sb's ears – be something that you are very pleased to hear

on closer reading – when read again more carefully, the first interpretation was wrong or incomplete

be in the doghouse – be disapproved of

keep track of sth – be continuously informed about something

a nudge in the right direction – a small effort to improve a situation

💡 EXTRA ACTIVITY

Write two lists on the board and divide the class into As and Bs:

Student A: extrapolate   trigger   finding   reinforce

Student B: exert effects   replicate findings   exacerbate

Ask students to check with a dictionary and write a synonymous paraphrase for each expression. In AB pairs, students explain the words in their lists to each other, using the context of the article.

d Ask students if the author believes in the link between cold and loneliness (generally, yes). Ask students to read the article in more detail and answer the questions. Check answers as a class.

Answers

1 It helps us see other perspectives and gives us a sense of social distance and separateness.
2 Loneliness makes people feel physically cold. Ostracised (lonely) people preferred hot food, and their skin temperature dropped.
3 Research which makes connections between things that don't logically seem to be connected, like loneliness and physical coldness, or words connected with old age and the speed we walk at. The research has lost popularity because scientists have not been able to repeat certain studies and get the same results.
4 Because temperature does, in fact, have an important link with loneliness.
5 Connections through social media make us feel lonely because they don't involve heat.
6 They warm us up and make us feel less lonely.

💡 EXTRA ACTIVITY

Put students into groups to discuss whether they would agree with these statements if they were presented with research evidence to back these claims up:

People will pay 50% more for a 10% improvement.

The happiest period of your life is between 35 and 40.

The more you pay people, the better their results at work.

Talking to flowers and plants helps them grow faster.

People with pets live 10% longer than people without pets.

e 💬 Ask students whether we can measure concepts like tolerance and loneliness in experiments. Put students into groups to discuss the questions. Take feedback as a class.

4 VOCABULARY Nouns with suffixes: Society and relationships

a Ask students if they know any of the highlighted words and if so tell them to explain the words to the class. Ask students to guess the meaning of the rest of the words from the context and check with a dictionary. Check answers as a class.

Answers

grasp viewpoints (C1): understand opinions
affable tolerance (C2): willingness to accept, in a friendly way, behaviour and beliefs that are different from your own, although you might not agree with or approve of them
prejudice (B2): an unfair and unreasonable opinion or feeling, especially when formed without enough thought or knowledge
perspectives (C1): particular ways of considering something
intimacy: a situation in which you have a close friendship with someone
loneliness (C1): the state of being lonely
ostracism: avoiding someone intentionally, or preventing someone from taking part in the activities of a group
exclusion: the act of not allowing someone or something to take part in an activity or to enter a place
social contact (B1): communication with people, relating to activities in which you meet and spend time with other people and that happen during the time when you are not working
security (B1): protection of a person, building, organisation or country against threats such as crime or attacks by foreign countries
isolated (C1): feeling unhappy because of not seeing or talking to other people

- Translation is an efficient way of concept checking vocabulary if you share the same L1 as the students and there is nothing in the communicative approach discouraging translation. However, you can use variations on the basic saying the word in L1 for students to then say the word in L2.

- Say the definition of the word in L1 rather than the word itself.

- Say an example sentence in L2 with the highlighted word in L1, e.g in Turkish: *There needs to be more hoşgörü of people from different cultures* (tolerance).

- Give a synonym or antonym of the highlighted word in L1.

- Say one of the words highlighted and give a list of three or four words in L1 for students to choose from. Alternatively, do the opposite: say a word in L1 and offer three or four of the highlighted words.

b Ask students to complete the phrases. Check answers as a class.

Answers
1 viewpoint   2 perspective   3 perspective; intimacy
4 social contact   5 security

c Ask students what the noun forms of the words are. Check as a class.

Answers
coldness; loneliness; ostracism; exclusion; isolation

d ▶ 3.36 Ask students to add the appropriate suffix from the nouns in 4c to each group of words. Play the recording for students to listen and check. Then tell students to check any new words in a dictionary.

Answers
1 -ism: materialism; optimism; socialism; separatism; capitalism
2 -ness: nervousness; rudeness; selfishness; fairness; closeness
3 -ion: collaboration; distribution; liberation; innovation; separation

CAREFUL!

A mistake students sometimes make is to use the wrong noun form: ~~I hope the city will accept the proposal that will benefit all of the residents and tourism that come to our great city the most.~~ (Correct form = *I hope the city will accept the proposal that will benefit all of the residents and* **tourists** *that come to our great city the most.*). ~~I handled the situation with calmness and professionality.~~ (Correct form = *I handled the situation with calmness and* **professionalism***.*).

e Tell students to study the examples and complete the rule. Refer students to the Learning Tip. Check answers as a class.

Answers
-ness   -ism   -ion

f Ask students what the difference between the meaning of the three nouns is, using a dictionary if necessary, and to make example sentences showing the differences.

Answers
separation (B2): a situation in which two or more people or things are separated; an arrangement, often legal, by which two married people stop living together as a couple
separatism: the belief held by people of a particular race, religion, or other group within a country that they should be independent and have their own government or in some way live apart from other people
separateness: the state of existing or happening independently or in a different physical space

FAST FINISHERS

Ask fast finishers to find three more nouns for each suffix, e.g. *tiredness, realism, decision.*

HOMEWORK ACTIVITY

▶ Ask students to read the information in the Learning Tip again and find five sets of words with the same base form but different suffixes, e.g. *collection* (a group of objects of one type that have been collected by one person or in one place); *collective* (an organisation or business that is owned and controlled by the people who work in it); *collectivism* (a theory or political system based on the principle that all of the farms, factories, and other places of work in a country should be owned by or for all the people in that country). Tell students to record the different meanings with example sentences. In the next class, ask them to share their words with a partner.

5 SPEAKING

a Ask students to look at the picture and ask how the man feels in such an isolated environment. Write this sentence on the board and ask students for nouns that would be suitable: _____ *is one way to make yourself unpopular and isolated.* (e.g. Selfishness, Rudeness). Tell students to complete the sentences using the words studied in the lesson or their own ideas, checking the form in a dictionary. Students then add two more sentences of their own on the same topic. Monitor and support students as necessary. Check that students' answers use appropriate suffixes.

b 💬 Put students into pairs to explain their ideas from 5a and then discuss and agree five key qualities and kinds of behaviour that are important to social relationships. Take feedback as a class.

c 💬 Put students into groups to choose one of the situations and decide how to deal with it, making a list of problems and suggestions. Tell each group to present their analysis of the situation to the rest of the class.

d 💬 Ask students to discuss in groups whether they have any personal experience of these situations. Ask students to share any interesting anecdotes with the class.

ADDITIONAL MATERIAL

▶ Workbook 7B
▶ Photocopiable activities: Grammar p.214, Vocabulary p.234

7C Everyday English
I was out of line

At the end of this lesson, students will be able to:

- apologise and admit fault in real-life contexts such as a telephone conversation using a range of functional language
- pronounce spellings with *ou* and *ough*

☉ OPTIONAL LEAD-IN

Books closed. Put students into groups and read out this situation:

It is late on Saturday night and Tom gets a phone call from his friend Sally saying she needs to see him urgently. Tom drives as fast as he can to Sally's, too fast to stop in time when he sees a barrier in the middle of the road the road workers had forgotten to remove. Tom's car crashes into the barrier. Sally then phones Tom to say she can wait until the morning.

Ask students to discuss whose fault the accident was: Sally's, Tom's, the road workers'.

1 LISTENING

a 💬 Draw arrows on the board to indicate four different intonation patterns: fall, rise, rise–fall, fall–rise. Get students to pronounce the word *Sorry* with the different intonation patterns and to say what the meaning could be: fall (normal pronunciation, an apology); rise (to get attention, *Sorry, are you Mrs Brown?*); rise–fall (sarcasm, *Sorry for giving my opinion.*); fall–rise (contradiction, *Sorry, B is the right answer.*). Put students into pairs to look at pictures a–d and discuss the questions. Take feedback as a class.

Suggested answers

1. a The elephant can't hear the mouse.
   b The child doesn't understand what the man is saying.
   c The shop assistant has made a mistake with the money.
   d The man is drawing the bus driver's attention to the fact that the bus's wheel is on his foot.
2. Students' own answers

b 💬 Ask students to look at the pictures and say who could be apologising for what. Take feedback as a class.

c ▶ **3.37** If you have the video, play it without sound first and ask students to say who looks as if they are apologising. Play Part 1 of the video or the audio recording. Check answers as a class. If necessary, pre-teach *call it a day* (stop the work you are doing) and *poke your nose into sth* (C2) (try to discover things that are not really related to you).

Answers

e Max is apologising to Sara for being on the phone.
f Sara is apologising to Max for talking about his book with Alex.

Videoscript/Audioscript (Part 1)

MAX Excuse me a moment, I'll have to take this ... Hi Wendy ... Yes, I agree, we do need to talk this through. I'm with someone right now though. Can I call you back? Yes. OK. Speak later. Bye. Sorry about that.

SARA No worries. Sometimes it can't be avoided.

M It was my publisher asking about another book.

S Oh? Most writers would be over the moon to get the opportunity to write a second novel.

M Yeah, but I'm not sure I could, even if I wanted to.

S I'm sure that's not true, Max. I'm sure you'll come up with something soon. Hey, y'know, Alex had a good idea yesterday, for more to the *Solar Wind* story.

M Alex?

S Yeah. You know how we said a sequel is impossible ... Well, he said you ought to write a prequel. Y'know ... Tell the story of what happens before *Solar Wind*.

M So, you've been talking this through with my sister's boyfriend?

S Well, yes, I thought it might be a good idea ...

M I think it's a bit out of order!

S Sorry?

M First, you hide the fact that you're a journalist. Then, you go gossiping about me to the whole world! It's not on!

S Well, I wouldn't say Alex is the whole world, exactly ...

M To be perfectly honest, I'm not sure I can go through with another interview.

S You're right. I was out of line.

M People poking their noses in! I've had it up to here with it!

S Max, please, it's not like that! I'm sorry, it was inexcusable of me to pretend I was a fan, but ... I think you're overreacting here.

M Maybe so, but I think we had better call it a day. Please don't bother me again.

d ▶ **3.37** Ask students what the outcome of the conversation is (Max doesn't want to speak to Sara). Play Part 1 of the video or the audio recording again for students to answer the questions. Check as a class. When checking question 2, ask students to explain these expressions Max used: *It's a bit out of order.* (It's not really correct behaviour.); *It's not on.* (It's unacceptable.); *I've had it up to here.* (I can't tolerate the ongoing situation.)

Answers

1. He's annoyed by them asking him about a second novel.
2. He's angry that she's discussed his problem about writing a sequel with Alex.
3. She's upset and disappointed.

e 💬 Ask students if they sympathise more with Max or Sara here. Put students into groups to discuss the question. Take feedback as a class.

2 PRONUNCIATION Sound and spelling: *ou* and *ough*

a ▶ **3.38** Write on the board:

Then, you go gossiping about me

Ask students if the pronunciation of the underlined *ou* sounds is the same or different (different: *you* = /uː/; *about* = /aʊ/). Play the recording. Ask students to note down one word spelled with *ou* in each sentence and to answer the question. Check answers as a class.

Answers and audioscript

1. I agree, we do need to talk this through.
2. I'm with someone right now though.
3. I'm not sure I could, even if I wanted to.
4. Well, he said you ought to write a prequel.
5. I think it's a bit out of order.

The sound of the letters *ou* in each word is different.

b ▶ 3.39 Ask students how many different ways *ou* is pronounced in the sentences in 2a (five). Students complete the table with words from the box and say which sounds are short and which are long (diphthongs count as long sounds). Play the recording for students to listen and check their answers. Drill all the words.

Answers
1 /ʊ/ could, should (short)
2 /uː/ soup, through, route (long)
3 /aʊ/ pronouncing, south (long)
4 /əʊ/ though (long)
5 /ɔː/ thought, ought, poor (long)
6 /ʌ/ tough, enough, rough, southern (short)
7 /ɒ/ cough (short)
8 /ə/ conscious, thoroughly (short)

c ▶ 3.40 Tell students to underline the *ough* words in the conversation. Play the recording. Drill the conversation line by line. Then put the students into pairs to practise the conversation.

LOA TIP DRILLING

- Drilling conversations containing the target sounds is useful as it is more natural to pronounce sounds in a context.
- Books closed. Write the conversation in 2c on the board. Drill it line by line and put students into pairs to read it out.
- Rub out several words from the conversation on the board. Drill it line by line again. Students will need to remember the missing words and their pronunciation.
- Rub out more words and drill the conversation in several stages until finally the whole board is blank and students are repeating the conversation from memory.
- Put students into pairs to practise the conversation. Then drill the conversation line by line a final time.

ⓦ EXTRA ACTIVITY

Put students into pairs to write a new conversation using as many words spelled with *ou* and *ough* as possible. Put pairs into groups of four. They take it in turns to read out their conversations to the other pair. Students listen and check the pronunciation.

3 LISTENING

a ▶ 3.41 Tell students to look at the photo and guess what Emma and Max are arguing about. Ask students to put the events in the order they think they will happen. Then play Part 2 of the video or the audio recording for them to check.

Answers
a 4 b 1 c 8 d 6 e 3,7 f 9 g 2,5

Videoscript/Audioscript (Part 2)

EMMA Oh, hello Max! Take a look at this house. Isn't it gorgeous?
MAX Yeah, nice.
E Look, it's dead cool. This website allows you to take a virtual tour around the house.
M Right. But surely that price is way out of your league.
E Yeah, but I thought … for you.
M Me? Why?
E Well, you need somewhere to live.
M Why don't you just come out with it? You're throwing me out!
E No, no, no, of course not. Look, there's no need to get so worked up about it!
M Why is everyone trying to organise my life for me today? First Sara, now you!
E Max!
M Why doesn't everyone just get off my back?!
E Look, calm down, Max. I'm sorry. That wasn't very tactful of me, was it? But, y'know, you do need a place of your own. We both do, to be honest.
M You're right. As always.
E Max.
M I'm sorry I overreacted. I don't know what came over me. I've just been really stressed recently. But I had no right to take it out on you like that.
E It's OK. We all lose it from time to time.
M Me more than most!
E Hmm. What were you saying about Sara?
M Oh. Apparently, she and Alex have been discussing my next book. Alex's got a brilliant idea, I'm told.
E Oh, I see. And what's that?
M Well, that I should write a prequel.
E Not a bad idea.
M Do you honestly think that that idea hasn't crossed my mind?!
E Oh, Max! Don't get all angry again, please!
M Well, for goodness' sake! I'm fed up of being completely misunderstood all the time!
E Well, if you've had that idea, why haven't you done anything about it?
M Well … you wouldn't understand.
E Try me! Y'know this is just typical you! Constantly whining about how nobody understands you, but given half the chance, you can't be bothered to explain what's going on in that big head of yours.
M Emma! All right then, fine. I'll tell you. I'm scared that I'll ruin *Solar Wind* by writing something rubbish that everyone hates.
E What?
M I'm scared, Em.
E Do you remember that time you wrote that short story for the school newspaper?
M Not really.
E Oh, come on, you do so. What was it called … ? Um …
M *Solar Breeze*.
E It wasn't, was it? Anyway, you write that story, the whole school loves it, Mum and Dad are beside themselves with pride, as are you, and Miss Hall suggests you enter the National Short Story competition. Do you remember?
M Yes.
E And what a hoo-ha that was! You were entering the competition, you weren't entering the competition, you were, you weren't. Mum, Dad and I had to endure listening to at least 30 versions of it – sometimes even in the middle of the night. We all went without sleep for about three weeks.
M Emma, look, I know where you're going with this, OK.
E Good! And in the end, you won first prize! And I was so proud of you, Max.
M You were?
E Yeah! Because the thing about my big brother is … he always pulls it off. Am I right, or am I right?
M You're right.
E And tell me, how did you leave it with Sara?
M Sara? I guess I overreacted there too, if I'm honest. Well, I had a bit of a go at her, actually. Stormed off … I know what you're thinking. Right again. I'd better ring and apologise.
E Yeah, I think you'd better do that, Max.

b ▶ 3.41 Ask students why Max mentions Sara (Emma is behaving like her and trying to organise his life). Tell students to watch or listen again and decide what Emma and Max agree about. Play Part 2 of the video or the audio recording again. Check answers as a class.

Answers
1 no 2 yes 3 yes

dead (adv., C1) – extremely

be out of your league – be too good or too expensive for you

worked up – upset or very excited about something

lose it – lose control of your behaviour

do sth about sth – take action to deal with something

whine – if you whine, you repeatedly complain in a way that is annoying to other people

be beside yourself with sth (C2) – experience a powerful emotion

hoo-ha – an occasion when there is too much interest in or discussion about something that is not important

go without sth (C2) – not have something that you usually have

where sb's going with sth – said during a long monologue, speech etc. to say what the speaker's eventual point will be

pull sth off – succeed in doing something difficult or unexpected

have a go at sb – attack/criticise somebody verbally during a disagreement

storm off – leave a situation angrily and without saying goodbye

c **Language in context** *Challenging*

Ask students how Max feels when he says these expressions (angry, aggressive). Tell students to say the expressions in other words. They could use the context in the audioscript on SB p.184 to help them. Check answers as a class.

Answers
1 Say what you really mean.
2 Stop interfering in my life.

 EXTRA ACTIVITY

There are a large number of idiomatic and informal expressions in this script. If students are interested, look at the expressions in the Vocabulary support box together with the script on SB pp.184–5. Ask students to find and underline the expressions, and then play the audio/video again and stop it after each phrase. Elicit the meaning of each expression.

d Ask students why they think Emma mentions the *Solar Breeze* episode (to make Max feel more confident). Ask students if the conversation ends better or worse than the one with Sara (better). Put students into pairs to discuss the questions. Compare ideas as a class.

Suggested answers
Students' own answers
calmer, better, more positive (about his next book), sorry/guilty

 EXTRA ACTIVITY

Tell students to write the last line of Max's short story *Solar Breeze*. Give some examples, e.g. *The breeze had gone but the wind was coming … .* Put students into groups to compare their last lines and say which one is the most interesting.

4 USEFUL LANGUAGE Apologising and admitting fault

a Ask students why the satnav might want to apologise (e.g. it has guided the driver into the sea / a river). Ask students which part of its words are apologetic and which admit fault.

Answers
apologetic: I do apologise
admits fault: it was my fault entirely

b ▶ **3.42** Tell students to complete the expressions. Play the recording for them to check. Drill the expressions.

Answers
1 inexcusable
2 line
3 tactful
4 came
5 right
6 guess

c Tell students to imagine that they were in a café and they shouted at a waiter because he brought white sugar not brown sugar. Ask students what expression from 4b they would use afterwards. Tell students to put expressions from 4b with the situations and say that more than one could be appropriate. Check answers as a class.

Suggested answers
a 4
b 5
c 3
d 4, 6
1, 2 possible for all

d Ask students if they think Sara is expecting Max's call and how she might react. Put students into pairs to plan and practise the phone call using the functional language. For variety, you could ask some students to behave as a relieved Sara, an unforgiving Sara, an indifferent Sara, etc. Choose several pairs to role-play the call in front of the whole class.

5 SPEAKING

▶ Divide the class into pairs and assign A and B roles. Student As read the Conversation 1 card on SB p.136 and Student Bs the Conversation 1 card on SB p.131. Student A starts the conversation. They then both read their Conversation 2 cards and Student B starts. Encourage students to use the functional language for apologising and admitting fault on SB p.87 and monitor. As part of the class feedback, ask students if they have ever been in any situations like this.

ADDITIONAL MATERIAL

▶ Workbook 7C
▶ Photocopiable activities: Pronunciation p.265
▶ Unit Progress Test
▶ Personalised online practice

7D Skills for Writing
It may result in improved cooperation

At the end of this lesson, students will be able to

- listen to professionals talking about the ingredients of a good team while using words and expressions appropriate to that sphere
- discuss characteristics of a good team, personality attributes and team-working strategies
- use devices for linking, highlighting and exemplifying ideas in writing
- write a formal proposal on the role and value of a team-building activity

OPTIONAL LEAD-IN

Books closed. Divide the class into groups of five. Tell students that the group is going to make a profit today. Tell them you will give them £25 or the local equivalent. They have five minutes to plan how they will use the money to make a profit. They should involve every person in the group in the plan. Stop students after five minutes. A speaker for each group explains the plans for the money. The class votes on the plan most likely to make the most profit. As feedback, ask students to describe how their group decided what to do and if they were happy with their plan.

1 LISTENING and SPEAKING

a Ask students what things are better to do alone and what things in teams. Put students into pairs to look at the pictures and answer the questions. Check ideas as a class.

Suggested answers
1 a team which is office-based, maybe quite traditional as leader is sitting at head of table
2 students or colleagues working closely, sharing information
3 two sports teams, friendly, competitive
4 colleagues working side-by-side, probably on different tasks, but cooperating to get a job done
Students' own answers

b Put students into groups to discuss the questions. Take feedback as a class.

c 3.43 Ask students what kind of teamwork might be important in an insurance company. Play the recording for students to listen to each speaker in turn and make notes for each question. If necessary, pre-teach *be/get caught up in sth* (C2) (become involved in something, often without wanting to) and *pull together* (work hard as a group in order to achieve something). Check answers as a class.

Answers
Claudio
1 Masha
2 stubborn, aggressive, too talkative, inflexible, no sense of humour
3 nice, good ideas, creative
Masha
1 Sam
2 funny habits, pays too much attention to detail, doesn't start a project until he understands everything about it, calls things to a halt / slows things down unnecessarily if something doesn't make sense to him, inflexible
3 old-fashioned, sweet, precise, asks the right questions, thinks ahead and predicts possible problems
Sam
1 Claudio
2 reads newspaper online when he should be working, strange, doesn't say a lot in meetings, seems to be laughing at colleagues, lazy, not sincere
3 quiet, says things worth listening to, good at solving problems, clever
Vicki
4 She thinks they aren't pulling together and can't communicate well with each other. She thinks they need to do a team-building course or something similar.

Audioscript

CLAUDIO Deep down, Masha is a nice person. I mean, if we go and have a coffee together and just talk about everyday things we get on just fine. But in meetings she really winds me up. She's the most stubborn person I know. What annoys me is that once she gets hold of an idea she won't let it go. She'll defend her idea and get quite aggressive about it. And sometimes she just won't stop talking and I'm sitting in a meeting and inside myself I'm saying 'Stop talking now, please!' Admittedly, she does have really good ideas sometimes. In fact, she's very creative, but she doesn't seem to understand that there can be other ways of looking at things. What she needs to do is lighten up – get a sense of humour. In this job, what you need more than anything else is the ability to laugh at yourself.

MASHA There's something a bit old-fashioned about Sam that I find very sweet. It's the thing I like about him the most. He has lots of funny little habits, like every morning he has coffee and a chocolate biscuit at exactly 9:45 am. It's always the same kind of biscuit, and only ever one. The trouble is that this kind of precision affects the way he works. His attention to detail is incredible, but it's a bit of a handicap. What frustrates me is the way he absolutely refuses to start work on a project until he understands absolutely everything about it. And then when a project is underway, if there's something that he thinks doesn't make sense, he'll call everything to a halt until he thinks it's sorted out. Sometimes it's just so unnecessary, and it really slows things down. But sometimes the question he is asking is the right one to ask. And I have to admit, he's really good at predicting where problems might come up. But I just wish he was a bit more flexible.

SAM I sit next to Claudio in the office. The one thing I really appreciate about him is he's quiet. I don't like working next to someone who talks all the time. However, I know for a fact that when it looks like Claudio is really concentrating on something, he's reading a newspaper online. I can see his screen. I don't really think he should be doing that. And in team meetings I find him a bit strange. What unsettles me is the fact he doesn't say a lot. He spends a lot of time sitting there looking bored or with a cynical smile on his face. I sometimes get the feeling that he's … well, that he's laughing at the rest of us. Still, when he does say something, it's usually worth listening to. Sometimes, when I notice a problem in a project, it'll be Claudio who comes up with the solution. Vicki, our team leader, she likes that. I always get the feeling that Claudio's her pet. He is clever, but I think he's a bit lazy and I'm not altogether sure he's sincere.

VICKI I'm really going to have to do something about the team I manage. We're supposed to be working on projects that improve business processes, but I feel like we spend more time managing each other than the project. We're not pulling together as a team. Team meetings have become really … painful – there's no other word for it. The main reason why this is happening is that they just can't seem to communicate well with each other. Masha talks all the time and wants everything done her way. Sam interrupts and goes off on tangents, and Claudio just sits there looking as though everything were beneath him. I mean they all have their strengths. Masha's a great ideas person, and Sam is brilliant at anticipating problems. And Claudio is the ultimate fixer – and he has a good sense of humour. But each individual is caught up in their own agenda. What we need to do is some kind of team-building course or something.

d ▶ **3.43** Ask students who they think sounds the most difficult person in the team. Tell students to complete the summaries with words from the box, using dictionaries if necessary. Then play the recording again for students to listen and check. Ask students to look at the audioscript on SB p.185 if necessary. Concept check some of the expressions, e.g. *makes (you) feel uncomfortable* (unsettles); *something which presents a problem* (bit of a handicap).

Answers
1 winds up
2 lighten up
3 attention to detail; bit of a handicap
4 unsettles; cynical smile
5 goes off on tangents
6 beneath him
7 caught up in their own agenda

💡 FAST FINISHERS

Ask fast finishers to add more phrasal verbs ending with *up* to the two in the box (*wind up, lighten up*), e.g. *bring up* (to care for a child until he or she is an adult); *cheer up* (to start to feel happier).

---

e 💬 Tell students to cover up d, look at the personality attributes and remember who has them, e.g. *pays a lot of attention to detail* (Sam). If necessary, pre-teach *tolerable* (of a quality that is acceptable, although certainly not good). Students rank the personality attributes according to their acceptability. They then compare their order with a partner and justify their ranking. Take feedback as a class.

2 READING

a Ask students if they have any experience of team building. Elicit how it is done or how they imagine it is done. Tell students to read the proposal and say why Vicki has chosen The Interpersonal Gym and how she thinks it will work. If necessary, pre-teach *absenteeism* (when people are not at work or at school when they should be) and *negotiate (obstacles)* (deal with something difficult, in this case things that are in the way). Check answers as a class.

Suggested answers
TIG have 12 years' experience in providing personal development programmes. Team-building programmes are their speciality, with games and problem-solving activities which will appeal to all team members. The programme is likely to increase sales, lower absenteeism and increase profits.
Her team will improve their active listening and collective decision-making. They will have effective professional development resulting in increased job satisfaction amongst team members.

b 💬 Put students into groups to discuss how Claudio, Masha and Sam will each react to the news. Students should base their ideas on the personality attributes of each person. Take feedback as a class.

3 WRITING SKILLS Proposals; Linking: highlighting and giving examples

a Ask students what the difference between a report and a proposal is (a report looks back, a proposal forward). Tell students to complete the headings in the proposal. Check answers as a class.

Answers
Training <u>needs</u>
The TIG programme – what they <u>do</u>
<u>Benefits</u> to our business

b Tell students to underline the phrases starting with *I* in the report and tick all the reasons for them. Ask students if the proposal is formal or neutral, giving an example (e.g. *to outline plans*), and explain why Vicki chooses this style. Check answers as a class and refer students to the Writing Tip.

Answers
I currently manage; I have identified; I believe; I believe; I hope
✓ to introduce her opinions
✓ to be more persuasive
formal, because the report is for senior management

💡 EXTRA ACTIVITY

Ask students to rewrite these parts of the proposal in a more relaxed style as if Vicki was writing to colleagues:

I currently manage (I'm in charge of at the moment)

The need for greater interpersonal awareness within a team framework has become apparent. (It's clear to me that we need to improve our ability to understand and communicate with each other as a team.)

activities that are likely to appeal to all team members (activities that everyone on the team will like)

from organisations similar to our own (from companies like ours)

therefore lower absenteeism (so fewer people missing work).

You could also do the activity the other way around: give students the suggested answers and ask students to underline the formal equivalents in the proposal.

---

c Students look at the highlighted words and phrases and match them with their functions. Check answers as a class.

Answers
1 For instance
2 As detailed in; as demonstrated by
3 Specifically; namely
4 in particular

d Ask students to complete the paragraph and add the words and phrases to their answers in 3c.

Answers
3d
1 especially
2 such
3 as shown by
3c
1 give an example: such as
2 give evidence: as shown by
4 highlight an individual thing: especially

e ▶ Students complete the exercises in Writing Focus 7D on SB p.173. Students read the table. Refer to the Language notes if necessary. Check answers to Exercise a and monitor Exercise b. After Exercise c, students could compare their achievements in English and discuss how to improve further. Tell students to go back to SB p.89.

Answers

a 1 For instance / Specifically
2 as demonstrated by / as shown by / such as / namely
3 as demonstrated by / as shown by
4 especially / in particular
5 such as / namely / especially / in particular
6 For instance / Specifically
7 as demonstrated by / as shown by / such as / namely / for instance

b, c Students' own answers

📖 LANGUAGE NOTES

Especially (one of the top 50 misspelt words in English) means particularly / in particular and *specifically* means for a particular reason/purpose or restricted, not general, in nature: *It was ~~a specifically~~ an especially warm welcome. The target market is specifically ~~especially~~ female.* A common mistake made by students is to use *especially* at the beginning of a sentence: *~~Especially,~~ In particular, the views were outstanding.*

---

4 WRITING

a Ask students if they think they have the skills to lead a team. Put students into pairs to choose one of the teams and discuss ways of helping them. Take feedback as a class for each team.

b ▶ Tell students to read the two programmes on SB p.136. Ask them to discuss the advantages and disadvantages of each with their partner and choose one. Take feedback on the advantages and disadvantages of each programme as a class. Tell students to go back to SB p.89.

c Students write their proposals individually. Tell them to read the prompts, and to use a structure with headings like Vicki's and formal language.

d 💬 Students read their partner's proposal, decide whether they will agree and tell their partner why.

🔄 LOA TIP REVIEW AND REFLECT

- When you give feedback on writing, encourage students to reflect on the process involved by writing multiple drafts, with each draft an improvement on the previous version. This is particularly helpful for weaker students.

- Students read one another's proposals and provide the first feedback, based on how persuasive the proposal is. Students rewrite their proposals.

- You give feedback on the content, including whether all the prompts in 4c have been covered, and the style. Students rewrite their proposals.

- Finally, give feedback on the language: mistakes and suggestions for more complex and descriptive language. Students now produce a final version.

- Ask students to compare their first and final proposals. They should see a clear development in content and language.

- The process of rewriting is smoother if students can use computers to edit and make changes.

💡 EXTRA ACTIVITY

For homework, ask students to imagine the training took place and write a report about its success. Tell students to look back at SB pp.28–29 for the structure of a report and useful language. When they have finished their reports, students give a mini-presentation to the class about their main findings and recommendations.

ADDITIONAL MATERIAL

▶ Workbook 7D

UNIT 7
Review and extension

1 GRAMMAR

a Write this sentence on the board and ask students how each modal makes the meaning different: *Jody should / must have told her.* (should = it was a good idea for Jody to tell her but he didn't; must = Jody definitely told her). Tell students to choose the correct options in the sentences. Check answers as a class.

Answers
1 will   2 couldn't   3 that flying cars will
4 may   5 must   6 should

b Write this sentence on the board and ask students to reorder it beginning with *It*: *with wanted to It who you speak I was* (It was you who I wanted to speak with.). Tell students to complete the sentences. Check as a class.

Answers
1 What
2 was
3 happened
4 It
5 All
6 not
7 to
8 only

2 VOCABULARY

a Say to students: *My uncle is weak-sighted and can't read the newspaper without his glasses.* and ask them to correct you (short-sighted). Tell students to correct the mistakes. Check answers as a class.

Answers
1 warm-hearted
2 back-breaking
3 absent-minded
4 mind-boggling
5 light-hearted
6 heart-breaking

> ### ⓦ FAST FINISHERS
> Ask fast finishers to identify the compound adjective in the sentences that can be correct in a different context and to give its meaning (*light-headed* = if you feel light-headed, you feel weak and as if you are going to lose your balance).

b Go through the words in the box and elicit the noun forms. Tell students to replace the words in italics with the noun forms. Check as a class.

Answers
1 nervousness
2 innovation
3 rudeness
4 collaboration
5 optimism
6 Selfishness
7 liberation

3 WORDPOWER *self-*

a ▶ 3.44 Concept check the adjectives in the box: *Which two are negative?* (self-centred, self-satisfied). *Which two are opposites?* (self-sacrificing, self-centred). *If a country is self-sufficient, does it need imports?* (no). *Someone who doubts herself all the time needs to be more …* (self-confident). *How is 'self-aware' different from 'self-conscious'?* (If you're self-aware, you have good knowledge and judgement about yourself. You concentrate on your own thoughts and don't worry what other people think about you. If you're self-conscious, you're nervous or uncomfortable because you know what people think about you or your actions.). Tell students to replace the words in italics in the sentences with the adjectives. Play the recording to check.

Answers
1 self-confident   2 self-aware   3 self-centred
4 self-satisfied   5 self-sacrificing   6 self-sufficient

b Tell students to read the text quickly and say what happened to change the person's life (a self-help course). Ask students to complete the text with adjectives from 3a. Check as a class.

Answers
1 self-confident   2 self-sufficient   3 self-centred
4 self-satisfied   5 self-sacrificing   6 self-aware

> ### ⓦ EXTRA ACTIVITY
> Put students into groups to discuss which of these self-help books they would read:
>
> *Improve your memory* (Get great marks in tests and never forget a face again!)
>
> *How to say no* (Stop people taking advantage of you)
>
> *Sleep less, work and play more* (Techniques to sleep less and still feel fresh)
>
> *Get in perfect shape in 30 days* (Ideal when a holiday is coming up)
>
> *Freedom from the Net* (End internet addiction and get a real life).
>
> Ask students if they would recommend any of these books to people they know.

c 🗩 Use an example of a well-known person all the students will have an opinion about and ask students to describe him or her using the adjectives in 3a. Give students time to write adjectives for each category of people. Put students into pairs to discuss their ideas. Take feedback as a class.

▶ Photocopiable activities: Wordpower p.247

> ### 🔵 LOA REVIEW YOUR PROGRESS
>
> Students look back through the unit, think about what they've studied and decide how well they did. Students work on weak areas by using the appropriate sections of the Workbook, the Photocopiable worksheets and the Personalised online practice.

UNIT 8
Body and health

UNIT CONTENTS

G GRAMMAR
- Gerunds and infinitives (simple, perfect, continuous; active and passive; uses)
- Conditionals (real and unreal, mixed)

V VOCABULARY
- Sleep: *be a light sleeper, be fast asleep, be restless, be wide awake, drift off to sleep, drop off to sleep, have a nap, not sleep a wink, oversleep, sleep like a log, suffer from insomnia, toss and turn*
- Ageing and health: *acne, arthritis, blotches, cardiovascular exercise, deteriorating eyesight, fine lines, freckles, glowing complexion, grey around the temples, heart trouble, inevitable part of ageing, moisturising, plastic surgery, poor circulation, rash, show your age, clear/dry/firm/oily/saggy/smooth skin, spots, strengthening and toning exercises, thinning hair, tighten/plump the skin, tooth loss, varied and balanced diet, weekly facials, weight loss, wrinkles, yellowing teeth*
- Language in context: Cause, origin and effect; Expressions with *fair*
- Wordpower: *and: bits and pieces; far and away; far and wide; part and parcel; sick and tired; wear and tear*

P PRONUNCIATION
- Main stress
- Tone: adding information
- Intonation in implied questions

GETTING STARTED

⚲ OPTIONAL LEAD-IN

Books closed. Put students into groups and read out the questions in this quiz (the correct answers are underlined).

1 Aged 72, Oscar Swahn won a silver medal in the 1920 Olympics in what sport?

   A <u>shooting</u>   B bowling   C golf

2 How old was Martina Navratilova when she won her last major tennis title?

   A 39   B <u>49</u>   C 59

3 In what film was 87-year-old Gloria Stuart nominated for an Oscar?

   A <u>*Titanic*</u>   B *Life Is Beautiful*   C *Jurassic Park*

4 What job was American Irving Kahn doing at the age of 108?

   A cleaning   B teaching   C <u>investment banking</u>

 UNIT OBJECTIVES

At the end of this unit, students will be able to:
- understand articles and interviews reflecting on the impact of historical changes in society on patterns of behaviour and the possibility of extended life expectancy, and evaluate different points of view and respond
- understand opinion and attitudes and follow broadcast material including in-depth interviews and detailed descriptions of unusual patterns of behaviour, lifestyle and diets and note the details
- use a range of lexis accurately to: describe sleeping habits and the superficial and health effects of ageing; discuss opinions on life expectancy and personal and societal attitudes to ageing
- understand and use a range of expressions to take part in negotiations over price and other terms of an agreement
- write well-organised and persuasive promotional material for the home page of a business

a Give students one minute to think about their answers to the questions before talking about the photo as a class. If you wish, give students information from the Culture notes below. As a class, take feedback on questions 1–3 and write the list of activities from 4 on the board. Ask the class to categorise the activities listed according to different criteria, e.g. for active people like the woman, for people with restricted movement.

🌍 CULTURE NOTES

This photo shows German Johanna Quaas, born in 1925 and the world's oldest active gymnast according to *Guinness World Records*, with her husband and trainer Gerhard. Johanna's first gymnastics competition was in 1934 and she still trains every day and takes part in competitions. Johanna has been a successful trainer and trainer-trainer herself, and millions have followed her workouts on YouTube.

b Put students into male/female pairs if possible to role-play a conversation between Johanna and her trainer/husband. Ask some pairs to repeat their conversation in front of the class.

c Put students into groups to discuss the question. Take feedback as a class.

⚲ EXTRA ACTIVITY

Ask students to write a speech bubble for the woman, e.g. 'What, 100 more?!', 'It's your turn next!', 'This isn't much of a date!' The class votes for the best speech bubble.

8A It's no use trying to go to sleep

At the end of this lesson, students will be able to:

- discuss the role and value of sleep and tips for helping with sleeplessness
- use different forms of gerunds and infinitives in complex sentences
- read an article and draw reasonable conclusions from the information presented
- listen to multiple speakers discussing sleep patterns and discuss the consequences of sleep patterns on everyday life
- use a range of expressions for discussing sleep patterns and identify the main stress

OPTIONAL LEAD-IN

Books closed. Tell students to write down how many hours in a typical day they spend on these activities:

- eating
- fitness
- sleeping
- travelling
- other (activities not mentioned).

- entertainment
- household tasks
- studying
- working

(the total should be 24!)

Tell students to compare with a partner. Ask students how much this pattern differs from two years ago and how they expect it to change in the future.

1 SPEAKING and READING

a Ask students how they slept last night and how many hours they slept. Put students into pairs to discuss the questions. Take feedback as a class.

b ▶ **3.45** Play the recording for students to listen and check their answers. You may wish to pre-teach these expressions: *go without sth* (C2) (not have something that you need), *get by on sth* (survive/manage with only this). Ask students what the longest they have gone without sleep is.

Suggested answers

1 We don't know for certain but there are theories, such as conserving energy and allowing the body, especially the brain, to repair and restore itself.
2 one third
3 11 days is the longest recorded time
4 people who sleep 6.5–7.5 hours may live the longest; 16–20 hours

Audioscript

PRESENTER We all sleep at night, but it's surprising how little most people know about sleep. We talked to sleep researcher Jonathan Wilson, to find out what science has to tell us about sleep. Jonathan, first of all, all animals including humans need sleep – but … why do we need it?

JONATHAN Well that's a surprisingly difficult question to answer. The simple answer is, we don't really know. But there are several theories about it. One is that it helps us to conserve our energy during the period when it's least useful to search for food, and another is that sleep provides a time when the body can repair and restore itself, and it seems this is especially important for the brain. One thing we know for sure is that we do need to sleep. Most people sleep for about 8 hours, which means we sleep for one third of our lives – so on average that's 25 years spent asleep. The other thing we know is you can't go for too long without sleep – it simply isn't possible. The longest recorded time that anyone has stayed awake continuously is 11 days.

P So what's the ideal length of time to sleep? Is it eight hours?

J Not necessarily. Again we don't know for sure, but research suggests that people who sleep six-and-a-half to seven-and-a-half hours live the longest. So it seems the popular idea that we need eight hours' sleep isn't really true and many people can easily get by on only six hours a night. Babies need most sleep, of course – about 16 to 20 hours a day for new-born babies, and that gradually decreases as they get older.

EXTRA ACTIVITY

Put students into pairs to tell each other about a dream they had recently. Give students these interpretations of things in dreams:

- family and friends = people you are worried about
- strangers = opportunities or threats
- animals = adventure or danger
- running/travelling = trying to find a solution to a problem
- eating/drinking = searching for new experiences
- work = pressure and/or responsibility.

Ask them to explain their dreams to each other and tell them to make up their own interpretations of things not mentioned.

c Ask students to look at the picture and say how they think the mother gets the baby to sleep. Put students into pairs to decide what they think each tip involves, read the article and match the headings with the tips. If necessary, pre-teach *catchy* (pleasing and easy to remember) and *silver lining* (said to emphasise that every difficult or unpleasant situation has some advantage). Check as a class.

Answers

A Compile a playlist
B Acknowledge distractions
C Everybody out!
D It is as it is

d Put students into pairs to discuss the question. Take feedback as a class. Ask students what they think the best tip is and if they have any tips of their own.

2 GRAMMAR Gerunds and infinitives

a Books closed. Write this mixed-up sentence from the article on the board and ask students to unscramble it: *to frustrating be sleep trying get very can to* (Trying to get to sleep can be very frustrating.). Ask students what forms the three verbs are in: gerund: *trying*; to + infinitive: *to get*; infinitive without to: *be*. Tell students to put the highlighted phrases into the three categories.

Answers

a 4 it's time   5 the best way
b 3 may as well get   6 'd better
c 2 it's no use   7 There's no point in

b Write on the board: *If I misbehaved, I used _____ to bed without any supper.* and ask students which form a–d of *send* would fit the sentence (a, *to be sent*). Tell students to match the verb forms in bold with a–d. Check answers as a class.

Answers

a 2   b 4   c 1   d 3

c Write these two sentences on the board and ask students what the difference in meaning is: *I'd like to know. I'd like to have known.* (*I'd like to know* = Tell me now; *I'd like to have known* = Why didn't you tell me before?). Put students into pairs to look at the examples and tell you what the difference is. Check answers as a class.

Answers

1 There is no definite difference in meaning between a and b, but the perfect form of the gerund in b stresses that he didn't say anything before he got out of bed, whereas in a he didn't say anything either before or during getting out of bed.
2 a The simple active infinitive makes it clear that the person sleeps well in general.
  b The perfect active infinitive makes it clear that the person has slept well on this particular occasion.
3 a The present active gerund makes it clear the person likes reading to herself in bed in general.
  b The present passive gerund makes it clear that the person likes other people reading to her in bed in general.
4 a The simple active infinitive makes it clear when the person wants to wake up but doesn't make it clear how or who is going to wake the person up.
  b The simple passive infinitive makes it clear that the person wants someone else to wake them up.

d Write this sentence on the board and encourage students to think of different ways of filling the gap: *I hate ____ just before I go to bed.* Ask students to complete the sentences in the exercise on their own and then compare with other students. Take feedback as a class.

e ▶ (▶)**3.46–3.47** Students read the information in Grammar Focus 8A on SB p.152. Play the recording where indicated and ask students to listen and repeat. Students then complete the exercises. Check answers as a class. Tell students to go back to SB p.93.

Answers (Grammar Focus 8A SB p.152)

a 2 Being picked   3 waiting   4 having misled
  5 to have been visiting   6 not to have known   7 to have
  8 complaining   9 to forget   10 describing
b 2 ~~to have fallen~~ falling   3 ~~to go~~ going
  4 ~~affecting~~ being affected   5 ~~carry out~~ to carry out
  6 ~~To not sleep~~ Not sleeping / Not having slept   7 ~~to feel~~ feel
  8 ~~being taken~~ taking   9 ~~doing~~ to be done   10 ~~being~~ to be
  11 ~~to be spending~~ to be spent

> ## ⊙ CAREFUL!
>
> Some students wrongly use an active gerund rather than a passive gerund: *My colleagues have even noticed instances of equipment mishandling.* (Correct form = *My colleagues have even noticed instances of equipment **being mishandled**.*). Another typical error is to use the simple infinitive rather than the continuous infinitive: *Please consider that you seem to break the terms of the contract.* (Correct form = *Please consider that you seem **to be breaking** the terms of the contract.*).

3 READING

a Ask students if they know any myths about health, e.g. *you can't drink too much water.* Put students into pairs to read the title, agree on two implications and then check with the text. If necessary, pre-teach some of the words from the Vocabulary support box.

Suggested answers

sleeping eight hours a night may be unnatural for humans
segmented sleep may be the human body's natural preference

> ## 📖 VOCABULARY SUPPORT
>
> *regulate* – control something so that it happens in a particular way
>
> *settle into a pattern* – reach and remain in a certain pattern
>
> *seminal (paper, work, etc.)* – (formal) containing important new ideas; influential
>
> *a wealth of sth* (C2) – a large amount of something good
>
> *unearth* – to discover information after carefully searching
>
> *a surge in sth* (C1) – a sudden and great increase in something
>
> *dwindle* – become (gradually) smaller in size/amount

b Ask students if this statement would be a reasonable conclusion from the article: *Roger Ekirch is an expert on the topic.* (yes, his book took 16 years of research and he found more than 500 references to a segmented sleep pattern). Put students into pairs to decide which statements are reasonable conclusions. Check as a class.

Answers

1 ✓   2 ✗ (because there wasn't street lighting; legitimate activity at night didn't happen until the 17th century)   3 ✓   4 ✓   5 ✗ (but relaxing during the waking period between sleeps in the past could have been a natural way of regulating stress)

c Language in context *Cause, origin and effect*

Ask students to look at *drawn from* and ask what it describes (a research paper) and what the origins were (16 years of research). Ask students what the synonym is (taken from) and why *drawn from* is preferred (it is more idiomatic and suggests selective reading of the research). Tell students to work out what the rest of the highlighted phrases mean in a similar way and to match the expressions with the synonymous phrases. Check answers as a class.

Answers

1 1 played an important part in   2 have roots in; be at the root of
  3 filtered down to   4 drawn from   5 attributes
2 *drawn from* suggests careful selection from a large body of research
  filtered down to shows how thinking about sleep patterns gradually changed over the course of time
  attributes highlights, in a more formal way, that this is Ekirch's opinion of where the changes come from
  have roots in and *be at the root of* are more colourful metaphors that improve the style
  play an important part in is a fixed phrase which improves style and precise meaning, but *be an important factor in* would work equally well.

d 💬 Ask students if they often wake up in the middle of the night and can't get back to sleep. Put students into groups to discuss the questions. Take feedback as a class.

> 💡 **FAST FINISHERS**
>
> Tell fast finishers to think of substitutes for *Lying awake* as the subject of the final sentence of the article, e.g. *Eating red meat could be good for you*, and compare ideas.

---

4 LISTENING and VOCABULARY Sleep

a 💬 Ask students if they think age or gender or anything else makes you more likely to wake up at night. Tell students to look at the speech bubbles and predict what each person will say.

b ▶ **3.48** Play the recording for students to check their ideas.

Suggested answers

Matt goes to bed about 10 or 11 but wakes up, restless, in the night. He doesn't want to disturb his wife so he goes out and takes photos. Last night he took some photos of a storm.

Saba wakes up in the night and goes to a yoga studio. There's a group of about 20 people who also do this. Sometimes her husband goes too.

Bernie is an artist. When he wakes up in the night he remembers the images from his dream and paints them, which he finds therapeutic.

Iain used to live in Papua New Guinea where he lived in a remote village. They'd go to bed after sunset and wake up in the night. Somebody would start a fire and sometimes they'd eat sweet potatoes.

Audioscript

PRESENTER Good afternoon. Well, some of you saw the article on our website last week. It explained how an eight-hour sleep may not be good for your health after all. And how people used to have what scientists call 'segmented sleep', which means they had two sleeps every night, not one. Well, we've had lots of people calling in to tell us that they do, in fact, sleep in two separate chunks and they've been filling us in on what they get up to at night. First of all, we've got Matt from Brighton on the line. Hi Matt … so, tell us what you do at night.

MATT Yeah I usually go to sleep around ten or eleven. I naturally wake up at about one in the morning or two in the morning. I feel quite wide awake and restless. Then I get tired again at around three am, I drop off to sleep until about seven o'clock or so. My friends have always made fun of my sleep patterns. My wife used to force me to get out of bed 'cause I would lie there tossing and turning all night and I couldn't sleep a wink and it would disturb her.

P Right, of course! So what did you do about that?

M Well, I actually decided to use the time creatively. Now, I walk around Brighton taking pictures in the night. Some people might be a bit nervous walking around at er, y'know, two in the morning, but it is actually a really beautiful time to be out, you have the whole city to yourself and it is really, really great for taking photos. There was a wild storm last night and a full moon, so I was itching to get out there with my camera.

P Right, well thanks Matt. So that's one idea if you're suffering from insomnia – get out there and take some photos. Now, we have Saba on the line from Amsterdam, in the Netherlands. Saba?

SABA Yes, hi, how are you?

P You also get up at night?

S Yes. I've always been a light sleeper, I don't really sleep much um … I wake up at about four am every night to practise er yoga. I, I love yoga. Most of the time I do it at home but er once a week, I drive to this really great yoga studio in Amsterdam, and I practise there with about 20 other people and we've all really become friends now.

P So they all get up, every night?

S Yes, er, we all have er the same pattern now. Sometimes I even get my husband to join us, if he's having trouble sleeping. But most of the time he's fast asleep and doesn't even notice when I get up. He sleeps like a log.

P OK, so you just slip away and go to your yoga class.

S Well I try to, yes. Depending on how busy the day is.

P And now we have Bernie from Manchester.

BERNIE Hi.

P Tell us about your sleep pattern.

B Well um … I'm an artist, er if that's not too bold a claim. I also work as an art teacher. And the way it works for me is most nights I tend to wake up in the middle of the night, feeling great, wide awake, full of beans, feeling very creative. Er … and usually I have a very strong image in my head that I've usually got from a, a dream. And what I do is I get up, er, get my paints out and I paint a picture.

P A picture? From your dream?

B Yes, that's right. Yeah, most of my work comes from dreams. Quite literally I'm a surrealist, I suppose. Yeah, it helps me to deal with issues and um … work through things. I find the whole process of dreaming very therapeutic.

P Interesting. And then you go to sleep again.

B Yeah, I mean what tends to happen is I go back to bed, and then I'll drift off to sleep for a couple of hours. But I'm, I'm always up at seven o'clock. After all, I've got to teach at art college.

P You never oversleep?

B No, no, I'm always fine. Er sometimes I will have a nap later in the day – I'm not as young as I was – y'know, after lunch.

P Thank you, Bernie. So Bernie has three sleeps, two at night and one in the afternoon. I think I'll try that one myself. And lastly we have Iain, who grew up in Indonesia.

IAIN Hi there, yes.

P Iain, tell us about it.

I Ah yes, um … well it's quite interesting. I grew up among the Yali people in Papua, which is er, part of Indonesia. My parents lived in a very remote area. My mum was a medical worker and Dad was an anthropologist, and we all lived in a remote village. I lived there until I was 16, and er, as a child I used to camp and go hunting with my, my friends in the Yali tribe. We would go to bed more or less after sunset and we always woke up during the night.

P The whole village?

I Yes. Um … we'd, we'd hear people talking, y'know, someone would start a fire. Sometimes we would eat er sweet potato before going back to sleep until about five thirty or six. At home with my parents, y'know, I would get the regular eight-hour sleep, but with my friends, I slept like they did – it just seemed more natural.

P OK, thanks Iain, very interesting. And now we're going to listen to …

> 📖 **VOCABULARY SUPPORT**
>
> *fill sb in on sth* – tell somebody something they don't know, but want/need to know
>
> *get up to sth* (C2) – (informal) do something interesting, surprising, naughty, etc.
>
> *be itching to do sth* – want to do something as soon as possible
>
> *slip away* (C2) – leave without disturbing others
>
> *too bold a claim* – an overstatement
>
> *be full of beans* – have a lot of energy and enthusiasm
>
> *a surrealist* – an artist who creates works in which unusual/impossible things are happening
>
> *work through sth* – understand and resolve a problem using a gradual process

c Tell students to categorise the expressions, referring to the audioscript on SB p.185 if necessary. Check as a class.

Answers
1 be fast asleep; sleep like a log; oversleep
2 be wide awake; be a light sleeper; be restless; not sleep a wink; toss and turn; suffer from insomnia
3 drift off to sleep; drop off to sleep
4 have a nap

LOA TIP ELICITING

- Use the audioscript on SB p.185 to elicit the meaning of the target vocabulary and draw students' attention to patterns of usage.
- Write on the board the sentence from the recording: *Sometimes I will have a nap later in the day … after lunch.* Ask students if from the context *have a nap* means a short or long sleep (short) and which category it is (4).
- Ask students: *Why does Iain say 'have a nap' and not just 'nap'?* Elicit some answers, then write this sentence on the board and ask students to choose the best alternative: *I was so exhausted I slept / had a sleep for 16 hours.* (slept).
- Elicit that phrases with *have* often mean a shorter activity. Point out that *have a nap* is more common than the verb *nap*.

EXTRA ACTIVITY

Highlight the simile *sleep like a log* and tell students to complete these other verb + *like* + noun similes:

eat like a (horse)

sing like (a bird)

watch something like a (hawk)

sink like a (stone)

have a face like (thunder).

Ask students if these similes are the same in their language.

d **3.49 Pronunciation** Ask students to identify the stressed syllables in *I'm trying to get some sleep.* Play the recording for students to underline the stressed syllables in the expressions in the extract. Check answers as a class.

Answers
<u>get</u> out of <u>bed</u>
<u>toss</u>ing and <u>turn</u>ing
<u>could</u>n't <u>sleep</u> a <u>wink</u>

e **3.50** Tell students to underline the syllables they think will be stressed. Then play the recording for students to listen and check. Drill all the expressions in 4d and 4e.

Answers
having <u>trou</u>ble <u>sleep</u>ing
he's <u>fast</u> a<u>sleep</u>
<u>sleeps</u> like a <u>log</u>

f Ask students if they or someone they live with snores (demonstrate!) and if this is, or would be, a problem. Put students into groups to discuss the questions. Take feedback as a class.

5 SPEAKING

a Ask students which people would benefit most and least from segmented sleep patterns, e.g. parents with young children would need to plan something for them in the breaks between sleep. Put students into groups to discuss the impact of segmented sleep patterns, using the factors listed as prompts. Take feedback as a class.

b Ask students if exercise is generally better done when someone is feeling fresh and full of energy or tired and in need of a stimulus. Each group plans a typical 24-hour day for a student, making time for the activities listed and rationalising their choices.

c One student from each group presents the timetable to the class. Encourage students from the other groups to ask questions.

d The class votes on the most practical and the most original plans.

EXTRA ACTIVITY

Tell students to make a sleeping log for a week and record this information:

- when and how long they sleep each day
- how well they sleep each time (are they woken up by anything?)
- any special circumstances, e.g. stress, illness
- any dreams they have
- how satisfied they feel after their sleep.

At the end of the week, put students into groups to present their information to one another and compare. Encourage students to use the expressions in 4c during the discussion. Take feedback as a class.

ADDITIONAL MATERIAL

▶ Workbook 8A
▶ Photocopiable activities: Grammar p.215, Vocabulary p.235

8B Suppose you could live forever

At the end of this lesson, students will be able to:
- talk about the effects of ageing on health and lifestyle and discuss experiences of and attitudes to ageing using a variety of words and expressions related to the topic
- read an article about medical science and discuss the extent to which it reflects students' opinions
- use a range of real and unreal conditions, with different conjunctions, to hypothesise and express opinions
- listen to a conversation about dietary habits and make notes on the content
- use a downward tone to signal extra information when speaking

OPTIONAL LEAD-IN

Books closed. Play the Queen song *Who wants to live forever?* to the class. Ask students to say how they feel as they listen. If students are interested in the song, encourage them to watch the film from which it comes, *Highlander*, about someone immortal.

1 SPEAKING and VOCABULARY
Ageing and health

a Ask students if they believe in the saying *You're as old as you feel*. Ask students to tell you how they feel about the pictures and the quote.

b Ask students to look at the pictures in the article and say how they might be related to treatment. Tell students to check by reading the text and then discuss the questions with a partner. If necessary, pre-teach *pout* (push both lips forward), *slime* (a sticky liquid substance that is unpleasant to touch, such as the liquid produced by fish and snails) and *sting* (a sudden burning pain on your skin, etc.).

c Draw a face with wrinkles on the board to elicit *wrinkles*. Tell students to match *wrinkles* with the correct definition (4). Ask students to match the other highlighted words and phrases with the definitions. Check answers as a class.

Answers
1 facial
2 fresh
3 circulation
4 wrinkles
5 rashes
6 scars
7 firm
8 facial
9 glowing complexion
10 youthful glow
11 sagging

FAST FINISHERS

Tell fast finishers to draw a *tattoo* (a permanent image, pattern or word on the skin that is created by using needles to put colours under the skin) which they think would represent their character or interests. Put them together to compare and explain their tattoos.

d **3.51–3.52** Students complete the exercises in Vocabulary Focus 8B on SB p.165. Play the recording for students to listen to the words and phrases in Exercise a and to listen and check answers in Exercise c. Check answers to Exercise a, b and d as a class. After the discussion in Exercise e, take feedback as a class. Tell students to go back to SB p.96.

Answers (Vocabulary Focus 8B SB p.165)
a youthful skin: a glowing complexion; smooth skin; spots/acne; firm skin; clear skin
mature skin: saggy skin; dry skin; wrinkles / fine lines
all ages: freckles; a rash; blotches; oily skin
b 1 dry skin; wrinkles; freckles; blotches; a rash
2 a rash; blotches; spots
3 saggy skin; dry skin; wrinkles / fine lines
4 oily skin; spots/acne
5 wrinkles / fine lines
6 saggy skin; oily skin; wrinkles / fine lines; spots
7 a glowing complexion; smooth skin; firm skin; clear skin
c 1 e 2 i 3 a 4 d 5 h 6 f 7 b 8 c 9 g
d Anti-ageing treatments/effects: moisturising; weekly facials; injections; whitening; tighten; plump; plastic surgery
Superficial effects of ageing: showing his age; yellowing teeth; tooth loss; hair was thinning; greying
Health problems caused by ageing: eyesight is deteriorating; heart trouble; poor circulation; 's got arthritis
Healthy living: strengthening; toning; weight loss; regular cardiovascular exercise; eating a varied and balanced diet

CAREFUL!

A mistake students sometimes make is to use verbs like *avoid* instead of *prevent*: ~~The station has no proper filters to avoid any gas or oil leakage into the soil.~~ (Correct form = *The station has no proper filters to **prevent** any gas or oil leakage into the soil.*). Students also sometimes use *deteriorate* incorrectly: ~~The aim of the law is not to deteriorate the position of the employees.~~ (Correct form = *The aim of the law is not to **worsen** the position of the employees.*).

2 READING

a Ask students when they think old age starts and what the signs are. Put students into pairs to discuss the questions. Take feedback as a class.

b Give students time to read the interview and answer the question. Use the Vocabulary support box to help with vocabulary if necessary. Check as a class.

Answer
very likely, with the high-tech intervention de Grey is working on

gerontology – the study of old age

robust opinions – strong opinions which will not be changed

transcend sth – go far beyond the limits of sth

accumulation (n.), *accumulate* (v.) – (C2) increase in number (gradual), build up over time

the dawn of time – the beginning of time / human history

in principle – fundamentally, in a way relating to the basic rules

a losing battle – when you try hard to do something with no chance of success

longevity (C2) – long life

within striking distance – very near to getting or achieving something

conceivable – possible to imagine or to believe

eliminate (C1) – cause something not to exist

infant mortality (C2) – the death of children under one year of age

c Tell students to summarise the main point made about the topic in each paragraph. Check answers as a class. Ask students what they found most controversial in the article.

Suggested answers

2 they are the result of lifelong damage and they aren't fun
3 it's nonsense not to recognise the possibility of being able to do something about ageing
4 anti-ageing mechanisms in our body aren't perfect and can't fight ageing successfully
5 he thinks we will soon be able to prevent the physical problems of ageing, but the medical profession doesn't agree
6 people who are now in their 40s have a 30–40% chance of benefiting
7 historically, humans have naturally managed increases in the population by reducing the birth rate so it shouldn't be a problem or a reason not to do something about our health

d 💬 Ask students what the world might be like in 1,000 years. Put students into pairs to discuss the questions. Take feedback as a class.

3 GRAMMAR Conditionals

a Ask students to tick the comments which they agree with and then compare with a partner. If necessary, pre-teach *a ripe old age* (an approving way of describing how old someone is/was). Take feedback as a class.

b Give examples of sentences that illustrate a–c: a *If I stop eating fast food, I might live longer.* b *If I saw Aubrey de Grey in the street, I'd recognise him by his beard.* c *If I had been born a few years later, I'd have more chance of benefiting from future medical advances.* Tell students to match sentences 1–7 in 3a with a–c.

Answers

a 3; 6   b 1; 2; 4; 5; 7   c 2

- Students can find the logic of conditional sentences difficult, so use percentage values to check the real/unreal distinction.
- Write these percentages on the board: *0%; 1%; 50%; 100%*.
- Say: *If your body can't fight disease any more, you die.* and ask students what the chance of this happening is in percentage terms (100%, it's a reality).
- Say: *If I live to 70, I'll be satisfied.* and ask what the chance of this happening is (50%, a real possibility).
- Say: *Supposing everyone could live forever, the world would get very crowded.* and repeat the question (1%, very unlikely).
- Say: *Had I been born in 1900, that would make me a very old person today.* and repeat the question (0%, the past can't be changed).
- Write the four conditional sentences on the board with the correct percentage values and check that students understand that the sentences with high percentage values are real and those with low percentage values are unreal.

c Tell students that conditional sentences have two clauses, a condition and a (real or imaginary) result. The condition clause is dependent so it is introduced by a word or phrase (usually a conjunction). Ask students to underline the word or phrase that introduces each condition. Check answers as a class.

Answers

1 if   2 If   3 Assuming   4 Supposing   5 Had
6 as long as   7 Even if

d ▶ 🔊 **3.53–3.54** Students read the information in Grammar Focus 8B on SB p.153. Play the recording where indicated and ask students to listen and repeat. Students then complete the exercises. Check answers as a class. Tell students to go back to SB p.96.

Answers (Grammar Focus 8B SB p.153)

a 2 c/h   3 f   4 a   5 c/h   6 i   7 d   8 g   9 b   10 e
b 2 If I were you, I would have a word with her.
3 You can stay as long as you keep quiet.
4 If anyone is to blame, it's me.
5 Sheila would have been disappointed if nobody had come.
6 I will only agree on the condition that this is kept confidential.
7 Should I find out, you will be the first to know.
8 It won't take long, assuming we have everything we need.

👁 CAREFUL!

A common student mistake is to use *in case* and *as long as* instead of *if*: ~~We have not received any special requests, but I will let you know in case there are some.~~ (Correct form = *We have not received any special requests, but I will let you know **if** there are some.*); ~~We need to choose the same one as long as we want to spend the holiday together.~~ (Correct form = *We need to choose the same one **if** we want to spend the holiday together.*). Another mistake students sometimes make is to write *under condition* instead of *on condition*: ~~It can be done under condition that we find a suitable person for this position.~~ (Correct form = *It can be done **on condition** that we find a suitable person for this position.*).

e Say some sentences about yourself using the phrases and suggested topics. One statement shouldn't be true or you don't really believe it and the students have to guess which one, e.g. *As long as I can still run 5 km without stopping, I feel fit.* (true); *Had I not met my husband, I would never have become a teacher.* (false). Put students into pairs to do the activity. In feedback, ask students to tell the class the statements which weren't true.

4 LISTENING

a Tell students this joke: *I'm on a special seafood diet. I see food and I eat it.* Ask students if the joke has a serious side (making fun of strange diets). Put students into groups to discuss the questions. Take feedback as a class, being sensitive to students who may have weight issues.

b Tell students to read the text and answer the question. Encourage them to list five things they think you can eat on this diet. Take feedback as a class.

> **Suggested answer**
> low-calorie foods, e.g. vegetables, beans, rice, fish, oats, etc.

c ▶ **3.55** Ask students if they have ever eaten any of the food in the captioned photos or would like to. Play the recording for students to listen and answer the questions. If necessary, pre-teach *abstraction* (considering a subject generally; not based on real situations), *appetising* (making you want to eat), *meticulous* (C2) (very careful and with great attention to every detail), *onerous* (difficult to do or needing a lot of effort) and *stave sth/sb off* (keep an unwanted situation away, usually temporarily). Check answers as a class.

> **Answers**
> 1 He mixes it up in a food blender with tomato paste, olive oil and pepper. He usually has the mixture for breakfast.
> 2 two or three big meals and ten smaller meals between 8 am and 5 pm

Audioscript

PETER BOWES And are you that meticulous about what you eat?

MARTIN KNIGHT I am – I weigh and measure everything I eat and almost never eat out. I eat about, maybe, instead of like two or three big meals throughout the day, I eat maybe, like ten smaller meals – it kind of staves off hunger that way. This is what I actually usually eat – first meal of the day – only about 170 calories. So the first thing I'm going to do is this kale and er chard mixture I kind of made myself, it's put in the food blender and I weigh out 55 grams – that'll be 30 calories.

P And you do this every morning?

M I do. Right first thing and then every time I eat – which sounds pretty onerous, but actually isn't so bad.

P And you're getting, I assume, mostly carbohydrates from this?

M I'm going to add olive oil here, so in fact, it's going to be about 50 per cent fats.

P So what else do you have with this?

M OK, well … Let me finish measuring out the kale here first. I have to measure it to the … to the gram, there we have it – that's about 30 calories. Then I have sprouted oats, 16 grams, so that's er that's about 70. Then this tomato paste here, and … 33 grams of that, and … almost done now. There we go. And then finally, add some olive oil, that's 9.2. Now oils you have to measure to a tenth of a gram, and be that accurate. And we're there!

P Can I taste it?

M Ah … if you'd like to, yes!

P I have to say it doesn't look hugely tasty to me, or appetising.

M No, no I can understand that perfectly, yeah. Um, here's a spoon.

P Here goes.

M It's very colourful anyway.

P It's actually not that bad.

M No, with the oil, so, so the pepper in it er gives it more of a flavour … more of a flavour than you might think.

P The oil helps. Not so sure about so much tomato in my breakfast like this.

M Oh, OK! That's one of my favourite things …

P But, y'know, really not as dreadful as I had expected.

M Oh, OK! Surprised you, huh? I try and actually have a kind of window of eating – from about eight till five in the afternoon, so maybe like eight or nine hours, and then I don't eat outside of that.

P Ever go to a restaurant for lunch?

M Ah … not very often. Maybe a few times a year.

P How do you cope with that?

M Er, like socially? Well, um, either take um some nuts, which I weigh beforehand – um maybe 200 calories of that. Or, um, I drink some water or tea round there. There's always some fluid there you can drink. It's … it's not as bad as it might sound.

P As well as his extreme diet, Martin Knight lives a Zen-like, stress-free existence in California. He practises yoga, goes jogging and lifts weights in his garden. And he says extending his life isn't his primary concern.

M For me, it's more about quality of life, right here and now, the daily. I don't really think about the abstractions of living longer, although that … that might happen.

P You're 49 now. How do you feel?

M Um I feel really good. I feel as good as I did ten, twenty years ago – I don't really feel any different.

P Do you feel better in a sense since your diet has changed?

M In some ways actually I do – I have a steadier energy level throughout the day, when before I maybe kind of dipped in the afternoon – y'know, it's more of a steadier level. And … I think um you more kind of have a higher alertness too. When you have a little bit of hunger in the background, then you're more aware, more alive.

🌍 **CULTURE NOTES**

Zen-like refers to Zen, a form of Buddhism originally developed in Japan, that emphasises that religious knowledge is achieved through emptying the mind of thoughts and giving attention to only one thing, rather than by reading religious writings. It was especially popular in the West in the 1950s and 1960s.

---

d ▶ **3.55** Ask students how old Martin is (49). Ask them if they think Martin will need to change his diet as he gets older. Play the recording for students to listen again and make notes on the topics. Check answers as a class.

> **Suggested answers**
> 1 never eats out; when goes to a restaurant for lunch, a few times a year, takes 200 calories of nuts or drinks water or tea
> 2 doesn't look tasty, or appetising, colourful, tastes better than it looks, flavoured with pepper, too much tomato for Peter, but not Martin
> 3 Zen-like; stress-free; does yoga, goes jogging, lifts weights
> 4 primary concern is improving quality of life, doesn't think about living longer although might happen
> 5 good, better than before; steady energy level; more alert; more alive

---

💡 **FAST FINISHERS**

Ask fast finishers to list five other ways in which people could improve their quality of life, e.g. *switch off their mobile phones at the weekend*. Tell students to compare their ideas with another fast finisher.

e 💬 Ask students if Martin's example is a good one. Put students into groups to discuss the questions. Take feedback as a class.

f ▶️ **3.56** **Pronunciation** Ask students why Martin includes the information in bold (he is very precise about how much he eats). Play the recording for students to listen and identify the pitch and its function.

Answers

1 lower   2 adds information

g 💬 Tell students:

I heat up some soup, from a can. That doesn't take long, about ten minutes. I might have some toast, usually brown, with it. What meal is this?

Elicit the answer (lunch) and write the three sentences on the board. Ask students to identify the extra information and the pitch (lower). Put students into pairs and ask them to describe how they prepare a meal to each other, using a lower pitch to add information. Tell students to guess each other's meal.

> 💡 **EXTRA ACTIVITY**
>
> Tell students to record a short extract, 30 seconds maximum, of a native speaker talking before the next class. They could ask a foreign friend to speak for a short time or use material from films, talks, etc. Tell students to listen again, transcribe the words and then mark the pitch changes. Students then practise repeating the text using the same pitch choices. When students feel confident of their pronunciation, ask them to record themselves repeating the text. Tell students to bring the original and their own recording into class and play them to other students to compare.

5 SPEAKING

a 💬 Ask students how old they have to be to drive, get married, etc. in their country. Put students into pairs to discuss the question. Take feedback as a class.

b 💬 Put students into groups of five to discuss the statements.

c 💬 Ask groups to choose one student for each statement. Tell students to take turns to present their group's views and experiences on each statement to the class. The class votes on whether they agree or disagree with each statement.

> 💡 **EXTRA ACTIVITY**
>
> Read out these instructions and tell students to work out their life expectancy, with men starting at 70 years, women at 75 years:
>
> - Add 2 years for each grandparent who has lived over those ages.
> - Add 5 years if you exercise at least three times a week.
> - Take off 10 years if you smoke or drink alcohol too much.
> - Add 4 years if you have or are planning higher education.
> - Add 3 years if you are married or in a relationship.
> - Take off 4 years if you sleep less than six or more than eight hours a night.
> - Add 3 years if you have reached Advanced level in English.

ADDITIONAL MATERIAL

▶ Workbook 8B

▶ Photocopiable activities: Grammar p.216, Vocabulary p.236, Pronunciation p.266

At the end of this lesson, students will be able to:

- negotiate more effectively, agreeing on the price of a product or service, using a range of functional language
- use intonation to signal implied questions

OPTIONAL LEAD-IN

Books closed. Put students into groups to discuss in which situation they'd feel confident they could negotiate a better price:

- checking into a hotel where they are the only guest
- buying a car with cash
- waiting 45 minutes for their main course at a restaurant
- buying a dress which was in the shop window
- agreeing to pay three months' rent in advance.

Ask students as a class if they have experienced these or similar situations.

1 LISTENING

a 💬 Ask students whether they still get as excited about presents as when they were children. Put students into groups to discuss the questions. Take feedback as a class.

b 💬 Ask students if they think Max's present could have been a *Star Wars* model. Put students into pairs to think of their own ideas. Take feedback as a class.

c ▶ **4.2** Play Part 1 of the video or the audio recording for students to check their answer to 1b and answer questions 2–4 in 1a. If necessary, pre-teach *tenuous* (a tenuous connection, idea or situation is weak and possibly does not exist). Check answers as a class.

Answers

a telescope
2 his father   3 he'd broken his leg
4 it's how he got into science fiction (he got ideas about life on other planets from looking at the night sky)

Videoscript/Audioscript (Part 1)

NADIA You're here late, Sara.
SARA Oh, hi Nadia. Yeah, I've got a lot on.
N How is the preparation coming along?
S Good, yeah. I'm just so grateful for this opportunity.
N Well, it could have gone either way with Paul, really. But he said he could see how much it meant to you, and the work you'd put into the presentation. He feels confident you can make the interview a success – we both do.
S Oh, thanks Nadia.
N So, what kind of stuff are you getting from Max?
S There's a couple of interesting angles we could take in terms of revealing his inspirations.
N Oh?
S Yeah, I asked him how he got into science fiction and he said he started getting ideas on life on other planets when he was a kid. He broke his leg, and to cheer him up his dad bought him a telescope. He said he couldn't sleep at night and he used to spend hours looking up at the night sky.
N Hmm …
S So maybe we could explore the idea that insomnia breeds creativity …
N Well, I'm not sure about the insomnia bit – it's a bit of a tenuous link … but overall I think you've got some really good material here.
S But you haven't heard the best bit yet!
N What's that?
S He has an idea for his next book, and, he's giving us the title of it first!
N Wow! What is it?
S It's … wait for it … *Gravity Zero*.

N Hmm. Interesting … Are you OK there, Oscar? I didn't hear you come in.
OSCAR Yeah, yeah, I'm fine. Just forgot my car keys … again!

N Anyway, Sara, I can't believe you've got us an exclusive on that! Well done! Good night, Oscar.
O Night.

d 💬 Ask students if they think Oscar meant to make a noise. Then put students into pairs to discuss the question. Check students' predictions as a class.

e ▶ **4.3** Play Part 2 of the video or the audio recording for students to answer the questions. Check as a class. If necessary, pre-teach *sneak preview* (an opportunity to see something new before the rest of the public see it) and *straight from the horse's mouth* (if you hear something straight from the horse's mouth, you hear it from the person who has direct personal knowledge of it).

Answers

1 c   2 b   3 Students' own answers

Videoscript/Audioscript (Part 2)

MIRANDA *Breaking News Online*. Can I help you?
OSCAR Hello, is that Miranda Hall?
M Yes, speaking.
O Oh, hello. This is Oscar Simmons. We met at a few press conferences. I don't know if you remember?
M Oh yes, Oscar Simmons, from *City FM*. Yes, I remember.
O Great, well, I'm calling because I've been doing a little, um, what you might call freelance work? Anyway, I've got some information you may be interested in – straight from the horse's mouth, I think it's fair to say.
M What kind of information?
O Exclusive information about our very own Max Redwood. Y'know, author of *Solar Wind*?
M Oh right, the guy who famously wrote the whole book staring out to sea from the end of the Palace Pier.
O Exactly. I can give you an article about him, including a sneak preview of his next book.
M I didn't know he was writing a second novel?
O He is! And I'm offering you the chance to be the first to announce it – with the title.
M The title? Well, yes, that would certainly be of interest. There's just the issue of how much you would like for it.

O Well, how much would you be willing to pay?
M Oh, I think we'd be prepared to offer, say, two fifty? Would that be a fair suggestion?
O Two fifty! Could you see your way to increasing that a little? I was kind of hoping for something more in the region of five hundred.
M No, out of the question. What would you say to three fifty? In principle, of course. I'd need to see the article first.
O Three fifty – is that your best offer?
M Fair's fair. Remember we haven't even seen what you're offering yet.
O OK, three fifty. We've got a deal.
M And I need it by one o'clock? I want it on the website by today.
O What? Today? Er, how flexible can you be on that?
M Well, if I don't get it by two and it's not the kind of thing I'm looking for, the deal's off.
O OK, fair enough. One last thing …
M What's that?
O Would you mind keeping my name off the article?
M Freelance and anonymous, eh?
O Yeah.
M No problem.
O Great. Thanks.
M Thank you.

f ▶ **4.3** Play Part 2 of the video or the audio recording again. Then write this answer on the board and elicit a question for it beginning with *Why*: *Oscar knows he is doing something unfair*. (*Why is Oscar embarrassed?*). Tell students to write a *Why* question for each answer. Check ideas as a class.

Suggested answers
1 Why does Oscar say he's been doing freelance work?
2 Why does Oscar say the information is straight from the horse's mouth?
3 Why does Miranda say she will pay three fifty in principle?
4 Why does she say the deal is off if she doesn't have the information by two?
5 Why does he want his name kept off the article?

💡 FAST FINISHERS

Ask fast finishers to make three more *Why* questions for these answers and then compare with other fast finishers:

Sara convinced Max his readers wanted to hear about this.

The 'Zero' suggests this is the first in a series.

Max is still thinking about the plot.

Suggested answers
Why does Max want to talk to Sara about his childhood?
Why will the book be called *Gravity Zero*?
Why hasn't Max started writing yet?

g Language in context *Expressions with* fair
Ask students to think of different meanings of *fair*, e.g. hair colour, a trade event. Tell students to match the expressions with the meanings. Check as a class.

Answers
a 3   b 1   c 2

💡 EXTRA ACTIVITY

Tell students that *fair* is a homophone and ask them what the other word with the same pronunciation is (*fare* = ticket price). Put students into pairs to think of as many homophone words and phrases as they can in a time limit. Take feedback to find the pair with the longest word or phrase that is a homophone.

h 💬 Ask students if Oscar's phone call to Miranda is just a case of Oscar showing initiative. Put students into groups to discuss the questions. Take feedback as a class.

2 USEFUL LANGUAGE Negotiating

a ▶ **4.4** Ask students why Oscar and Miranda need to negotiate (there is no set price for inside information!). Tell students to complete the conversation from Part 2. Play the recording for them to check. Check answers as a class.

Answers
1 issue
2 willing
3 prepared
4 fair
5 way
6 hoping
7 out
8 say
9 best

b Tell students to write the number containing the expression into the table. Check answers as a class and refer students to the Language notes. Drill the expressions.

Answers

Opening negotiations	Making and accepting offers
There's just the issue of … How much would you be willing to pay?	We'd be prepared to offer … Would that be a fair suggestion? What would you say to … ?

Asking for more	Declining offers
Could you see your way to increasing that? I was kind of hoping for something more in the region of … Is that your best offer?	Out of the question.

📖 LANGUAGE NOTES

The expression *How much would you be willing to pay?* shows three ways of being polite: a modal verb (*would*), a past tense (*would* not *will*), the polite phrase *be willing to*.

c 💬 Tell students to complete the conversation with words from the table in 2b. Check answers as a class. Put students into pairs and ask them to practise the conversation.

Answers
1 open   2 worth   3 accept   4 flexible
5 position   6 authorised

d 💬 Read out the conversation with very flat (rude/bored) intonation. Put students into pairs to answer the questions. Check answers as a class.

Suggested answers
1 same: it's a negotiation, with the same information; different: it's very abrupt
2 the conversation in 2a: it's important to be polite and show a willingness to make concessions

e 💬 Put students into pairs to role-play the negotiation, covering 2a but looking at the functional language in 2b and the structure of the conversation in 2d. As feedback, ask some pairs to role-play their conversation in front of the class.

Dictate this ineffective negotiation to the class:

A The delivery time will be 30 days.
B 30 days?!
A What's that supposed to mean?
B We need it asap.
A All right, 25 days.
B Are you serious?
A 20 days and that's the best you'll get from us.
B And that's it?
A Take it or leave it.

Put students into pairs to rewrite and role-play a more effective negotiation.

Suggested answer
A We could deliver it in 30 days, just for you.
B That's out of the question.
A I'm not sure I follow you.
B Could you see your way to reducing the delivery time?
A I'd be prepared to agree to 25 days.
B Is that your best offer?
A I'm not authorised to agree to less than 20 days.
B I think our business is worth much more than that.
A I'm not in a position to improve on my previous offer, I'm afraid.

3 PRONUNCIATION
Intonation in implied questions

a ▶ 4.5 Say to students with a rising intonation:

The homework needs to be in by tomorrow.

Ask if this is a question in form (no), in meaning (yes) and why (the intonation rises as in most questions). Ask students to rephrase the statement as a question (Can you give me the homework by tomorrow?). Play the recording for students to listen and notice the intonation. Drill the implied questions with first the normal (falling) intonation and then rising intonation to highlight the difference.

Answer
rising

b ▶ 4.6 Play the recording for students to tick the statements with rising intonation.

Answers
1 ✓   2 ✓   5 ✓   6 ✓   7 ✓   9 ✓

c 💬 Put students into pairs to practise the dialogue. Monitor and make sure students are using the appropriate intonation.

4 SPEAKING

a Give students some ideas of attractive products or services, e.g. ice cream which has minus calories, a hotel for stressed-out pets. Put students into groups to think of more things to sell. Tell students to choose one of these, one of the items listed in 4a or think of their own ideas. Students then work individually and list some selling points, including setting a price and another aspect to negotiate.

b 💬 Put students into pairs to sell to each other, negotiating the price and another aspect. Encourage students to use the negotiation language and implied questions. As feedback, tell some pairs to role-play their dialogues in front of the class.

Put students into pairs. Give them these difficult things to sell:

- a round-the-world plane ticket to someone who is scared of flying
- a chocolate cake to Martin Knight (SB p.97)
- a smartphone to a technophobe
- garlic to a vampire.

Student A has to sell first the plane ticket and then the smartphone; Student B the cake and then the garlic. Tell students to take it in turns and use their negotiating language and skills to sell each thing to their partner.

ADDITIONAL MATERIAL

▶ Workbook 8C
▶ Unit Progress Test
▶ Photocopiable activities: Pronunciation p.267
▶ Personalised online practice

8D Skills for Writing
It's a unique dining experience

At the end of this lesson, students will be able to:

- **discuss and evaluate eating-out experiences**
- **listen to an interview comparing modern dietary habits with those of primitive humans and form their own opinions on the content**
- **write a promotional text for a restaurant website using persuasive language**

💡 OPTIONAL LEAD-IN

Books closed. Put students into pairs to work out the meaning of these menu items in bad English: *sweat and sour chicken, soap of the day, French flies, baby sheep, New York chess cake, thrown salad, beef in hot sores*. Ask students to tell the class about any strange translations they've seen on menus.

Answers

sweet and sour chicken, soup of the day, French fries, lamb, New York cheesecake, tossed salad, beef in hot sauce

1 LISTENING and SPEAKING

a 💬 Ask students to tell you whether people in their country eat out much and the last time they ate out. Put students into groups to discuss the questions in 1 and go through the criteria in 2 and agree on five. Take feedback as a class. Ask questions about some of the criteria, e.g. *What types of cuisine are most popular where you live?*

🔄 LOA TIP MONITORING

- You need to have strategies for dealing with fast finishers and slow workers in an open-ended task like 1a.
- Think about how you arrange groups so they are more or less equally divided in terms of ability and speed of working (by this stage of the course you will know students quite well).
- Set a time limit for both parts of 1a and signal the end of stage 1 so that everyone moves on to stage 2 at the same time. Use a consistent signal to show the beginning and end of activities, e.g. clapping your hands once to start and twice to stop.
- Monitor groups and set an extra speaking task for groups that finish early, e.g. for 1, *What kind of people eat out the most?* and 2, *Can you add any more criteria to the list?*
- Do not wait for all groups to agree on five criteria before you stop the second stage. Stop when the time limit is up or you feel that discussion is slowing down.

b 💬 Ask students what period the Stone Age refers to (the Palaeolithic /pæliəʊˈlɪθɪk/), what they know about life then and what people used to eat. You could show an excerpt from a *Flintstones* cartoon for a funny (and satirical) perspective on the Stone Age.

c ▶️ **4.7** Play the recording for students to answer the questions. Check answers to 1–4 as a class and take feedback on 5.

Answers

1 Because it lasted for over a million years, human beings learned to cook and their bodies adapted to their diet.
2 Wild meat, fish, vegetables, seeds, nuts and fruit are healthy because our bodies are still adapted to life in the Stone Age.
3 Dairy products and refined grains like wheat and rice were developed later, so are not 'natural'; they are difficult to digest and cause people to gain weight.
4 The ingredients are based on the Stone Age, so people are eating healthily; the food is prepared in a modern, sophisticated way to produce tasty dishes.
5 Students' own answers

d 💬 Ask students whether an obsession with diet is a characteristic of the Western world. Put students into groups to discuss the questions. Take feedback as a class.

2 READING

a 💬 Ask students what kind of information a home page for a restaurant should contain, e.g. pictures of unusual or special dishes. Tell students to read the home page and discuss the questions with a partner. Check the answer to 1 as a class and take feedback on 2.

Suggested answers
1 city-centre restaurant; Stone Age diet included grains; seasonal menu; details of signature dishes; sample menu available; drinks served are natural fruit and vegetable juices, teas, coffee, herbal teas; fixed-price early evening menu; cookbook containing *Ancestors* recipes; sample pages from cookbook available
2 someone health-conscious and interested in a new culinary experience because the food is good for you and unusual; students' own answers

b 💬 Ask students whether or not these are possible dishes at *Ancestors*, and why: *fried dinosaur leg* (no, fried food is unhealthy), *rice pudding* (no, rice is a refined food), *rock cakes* (the name is appropriate so yes, if they can be made out of fruit, seeds, nuts and vegetable oil, and no flour or dairy products). Ask students to think of a starter, main course and dessert individually and then compare their ideas in groups. Take feedback as a class.

3 WRITING SKILLS Promotional material; Using persuasive language

a Ask students to choose the main purpose. Check as a class. Elicit why the other purposes are less important (people won't have time to read detailed information; few people use restaurant websites to get advice).

Answer
to promote the restaurant

b Ask students how the home page is organised (headings, sections, links) and why it uses headings and sections. Check answers as a class. Ask students which of the links they would follow.

Answers
so people can quickly find out about the features they are interested in; so it looks easy and engaging to read – more so than a block of text

c Tell students to match the features with the purposes. Check answers as a class.

Answers
1 c   2 d   3 b   4 a

d Ask students to tell the class any slogans they like. Put students into pairs to choose one of the slogans for *Ancestors* and say why they have chosen it. Take feedback and ask the class if they can think of a better slogan.

Suggested answer
Pure enjoyment, pure health – because eating at *Ancestors* is an enjoyable experience and the food is healthy and contains only the purest ingredients

e Tell students to look at the opening phrase *Our city-centre restaurant* and ask: *Is the message that* Ancestors *is easy to get to or that you should come early to avoid the traffic?* (it's easy to get to). Students match the phrases with the messages. Check answers as a class.

Answers
1 c   2 b   3 d   4 a

f Write these two sentences on the board and ask students to say which is more positive, why, and how its structure is different:

When you enter Ancestors, you feel like you're in a new world.

Entering Ancestors, you feel like you're in a new world.

(The second is more positive because of the structure of the opening adverbial. The first has a conjunction and pronoun; the second, with no conjunction or pronoun but an *-ing* participle clause, is more concise and has more impact.) Put students into pairs to do the same with the sentences in the exercise. Tell students to find three more examples in the text of descriptive clauses or phrases which start sentences. (Note that they are all in the last two sections.) Check answers as a class.

Suggested answers / Answers
1 The first is more effective. Putting vivid description at the start of a sentence immediately gets the reader's attention. The second sentence has two main clauses and this is less efficient as the subject is the same in both.
Based in the city centre, ANCESTORS is …
Tasty and fresh, the early evening menu offers …
Tried and tested by our team of cooks, our recipes will enable …

g ▶ Students complete the exercises in Writing Focus 8D on SB p.174. Refer students to the table and the Writing Tip. Students complete Exercise a–c, using a dictionary if necessary. Check answers as a class. Monitor Exercise d and then ask students to compare ideas in Exercise e. Tell students to go back to SB p.101.

Answers

a 1 freshly; lovingly
2 most exacting; highest
3 serve; offer
4 perfect; ideal
5 complete; total
6 away from it all; far from the bustle of the city

b 1 a hotel
2 a furniture shop
3 a duty-free shop
4 a music venue
5 a language school
6 an airport lounge
7 a bank

c 1 Tastefully furnished; truly relaxing
2 manufactured to the highest standards; stand the test of time
3 an extensive range of; globally recognised
4 an ideal venue
5 fully; highly qualified; a unique learning experience
6 A warm welcome awaits you; while away; luxurious
7 Our mission is; a secure home

4 WRITING

a 💬 Ask students to think of a concept for a restaurant where they live, e.g. a vegan restaurant, a slow-food café, a make-it-yourself pancake place. Put students into pairs or groups to decide on a concept and make notes for the website, using the prompts and looking back at the criteria in 1a on SB p.100. Tell pairs or groups to give a brief presentation to the rest of the class of their concept and promotional ideas.

b Tell pairs or groups to write a promotional text with a name, slogan and sections with headings. Tell students to divide up the sections so that they each write a short paragraph. Stronger students can write more than one section. Encourage students to use structures which emphasise the positive features. You could also give weaker students a paragraph frame based on the model text for them to change and expand, e.g. *Based in _____ , [name] is the ideal place for _____ . The early lunch menu offers _____ . You will also find _____ exciting selection of _____ .*

c Ask groups to pass round their texts, read one another's and write questions on the text that they'd like answered. Groups then tell the class their answers to the questions on their text and anything else they'd like to make clear. The class votes on the best restaurant.

💡 **EXTRA ACTIVITY**

If possible, follow up this writing activity with a visit to a restaurant. Put students into groups to look at different restaurant websites and ask them to present to the class the best place to go based on the criteria in 4a. The class then votes on the best restaurant. Go to the restaurant and then ask groups to write an English version (or a new English version) of the restaurant website. (The restaurant may be interested in this text if it is positive enough!)

ADDITIONAL MATERIAL

▶ Workbook 8D

UNIT 8
Review and extension

1 GRAMMAR

a Write this sentence on the board: *Tracy is glad not to have been playing / be playing / have played next weekend.* Ask students to choose the correct option and explain why (be playing – present continuous for future arrangements). Tell students to choose the correct option. Check answers as a class.

Answers
1 Waking
2 Being sent
3 getting
4 to listen
5 having
6 to have met
7 of saving

b Write this sentence on the board and ask students to complete it with one word: *Had Oscar given his name, he _____ have got into trouble.* (would). Tell students to complete the sentences with one word. Check answers as a class.

Answers
1 didn't 2 have 3 Had 4 asks 5 otherwise/or 6 Were

2 VOCABULARY

a Ask students to cover the endings, look at the sentence halves and think of the word or phrase which comes next. Students then match the sentence halves with the endings. Check as a class.

Answers
1 c/f 2 h 3 a 4 e 5 g 6 b 7 c/f 8 d

ⓦ FAST FINISHERS
Ask fast finishers to think of interesting new similes for *sleep like* (a log), e.g. a bear in winter, my gran after Sunday lunch, a bored student in a library. Tell them to compare ideas with another fast finisher.

b Ask students which of these words is the odd one out: *thinning, loss, grey, glowing* (glowing, the others can be about hair). Put students into groups to find the odd word out and explain why (there may be different answers but students need to justify them). Check answers as a class.

Suggested answers
1 saggy; it's the only negative adjective
2 scars; they are permanent, not temporary marks
3 strengthen; it is part of healthy living and not an anti-ageing treatment
4 weight loss; it isn't usually a result of ageing
5 yellowing; it's a superficial effect of ageing, not a way of looking/feeling better
6 poor circulation; it's a health problem caused by ageing, not a superficial effect of ageing

3 WORDPOWER *and*

a ▶4.8 Ask students to describe the pictures and say what the people might be saying. Tell students to match the sentences with the pictures. Students may remember that *bits and pieces* was in 1C Ex 2b on SB p.15. Play the recording for students to listen and check. Drill the expressions.

Answers
1 b 2 f 3 a 4 c 5 d 6 e

b Ask students to think of their own paraphrases for the idioms. Then tell students to replace the idioms with the expressions in the box. Check as a class.

Answers
1 small things of different types
2 many places
3 easily
4 annoyed by
5 damage caused by everyday use
6 a normal part of

c ▶4.9 Ask students if they know any other expressions with *and*, e.g. *first and foremost, heart and soul*. Tell students to complete the sentences with the adjectives in the box. Play the recording for students to check.

Answers
1 clear 2 tidy 3 sweet 4 safe

d Write this sentence on the board and ask students to fill in the missing word: *Apart from some _____ and tear, it's in good condition.* (wear). Tell students to choose four expressions from 3a or 3c and do the same.

e 💬 Put students into groups to read out their sentences for other students to guess what goes in the gap.

ⓦ EXTRA ACTIVITY
Put students into pairs. Tell them to write a dialogue using as many of the *and* expressions as possible. First they plan the dialogue, making notes, then they practise it and finally they role-play it in front of the whole class.

▶ Photocopiable activities: Wordpower p.248

🔄 LOA REVIEW YOUR PROGRESS
Students look back through the unit, think about what they've studied and decide how well they did. Students work on weak areas by using the appropriate sections of the Workbook, the Photocopiable worksheets and the Personalised online practice.

UNIT 9
Cities

GETTING STARTED

 OPTIONAL LEAD-IN

Books closed. Write these criteria for a good city to live in on the board:

- transport links
- safety
- affordable housing
- friendly locals
- shopping
- entertainment options
- multiculturalism
- atmosphere

Elicit some more criteria from students. Ask students to give each criterion a mark from 1–5 (1 = terrible, 5 = excellent) for the city they live in or their closest city. Put students into pairs to compare marks and discuss.

a Put students into pairs to describe the photo. Take feedback as a class.

b Give students one minute to think about their answers to the questions before talking about the photo as a class. If you wish, give students information from the Culture notes below.

CULTURE NOTES

This photo shows a house in the middle of a housing development in southern China. The owners of the house have refused to let the property be demolished. Originally, the house was part of a village but all the other residents were relocated in the 1990s. The owners don't even live in the house now but the property company have no legal way of getting rid of the house and essential maintenance work can't be carried out on the road it occupies. A similar inconvenient property is Stott Hall farmhouse in the middle of a major motorway in the north of England. Drivers often stop there, for fuel and repairs, but the farmer does not seem to mind, in fact he helps them out however he can.

c Put students into groups to discuss in what situation they would agree to their family home being demolished. Take feedback as a class.

EXTRA ACTIVITY

Put students into groups. Ask them to think of legal ways of putting pressure on a homeowner to move, e.g. organising a petition signed by as many local residents as possible. Ask each group to share their ideas with the class and choose the best suggestion.

9A They did it all themselves

- read an article about urban development and decide how convincing the arguments put forward are
- use a range of verbs with *re-* relating to urban development, saying them with the different pronunciations of *re-*
- discuss improvements and challenges to cities and the urban environment
- use reflexive and reciprocal pronouns for a range of functions
- listen to a podcast and reactions to the influence of technology on cities
- prepare and present an idea for improving their local urban area

OPTIONAL LEAD-IN

Books closed. Give students two minutes to draw and label a rough map of an urban area they know well, e.g. their neighbourhood, including main buildings, transport links, parks, etc. Put students into pairs to show each other their maps and suggest how the area could be improved, e.g. adding roads, making the hospital more central, etc. Take feedback as a class.

1 READING

a Tell students to look at the picture and say how it looks different from the street where they live. Put students into pairs to discuss the questions. Take feedback as a class.

b Ask students why they think the street is called Exhibition Road (possible answer: it's a model for other streets) and tell them the real reason (see the Culture notes below). Give students time to read the article and answer the questions individually. Check the answer to question 1. Then put students into groups to compare and explain their answers to the second question. Take feedback as a class.

Answers
1 It improves safety.
2 Students' own answers

CULTURE NOTES

Exhibition Road is in the centre of London. Three of London's important museums, the Science Museum, the Natural History Museum and the Victoria and Albert Museum, are on it. It is named after the Great Exhibition of 1851, which was held at Hyde Park, to the north of the road. The shared space project was completed in time for the 2012 London Olympics.

c Ask students if this is the first street of its kind (no, the idea comes from the Netherlands). Tell students to answer the questions, using a dictionary if necessary. Use the Vocabulary support box to help students with vocabulary if necessary. Check answers as a class.

Answers
1 Suggested answers: traffic signals, kerb marking (in the text); advertising boards, benches, litter bins, parking meters, railings
2 They control and threaten people and treat them like children. Students' own answers
3 We wouldn't expect it to work; others should copy the example.
4 Drivers don't drive irresponsibly when the road markings are taken away / they aren't allowed to drive dangerously (although this is not explained further in the text, logically, normal road safety laws would apply)
5 Having space dedicated to traffic and controlled by signs and green traffic lights makes motorists feel that the space belongs to them.

VOCABULARY SUPPORT

kerb – the edge of a raised path nearest the road

tactile – designed to be perceived by touch

strip (C1) – a long, flat, narrow piece

hectoring – communicate in an unpleasantly forceful way, in order to get somebody to do something

nannying – giving too much advice or making too many rules so that people are treated like children and not allowed to think for themselves

co-exist harmoniously – exist together in a friendly and peaceful way

eye contact (C2) – when people look directly at each other's eyes during communication; lack of eye contact implies low confidence / poor communication

counter-intuitive – something that is counter-intuitive does not happen in the way you would expect it to

blueprint – plan or design that explains how something can be achieved

a jigsaw of sth – made up of a large number of small pieces which are designed to fit together

free-for-all – a situation without limits or controls in which people can have or do what they want

in a similar vein – in a similar way

invade sb's space (C2) – enter into an area around somebody, or that somebody feels is theirs, in a way that makes the person feel uncomfortable, angry, etc., e.g. the space closest to their body, car, etc.

FAST FINISHERS

Point out the phrase *stretch of road* and ask fast finishers what it means (a continuous section of road). Ask them to complete these other quantifying phrases, using a dictionary if necessary: *a _____ of luck, a _____ of grass, a _____ of thunder, a _____ of land, a _____ of fresh air, a _____ of anger.*

Suggested answers
stroke, blade, clap, plot, breath, fit

d Ask students if they would feel safe walking down Exhibition Road. Put students into groups to discuss the questions. Take feedback as a class.

2 VOCABULARY Verbs with re-

a Ask students how the words in bold are similar in meaning. Check answers as a class. Ask how they are similar in form (they both start with *re-*) and how they are different (in these sentences *revamped* is an adjective, *redeveloped* is a verb).

Answers

Both words refer to processes that make something that was old, or had deteriorated, good again.
revamp: change or arrange something again, in order to improve it
redevelop (C1): change an area of a town by replacing old buildings, roads, etc. with new ones

b ▶ **4.10** Tell students to replace the words in italics with the correct form of the verbs in the box. Play the recording for students to listen and check.

Answers and audioscript

1 The council's policy is to <u>regenerate</u> the port area of the city.
2 It's a beautiful old building. They just need to <u>renovate</u> it.
3 It's good that students are moving into this area. It will help to <u>rejuvenate</u> it.
4 There's a place in China where they've <u>recreated</u> a traditional English town, with authentic materials and architecture.
5 The fountain in the main square was dry and falling to pieces. Now they've <u>restored</u> it.
6 The town needs new industries so it <u>regains</u> its appeal as a place to live and work.
7 Removing the speed limit led to so many accidents that they decided to <u>reinstate</u> it.

> **LOA TIP ELICITING**
>
> • Use the general meaning of *re-* to elicit the meanings of the words.
> • Give students simpler examples with words they already know: *If you 'retake' a test, what do you do?* (do it again). *Can you think of a 'remake' of a famous film?* (*King Kong*). Elicit the general meaning of *re-*, to do something again, often to do it better.
> • Tell students to read question 4 and ask *Is this a new idea?* (no). *Are they repairing something?* (no). *Are they building something which already exists somewhere else?* (yes). Then ask students to choose the best word to replace the phrase in italics and put it in the appropriate tense (recreated).
> • Point out that this meaning does not apply to all verbs with *re-* and elicit examples, e.g. you usually only *resign* from your job once.

> **LANGUAGE NOTES**
>
> Highlight that *rejuvenate, renovate* and *revamp* cannot be used without *re-*: ~~juvenate, novate~~ and ~~vamp~~ are not words.

c Pronunciation

1 ▶ **4.11** Play the recording for students to listen to the pronunciation of *e* in *re-* in the verbs in the table. Ask students in which word the *e* sound is longer (redevelop). Drill the two verbs.

2 ▶ **4.12** Tell students to add the other verbs with *re-* in 2a and 2b to the table and identify which verb has a different sound and can't be added. Play the recording for students to check. Drill the words.

Answers

1 /iː/	**2** /ɪ/
revamp	restore
recreate	regain
reinstate	regenerate

Different: /e/ renovate

> 💡 **FAST FINISHERS**
>
> Tell fast finishers to add these verbs to the table: *relax, repeat, re-educate, refund, reject, rehouse, require, result.* Check and drill the words.
>
> **Answers**
>
> /iː/: re-educate, refund, rehouse
> /ɪ/: relax, repeat, reject, require, result

d 💬 Tell students to look around their classroom/school and say if any renovation or any other changes are needed. Put students into groups to discuss the questions. Take feedback as a class.

3 READING and SPEAKING

a 💬 Put students into pairs to look at the pictures and discuss the questions. Take feedback as a class.

b ▶ Divide the class into groups of four and assign A, B, C and D roles (students can share a role if necessary). Student As go to SB p.128. Student Bs go to SB p.133. Student Cs go to SB p.134. Student Ds go to SB p.136. If necessary, put the following words and definitions on the board for students' reference during the task: *carbon emissions* (carbon released into the atmosphere by, e.g., burning fuel), *turf* (the surface layer of garden lawns and sports pitches: the grass, its roots and the attached soil), *makeover* (a process within a certain timeframe involving a series of changes intended to make something more attractive), *developers* (C2) (businesses that profit from buying land or buildings, improving them and then selling on to a new owner). Tell students to read their fact files and make notes to help them retell the information. Tell students to go back to SB p.105.

c 💬 Tell students to explain the ideas they read about to one another in their groups, using the prompts given. Take feedback as a class.

4 GRAMMAR Reflexive and reciprocal pronouns

a Ask students which picture this comment could refer to: *You can just help yourself to refreshments.* (B). Tell students to read the comments and say which picture they could refer to. Take feedback as a class.

Suggested answers

1 C;D   2 A;B;D   3 C;D   4 C   5 B;D   6 C

b Put students into pairs to look at the words and phrases in bold and answer the questions. Check answers as a class.

Answers

1 a 6 (themselves)   b 3 (itself)   c 1 (by yourself)
  d 2 (for themselves)
2 a *we support ourselves*: we don't need other people's help; *we support each other*: I help them and they help me
  b *they talk to themselves*: they speak as if they were alone, not to another person; *they talk to one another*: they speak with another person / other people

c ▶ ⏵ **4.13–4.14** Students read the information in Grammar Focus 9A on SB p.154. Play the recording where indicated and ask students to listen and repeat. Students then complete the exercises. Check answers as a class. Exercise c could lead to a discussion in groups of how cities will cope with an increasing global population. Tell students to go back to SB p.106.

Answers (Grammar Focus 9A SB p.154)

a 1 a2 b1 2 a1 b2 3 a1 b2 4 a2 b1 5 a2 b1 6 a2 b1
b 1 ourselves 2 John himself 3 herself 4 myself 5 myself
6 himself 7 one another 8 each other's
c towns and cities find <u>themselves</u> under tremendous pressure …
let alone enjoy <u>ourselves</u> there … But, let's just remind
<u>ourselves / one another / each other</u> of the challenges ahead.
The technology (<u>itself</u>) may be there but we would be opening
<u>ourselves</u> up to lots of problems … The world needs to sort <u>itself</u>
out and we need to learn to live with <u>one another / each other</u>. I
hope I've made <u>myself</u> clear.

⊙ CAREFUL!

Students often use a reflexive pronoun after verbs which don't need them, especially *feel*: *How do they feel themselves being in a group?* (Correct form = *How do they* **feel** *being in a group?*). Another typical mistake is not to use the reflexive pronoun when it's necessary, especially after *enjoy*: *The performance went well, and the spectators enjoyed a lot.* (Correct form = *The performance went well, and the spectators enjoyed* **themselves** *a lot.*). Some students also confuse the reflexive with the object pronoun, especially *myself/me*: *His knowledge of geography often impressed myself.* (Correct form = *His knowledge of geography often impressed* **me**.). Another typical error is to put the reflexive pronoun between the verb and the object: *It means you should yourself organise your leisure time.* (Correct form = *It means you should* **organise** *your leisure time yourself.*). A further common error is to use a reflexive pronoun instead of a reciprocal pronoun: *Our students can meet themselves during the break.* (Correct form = *Our students can meet* **each other** *during the break.*).

---

5 LISTENING

a 🗨 Ask students what their favourite apps are. Ask students to discuss in pairs what they think the app in the photo is for. Then take feedback as a class. Elicit students' ideas and ask them to justify their suggestions.

b ⏵ **4.15** Play the recording for students to listen and answer the questions. You may wish to pre-teach some of the expressions in the Vocabulary support box. Tell students to work individually and then compare their answers in pairs. Check answers as a class.

Answers

1 You go on the app, take a photo of a maintenance problem in the city, choose the appropriate issue category and send off the photo. Receipt of the photo is immediately acknowledged and you can track the issue to see if it's 'In process' or 'Fixed'.
2 It's an example of democracy in action, which she approves of and it also saves the city money.
3 Students' own answers

Audioscript

PRESENTER Cities around the world are growing more crowded by the day. All us city dwellers experience the frustration of ever-increasing traffic on our roads, and wear and tear on our amenities. Keeping transport moving, and public amenities functional, is an ongoing problem the folks who run our cities have to deal with. With an estimated five billion inhabitants of the world's cities by 2030, the challenge has never been greater … So, today … many major cities around the world are looking to mobile technology for their solutions. And there are a handful of products out there already that are aimed at helping to optimise the way we live in cities. One example is an app called 'click-and-fix'. It's in use in a number of cities and what it does is to let you communicate with your city maintenance services. People use their mobiles to let the city know where there's a problem – something's broken or out of service – and then the idea is it'll get fixed straight away. Or at least they get updated on what's being done about it. Michelle Thornton in Boston, USA shows us how it works.

MICHELLE Well, look I'm just going along the street and if I see something that needs fixing I can report it. It could be anything, like a pothole, or graffiti on a wall, or if something's been vandalised, or even a place where you're repeatedly having to risk your neck to get across the road – anything like that. So, right now, we're going past a park and there's a railing that's been smashed in here – it's all bent. So I'll go on the app and then I just take a snap of it – and I'll choose the most appropriate issue category, so I'll choose 'park issue' – the app knows where I am of course, and then … just send it off. And you can see it comes up here, it's saying it's received. Then I can look it up later and it will tell me if it's 'in process' or hopefully 'fixed'. I think it's a great idea. It means that I, as a citizen, can be more involved. So it's a kind of democracy in action if you like, and it also saves the city money.

📖 VOCABULARY SUPPORT

city dwellers – people who live in a city

wear and tear – the damage that happens to an object with ordinary use over time

amenity – desirable or useful features and facilities of a place – such as parks, swimming pools, public toilets

optimise sth – make something as good as possible

pothole – a hole in a road surface

vandalise – intentionally damage the property of others

democracy in action – when the opinions of a number of ordinary members of a population are listened to by the government and they get what they want

---

c ⏵ **4.16** Play the recording and ask students to choose the idea which has been invented. If necessary, pre-teach *canopy* (the branches and leaves that spread out at the top of a group of trees forming a type of roof), *commute* (C1) (make the same journey regularly between work and home) and *have a mind/memory like a sieve* /sɪv/ (forget things very easily). Put students into pairs to compare what they have chosen. Tell students to check the answer on SB p.128.

Audioscript

FRANK I've got an app here, on my phone, called *Trainspotting*. I use this all the time – in fact I couldn't manage without it. I commute into town and it actually shows me, not just when the train's due, but exactly where it is – which is great because sometimes the station announcements are basically all over the place. You can't really trust them. So, I can get the map here, blow it up a bit like that and, yeah, there's my train! It's just left the last station and it's due in … two minutes.

RITA OK, this isn't an app, but it's an information screen. And they've got these screens all around the city – they're all over the place. And it can tell you whether your health is OK, which is really useful – especially for elderly people. So you press this panel here and it reads your blood pressure, and your body mass index, blood sugar level, pulse – all those things. And it also tells you how stressed you are. It reads the whole thing just from contact with your finger – it's a touch screen. It's amazing! So let's give it a whirl … I put my finger on it … Press OK … Print … OK, it's printing it out now … There we go. Let's see if I'm OK or whether I'm about to keel over. No, it says everything's normal, that's a relief – but 'stress level high', it says. Ah well … what can you do?

NICK Yes, well this isn't an app, but it's a cool idea. It's called *Strawberry Tree*, and these are artificial trees and they're dotted around the city. They're basically solar-powered phone charging points. They're shaped like trees, so they blend in. And the canopy consists of solar panels, which feed into batteries for charging your mobile or your laptop. It's all free, of course. So you can go to the park, sit and chat to people, or you can drink coffee, and they charge up your phone for you. It suits me because I've got a mind like a sieve – I'm always going out without charging my phone, so it's a real life-saver for me.

d ▶ **4.16** Ask students: *Which app would be useful for punctual people?* (Trainspotting). Play the recording again for students to write the app idea next to each function. Check as a class.

Answers
1 Trainspotting; health information screen
2 Strawberry Tree   3 Trainspotting   4 Strawberry Tree
5 health information screen   6 Strawberry Tree

e 💬 Put students into groups to discuss the questions. Take feedback as a class.

f 💬 Ask students if apps are like toys for some people. Put students into groups to answer the questions. Take feedback as a class.

g Language in context *Colloquial expressions*
1 ▶ **4.17** Tell students to complete the expressions in bold with the words from the box. Play the recording for students to check. Concept check some of the expressions, e.g. *Which phrasal verb means to make bigger?* (blow up).
2 Read the Learning Tip with the class and tell students to answer the question. Check answers as a class.

Answers
1 a neck   b smashed   c blow   d place   e whirl   f keel
   g dotted   h blend   i life
2 collapse: keel over; enlarge: blow up

💡 FAST FINISHERS

Tell fast finishers to look at the audioscript on SB p.187, underline the other example of *all over the place* (sometimes the station announcements are basically <u>all over the place</u>) and say what it means in this context (not correct or suitable).

💡 EXTRA ACTIVITY

Tell students that you have an app to calculate stress levels. Pretend to read this information from your mobile device. *Start with 0 points. Add 1 point for any of these factors: you have more than 2 children, you work over 40 hours a week, you live in a city, you have recently moved flat/house, you have recently changed jobs, you have bad neighbours, you drive in the rush hour, you are getting married soon, it rains a lot in your country. Result: more than 6 points means your stress levels are high; zero points means you are very relaxed.* Put students into groups to discuss how accurate this 'app' is and to think of other factors that could increase stress levels. Take feedback as a class.

💡 HOMEWORK ACTIVITY

▶ Tell students to find five phrasal verbs connected with the topic of urban development or technology. Ask them to write them down in their vocabulary notebook with their single-word equivalents and example sentences. Examples: *do up*: repair; *move in*: occupy; *put up*: build; *set up*: found; *take down*: destroy. In class, put students into groups to teach one another their phrasal verbs.

6 SPEAKING

a 💬 Tell students to read the list of ideas. Pre-teach *impending* (used to refer to an event, usually something unpleasant or unwanted, that is going to happen soon). Put students into groups of three to discuss the questions.

b 💬 Tell each group of three to choose one idea and prepare to tell the class how useful it would be. They should use the prompts to make notes and then practise their presentation. Monitor and encourage students to use the colloquial expressions in 5g.

c 💬 Each group should present their idea in turn, with each student in a group presenting one of the bullet points. The class then votes on the most useful idea.

💡 EXTRA ACTIVITY

Put students into groups to discuss which of these apps is the most useless. Take feedback as a class.
An app which …
says when it is feeding time at the nearest zoo
counts down how many seconds you have left to live
tells you the birthday of the person physically closest to you
teaches you a new mathematical formula every day
translates cat sounds into dog sounds.

ADDITIONAL MATERIAL

▶ Workbook 9A
▶ Photocopiable activities: Grammar p.217, Vocabulary p.237, Pronunciation p.268

At the end of this lesson, students will be able to:

- talk about the design and function of local and iconic buildings using a range of descriptive vocabulary with the correct syllable stress
- use ellipsis and substitution to make their language more concise and coherent
- read an article about an architect and work out the meaning of the metaphorical phrases
- discuss a scenario for dealing with an urban challenge and present a solution

OPTIONAL LEAD-IN

Books closed. Put students into groups. Ask students to imagine that they have travelled forward in time from Ancient Greece and find themselves in their local town today. Students should discuss what they find most surprising and most impressive as they look around town.

1 SPEAKING and VOCABULARY

Describing buildings

a 💬 Put students into groups to look at the pictures and answer the questions. Check answers and take feedback as a class. If you wish, give students information from the Culture notes below.

Answers

Triumph Palace, Moscow, Russia; apartments and hotel
Krzywy Domek (The Crooked House), Sopot, Poland; restaurants, shops and offices
L'Hemisfèric and El Palau de les Arts Reina Sofía, Valencia, Spain; L'Hemisfèric is a cinema and projections hall; Palau de les Arts Reina Sofía is an opera house and cultural centre
Torre Velasca, Milan, Italy; shops, offices, exhibition spaces and apartments
The Barbican, London, the UK; multi-arts cultural and exhibition centre
Museo Soumaya, Mexico City, Mexico; museum

CULTURE NOTES

Triumph Palace, built in 2003, is the tallest apartment building in Europe. It is known as the Eighth Sister because it is similar to the Seven Sisters skyscrapers built in Moscow in the 1950s.

The Crooked House, built in 2004, was inspired by fairy stories. L'Hemisfèric and El Palau de les Arts Reina Sofía are part of an entertainment and cultural complex completed in 2005, following considerable controversy over the expense.

The 100 m Torre Velasca was built in the 1950s on the model of a medieval castle. Right in the centre of historic Milan, it is considered an eyesore by some people.

The Barbican, the largest performing arts centre in Europe, was opened in 1982. The concrete functional style is typical of an architectural movement popular between the 1950s and 1970s (Brutalism).

Museo Soumaya, completed in 2011, is mainly an art museum. Most of the collection is of European art from the 15th to 20th centuries.

b Read out the definition for *imposing* from the Vocabulary support box and ask students if *imposing* is positive or negative (usually positive). Tell students to mark the words in the box as positive or negative, using a dictionary if necessary. Check answers as a class.

Answers

positive: 1; 3; 4; 9
negative: 2; 5; 6; 7; 8

VOCABULARY SUPPORT

imposing – impressive/powerful because it is very large and magnificent and looks important – people can't ignore it

nondescript – very ordinary, or having no interesting or exciting features or qualities

graceful (C1) – having a smooth, attractive shape

innovative (C1) – using new methods or ideas

tasteless (C2) – not stylish

over the top (C2) – too extreme and not suitable

dated (C2) – old-fashioned in a way that is bad

out of place (C2) – in the wrong place or looking wrong

stunning (B2) – extremely beautiful or attractive

c ▶ 4.18 **Pronunciation** Ask students to mark the stressed syllable in each word or phrase. Play the recording for students to listen and check. Drill the words and phrases.

Answers

1 im<u>pos</u>ing   2 <u>non</u>descript   3 <u>grace</u>ful   4 <u>inn</u>ovative
5 <u>taste</u>less   6 over the <u>top</u>   7 <u>da</u>ted   8 out of <u>place</u>
9 <u>stun</u>ning

d 💬 Put students into pairs to describe the buildings, using the words and phrases in 1b and other adjectives or phrases they know. Take feedback as a class. Ask students to choose one of the buildings to visit.

e ▶ 4.19–4.20 Students complete the exercises in Vocabulary Focus 9B on SB p.166. Play the recording for students to listen and check their answers to Exercise a and b. Check the answers to Exercise c. Take feedback as a class after the discussion in Exercise d. Tell students to go back to SB p.107.

Answers (Vocabulary Focus 9B SB p.166)

a 1 innovative   2 imposing; out of place   3 nondescript; dated
4 tasteless; over the top   5 graceful; stunning
b 1 e   2 k   3 j   4 a   5 c   6 h   7 l   8 g   9 f   10 b
11 i   12 d
c 1 cabin; skyscraper; housing estate; tower block; penthouse; studio; bungalow; semi-detached; mansion
2 power station; warehouse; retail park
3 cabin; skyscraper; warehouse; tower block; studio; mansion

f 💬 Check students remember *iconic* from Lesson 6A. Put students into pairs. Tell them to take turns to describe a building, using the new vocabulary and other words and phrases they know, for their partner to guess. As feedback, ask students to say their descriptions again for the whole class to guess.

2 GRAMMAR Ellipsis and substitution

a 💬 Tell the students to read the sentences and tick the ones that are true for them. Put students into pairs to compare. Take feedback as a class.

b Ask students to work in the same pairs and decide which words and phrases have been left out or replaced with the words in bold, and why. Check answers as a class.

Answers

1 dislike modern architecture
2 consult residents about new buildings   3 they've   4 buildings
5 built more houses
6 (They) (are)n't (likely to) build anything new around here for ages.
Words have been omitted or substituted to avoid repetition and to make the sentences more concise.

c ▶ 🔊 **4.21–4.26** Students read the information in Grammar Focus 9B on SB p.155. Play the recording where indicated and ask students to listen and repeat. Students then complete the exercises. Check answers.

▶ For Exercise d, divide the class into pairs and assign A and B roles. Student As go to SB p.131 and Student Bs to SB p.135. Tell students that they are neighbours complaining about changes in their neighbourhood. If necessary, pre-teach *petition* (a document signed by a large number of people demanding or asking for some action from the government or another authority). Tell Student A to start first and then Student B to respond, taking it in turns to listen and reply using ellipsis and substitution to make their sentences more natural. They then change roles. Monitor and make sure students are using ellipsis and substitution. Tell students to go back to SB p.108.

Answers (Grammar Focus 9B SB p.155)

a 1 The president arrived and ~~he~~ made a speech.
 2 You don't know and ~~you~~ never will ~~know~~.
 3 I will tell you because I value and ~~I~~ respect your opinion.
 4 We have been thinking about our reputation, ~~we have~~ not ~~been thinking about~~ money.
 5 I said I would be volunteering so I will ~~be volunteering~~.
 6 If they are (hungry), bears can be dangerous and ~~they can be~~ unpredictable.
 7 My first impression was very positive but my second wasn't ~~very positive~~.
 8 We can meet up at seven if you'd like to ~~meet up tonight~~.
 9 'Are we in room six?' 'I guess ~~we are~~ not ~~in room six~~.'
 10 The Amazon is the longest river in the world and the Nile ~~is the~~ second longest ~~river in the world~~.
b 2 'Is this the right page?' 'I think ~~it is the right page~~ so.'
 3 'I don't know where we are.' '~~I don't know where we are either~~ Neither/Nor do I.'
 4 I love holidays abroad, especially long ~~holidays abroad~~ ones.
 5 'Who's got a dress with short sleeves?' 'Borrow ~~my dress with short sleeves~~ mine.'
 6 'Did you get my message?' 'I'm afraid ~~we didn't get it~~ not.'
 7 'George has got married.' 'I didn't know ~~George had got married~~ that.'
 8 Klaus is very enthusiastic, and ~~his sister is very enthusiastic too~~ so is his sister.
 9 Tina had always wanted to go parachuting and one day she ~~went parachuting~~ did.
c **D** The place where we are going to work and ~~where we are going to~~ do business say fifty years from now. Those offices will look completely different compared to the ~~offices~~ ones today.
 R I expect ~~they will look completely different~~ so.
 D For example, imagine there are no walls and ~~there are~~ no doors. All barriers to communication will be broken down and ~~all barriers to communication will~~ be a thing of the past. This is hard to imagine but you don't need to ~~imagine it~~. Just go to any successful company today.

R I think ~~successful companies today~~ they have walls and ~~have~~ doors.
D You are being sarcastic and ~~you are~~ trying to make fun of me.
R Sorry, I didn't mean to ~~make fun of you~~. I'd like to travel in time and ~~I'd like to~~ visit an office of the future. Tell me when you have built ~~an office of the future~~ one.

👁 CAREFUL!

Students sometimes leave out the subject, especially *it*, after *and* and *but* when the subject of the new clause is different: ~~*I can't rely on public transport and is expensive for me to take taxis.*~~ (Correct form = *I can't rely on public transport and **it** is expensive for me to take taxis.*). Students also leave out the subject, especially *it*, after *because* and *if*: ~~*The training was too short because lasted only eight hours.*~~ (Correct form = *The training was too short because **it** lasted only eight hours.*).

💡 EXTRA ACTIVITY

Give students an example of a sentence containing ellipsis and substitution and how it can be expanded, e.g. *Mike hasn't been to one but I have.* (Mike hasn't been to an interactive museum but I have been lucky enough to go to several.), pointing out that different ways of expanding are possible. Put students into two groups, A and B, and give each group four sentences:

Group A

1 *The first place was but the second wasn't.*

2 *I never did and I don't regret it.*

3 *Are you? I'm not.*

4 *If Lucy said so, she must have.*

Group B

a *I will as long as you will.*

b *I suspect not but ask her.*

c *She hasn't yet but she might.*

d *If so, take mine.*

Ask groups to expand their sentences and to write the expanded sentences on a separate piece of paper. Group As then swap their expanded sentences with Group Bs and use ellipsis and substitution to reduce them. Groups then compare their reduced sentences with the original reduced sentences.

---

3 READING

a Ask students if they know any famous architects, current or past. Tell students to read the article and choose the best summary. Check as a class.

Answer

2

b Ask students which of Zaha's projects could be considered a failure and why (the fire station in Germany because it wasn't used for this purpose). Tell students to read the text again and make notes using the prompts. The praise and criticism of Zaha Hadid's work contains vocabulary which may be unfamiliar. Encourage students to note whole descriptive phrases as well as words, e.g. *shamelessly flamboyant*, and decide if these are positive or negative using the context. Ask them to check their ideas in a dictionary. Use the Vocabulary support box to help with vocabulary if necessary. Put students into pairs to compare notes. As feedback, ask some students to read out their notes.

the praise of Zaha Hadid's work: ruthless genius; fluid solutions to rectangular problems; astonishing, graceful, streamlined, sensual, intoxicating buildings, aesthetic triumph

the criticism of Zaha Hadid's work: showboating 'starchitect'; overly complex, vain fantasies; experimentation put ahead of functionality; abstract art

Zaha Hadid's reactions to these views: although rectangle = best use of space, the world is not a rectangle; buildings are practical, constructed around different organisational patterns; Vitra fire station not a failure

📖 VOCABULARY SUPPORT

ruthless (C2) – not thinking or worrying about any pain caused to others; cruel

showboating – a slightly annoying form of behaviour that is intended to attract attention or admiration because it is very skilful

be better off as sth – be more suitable in a different form/ situation

spookily – in a way that is strange and surprising because it doesn't seem possible

streamlined – designed in a smooth, simple shape, without corners and flat surfaces

intoxicating – something intoxicating makes you feel excited and emotional

brazen – obvious, without any attempt to be hidden

flamboyant – very confident in behaviour, and liking to be noticed by other people

put sth ahead of sth – decide one thing is more important than another thing

relish (C2) – enjoy something very much

on a (certain *e.g. aesthetic*) *level* – only in this aspect, without considering other aspects

make sth over as sth else – change something superficially so it can be used for a different function

if sth was no object – if there were no limits on a resource, e.g. money, time

c 💬 Put students into groups to look at the pictures of the Vitra fire station and the Heydar Aliyev Centre and ask them to discuss the questions. Encourage students to use vocabulary from the text. Take feedback as a class.

🔄 LOA TIP MONITORING

- When you monitor group work, make sure that students take turns appropriately. An important part of turn-taking is everyone contributing equally.

- To raise awareness, ask students to time how long they are speaking for on their stopwatches on their mobile devices (or watches). Tell each student to start the stopwatch when they begin speaking, pause it when they stop and restart when they speak again. Monitor to check that students are using their stopwatches and note down any problems in turn-taking, e.g. particular students dominating or periods of silence.

- At the end of the discussion, ask students to compare how long each person in the group spoke for. See which group had the most equal interaction.

- Tell the students what you noticed as you monitored and elicit solutions to the issues from the class.

d **Language in context** *Metaphorical phrases*

1 Write on the board:

   1 I saw a burning building.

   2 This is a burning issue.

   Ask students how the meaning of *burning* is different in the two sentences (1 on fire; 2 very important) and say that the first usage is literal and the second is metaphorical. Tell students to say whether the meaning of the words in phrases a–g matches those in the text. Check answers as a class.

2 Students then match the highlighted metaphorical expressions in the text with the definitions. Check as a class and read the Learning Tip.

Answers

1 No: they are used in a literal sense in a–g and in a metaphorical, or indirect, sense in the text.

2 a run the risk of
  b upturned the apple cart
  c let her imagination run wild
  d blossomed into
  e walk away with
  f broke the mould
  g draw the line at

💡 HOMEWORK ACTIVITY

▶ Tell students to find a short written piece or an audioscript of spoken text which contains metaphorical language (descriptive texts like advertisements and promotional work are often good sources). Ask students to underline the metaphorical language and next to it make a note of the literal and metaphorical meaning, making up an example which will help them understand the indirect meaning, e.g. *The Taj Mahal is the face of India.* (face = front of the head/ image; your face is your appearance and how other people see you and judge you). Tell students to bring their texts to class and put them up on the classroom walls. Tell students to go round the class, reading the texts and noticing the metaphorical language.

▮4▮ LISTENING

a Ask students why they think the building is called the Gate to the East and use the Culture notes to check answers. Put students into groups to look at the photo and discuss the question. Take feedback as a class.

🌍 CULTURE NOTES

The Gate to the East is 302 metres high and was completed in 2015. The form is meant to symbolise east meeting west as the building itself bridges an important east–west route in Suzhou.

b ▶ 4.27 Ask students to predict any criticisms that different people, e.g. local citizens or architects, may have. Play the recording for students to check their ideas and tick the criticisms they hear. Use the Vocabulary support box to help with vocabulary if necessary. Check as a class.

Answers

1, 4

Audioscript

NEWSREADER As Chinese tower blocks get higher and stranger, the debate is getting fiercer. The architects of this building in the city of Suzhou say it's a mix of western form and Chinese subtlety. Local residents see it differently.

LOCAL MAN [Speaking in Chinese]

NR 'We call it the giant pair of pants,' this man says. 'The giant pair of pants' isn't the only iconic modern building to have come in for a barrage of barbed criticism from Chinese Internet users – complaining about what they see as increasingly outlandish foreign designs, completely out of keeping with Chinese culture and architectural heritage.

DR ZHENG SHILING The danger is er for some cities – they don't have this need and they just construct so many high-rise buildings as a symbol. Er … one city constructed a, a 300 high-rise building … Another city would like to construct a 400 metres, and another 600, and so on. This competition is nonsense.

NR But the Chinese skyscraper is sprouting fast and might soon get even faster. This took little more than a week and now the company behind it says it will build the world's tallest skyscraper in just three months. Heritage is important, some experts say, but so too is solving the problem of China's overcrowded cities.

TIMOTHY JOHNSON A city like Shanghai – 20 million people already, could easily go to 30 to 40 million people, and I, I would subscribe that spreading that out further and further away from a kind of central core is more detrimental, it's less sustainable, than keeping things more dense, and going vertical.

NR But with more than 300 skyscrapers currently under construction in China, the debate is only going to intensify. Is the country laying the foundations for a well-planned urban future, or flying by the seat of its architectural pants?

c ▶ **4.27** Play the recording again for students to listen and summarise the points according to the three views. Check answers as a class.

Suggested answers

1 Increasingly outlandish foreign designs are inappropriate and architects should take into account traditional Chinese culture and architecture.
2 High-rise buildings aren't always needed but cities are competing with each other to build higher and higher buildings as a symbol of their success.
3 The large increase in the population of cities means that building upward is preferable to further and further outward from the centre.

📖 VOCABULARY SUPPORT

a barrage of criticism – a large volume of criticism from many different people

barbed criticism – unkind, angry or resentful criticism

outlandish – strange and unusual and difficult to accept

heritage (C2) – the buildings, paintings, customs, etc. which are important in a culture or society because they have existed for a long time

sth is a symbol – something that represents an idea, e.g. skyscrapers are a symbol of wealth, business, modernity, etc.

out of keeping (with sth) – not suitable for a particular situation

sprout – if a large number of things sprout (up), they suddenly appear or begin to exist

subscribe to sth – agree with or support an opinion, belief or theory

fly by the seat of your pants – do something difficult without the necessary skill or experience

💡 FAST FINISHERS

Ask fast finishers what the British English equivalent of the American English *pants* would be (trousers). Tell students to write down as many American/British alternatives for clothing as they can.

Suggested answers

American/British: pantyhose/tights, sneakers/trainers, suspenders/braces, undershirt/vest; vest/waistcoat; robe/dressing gown; diaper/nappy; anorak/parka; rain boots / wellingtons or wellies

d 💬 Put students into groups to discuss examples of controversial urban development similar to the controversy over the Gate to the East. Take feedback as a class.

5 SPEAKING

a 💬 Pre-teach *derelict* (derelict buildings or places are not cared for and are in bad condition) and *repurpose* (find a new use for an idea, product or building). Ask students how the *re-* in *repurpose* is pronounced (/riː/). Put students into groups of four. Tell them to read the scenario, discuss solutions based on the points to consider and then plan an individual proposal.

b 💬 Students work in their groups of four and present their individual proposals to one another. Each group then chooses the best proposal to tell the rest of the class. The class votes on the best proposal.

💡 EXTRA ACTIVITY

Put students into groups. Explain that they are renting out eight floors, floors 33–40, at the top of a skyscraper and need to decide which floor to allocate to eight new clients:

- a law company needing quiet neighbours
- a private detective firm with lots of strange visitors
- a penthouse for a millionaire who loves giving parties
- the head office of the national vegetarian association
- a studio for an eccentric artist who wants the best view
- an exclusive 24-hour fitness studio
- a man always dressed in black who won't give his real name
- an expensive steak restaurant which gives off very strong smells.

Each group should draw a plan of the eight floors labelled with their allocations and present it to the other groups, explaining their decisions. The class votes on the best solution.

ADDITIONAL MATERIAL

▶ Workbook 9B
▶ Photocopiable activities: Grammar p.218, Vocabulary p.238

9C Everyday English
Let's not jump to conclusions

OPTIONAL LEAD-IN

Books closed. Put students into pairs. Tell them to discuss a situation when they felt really angry: what happened, why did they feel that way and how did they deal with the situation? Take feedback as a class.

1 LISTENING

a ⬤ Ask students if their picture or personal details have ever been used anywhere without their permission. Put students into groups to discuss the questions. Take feedback as a class.

b ⬤ Tell students to look at the picture. Elicit ideas of what students think is happening.

c ▶ 4.28 Play Part 1 of the video or the audio recording for students to check their answer to 1b. Use the Vocabulary support box below to help students with vocabulary if necessary but don't explain the animal idioms as these are dealt with in 1e. Check answers.

Answer

Emma is showing Max a news article about him. He is very angry because it includes exclusive information he had given to Sara.

Videoscript/Audioscript (Part 1)

EMMA You're cheerful today!

MAX Yeah, well, I am. It seems like everything's falling into place, at last.

E Oh?

M Yeah! My new book's coming together well and I really think it's going to work. And, guess what? I think I've found a place to live.

E Wow, that's brilliant!

M Yeah, it's in a renovated warehouse, down by the marina.

E Sounds very avant-garde! Hey, Max ... there's an article about you on *Breaking News Online*. Look!

M But ... I've never even spoken to anyone at *Breaking News Online*! This is outrageous! Listen: 'Night owl Max Redwood spent his childhood gazing up at the night skies ...' This is beyond belief!

E But it's true. I remember when Dad gave you that telescope.

M They've got no right to publish this! Where on earth did they get this from?! Who wrote it?

E There's no name.

M I don't believe it! They've even got the title of my next book in here!

E Let's see ... 'Gravity Zero ...' So they do!

M But I haven't told ... Sara! It's disgraceful! How dare she?! ...

E Sara? But she doesn't work for *Breaking News*!

M No, but she's the only person I've told.

E Hmm, let's not jump to conclusions. There's something fishy about this. Why would Sara give the exclusive information that she needs for her big break to someone else?

M I don't know ... I'm lost for words!

E I smell a rat.

M What do you mean?

E Someone else at *City FM* must have leaked the information.

M Maybe ... Anyway, whoever it was, they've got no right! I'm ringing them right now!

E Hold your horses, Max! Think about what you want to say first.

---

d ▶ 4.28 Ask students who or what the pronouns refer to. Play Part 1 of the video or the audio recording again for students to check.

Answers

1. his new book
2. (the news that) Max has found a place to live
3. the fact there's an article about him on *Breaking News Online*
4. the fact Max spent his childhood gazing up at the night skies
5. Sara
6. *City FM*

EXTRA ACTIVITY

Ask students where Max is going to move to (a renovated warehouse) and whether they think that would make a good home for him. Put students into groups to design Max's living space. Encourage them to use the vocabulary from Lesson 9A. Ask groups to present their ideas to the class.

e **Language in context** *Animal idioms*

1. ▶ 4.29 Ask students to correct the idioms and then play the recording for them to check.
2. Ask students to say what the idioms mean. Tell them to look at the audioscript on SB p.187 and a dictionary if necessary.

Answers and audioscript

1. a Night owl, Max Redwood.
   b There's something fishy about this.
   c I smell a rat.
   d Hold your horses, Max.
2. See the Vocabulary support box.

VOCABULARY SUPPORT

fall into place (C2) – when events or details that you did not understand before fall into place, they become easy to understand

come together – when different things start working successfully and effectively together

night owl – a person who prefers to be awake and active at night

fishy – seeming dishonest or false

smell a rat – recognise that something is not as it appears to be or that something dishonest is happening

leak (v.) (C2) – allow secret information to become generally known

hold your horses – used to tell someone to stop and consider carefully their decision or opinion about something

- Encourage students to think about the meaning behind the idiom as you concept check. This will help students to remember the animal expressions.

- Ask students: *Do you usually see owls at night or day?* (night). *So is a 'night owl' someone who likes to work early or late?* (late). *Would you be happy to see a rat in your home?* (no). *So if you 'smell a rat' do you have a good or a bad feeling?* (bad). *What would you want to do next?* (find out what's happening). *If fish was left on a table for a few days, how would it smell?* (terrible). *So if a situation is 'fishy', do you feel comfortable about it?* (no). *Are horses strong animals?* (yes). *If someone didn't control their horse, what could happen?* (they could have an accident). *So would you advise someone to 'hold their horses' before making a difficult decision?* (yes).

f (▶) **4.30** Ask students whether they think Nadia will take any complaint that Max makes seriously. Put students into pairs and play Part 2 of the video or the audio recording for them to answer and discuss the questions. If necessary, explain *get the lie of the land* (wait until you have all the available information about a situation before you take any action). Take feedback as a class.

Answers
1 c   2 Students' own answers   3 Students' own answers

Videoscript/Audioscript (Part 2)

MAX This is Max Redwood, and I'm calling to express my dissatisfaction … No … no … This is Max Redwood and words cannot express my anger … Oh, for goodness' sake. Hello, is that the editor-in-chief at *City FM*?

NADIA Yes, speaking.

M This is Max Redwood. I really feel you owe me an explanation for the article which appeared on *Breaking News*.

N Yes, I've just seen that. I can assure you that we are just as upset as you are.

M Really? Well … I spoke in confidence to Sara Neroni. The next thing I know, I'm in an anonymous story online, and the title of my next book has been announced! It's totally unacceptable! Don't you think you should take full responsibility for this?

N There's no need to raise your voice, Mr Redwood. I do understand, and I have every intention of investigating the matter. Should I discover that any of the team have been involved, I can assure you, there will be consequences.

M How would you feel about someone you trusted revealing your confidential information in the press?! You've failed to fulfil your responsibility to protect my privacy!

N I really don't know what else I can say … Once I get the lie of the land, I'd like to invite you in and we can discuss it face-to-face.

M Absolutely not. And I'd appreciate it if you didn't try to contact me again. It's over. Finished. Finito. The end.

2 USEFUL LANGUAGE
Dealing with conflict

a (▶) **4.28** (▶) **4.30** Ask students to try to complete the expressions before they listen. Then play Parts 1 and 2 of the video or the audio recording again for them to complete the expressions and check. Drill the expressions.

Answers
1 beyond   2 earth   3 words   4 disgraceful
5 dissatisfaction   6 anger   7 unacceptable

b Tell students to think about possible differences between a spoken and written complaint (written would usually be more formal). Tell students to answer the questions. Check answers as a class.

Answers
5 I'm calling to express my dissatisfaction.
6 Words cannot express my anger.
The expressions are too formal for a conversation of this kind.
I'm calling would need to be changed to *I'm writing* in a written complaint.

c (▶) **4.31** Tell students to complete the sentences. Then play the recording for students to check.

Answers
1 jump to
2 to raise
3 right
4 explanation
5 take full responsibility
6 to fulfil your responsibility

📖 **LANGUAGE NOTES**

Students often get confused between *arise, rise* and *raise*. Point out that *arise* (C1) is formal, takes no object and means to happen, e.g. *Should the opportunity arise, I'd like to go to China*. Highlight that *raise* (B1) and *rise* (B2) both mean increase but *raise* (= to cause something to increase or become bigger, better, higher, etc.) needs an object whereas *rise* doesn't take an object.

---

d Ask students to categorise the comments under Max's and *Breaking News Online / City FM*'s behaviour. Check as a class.

Answers
Max's behaviour: 1; 2
Breaking News Online / City FM's behaviour: 3; 4; 5; 6

e (▶) **4.32** Ask students what Nadia suggests at the end of the conversation with Max (a face-to-face meeting with Max at *City FM* once she has all the information she needs about the situation). Ask the students to complete the sentences. Then play the recording to check.

Answers
1 intention   2 can assure   3 Absolutely; appreciate

f 💬 Put students into pairs to role-play the conversation between Max and Nadia using the language from the exercises but ending with Max reacting positively. As feedback, ask some pairs to role-play their conversation in front of the class.

3 LISTENING

a (▶) **4.33** Ask students to look at the picture and say what they think is going on between Nadia and Oscar. Play Part 3 of the video or the audio recording for students to find Nadia's two reasons for suspecting Oscar and what she wants from Oscar. Check answers as a class.

Answers
Oscar was the only other person in the office and Nadia knows he overheard Sara's conversation with her. Nadia found the business card of *Breaking News Online*'s editor on Oscar's desk.
Nadia wants Oscar's letter of resignation the next morning.

Videoscript/Audioscript (Part 3)

NADIA Oscar.

OSCAR You wanted to see me?

N Take a seat. Have you got something to tell me, Oscar?

O Er, no, should I?

N There's an article on *Breaking News Online* about Max Redwood.

O Oh?

N Yes. It gave me a strong sense of déjà vu actually … it's full of Sara's information – including the title of the book.

O Really?

N Yes.

O So, are you thinking someone leaked it?

N Yes, I am, Oscar. You were the only other person in the office last night. I know you overheard our conversation.

O What are you saying?

N What's more, I happened to find this business card on your desk – 'Miranda Hall, Editor-in-Chief, *Breaking News Online*'. … Had a little rendezvous with Miranda, have we?

O I don't know what you're talking about.

N Oscar, by selling information to other organisations, you are in breach of your contract.

O You can't sack me. I'll take you to court!

N I'm not going to sack you, you're right. You're going to resign. If you take us to court, you'll lose, and you'll never work in journalism again. I'll expect your letter of resignation in the morning.

b ▶ **4.33** Play Part 3 of the video or audio recording again for students to answer the questions. Check as a class.

Answers
1 Because the article contained the information Sara told her.
2 They had a meeting.   3 He'd lose.

📖 LANGUAGE NOTES

Ask students to underline the tag question in the audioscript on SB p.187 (*Had a little rendezvous with Miranda, have we?*) and ask what is unusual about the form: the use of the plural *we*; the direction of the tag (after a positive statement there is usually a negative, not positive, tag). Elicit that the *we* is sarcastic and patronising and that same-direction tags can be used as a reaction to what we already know. Here the same-direction tag is used as an accusation.

c 💬 Put students into groups to discuss Nadia's treatment of Oscar. Take feedback as a class.

💡 FAST FINISHERS

Ask fast finishers to think of how Oscar could get his revenge on Nadia and *City FM*, e.g. send an email to everyone on the company's address list telling them that they have won a thousand euros in a *City FM* competition.

4 PRONUNCIATION Sound and spelling: foreign words in English

a ▶ **4.34** Ask students what you call the thing that protects you from the rain (*umbrella*) and if they know what the origin of this word is (*ombrello*, Italian). Play the recording for students to listen to the words. Ask students to say the origin of the words and which four were used in Parts 1–3. Tell them to look at the audioscript on SB p.187 if necessary. Check answers.

Answers
1 French   2 Spanish   3 French   4 Italian   5 Italian
6 French   7 French   8 Spanish (it is also a common word in Italian, but not with the same meaning)
In Parts 1–3: avant-garde (Part 1); finito (Part 2); déjà vu; rendezvous (Part 3)

🌍 CULTURE NOTES

English has absorbed a large number of foreign words throughout its history. Approximately 60% of English vocabulary comes from French or Latin.

b Tell students to match the words and phrases with their meanings. Check answers as a class.

Answers
a 3   b 7   c 4   d 5   e 2   f 1   g 6   h 8

c ▶ **4.34** Play the recording again for students to listen and underline the consonant sounds which are unusual for English. Check as a class.

Answers
cappu<u>cc</u>ino   déjà vu   rende<u>z</u>vou<u>s</u>   ava<u>nt</u> gar<u>de</u>

d Put students into pairs to answer the questions and check in a dictionary. Check as a class.

Answers
c'est la vie /seɪlæˈviː/ (French): used to say that situations of that type happen in life, and you cannot do anything about them
kaput /kəˈpʊt/ (German): not working correctly
aficionado /əfɪʃiəˈnɑːdəʊ/ (Spanish): someone who is very interested in and enthusiastic about a particular subject
faux pas /fəʊˈpɑː/ (French): words or behaviour that are a social mistake or not polite
kindergarten /ˈkɪndəɡɑːtən/ (German): a nursery school
tsunami /tsuːˈnɑːmi/ (Japanese): an extremely large wave caused by a violent movement of the earth under the sea
paparazzi /pæpərˈætsi/ (Italian): the photographers who follow famous people everywhere they go in order to take photographs of them for newspapers and magazines
Schadenfreude /ˈʃɑːdənfrɔɪdə/ (German): a feeling of pleasure or satisfaction when something bad happens to someone else
typhoon /taɪˈfuːn/ (Cantonese Chinese): a violent wind that has a circular movement, found in the West Pacific Ocean
karaoke /kæriˈəʊki/ (Japanese): a form of entertainment, originally from Japan, in which recordings of the music but not the words of popular songs are played, so that people can sing the words themselves
siesta /siˈestə/ (Spanish): a rest or sleep taken after lunch, especially in hot countries

e ▶ **4.35** Play the recording for students to listen and repeat the words and phrases.

5 SPEAKING

a Ask students to read the example situations and think of a situation where they need to complain. Tell them to make notes about what has happened, who is responsible and the response they want.

b 💬 Put students into pairs. Ask them to take turns role-playing the complaints using the structure given in the bullet points and the language in 2. As feedback, tell some pairs to role-play their conversation in front of the class.

ADDITIONAL MATERIAL

▶ Workbook 9C
▶ Photocopiable activities: Pronunciation p.269
▶ Unit Progress Test
▶ Personalised online practice

At the end of this lesson, students will be able to:

- listen to a comparison of different living environments and give advice to the speakers
- understand the structure of a discussion essay on urban migration and the linking devices used to express reasons and results
- write a discussion essay about social change based on the structure and language of a model

💡 OPTIONAL LEAD-IN

Books closed. Tell students to make a list of the best places in the world to live, and be specific, e.g. a beach on Hawaii. Put them into groups to compare lists and point out any potential problems, e.g. a beach home could get flooded.

1 LISTENING and SPEAKING

a 💬 Ask students if the capital of a country is always the best place to live. Put students into groups to discuss the questions. Take feedback as a class.

b 💬 Ask students to look at the photos and elicit answers to the question. If you wish, give students information about New Zealand from the Culture notes below.

🌍 CULTURE NOTES

New Zealand is in the Southwest Pacific Ocean and has a population of about 4.5 million. While Auckland is the largest city, Wellington is the capital. Because New Zealand was one of the last places settled by humans, it has a very diverse animal and plant life. Historically, agriculture has been an important part of New Zealand's economy.

c ▶ 4.36 Ask students why they think Lizzie and Ron look so pleased in the photo. Play the recording for students to answer the questions. If necessary, pre-teach *leave the nest* (when children leave home), *sit tight* (stay where you are) and *the Big Smoke* (a large city). Check answers as a class.

Answers

1. Her son Josh has won a scholarship – University of Auckland Academic Excellence. She feels proud, but thoughtful / a little sad as it's her first child to be leaving home.
2. They can't get a good education in the small town where they live.
3. They won't be able to find the kind of jobs they would like.
4. House prices are much higher in big cities; life is less stressful; they have good friends.
5. The population will keep getting smaller.

Audioscript

CAFÉ WORKER So … a flat white and a long black. That's $7.50.

LIZZIE Here you are.

RON But isn't it my turn?

CW Thanks.

L The coffee's on me, Ron.

R You sure, Lizzie?

L Well, look on it as a kind of celebration.

R Really?

L Yeah.

R Shall we sit here?

L Yep.

R So … What's up?

L What do you mean?

R Well, you don't exactly look like you're jumping for joy. In fact, I'd say you almost look a bit miserable.

L Thoughtful – not miserable.

R OK. But you still haven't told me – what are we celebrating?

L It's Josh – he's won a scholarship – University of Auckland Academic Excellence.

R Lizzie, that's great! Pass on my congratulations to him. Oh, that's wonderful – proud mum, eh?!

L Yeah, yeah – I do feel proud. He's studied hard and done really well.

R So why the long face?

L Well, it just hit me, y'know, this whole thing of Josh leaving home – off to the Big Smoke …

R Yeah nah, it's hard when they leave the nest. When Jessica went off to uni last year it took me a while to get used to her … not being there.

L Yeah, I remember.

R It did mean I was able to reclaim the bathroom for myself!

L A lot to be said for that!

R But I still miss her.

L Yeah, Josh is my first to go.

R Well, they'll probably all go and live elsewhere in the long run – all our kids.

L Yeah – they've got to really, though, don't they?

R Well, they can't stay in this town and hope to get a decent education!

L Problem is – and this is what I've been thinking about – nor are they likely to return. I mean, even if Josh did want to come back and live here, there wouldn't be any jobs for someone with an engineering degree.

R Yeah, Jessica reckons she wants to get into marketing or something like that. Don't see much chance of her coming back here to do that.

L But that's the thing – see, everyone just goes off to Auckland or Wellington and they never come back. And then small towns like these – they just get smaller and smaller.

R But it's not just the kids going off to study, is it? What about when they shut down the timber mill – that meant a big exodus.

L Yeah, we've lost just over a thousand people in the last five years. Makes me feel like packing up myself and moving on.

R Yeah, I have to say the thought has crossed my mind.

L But imagine – the price you'd get for your house here and then the price of houses in a place like Auckland. I just couldn't afford to do it.

R Nope, we're better off sitting tight.

L Yeah nah, you're probably right.

R And the truth is, I'm not unhappy – life's a whole lot less stressful here.

L That's certainly true.

R And I've got some good friends – like yourself. We can keep each other sane.

L Yeah, but this scholarship thing – it just made me think. Like, I could see we might end up being the last generation that lives in a town like this. I mean, will the population just keep getting smaller and smaller – and then what?

R To the point that we don't exist any more?

L Yeah, something like that.

R But, hey, enough of these pessimistic thoughts – let's just celebrate Josh doing well for himself.

L Yeah. I must have done something right bringing him up.

R Maybe, but any kid's only as smart as their mother! Or their father!

L Absolutely!

d 💬 Ask students if house prices vary a lot in their country. Put students into groups to give advice. Take feedback as a class.

💡 EXTRA ACTIVITY

Ask students to underline these colloquial expressions in the audioscript on SB pp.187–188 and say what they mean: *The coffee's on me*; *Yep*; *what's up?*; *uni*; *reckons*; *Nope*.

Answers

The coffee's on me: I'll buy the coffee; *Yep*: yes; *what's up?*: What's the problem?; *uni*: university; *reckons*: thinks; *Nope*: no

2 READING

a Ask students if urban migration is more of a problem in smaller countries like New Zealand. Tell students to read the essay and put the points in the order they are mentioned. If necessary, pre-teach *ghost town* (a town where few or no people now live), *incentive* (C2) (something that encourages a person to do something) and *subsidy* (C1) (money given as part of the cost of something, to help or encourage it to happen). Check answers as a class.

Answers
5
6
2
3
1
4

b 💬 Ask students if they know anybody who has moved to a bigger town and what issues they had. Put students into groups to discuss the challenges faced in moving. Take feedback as a class.

3 WRITING SKILLS Discussion essays; Linking: reason and result

a Ask students how many paragraphs there are in the essay (five). Elicit the function of each paragraph.

Suggested answers
paragraph 1: to introduce the topic
paragraph 2: to explain why people move to cities
paragraph 3: to describe the (negative) effects of migration on cities
paragraph 4: to describe the (negative) effects of migration on small towns / rural communities
paragraph 5: to summarise and suggest a plan of action

b Write these sentence headers on the board:

In my opinion,

It could be said that

Ask students which expresses a writer's view directly (In my opinion) and which indirectly (It could be said that). Ask the same question for the phrase in italics in the first paragraph. Check the answer and then tell students to match the other phrases in italics with the meanings. Check answers and then read through the Writing Tip with the class.

Answers
indirectly
1; 4 you can see clearly
3 I've looked
2; 5 I think

c Ask students what would be the formal synonyms of these words used about the structure of an essay: *start* (introduction), *ending* (conclusion), *part* (section), *main part* (body). Tell students to put the formal synonyms from the box into the sentences. Check as a class.

Answers
1 noticeable
2 outcome
3 appear
4 outlining
5 claimed

d Ask students to look at the first highlighted phrase and ask if it introduces a reason or indicates a result (introduces a reason) and why (*factor* is similar in meaning to *reason* in this context). Tell students to put the rest of the highlighted examples into two lists: introduce a reason, indicate a result. Check as a class and drill the phrases.

Answers
Introduce a reason: One key factor; because of; due to
Indicate a result: leads to; causing; As a result; results in; which, in turn, means; As a consequence; can lead to

💡 FAST FINISHERS
Ask fast finishers to replace three of the highlighted examples in the essay with other examples from the list. Tell them to write the relevant part of the sentences and add them to their list, e.g. *This exodus leads to the closure of businesses.*

e Tell students to read the sentences and underline the reason or result language. Check answers as a class. Ask students which language shows result and which shows reason (reason: 1, 5; result: 2, 3, 4). Tell students to add the words and phrases to their lists in 3d.

Answers
1 owing to
2 Consequently
3 causes
4 Hence
5 as a direct consequence of

f Ask students which expressions in 3e can be used in the same way as the examples. Check answers as a class. Tell students to add the expressions to their lists in 3d.

Answers
1 causes
2 owing to, as a direct consequence of
3 Consequently, Hence

g Tell students to choose the best word in italics. Check answers as a class. In item 3, *thus* is a better choice, because it refers to the process by which a result happens; however, *therefore* would not be wrong here. See the Writing Tip on SB p.175.

Answers
1 creating
2 Thus
3 thereby

📖 LANGUAGE NOTES
Highlight that *thereby* (C1) (formal, as a result of a particular action or event) is used before a verb. *Therefore* and *Thus* can be used as comment adverbs or before a verb.

h ▶ Students complete the exercises in Writing Focus 9D on SB p.175. They read the table and the Writing Tip and then complete the exercises. Check answers to Exercise a and b as a class. Monitor Exercise c and take feedback as a class. Tell students to go back to SB p.113.

Answers

a 1 One of the main reasons   2 resulted in   3 Thus
4 due to   5 cause   6 thereby

b 1 The recent arrival of large numbers of people from the
countryside ~~leads~~ has led to the current shortage in housing.

2 Increased pressure on city infrastructure often causes ~~that~~
~~there is~~ a rise in taxes.

3 There are fewer jobs in small towns because <u>of</u> the closure of
so many businesses.

4 As a result <u>of</u> the arrival of rural migrants, city schools have
many more children on their roll.

5 Youth unemployment is very high in the town~~, thereby~~.
<u>Therefore/Thus,</u> there's a lot of competition for jobs.

4 WRITING

a Tell students to read the examples and think about
a social change in their country, the reasons and results.
Put students into pairs to talk about them.

b Tell students to follow the steps and write a discussion
essay with five paragraphs as in the model. As a more
interactive alternative, or if you have less class time
available, you could put students into groups of five,
tell them to choose one of their ideas for social change
and ask each student to write one paragraph (in
smaller groups stronger students could write an extra
paragraph). Ask students to check one another's work
before the next stage.

c Tell students (or groups) to swap essays and read them.
Put students into pairs (or two groups together) to
answer the questions and say what they think about the
issues raised.

 LOA TIP REVIEW AND REFLECT

- Encourage students to check their writing thoroughly
  before they give it to someone else to read.

- Give students a checklist to go through. They should be
  able to answer *yes* to all these questions.

  Have I followed all the steps in 4b?

  Will my partner want to read my essay?

  Will my partner learn anything new about this issue?

  Is the grammar accurate?

  Is the grammar complex, e.g. complex noun phrases?

  *Have I used a range of vocabulary, including new words and
  expressions from this unit?*

  Have I checked for spelling and punctuation mistakes?

- Students could use the same checklist to evaluate each
  other's essays in 4c.

💡 EXTRA ACTIVITY

Tell students to watch on YouTube an episode from the
British 1970s comedy *The Good Life*, about a couple who
try to lead a self-sufficient life while staying in their house
in a suburb of London. A lot of the humour comes from
the naivety of people as they attempt to adopt a simple
lifestyle. Put students into groups to say what happened in
the episode they watched and what it said about adopting a
sustainable life.

ADDITIONAL MATERIAL

▶ Workbook 9D

UNIT 9
Review and extension

1 GRAMMAR

a Write these sentences on the board and ask students what the difference between them is: *1 Karen and Simon are proud of themselves. 2 Karen and Simon are proud of each other.* (1 they feel proud as individuals and/or as a couple; 2 each feels proud of the other person). Ask students to complete the sentences with pronouns. Check as a class.

Answers
2 himself   3 herself   4 each other   5 ourselves
6 each other; each other   7 ourselves

ⓦ FAST FINISHERS

Ask fast finishers to write down three things that are better to do by yourself, e.g. wash up, and three things that are better to do with other people, e.g. karaoke. Tell students to compare their ideas with another fast finisher.

b Dictate this sentence to students and ask them to write it down more concisely: *I got up and I looked and then I heard a familiar sound but I was confused by the familiar sound.* (I got up, looked and heard a familiar sound but was confused by it.) Tell students to correct the mistakes. Check as a class.

Answers
1 Kate wanted to put in new windows but I didn't ~~want~~.
2 'I'll never listen to her advice again.' '~~So~~ Neither will I.'
3 It was a beautiful morning although ~~it~~ was rather cool outside.
4 ~~He~~ Living nearby, Frank had no problem getting in early.
5 So they wouldn't get bored, they were listening to the radio.
6 'Kelly hasn't read the contract properly.' 'I ~~don't suspect~~ suspect not.'
7 She became a famous actress, as did/was her mother.
8 Take the clean mug, not the dirty one.

2 VOCABULARY

a Ask students to complete the sentences. Check answers as a class.

Answers
1 redevelop   2 reinstate   3 restore   4 recreate   5 regain
6 renovate

b Tell students to match the sentence halves. Check as a class.

Answers
1 b   2 d   3 f   4 a   5 c   6 e

ⓦ EXTRA ACTIVITY

Ask students to choose one of the buildings in a–f in 2b. Tell them to write three adjectives, from 9B Vocabulary Focus or other adjectives which could describe it, e.g. *imposing/practical/ugly* (power station). Put students into groups. They take turns to read out their three adjectives for the other students to guess the building.

3 WORDPOWER *build*

a Ask students which of these words can't follow *build*: *trust, safety, goodwill, momentum* (safety). Tell students to read the multi-word verb collocations with *build* and then match them with the meanings. Check answers as a class.

Answers
a 4
b 1
c 6
d 5
e 3
f 2

b ▶ **4.37** Tell students to complete the sentences with the words and then play the recording for them to check.

Answers
1 up
2 in
3 up
4 on
5 around
6 up
7 up

c Tell students to complete the statements with their own ideas, using a dictionary if necessary to help them understand the expressions.

d ⏺ Put students into pairs to compare their answers. Take feedback as a class.

▶ Photocopiable activities: Wordpower p.249

🔄 LOA REVIEW YOUR PROGRESS

Students look back through the unit, think about what they've studied and decide how well they did. Students work on weak areas by using the appropriate sections of the Workbook, the Photocopiable worksheets and the Personalised online practice.

UNIT 10

Occasions

GETTING STARTED

☉ OPTIONAL LEAD-IN

Books closed. Put students into pairs and ask them to make a list of things that could go wrong at a wedding, e.g. terrible weather, forgetting the rings, someone dropping the wedding cake. Write the list on the board and ask the class if they have ever experienced any of these things at a wedding.

a ☐ Elicit *bride* (B1) and *bridegroom* (a man who is about to get married or has just got married). Give students one minute to think about their answers to the questions before talking about the photo as a class. If you wish, give students information from the Culture notes.

◯ UNIT OBJECTIVES

At the end of this unit, students will be able to:

- understand instructional texts about presentations and speeches, articles about sports psychology and detailed film reviews
- follow and understand details including the attitudes of the speakers in narratives about socially awkward public speaking situations and radio discussions of the origins of superstitions
- use a range of lexis to: describe communication, regrets and criticisms and customs, beliefs, rituals in their own and other cultures and respond to these ideas and discuss possible origins; give a short talk using anecdotes to illustrate main points
- follow an interview and an idiomatic social interaction in which speakers congratulate each other on their success
- use a range of expressions and strategies for turn-taking in more formal conversations and interviews to continue speaking, interrupt and encourage others
- write an informative review of a film or TV series using a range of devices to make description concise and effective

🌍 CULTURE NOTES

This photo shows a couple getting married in the London Aquarium on 14 February, 2011. The man outside the tank is the wedding official and he is using signs to give the instructions. In the UK, you can get married outside a church or official registry office if the place is a permanent structure with a roof (this rules out many outside locations such as beaches and forests) and if it has been approved for purpose. As other examples of non-traditional wedding locations, couples regularly get married on the route of the London Marathon course, running the whole way in wedding clothes; a Russian couple got married while cycling around their home city; a Belgian couple got married on a bungee-jump platform.

b ☐ Put students into groups to discuss the questions. For questions 1 and 2 take feedback as a class. For question 3 tell students to share their suggestions and ask the class which is the most original and interesting.

☉ EXTRA ACTIVITY

Tell students that there is a (not very well-followed) tradition to give anniversary presents according to the number of years of marriage: 1st = paper, 2nd = cotton, 3rd = leather, 4th = fruit/flowers, 5th = wood. Put students into pairs to think of more modern equivalents for the first five years, e.g. 1st = digital, 2nd = environmentally friendly, 3rd = sporty.

10A I really wish I'd been on time

At the end of this lesson, students will be able to:

- read, listen to and discuss factors that make a successful speech or presentation using a range of communication verbs
- speak about regrets for past situations using a range of structures to express regret and criticism
- use main stress appropriately in regrets and criticisms
- give a one-minute speech based on a personal experience

ⓦ OPTIONAL LEAD-IN

Books closed. Ask students to remember what Sara's presentation in Lesson 6C was about (Max), and why she made it (to convince everyone he was worth interviewing again). Put students into groups to write down the expressions they learned about organising a presentation in 6C, e.g. *My focus today is … .* Check answers as a class. Then tell students to go back to SB p.74 and find the expressions they couldn't remember.

1 SPEAKING and VOCABULARY
Communication verbs

a 🗩 Ask students what kind of situations people need to give speeches or presentations in, e.g. a wedding, winning an Oscar. Tell students to discuss the questions in pairs. Take feedback as a class.

b 🗩 Ask students why they think people use speechwriters. Tell students to read the quotes. Then put students into groups to discuss the questions. If necessary, pre-teach *embodiment* (someone or something that represents a quality or an idea exactly) and *sway* (persuade someone to believe or do one thing rather than another). Take feedback as a class.

Suggested answers
Emma Watson: self-belief can overcome any nervousness
Sir Winston Churchill: you need to believe in the message yourself
Ashley Ormon: it's important not to try to please everyone
Chris Anderson: good speeches make a difference
Students' own answers

🌍 CULTURE NOTES

Emma Watson (born 1990) is a British actress most famous for her role as Hermione in the *Harry Potter* film series.

Sir Winston Churchill (1874–1965) was the UK Prime Minister during the Second World War, famous for his wartime speeches.

Ashley Ormon is an editor and a writer of poetry, books and articles, mostly on religious topics.

Chris Anderson (born 1957) bought the TED concept, first launched in 1984, in 2001 through the media company which he founded and then greatly expanded TED on a non-profit basis.

c 🗩 Ask students if they've ever had to listen to a really bad presentation. Put students into groups to discuss the questions. Take feedback as a class.

🔄 LOA TIP ELICITING

- A 'pyramid' discussion is an effective way of eliciting as many different ideas as possible from students, maximising a discussion and varying the interaction pattern.
- Arrange students into pairs and give them a time limit to discuss 1c.
- At the end of the time limit, or when students start to run out of ideas, put two pairs into a group to compare ideas.
- Then put students into new groups of four made up of students from different groups to compare what they have discussed.
- Finally, tell a student from each group to present the group's ideas to the whole class. Ask a volunteer to write the ideas on the board in note form in two lists: what makes a good presentation; what can go wrong.

d Tell students to read the sentences to see if their ideas are mentioned.

e ▶ 4.38 Check students understand *finer* (C1) (needing to be considered very carefully) and *throwaway* (something that someone says without thinking carefully and is not intended to be serious). Tell students to match the verbs and verb phrases in bold from 1d with the phrases 1–7. Check answers as a class.

Answers
1 present 2 demonstrate 3 address 4 move on to
5 go into 6 illustrate 7 make

f ▶ ▶ 4.39 Students complete the exercises in Vocabulary Focus 10A on SB p.167. Play the recording for students to check their answers to Exercise a. Check answers as a class after Exercise b. Put students into pairs to do Exercise c and then put them into groups to discuss the questions in Exercise d. Take feedback as a class after both Exercise c and d. Tell students to go back to SB p.116.

Answers (Vocabulary Focus 10A SB p.167)
a 1 demonstrated 2 address 3 move on to 4 made
  5 presented 6 illustrate 7 go into
b 1 c 2 h 3 g 4 b 5 f 6 a 7 e 8 d

2 READING

a Ask students if they have heard about TED talks. Tell them to read *TED* and the first column of the article *How to Give a Killer Presentation* and then answer the questions. Pre-teach *halting* and *tumble out* if necessary (see the Vocabulary support box below). Check answers as a class.

Answers
1 through short talks (up to 18 minutes)
2 He was very shy, spoke English haltingly and was incoherent. His talk was a great success and he received a standing ovation.

📖 VOCABULARY SUPPORT

an unlikely candidate – not the usual type of person to do a certain thing

halting – stopping often while you are saying or doing something, especially because you are nervous

tumble out – (speaking) if somebody's words tumble out, they speak quickly and the ideas don't come in a logical order

frame sth – organise ideas in a clear structure

incoherently – in a way that is not clear, especially with words or ideas that are joined together badly

compelling – very exciting and interesting and making you want to watch or listen

hang on sb's every word – listen carefully and with fascination

sustained – lasting a long time

a standing ovation – when an audience stand and clap and cheer to show their appreciation

muddled – things that are muddled are badly organised

mesmerising – very attractive, in a mysterious way, making you want to keep looking

b Tell students to read the rest of the article (*Chris Anderson's advice on giving presentations*) and match the headings with the advice. Check as a class.

Answers
1 Frame Your Story
2 Plan Your Delivery
3 Develop Stage Presence
4 Plan the Multimedia
5 Putting It Together

💡 FAST FINISHERS

Tell students that there are nine words or phrases you are going to check the class understands before students read the text again in detail in 2c (the words are listed in the Vocabulary Support box below). Ask them to underline the words or phrases that they think have been chosen and guess their meaning.

c If you used the activity for fast finishers above, elicit the words and phrases fast finishers have underlined in the text and write them on the board. Go through the words and phrases in the Vocabulary support box and elicit or give their meaning. Then tell students to read the text again and make notes on how the ideas will improve presentations. Put students into pairs to compare notes. Check answers as a class.

Suggested answers
1 people love listening to stories
2 avoids a long and complicated talk with information on too many different subjects
3 keeps the audience's attention and gives the impression you are a strong speaker
4 helps you make eye contact with people in different parts of the audience, so people feel you are speaking personally and directly to them
5 avoids using the wrong technology and makes you think about keeping things short and simple
6 starting to prepare six months or more in advance allows time to perfect the talk
7 avoids the talk being formulaic and makes it your own

📖 VOCABULARY SUPPORT

abound – exist in large numbers

be wired to do sth – automatically behave in a certain way as a result of genes or design

cover (too much) ground – describe (too many different) areas of expertise or knowledge

scope (C2) – the range of a subject covered

painstakingly – thoroughly, with a lot of care and attention to detail

map sth out – plan in a detailed, well-organised form

formulaic – organised mechanically according to a standard pattern or style

emulate – copy something achieved by someone else and try to do it as well as they have

take sth on board (C1) – understand or accept an idea or a piece of information

d 💬 Ask students which heading in 2b the advice *Look at the audience, not the slides* would come under (Develop Stage Presence). Put students into pairs to discuss the most relevant piece of advice in the article for them. Take feedback as a class.

💡 HOMEWORK ACTIVITY

▶ Tell students to watch Richard Turere's TED talk *My invention that made peace with lions* at home on YouTube if they have the technology. In class put students into groups to discuss whether they were as impressed with Richard's speech as Chris Anderson was.

3 LISTENING

a 💬 Ask students if they would feel more nervous giving a speech or presentation to people they knew or to strangers. Tell students to discuss which of the situations in 3a they would feel most comfortable in. Take feedback as a class.

b ▶ 4.40 Ask students what they think the situations are in the photos. Play the recording for students to listen and answer the questions. Check answers as a class.

Answers

1 Rob: was best man at his friend's wedding
  Chantal: was giving a presentation to her managers
  Milos: was fundraising
2 Rob: didn't have one of his speech cards and didn't thank the bride's parents
  Chantal: didn't have any PowerPoint slides because they weren't on the memory stick her colleague brought into work on the morning of the presentation after working on them at home the previous evening
  Milos: got distracted by a beautiful girl he knew in the audience
3 Rob: has a difficult relationship with the bride and groom
  Chantal: got promoted
  Milos: hasn't been asked to make any more speeches

🌐 CULTURE NOTES

The best man at a wedding is usually a close friend or relation of the groom (the man about to be married). His main duties are to support and help the groom, keep the wedding rings safe and make a speech at the reception.

Audioscript

ROB I agreed to be best man at my friend Dan's wedding. I mean, I was really thrilled that I was asked – it was a great honour. I was fine with the whole thing – you know, organising the pre-wedding party, the ring – everything. I just threw myself into it. But the one task that really unnerved me was having to give a speech at the reception. I'm just hopeless at giving speeches – they make me feel right out of my depth. I should never have agreed to be best man, but, like, Dan's my best mate. Anyway, I decided to get organised and I planned the whole thing out. Y'know, I thought of some funny stories about Dan and all that sort of thing. And I worked out who I needed to acknowledge and say thanks and all that stuff. I put it all on little cards, so by the time the big day came around, I was feeling reasonably on top of things. Just before going to the church, I started feeling really jittery, and while I put all the cards in the pocket of my jacket, I forgot to check they were all there. I really regret not doing that. Anyway, we got to the reception and I somehow managed to get through the speech … Got a few laughs at my jokes. I thought I'd made a good job of it. But Dan was giving me these funny looks. The card I forgot was the one where I thanked the bride's parents and all that sort of thing. And the bride, Jessica, was not impressed. So now there's this strange tension between Dan and me, and Jessica is very cool with me. It's all a bit awkward. I mean, it was a genuine mistake. If only I'd checked those cards. And I have to say that part of me wishes that Dan hadn't asked me to be best man. Oh well, I guess they'll get over it. Eventually.

CHANTAL Ever since I started my present job, I've had this really strange relationship with this colleague of mine, Martin. Back then, we were both at the same level in the company and it's like he somehow resented that – like I should have started out on a lower level or something. Who knows? We had to do this joint presentation to managers on a project to upgrade the IT systems in the company. We worked out the content together – well, actually, a lot of the ideas were my ideas. And then, Martin agreed to make our PowerPoint slides look good – he's good at that kind of thing. So anyway, everything was on a memory stick and Martin said he'd take it home and work on it and make it look really professional. I really wish I'd copied the presentation on to my hard drive. You know the golden rule – always make a copy, otherwise it's a recipe for disaster. So, the next day, we go upstairs to this meeting room to give our presentation. Martin plugs the memory stick into the laptop and … it's just not there. He's incredibly apologetic and says he can't understand what went wrong and all that sort of thing, but … I have my suspicions … For a minute I was in a state of absolute panic and then I thought 'I can do this.' So when all the managers came in I just told them the truth – that we'd had a problem with IT, but that I would

give the presentation anyway. You see, the one thing Martin didn't know about me is that I'm very good at improvising. And I just explained the whole project and it went like clockwork. The managers were all impressed and I really made my mark. In fact, I'm pretty sure my presentation led to my promotion and I became manager of the project we were presenting. If it **was** Martin who sabotaged the presentation, I've no doubt he now regrets deleting all that data. Not me! Had he been less underhand, I might not have the job I've got now.

MILOS I'm a volunteer paramedic on an air ambulance service. It's very costly to run a service like this, so we need to do quite a bit of fundraising. One of the ways we can do this is by going around to different community groups and talking about our work. It's not something I'd say that I enjoy, but I can do it well enough. This friend of mine, Teresa, has given me a few tips. She told me to look at a point towards the back of the room, and avoid looking at people's faces – it can put you off. Anyway, I was giving a speech to a Parent–Teacher Association at the local primary school, and about half-way through, for some reason, I looked down at people in the front row. And there she was – Ivana – looking up and giving me a gorgeous big smile. Ivana was the most beautiful girl in our class at school. She wasn't my girlfriend, but I used to wish she were. So in the middle of the speech, my heart melted, I turned to jelly … I couldn't go on – I was completely lost for words. I just sort of stood there like an idiot and grinned back at her. I grinned and she grinned and … well, what a romantic fool! I was sort of saying to myself, 'C'mon, get a grip on yourself!' But, no way. You know, if I had listened to Teresa's advice, I might have been OK. In the end, I think I … sort of apologised and told people to look at the website, and then I made a pretty quick exit. Needless to say, we didn't get many donations from the Parent–Teacher Association. If it wasn't for my stupidity, we could have raised more money that day. They haven't asked me to give any more speeches – a good thing – I'm just sticking to being a paramedic these days.

📖 VOCABULARY SUPPORT

unnerve sb – make somebody feel less confident and slightly frightened

jittery – nervous

give sb funny looks – looking at somebody in a way that implies there is something wrong

be cool with sb (C2) – behave in an unfriendly way towards somebody

the golden rule – an important rule or principle, especially in a particular situation

sabotage – intentionally prevent the success of a plan or action

underhand – done secretly and dishonestly in order to achieve an advantage

put sb off – distract somebody from something

turn to jelly – start to feel weak

grin (C2) – smile widely

stick to sth – limit yourself to doing just a particular thing, or things

---

c 💬 Students may want to listen again before doing this activity. If so, you could write some of the expressions from the Vocabulary support box up on the board, and ask students to listen for what they refer to in the text. Ask students which situation interested them the most. Put students into groups to discuss the questions. Take feedback as a class.

Tell fast finishers to write two reactions from people listening to each person: Rob, Chantal and Milos, e.g. Rob: *Aren't you going to mention us? That one about the zookeeper on his wedding night was funny.* Chantal: *Very cool given the circumstances. My trick didn't work!* Milos: *Why do you keep looking at me? I'm not giving any money after that!* Compare reactions with another fast finisher.

d **Language in context** *Idioms: Plans into action*

1 ▶️ **4.41** Tell students to complete the idioms. Play the recording for students to check. Drill the idioms.

2 Tell students to match the idioms with the meanings. Check as a class.

Answers

1 1 threw 2 out 3 good 4 recipe 5 went 6 made
  7 words 8 yourself
2 a 4 b 7 c 3 d 8 e 1 f 5 g 6 h 2

4 GRAMMAR

Regret and criticism structures

a Tell students to read the sentences and decide which one doesn't show regret. Check as a class.

Answer

5 Had he been less underhand, I might not have the job I've got now. (She is glad he was underhand as it led to her promotion).

b Tell students to underline the structures for regret. Check as a class. Ask students to give an example of a third conditional and then ask them to mark the sentences with a third conditional. Check answers as a class.

Answers

1 I should never have agreed to be best man.
2 If only I'd checked those cards.
3 Part of me wishes that Dan hadn't asked me …
4 I really wish I'd copied the presentation …
6 She wasn't my girlfriend, but I used to wish she were (my girlfriend).
7 If I had listened to Teresa's advice, I might have been OK.
8 If it wasn't for my stupidity, we could have raised more money …
  third conditional: 7 and 8 (in 8 *wasn't = hadn't been*)

c ▶️ **4.42** **Pronunciation** Tell students to mark the word groups and underline the main stress in the two sentences. Play the recording for students to listen and check. Drill the sentences.

Answers

1 If I had listened to Teresa's advice, | I might have been OK.
2 If it wasn't for my stupidity, | we could have raised more money.

d ▶ ▶️ **4.43–4.47** Students read the information in Grammar Focus 10A on SB p.156. Play the recording where indicated and ask students to listen and repeat. Students then complete the exercises. Check answers as a class. Tell students to go back to SB p.118.

Answers (Grammar Focus 10A SB p.156)

a 1 a2 b1 2 a2 b1 3 a1 b2 4 a1 b2
b 2 hadn't dropped
  3 ought not to
  4 would
  5 should have waited
  6 might
  7 have heard
  8 wish
  9 could
  10 cleaned
c 2 had 3 rather 4 ought 5 should 6 were 7 should
  8 only 9 time

A common mistake students make is to use *wish* instead of *hope*: ~~I wish you can understand my position.~~ (Correct form = *I hope you can understand my position.*).

e 💬 Put students into groups to talk about the regrets. Monitor and encourage students to use different structures for regrets and criticism. Take feedback as a class.

Write a list of negative events on the board, they can be real or unreal, or a mixture, e.g.

We lost the World Cup on penalties!

1503 people died when the Titanic sank.

We're in an economic recession.

My wife's had a terrible hair cut.

Ask students how these things might have been prevented and what is regretful about what happened. Elicit a range of regret and criticisms for each item, e.g. *If only our goalie hadn't jumped left. If the team hadn't been under so much pressure, I'm sure we would've won.*, etc.

5 SPEAKING

a Tell students to plan a one-minute speech *Learning from my mistakes*, thinking about what they said in 4e and following Chris Anderson's advice. You could put students into pairs to practise giving the speech before the next stage.

b 💬 Put students into small groups to give their speeches and answer follow-up questions. Ask groups to choose the best speech and ask students to give some of the best speeches to the class.

ADDITIONAL MATERIAL

▶ Workbook 10A

▶ Photocopiable activities: Grammar p.219, Vocabulary p.239, Pronunciation p.270

At the end of this lesson, students will be able to:

- discuss superstitions, customs and beliefs in their own and different cultures using a range of words and phrases connected with luck, magic and customs
- pronounce consonant groups in and across words
- read about the significance of ritual in sport and discuss the motivation behind rituals
- use passive reporting structures to be more objective and distance themselves from the facts reported
- listen to and speak about superstitions connected with the theatre and discuss and write about where they originate from

⚲ OPTIONAL LEAD-IN

Books closed. Tell students you are going to do some magic. Ask them to write down any number between 1 and 9, e.g. 3. Tell them to multiply this number by 9, e.g. 3x9 = 27. Tell students to make the answer one digit if necessary by adding the two digits together, e.g. 2+7 = 9. Tell students to subtract 5 from this number, think of the corresponding alphabet letter, e.g. 9–5 = 4, 4 = D, and think of a country in Europe beginning with this letter. Tell students to add 1 to their number, e.g. 4+1 = 5, think of an animal beginning with the corresponding alphabet letter, and then the usual colour of this animal. Finally, tell students to write down the country, the animal and the colour, and then say: *Does anyone have a grey elephant from Denmark?* As if by magic, most students will if they have followed the steps because when they multiply their first number by 9 the two digits always add up to 9.

1 SPEAKING and VOCABULARY

Superstitions, customs and beliefs

a 💬 Ask students in what situations they might need some luck, e.g. when buying a lottery ticket, for getting good weather on holiday. Tell students to look at the pictures and discuss the questions. Take feedback as a class.

b 💬 Ask students which objects they think the sentences describe. Tell students to compare their answers in pairs.

c ▶ 4.48 Play the recording for students to listen and check their answers in 1a and 1b. If necessary, pre-teach *beckon* (move your hand or head in a way that tells someone to come nearer) and *paw* (the foot of an animal that has claws or nails, such as a cat, dog or bear) and refer to the Culture notes for *feng shui*. Drill the words and phrases.

Answers

1a 1 They are all lucky charms, supposed to bring luck and protect people.
    2 Ba Gua mirror: China; Horseshoe: Britain, the USA; Maneki-neko: China, Japan; Wish bracelet: Brazil
1b 1 Wish bracelet 2 Horseshoe 3 Horseshoe
    4 Ba Gua mirror 5 Maneki-neko 6 Wish bracelet
    7 Ba Gua mirror

🌍 CULTURE NOTES

Feng shui /fʊŋˈʃweɪ/ is an ancient Chinese belief that the way your house is built or the way that you arrange objects affects your success, health and happiness. Feng shui is widely practised today, e.g. the Disney company changed the location of the main gate to Hong Kong Disney in its building plans because of Feng shui principles.

Audioscript

SPEAKER All these objects are lucky charms from different parts of the world. They're all supposed to bring luck or protect you in some way. This is a horseshoe, and these were traditionally nailed above doorways in Britain and also in the USA, and they bring good luck to the household. Because they're over the door, they stop bad luck entering the house and they protect it against magic spells. Some people say it's important that the open side should be upwards, so the luck doesn't 'run out'. In other words the horseshoe collects the luck for you.

Now this one is a special kind of mirror, which are traditionally used in China, and they're an important part of feng shui. It's customary to hang them above the front door of a house, and they always face outwards so they can ward off evil and protect the house. The idea is that the mirror deflects any bad energy coming towards the house, so it's very important that you should hang them outside the house, not inside.

And this figure of a cat is called *maneki-neko*, which literally means 'beckoning cat'. You may see these if you go to a Chinese or Japanese shop or a restaurant – they're often just by the door. They come from Japan originally, and they're supposed to bring good fortune to the owner. You see the cat's paw is raised – sometimes it's the left paw and sometimes it's the right paw. If it's the left paw, this attracts customers. And if the right paw is raised, it invites good fortune and brings wealth to the owner – so it's a good idea to have both kinds!

And these are wish bracelets, which are worn as a good-luck charm in Brazil. And they're also worn just as a fashion accessory because they look good. The idea of these is, you tie the ribbon three times round your wrist and you make a wish with every knot you tie. If the ribbon wears out naturally and falls off your wrist, your wishes will come true. So it's really important not to cut the ribbon off.

d Ask students which of the words and phrases are connected with luck and magic and which with customs. Check answers as a class.

Answers

luck and magic: make a wish, magic spells, good fortune, good luck charm, ward off evil
customs: traditionally, customary

LOA TIP CONCEPT CHECKING

- When you are concept checking whether words and phrases belong to one category or another, you can appeal to a variety of learning styles, visual, auditory and kinaesthetic, for students to form strong associations with the language and have some fun. Read out each of the words and phrases and tell students to do one of the following:

  Click their fingers once if it belongs to 'customs' and twice if it belongs to 'luck and magic'.

  Move to the left side of the room for 'customs' and right for 'luck and magic'.

  Stand up for 'customs' and remain sitting for 'luck and magic'.

  Repeat back the 'customs' in a loud voice but whisper back the 'luck and magic'.

  Write down the 'customs' in one colour and 'luck and magic' in another.

EXTRA ACTIVITY

Write this magic spell for good weather (check students understand the pun: *spell* = a period of weather / a magic spell) on the board:

1 cup of 6-day old milk (low-fat or full-cream)

3 tablespoons of baby's tears

2 donkey hairs

half a glass of fresh air

Mix together under a full moon while reading the alphabet backwards. Then burn your umbrella.

Put students into pairs to make spells for things they'd like to have or to happen.

---

e ▶ ⏺ **4.49–4.50** Students complete the exercises in Vocabulary Focus 10B on SB p.168. Play the recording for students to check their answers to Exercise a and b. Play it again for students to listen and repeat the words in Exercise b. Check answers to Exercise c. Take feedback as a class after the discussion in Exercise d. Tell students to go back to SB p.119.

Answers (Vocabulary Focus 10B SB p.168)
a 1 good luck charm 2 good fortune 3 traditionally
4 customary 5 ward off evil 6 make a wish
c 1 convincing/persuasive/plausible 2 gullible
3 convincing/persuasive/plausible 4 convincing/persuasive/plausible 5 dubious/far-fetched 6 convinced
7 dubious/far-fetched
Similar: convincing/persuasive/plausible; dubious/far-fetched

f Cross your fingers and ask students why people do this (for good luck). Tell students to match the expressions with their function. Check answers as a class.

Answers
1 fingers crossed, touch wood, third time lucky
2 you're tempting fate
3 to be on the safe side

g ⏺ **4.51** Tell students to complete the sentences with the expressions. Play the recording for students to check.

Answers
1 touch wood 2 third time lucky 3 fingers crossed
4 you're tempting fate 5 to be on the safe side

h ⏺ **4.52 Pronunciation** Ask students to underline the consonant groups in *magic spells*. Tell students to do the same for the words and expressions in 1f. Play the recording for students to check. Point out that the /d/ in *third* isn't usually fully pronounced before the /t/ of *time* (see 2c and 2d on SB p.38). Then drill the expressions.

Answers
fingers crossed
to be on the safe side
touch wood
third time lucky
you're tempting fate

i 💬 Put students into pairs to take it in turns to say what they are planning and respond using an expression from 1f.

FAST FINISHERS

Ask pairs of fast finishers to think of a situation where they would need a lot of luck, e.g. asking the boss for a pay rise, and to do the role play in i in the new situation.

---

j 💬 Ask students if they believe the saying *You make your own luck*. Put students into groups to discuss the questions. Take feedback as a class.

2 READING

a 💬 Ask students why many sports teams and even competitions, like the Olympics, have a mascot (a person, animal or object that is believed to bring good luck, or one that represents an organisation). Ask students to look at the photo of Nadal and say what he's doing, and why. Take feedback as a class. If you wish, give students information from the Culture notes below about Rafael Nadal.

CULTURE NOTES

Rafael Nadal (born 1986) is one of the greatest tennis players of all time. He has won every major tennis championship, Olympic gold, and team competitions for his country, Spain.

---

b Tell students to read the introduction to the text to check their answers and say why he is doing this and how effective it is. Check answers as a class.

Answers
lining up his water bottles; belief in the power of rituals to bring luck
This behaviour can give an illusion of control and of a way to contribute to success, thus reducing anxiety, so it probably is effective.

c Ask students what they know about the other sports stars in the pictures. Tell students to read the article to find examples of the rituals and say which one isn't mentioned. Check answers as a class.

Answers

2 Serena Williams: bouncing the ball five times before her first serve, twice before her second
3 Cristiano Ronaldo: goes onto pitch first when playing for Portugal, last when playing for Real Madrid
4 Lewis Hamilton: used to have a conker with him
5 Serena Williams: ties her shoelaces in a particular way, wears same pair of socks during a run of wins; Cristiano Ronaldo: only player to start match in long-sleeved shirt when playing for Portugal; Lewis Hamilton: used to wear the same underwear, put one sock on a certain way before adjusting his helmet
6 Cristiano Ronaldo: sits at back of team bus or plane
7 Cristiano Ronaldo: gets his hair done (in a different style) during half-time
1 touching yourself or other people isn't mentioned

📖 VOCABULARY SUPPORT

line sth up – put things into a line

go through sth – practise or perform a prepared sequence, e.g. a script, a presentation, a ritual

come about (C2) – originate, start to happen

an illusion of sth (C2) – a false belief that something is real

drive (n., C1) – energy and determination to achieve things

a run of sth (C2) – a continuous period in which something, e.g. successes, losses, luck, etc., is repeated or lasts

abide by sth – (formal) to obey a rule

conker – the shiny, brown, poisonous nut of a horse chestnut tree

get in sb's way – stop somebody from achieving something

---

d 💬 Ask students if they think rituals could help average players, too. Put students into groups to discuss the question. Take feedback as a class.

💡 FAST FINISHERS

Ask fast finishers to think of a ritual which would help them in English tests, e.g. always walking around the room clockwise before they sit down at their desk.

---

3 GRAMMAR Passive reporting verbs

a Write these sentences on the board and ask students to compare the structures:

Hamilton broke the record. (active)

The record was broken by Hamilton. (passive)

Hamilton is reported to have broken the record. (passive reporting verb)

Tell students to read the sentences and choose the two reasons for using passive reporting verbs.

Answers
to show the information comes from someone else
to show this is not necessarily what they believe

b Ask students to rewrite *Hamilton is thought to have broken the record.* beginning with *It* (It is thought that Hamilton has broken the record.). Tell students to answer the questions individually. Then go through the questions with the class and check answers.

Answers

1 1 a
  2 a
  3 b
  4 b
  5 a
  6 b
2 1 a
  2 a
  3 a
  4 a
  5 a
  6 b
3 2 The champion tennis player is even reported to wear the same …
  3 It is claimed that Williams is so convinced …
  4 It is believed that he insists on sitting …
  5 When playing for Portugal Cristiano Ronaldo is said not to allow any other player to start …
  6 It's said that Lewis Hamilton has overcome the superstitions …

c 💬 Ask students to say some of the sentences from 3a in a more conversational style. Check answers as a class.

Suggested answers

1 They reckon that 'lucky' routines make you more relaxed.
2 I've heard that she wears the same pair of socks all the time when she's winning.
3 They say Serena Williams is so superstitious that she blames herself when she loses.
4 People say he has to sit on the back row whenever they're off to a match.
5 It's common knowledge that Cristiano Ronaldo doesn't allow other Portugal players to start the match in long sleeves.
6 I read in the paper that Lewis Hamilton isn't superstitious any more.

d ▶ Students read the information in Grammar Focus 10B on SB p.157. Play the recording where indicated and ask students to listen and repeat. Students then complete the exercises. Check answers as a class. Tell students to go back to SB p.121.

Answers (Grammar Focus 10B SB p.157)

a 2 It 3 that Sam 4 revealed 5 was regarded
  6 that mistakes will be made 7 been shown to
b 2 He is said to have lived in a cave. / It is said that he lived in a cave.
  3 Basketball is seen as / seen to be very popular in Asia.
  4 It was not reported what her reply was.
  5 It is suspected that the people responsible have left the country. / The people responsible are suspected to have left the country.
  6 It is thought that the winters get very cold in this part of the world. / The winters in this part of the world are thought to get very cold.
c 2 known 3 seen 4 considered 5 expected 6 implied
  7 not understood 8 explained

👁 CAREFUL!

Students sometimes make the mistake of not putting *it* before the passive reporting verb: ~~Don't wear anything red because is believed that it brings bad luck.~~ (Correct form = *Don't wear anything red because **it** is believed that it brings bad luck.*).

---

4 LISTENING

a 💬 Ask students what Shakespeare plays they can name. Put students into groups to say what they know about *Macbeth*. In class feedback give students information from the Culture notes.

> 🌐 **CULTURE NOTES**
>
> *Macbeth*, written about 1606, is set in Scotland and very loosely based on history. A general, Macbeth, driven by the prophecies of three witches and the ambition of his wife, Lady Macbeth, kills the king of Scotland, Duncan, to become ruler himself. Macbeth, tormented by guilt and paranoia, murders more people to keep power, including another general, Banquo. In the end, Lady Macbeth commits suicide and Macbeth is killed by Macduff, a supporter of Malcolm (Duncan's son), who becomes the next king.

b ▶ 4.54 Play the recording for students to listen and answer the questions. If necessary, pre-teach the different meanings/uses here of *curse* (n. a cause of trouble or unhappiness; v. 1 say magic words that are intended to bring bad luck to someone; 2 use a word or expression that is not polite and shows that you are angry; *cursed* adj. experiencing bad luck caused by a curse), *a curse* n. (supernatural power of magic words intended to cause harm or punish) and pre-teach *spit* (C2) (force out the contents of the mouth, especially saliva) and *curse* v. (US) (UK, usually *swear* v., say a word that is considered extremely rude). Check as a class.

Answers

1 It brings bad luck.
2 Three witches are cooking a magic potion.
3 Leave the theatre building straight away, spin round three times in the street, spit, curse and then knock on the door to be allowed back in.
4 a, c, d

Audioscript

PRESENTER Even if you don't go to the theatre or know much about Shakespeare, you've probably heard of Shakespeare's character, Macbeth, who murders the king of Scotland and then becomes king himself, only to be destroyed by his enemies and by his own guilt. What is not so well known is that *Macbeth* is also considered an unlucky play by actors. Actor Naomi Atkins is about to play the role of Lady Macbeth in a new production at the Cavendish Theatre. Naomi, tell us about the superstition – the play is supposed to be cursed, isn't it?

NAOMI Yes, that's right. And especially it brings bad luck if you mention the play by name when you're in the theatre. So, we always refer to it indirectly – we always call it 'the Scottish play' or 'that play'. Some actors even avoid quoting lines from it before a performance. As you know, the play opens with a scene with three witches cooking a magic potion, and people say it's especially unlucky to quote the witches' lines at the opening of the play.

P And what happens if you say the word, *Macbeth* – are you cursed?

N Yes, or the production is – something's bound to go wrong. But, there's a kind of penalty you can pay, to make it all OK again. This actually happened to me. I said the name of the play by mistake during rehearsals.

P What happened?

N Well, to stop the curse, I had to leave the theatre building straight away, then when I was out in the street, I had to spin round three times, spit, curse and then knock on the door to be allowed back in.

P And that neutralised the curse?

N That neutralised it, yes. We had a good laugh about it. It was a bit of a joke, but you'd be surprised how seriously some people take it.

P Do we know where this comes from? Why is the play cursed?

N Well no one knows for certain, but as I said the play does start off with a scene where witches are casting spells, and Shakespeare is believed to have got the words from real witches. And then the witches saw the play, and they put a curse on it because, of course, the play revealed their spells.

P Another explanation I heard was there's a lot of sword-fighting in the play, so people think there's more chance for someone to get injured. So it's unlucky in that way.

N Yes, there are lots of different ideas. Another explanation is that the play was very popular, so it was often put on by theatres that were in debt as a way to increase their audience numbers. But then of course, the theatres normally went bankrupt anyway, so they put the blame on the play and they said it was cursed.

P That's a nice idea.

N Yes, I like that one. As I say, nobody really knows.

5 SPEAKING

a 💬 Ask students why they think actors are so superstitious. Tell students to read the superstitions and say where they might come from. Take feedback as a class (the correct explanations are given in 5d).

b Put students into pairs to choose one of the superstitions. Tell them to write an explanation for it, using passive reporting verbs as in the example.

c 💬 Ask one student from each pair to read out their explanation. Ask the class to vote for the best explanation for each superstition in 5a.

d ▶ Tell students to turn to SB p.131 and read the real explanations. If you wish, give students information from the Culture notes below.

> 🌐 **CULTURE NOTES**
>
> There are other possible explanations for the superstitions, e.g. the *leg* in *Break a leg* may be a chair leg as theatregoers sitting on chairs used to bang their chairs on the ground rather than clap, which could break the chair legs if the audience was really enthusiastic. You could also point out that people use *Break a leg* in everyday usage to wish someone good luck before anything, not necessarily a performance.

ADDITIONAL MATERIAL

▶ Workbook 10B
▶ Photocopiable activities: Grammar p.220, Vocabulary p.240

10C Everyday English
Before we move on

At the end of this lesson, students will be able to:

- use turn-taking language and strategies in conversations and interviews to continue speaking, interrupt and encourage others
- use the appropriate tone in question tags to ask for clarification or confirmation
- take part in a more formal interview in which turn-taking is required

OPTIONAL LEAD-IN

Books closed. Put students into groups to discuss what the best end to the *Solar Wind* story would be for the remaining main characters (Alex, Emma, Max, Sara). Take feedback as a class.

1 LISTENING

a 💬 Ask students what they would do if they had their mobile and it rang right now in the middle of English class. Tell students to look at picture a and discuss the question. Take feedback as a class.

b ▶4.55 Play Part 1 of the video or the audio recording and ask students what the two reasons for the call are. Check answers as a class.

Answers

She's tracked down the source of the leaked story about Max. She'd like Max to at least consider coming for his interview with Sara the next day.

Videoscript/Audioscript (Part 1)

MAX I asked you not to contact me again, didn't I?

NADIA I know that, Mr Redwood, but I just wanted to –

M You've got a nerve!

N Sorry, if I could just finish what I was saying, Max!

M Oh, go on then!

N I've managed to track down the source of the leaked story about you …

M Don't tell me! Sara was gossiping about me again –

N Sorry to interrupt, but Sara wasn't idly gossiping. She was updating me on her research

and was overheard by another journalist, who showed some very poor judgement. He's no longer a member of our team, I hasten to add.

M I see.

N I'd like you to at least consider coming in for your interview with Sara tomorrow. I know how much she was looking forward to it. And I think it would be refreshing for all of us, after our experiences with Oscar Simmons!

M Hmm …

c ▶4.55 Play Part 1 of the video or the audio recording again and tell students to answer the questions. Check answers as a class.

Answers

1 He thinks it's over-confident and rude of her to call because the last time they spoke he asked her not to try to contact him again.
2 idly gossiping
3 *refreshing* (C1): adjective to describe a welcome improvement; a pleasant change from previous events/situation

📖 VOCABULARY SUPPORT

track sb/sth down (C2) – find someone or something after looking for them in a lot of different places

idly (C2) – in a way that is not serious or has no real purpose

judgement (C2) – the ability to make good decisions

hasten to say, add, etc. – used when we need to avoid misunderstandings by giving somebody some more information quickly

d 💬 Tell students to look at the picture and say why they think Max changed his mind about the interview. Take feedback as a class.

e ▶4.56 Play Part 2 of the video or the audio recording and ask students to put the topics in the order they're mentioned. If necessary, pre-teach some of the expressions from the Vocabulary support box on p.168. Check answers as a class.

Answers

a 3
b 4
c 1
d 2

Videoscript/Audioscript (Part 2)

SARA Thanks for this, Max.

MAX No worries.

S Hello. My name is Sara Neroni, and I'm going to be talking to Max Redwood, author of the best-selling science fiction novel *Solar Wind,* and who is in the process of writing his second novel, *Gravity Zero.* Good to see you, Max!

M Thanks. And good to see you too, Sara.

S Now, as anybody who's read your first book will know, you're an incredibly imaginative, creative person, Max, but where do you get your inspiration from? Could you tell us a little bit about that, please?

M Before we get started, can I just make a point about creativity? I just wanted to say that … it doesn't come easily all the time. I was in a bad place up until recently. I thought all of my ideas had dried up … but, my fans got me through that and encouraged me to keep at it.

S Oh, really? I'm glad to hear that.

M But anyway, to answer your question about inspiration, I think I first got interested in space travel when I was growing up.

S Speaking of which, you grew up here in Brighton, didn't you?

M Yeah, that's right. It was really my dad who got me into space – I mean, first got me interested in space! He bought me this telescope and we would look up at the stars at night together. I'd imagine all sorts of weird and wonderful worlds up there.

S AND M And did you say / And I never …

S Please, after you.

M Yeah, as I was saying, I never forgot those worlds.

S Now if you don't mind me coming in here, you had trouble sleeping as a child, didn't you?

M Yeah, that's right. So I spent more time than most kids that age in my own little world …

f ▶4.56 Play Part 2 of the video or the audio recording again and tell students to make notes under each topic in 1e. Check answers as a class.

Answers

a father bought him a telescope, they looked at stars at night
b had trouble sleeping as a child, spent time in his own little world
c thought ideas had dried up, but fans got him through, encouraged him to keep writing
d grew up in Brighton

g 💬 Replay the interview between Oscar and Max on SB p.38 (video or audio recording 2.2) as a contrast. Put students into pairs to discuss whether the interview with Sara was successful. Take feedback as a class.

Suggested answers

Yes. They are relaxed and friendly. Max acknowledges Sara's support without mentioning her name, which surprises and pleases her. There are no awkward pauses and they even accidentally interrupt each other in their eagerness to speak.

💡 **EXTRA ACTIVITY**

Put students into pairs to continue the interview between Sara and Max from where it stops, talking about what Max did when he couldn't sleep. Ask students to write three lines for Sara and three lines for Max, practise reading the dialogue out loud and learn it by heart to act out in front of the whole class.

2 USEFUL LANGUAGE Turn-taking

a Tell students to match the expressions with their uses. Check as a class. Drill the expressions.

Answers

1 a,c   2 a   3 b,c   4 b   5 c   6 a

b Elicit some more formal types of conversation from the students, e.g. a business meeting, a job interview. Ask students to discuss the question in pairs, using the categories a–c in 2a as a starting point for their answers. Take feedback as a class.

Answers

1 when you are encouraging somebody to continue with what they are saying, perhaps after an interruption
2 when you have a formal agenda or a task to perform and you want to say something first
3 when you feel a topic under discussion is coming to a close, to continue speaking about a topic

c ▶4.57 Tell students to read the conversation. Elicit the interviewee's profession (mountaineer). Ask students to complete the conversation with expressions from 2a. Play the recording for students to check.

Answers

1 Sorry to interrupt, but   2 as I was saying   3 Go on.
4 If you don't mind me coming in here   5 Sorry, if I could just finish

💡 **FAST FINISHERS**

Ask fast finishers to think of what people in these different professions could teach business people: a mountaineer, a chef, a clown, a nanny, a gardener, e.g. a mountaineer could teach business people about the determination required to get to the top.

d 💬 Put students into pairs to act out the conversation. Tell them to change the profession of the interviewee.

3 LISTENING

a ▶4.58 Play Part 3 of the video or the audio recording and ask students to choose the best answers to the questions. If necessary, pre-teach *gushing* (expressing a positive feeling, especially praise, in such a strong way that it does not sound sincere). Check answers as a class.

Answers

1 c   2 b   3 d

Videoscript/Audioscript (Part 3)

SARA Thanks, Max. I think that went really well.

MAX Yeah – seemed to go OK. I quite enjoyed it actually!

A Hats off to you both!

S Well, credit where credit's due – Max made it so easy.

M Well …

S You were so different this time, weren't you? Y'know, from that interview with Oscar?

A Well, that's because you're a better interviewer than Oscar.

M That's right, you are.

A And I'll tell you what, I overheard Nadia singing your praises this morning.

S Really?

A Gushing, she was. Thinks you're the best thing since sliced bread!

S Do you think my job is safe then?

A Definitely.

M Listen, Sara … Alex and Emma are coming over to my new place tonight. You'd be very welcome.

S Thanks very much, Max. I'd love to.

M Great.

A Oh, wait till you see the place, Sara. It's a converted warehouse. It's massive, isn't it, Max?

M I suppose so.

S Oh, plenty of room for dancing then!

M Well, it's not going to be that kind of thing, really.

A No?

M Well, I thought we could all sit down together and watch *Moon Station X*.

S AND A Oh … Great …

b 💬 Ask students how Sara and Alex feel about Max's way of celebrating (unenthusiastic). Elicit some achievements, e.g. passing a test, and put students into pairs to discuss how they celebrate them. Take feedback as a class.

c **Language in context** *Praising idioms*

▶4.59 Make sure that students understand *praise* (C1) (things you say that express your admiration and approval for someone or something). Tell students to match the two halves of the idioms. Then play the recording for students to check. Drill the expressions.

Answers

1 b   2 d   3 a   4 c

4 PRONUNCIATION
Tone in question tags

a Say: *We're near the end of the last unit in the book, aren't we?* with a falling tone on the question tag and *You're going to carry on studying English, aren't you?* with a rising tone on the question tag. Elicit which question you don't know the answer to (the second question) and whether the tone went up or down at the end (up). Ask students whether the tone went up or down for your first question and why (down, because the answer is obvious). Play the recording for students to say whether the tone rises or falls on each question tag. Check as a class and drill the sentences.

Answers
1 fall   2 rise   3 rise   4 fall   5 fall

b Tell students to complete the rules. Check as a class.

Answers
rising; falling

c ▶ 4.61 Play the recording for students to say whether the tone is rising (A) or falling (B). Check as a class. Drill the sentences.

Answers
1 B   2 A   3 A   4 B   5 A   6 B

↻ LOA TIP DRILLING

- When drilling sentences, ask students to identify the word groups and the tone changes in each sentence.
- Ask students how many word groups there are in the questions in 4c (two) and what they are (statement + question tag).
- Ask students what the tone is at the end of the first word group (falling) and at the end of the second word group (rising or falling, depending on the meaning).
- Do a choral drill of the questions using your hands like a conductor to show the two word groups and the tone changes: *You did, didn't you?*: sweep your hands down in one movement for *You did* and then down again in a separate movement for *didn't you?*; *You can't, can you?*: hands down for *You can't* and then back up for *can you?*. Make sure students repeat first with you and then after you, using the correct tone for both word groups.

---

d Put students into pairs to take turns saying sentences from 4c, using different tones for the question tag. Their partner says *A* or *B*. As feedback, say some of the sentences yourself with different tones for students to say *A* or *B*. Then say the number of a sentence and *A* or *B*, e.g. *2B*, and ask individual students to say the sentence with the appropriate tone.

e ▢ Say to students: *Max is quite an unusual person, isn't he?* with a falling tone and elicit agreement from the class. Ask students whether the tone was rising or falling, and why (falling, because it's an opinion to elicit agreement). Put students into pairs to give their opinions on the topics and agree with each other.

5 SPEAKING

a Ask students to invent a sporting celebrity. Tell them to make notes on their answers to the questions.

b Ask students to think of some more questions, different from those in 5a, to ask another sporting celebrity.

c ▢ Put students into pairs to take turns interviewing each other. Encourage students to use turn-taking expressions and tag questions.

💡 EXTRA ACTIVITY

Ask students to think of a world-famous sportsperson, past or present. Put students into pairs. Tell them to try and guess each other's sportsperson by asking their partner *Yes/No* tag questions, e.g. *You're a footballer, aren't you? Your sport is connected with water, isn't it?* See which student can guess the sportsperson in the least number of tag questions.

ADDITIONAL MATERIAL

▷ Workbook 10C
▷ Photocopiable activities: Pronunciation p.271
▷ Unit Progress Test
▷ Personalised online practice

10D Skills for Writing
It's an intense and inspiring story

At the end of this lesson, students will be able to:

- read and compare film reviews, discuss their content and analyse their structure
- write a review of a film or TV series using adjectives to give an intense description and being as concise as possible

⚲ OPTIONAL LEAD-IN

Books closed. Ask students to tell you films with really good names, even if the films themselves weren't great, e.g. *One Flew Over the Cuckoo's Nest*; *Honey, I Shrunk the Kids*. Ask students if they have ever chosen to watch a film just because of the title and how they usually decide whether to watch a film or not.

1 SPEAKING and LISTENING

a 💬 Tell students what *whiplash* means (a neck injury caused by a sudden forward movement of the upper body, especially in a car accident). Ask students what genre a film with this name could be (e.g. thriller, horror). Then tell students to look at the photo and poster and say what they think the film is about.

b Tell students to check their prediction in 1a against the descriptions and to match the descriptions with the places you would find them. Check answers as a class. You could show a clip from *Whiplash* if you have the technology in order to give students a flavour of the film.

Answers

1 A   2 B   3 D   4 C

c 💬 Ask students if they have ever read a film review which they completely disagreed with. Put students into pairs to discuss the questions. Take feedback as a class.

d ▶ 4.62 Play the recording for students to listen, make notes to answer the questions and see if any of the speakers agree with their opinions about reviews. Take feedback as a class.

Answers

1 Sasha: online reviews; they are more reliable as you get a range of different opinions from ordinary people
  Marie: newspaper and magazine reviews; there are particular reviewers she thinks are reliable; doesn't read amateur reviews as you don't know the people's tastes
  Kim: doesn't read reviews; films shouldn't be taken too seriously
  Isser: never reads a review before seeing a film, wants to see a film 'fresh', without preconceived ideas; reviews often contain 'spoilers', information about what's going to happen
2 Sasha: before going to the film
  Marie: after going to the film
  Kim: never
  Isser: perhaps after seeing the film
3 Sasha: reviews for accommodation, travel destinations, products, electronic equipment
  Marie: not mentioned
  Kim: reviews of things you spend a lot of money on where there are definite differences between the products, e.g. a laptop or TV
  Isser: not mentioned
  Students' own answers

Audioscript

SASHA I'm a review addict. I'd never dream of going to see a film without checking the reviews online first. I think it's worth seeing whether a film has good reviews or bad reviews. Even if someone has recommended it to me, I like to read the review first before I … see it myself. And I find that online reviews are good because I get a very wide range of different opinions. I like this because it's more

reliable than the newspaper reviews that are written by the so-called experts. Y'know, the online reviews are written by ordinary people like me. I also like reviews um, for accommodation and travel destinations, products, electronic equipment. It's one of the incredible things about the Internet – everything's been reviewed by someone, somewhere in the world.

MARIE I read a lot of film reviews, mainly in newspapers and magazines. I trust a professional opinion and there are actually some reviewers that, er I can really rely on to recommend some good films. But I don't read the reviews to help me decide whether I should watch a film or not – I read it afterwards so it doesn't spoil it. I think, also it's interesting to compare the review with what I initially thought of the film. And er, it can usually help me understand the film better, especially if it's a, a more obscure or complex film. And also reading the review can sometimes help me in case I missed something in the original film. I, I don't like the er … kind of Internet, amateur reviewers because I mean you don't even know who these people are – and er, they may not even have the same taste in cinema that I might have.

KIM I can never be bothered with reviews. I mean I usually download films and watch them at home. I hardly ever go to the cinema any more. I choose something that I like the look of – it doesn't have to be great – it's just a way for me to switch off completely after work and wind down, y'know – it's just relaxation. I really don't understand why some people take films so seriously. I do look at reviews for some things. I mean if I'm going to buy a laptop or a TV and I'm spending that much money on something then, yes, there's a difference between the products. But, not for films.

ISSER I avoid reading reviews of films or TV series, especially TV series, because I just don't trust them because I think it's just one person's opinion and I'd rather go and see a film with an open mind – without any preconceived ideas about what it might be like. Reviews nearly always contain spoilers of some kind. They mention something about a character or something that is about to happen. I don't like that. I'd rather start watching a film without knowing anything about it. And … sometimes, if I really like the film, I would like to go and read the review after I've seen it, er, but definitely not before.

📖 VOCABULARY SUPPORT

wouldn't dream of doing sth (C2) – used to say that you would not do something because you think it is wrong or silly

obscure – not widely popular because it is unusual and difficult to understand

like the look of sth – be attracted to something because it seems suitable

switch off (from sth) – stop thinking about something and relax

wind down – relax after a stimulating/demanding situation or activity

pre-conceived ideas (about sth) – ideas and opinions you have in advance of actually experiencing something

spoiler – information about an important part of a story, e.g. the ending, which, if known before watching, will make the film/book/TV show less enjoyable

e 💬 Put students into pairs to discuss the questions. Take feedback as a class.

2 READING

a Tell students to read the reviews. Put students into pairs to discuss which film is more positive and what the main differences in the reviewers' feelings are. Encourage students to guess the meaning of the words and phrases in the Vocabulary support box if they ask about them. Check answers as a class.

> **Answers**
> Reviewer A is more positive; liked the exploration of the teacher–student relationship.
> Reviewer B found the film a bit simple and unrealistic; the message was depressing.

📖 VOCABULARY SUPPORT

elite (adj.) – describing a school, club, etc. which is high-status because membership requires that you fulfil some very rare criteria, e.g. be one of the most talented in the country, etc.

subject sb to sth – cause somebody to experience something unpleasant

ferocious – frightening and violent

push sb to the limit – force somebody to work so hard they are likely to break down (either physically or emotionally)

uncompromising – unreasonable; unwilling to change your ideas/methods when they conflict with what other people want

portrayal of sth/sb – a representation of something/somebody, such as a performance by an actor, in a book or film

sadistic – getting pleasure by being cruel to / hurting another person

sb's vision of sth – somebody's specific or detailed idea/plan of how the future of something will develop

single-minded – completely focused on achieving one thing, whilst ignoring everything else

sb's pursuit of sth (C2) – when somebody tries to achieve something over a long period of time

thought-provoking – stimulating questions and ideas in the mind of the viewer/reader/listener, etc.

💡 FAST FINISHERS

Ask fast finishers to imagine that a film is being made about their life. They must write down the five main characters and the actors to play them, e.g. me – Mario Casas; my boss – Julia Roberts. Students can then compare casting with another fast finisher.

---

b 💬 Ask students if they know any other good films about music. Put students into groups to discuss whether or not they would like to see the film. Take feedback as a class.

3 WRITING SKILLS
Film reviews; Concise description

a Ask students what elements they would expect to see in a review, e.g. overall impression. Tell students to tick the elements that are in the reviews and say if the elements are in the same order in both reviews. Then ask them if the elements they haven't ticked should be included in a review. Tell them to justify their opinions. Check answers as a class.

> **Answers**
> Ticks: 2, 3, 5, 6, 7, 8
> They aren't in the same order in both reviews. In Review B, the names of the actors are given after information about the plot.
> 1 when and where the writer saw the film is irrelevant
> 4 how the film ends would be a spoiler

b Ask students to write *A*, *B* or *both* to indicate which reviewer mentions strengths and weaknesses in the areas given. Check answers as a class.

> **Answers**
> 1 both 2 both 3 both 4 B 5 both 6 B

c Ask students to underline two or three useful expressions to talk about films, e.g. *well worth a watch*, and compare with other students.

d Ask students to read the first sentence of Review B. Ask students to expand the part in commas without changing the meaning (Whiplash, *which is a new film by director Damien Chazelle, is set in a top music academy in New York.*). Then tell students to compare the excerpts with the actual words in the first paragraph of Review A and choose the reason for the difference.

> **Answer**
> 2

📖 LANGUAGE NOTES

Terence Fletcher, a jazz teacher at the school is an example of apposition: two noun phrases in parallel, the second describing the first. The other examples are participle clauses, often used in writing in order to be more concise (see 6B, SB p.73 and Writing Focus 10D).

💡 EXTRA ACTIVITY

Books closed. Read out Review B but change or leave out some words so that there are mistakes, e.g.:

Whiplash, *a new film by director Damien Chazelle, is set on a top music academy in New York.* (Whiplash, a new film by director Damien Chazelle, is set ***in*** a top music academy in New York.)

Ask students to listen carefully and stop you as soon as they hear a mistake by raising a hand. Elicit the correction from one student and continue to the end of the review.

---

e ▶ Students complete the exercises in Writing Focus 10D on SB p.175. Students read the table and make the sentences in Exercise a more concise. Check answers as a class. Monitor Exercises b–d and take feedback as a class. Tell students to go back to SB p.125.

Suggested answers

a 1 *Manhattan*, a classic Woody Allen movie, now appears a bit dated.

2 Realising he has only a few months to live, he decides to make as much money as possible.

3 British director Mike Leigh is planning to make a new film.

4 Determined to solve the crime, she works on the case night and day.

5 Nina, a promising young dancer played by Natalie Portman, lives with her mother. / Nina, played by Natalie Portman, is a promising young dancer who lives with her mother.

6 Set in the future, Panem is a totalitarian country divided into 12 districts.

7 Trapped in the mountains and running out of food, they send four people off to get help.

4 WRITING

a Ask students what films or TV series they particularly recommend or don't recommend. Ask students to choose a film or TV series they know and to plan a review for someone who hasn't seen it. Tell them to include the main strengths and weaknesses and other elements from 3a in their review, and to structure it into four paragraphs.

b Write on the board this sentence describing the plot of a film and ask students to make the first clause more effective: *After she has escaped from her bad stepmother, Cinderella goes for a ride in the woods.* (Having escaped from her wicked stepmother …). Tell students to write their review using adjectives for more intense description and making the information as concise as possible. Weaker students could use their notes from Writing Focus 10D Exercise d on SB p.175 as the basis for their review.

c Put students into pairs to read each other's reviews. If they have seen the film or series, they should say if they agree with the review; if they haven't, they should decide whether they would like to see it.

LOA TIP REVIEW AND REFLECT

• The end of the course is a good time for students to reflect on their progress and review their achievements and goals.

• Write some prompts for students to think about on the board: *grammar, vocabulary, pronunciation, listening, speaking, writing, reading*.

• Give students time to reflect on their progress in these areas, how the course helped them and how they can improve in the future. Encourage students to be specific, e.g. grammar, *I have trouble with articles, I could get an app and do some practice exercises.*

• Put students into groups to compare and make a list of suggestions which could benefit the whole class, e.g. for future motivation, take an advanced English exam.

• Students share their suggestions with the class and discuss general issues about the course and their language learning.

ADDITIONAL MATERIAL

▶ Workbook 10D

UNIT 10
Review and extension

1 GRAMMAR

a Read out this sentence and ask students for a suitable word to complete it: *I think it's ___ time we repainted the bedroom.* (about/high) Tell students to complete the sentences, using the words in the box. Check answers as a class.

Answers
1 have
2 rather
3 It
4 only
5 time
6 wish
7 needn't
8 ought to

b Tell students to rewrite the sentences, using the words in brackets. Check answers as a class.

Answers
1 You should have phoned me.
2 You needn't have met me.
3 It is said that the president owns a private zoo. / The president is said to own a private zoo.
4 I wish we lived closer.
5 Alex couldn't have been on time.
6 If only Sarah hadn't lost her temper.
7 It is thought that she died in a car crash. / She is thought to have died in a car crash.

💡 FAST FINISHERS

Ask fast finishers to make up two sentences that either go before or come after three of the sentences in 1b. Students compare their sentences with another fast finisher and say which sentences in 1b their partner's sentences come before or after, e.g. *It takes me two bus rides to come and see you.* (I wish we lived closer.).

2 VOCABULARY

a Ask students to cover endings a–f and try to complete 1–6 with their own ideas. Then tell students to uncover a–f and match 1–6 with a–f. Check answers as a class.

Answers
1 e   2 c   3 a   4 d   5 f   6 b

b Tell students to complete the sentences using the first letter of the words as a clue. Check answers as a class.

Answers
1 fingers
2 time
3 tempting
4 convincing
5 side
6 make

3 WORDPOWER *luck* and *chance*

a ▶ 4.63 Go through the phrases and ask students to use them to replace the words in italics. Play the recording to check. Drill the phrases.

Answers
1 count yourself lucky
2 on the off chance
3 a fighting chance
4 it's tough luck
5 blow my chances
6 're in luck
7 don't stand a chance

📖 LANGUAGE NOTES

Tough luck is often used as a fixed expression, without a subject or verb. It usually signifies a lack of sympathy for someone's problems or difficulties, but spoken with sympathetic intonation can also be used to express sympathy.

b ▶ 4.64 Ask students to complete the dialogues using the correct form of the phrases. Tell them to use one word in each gap. Play the recording for students to check.

Answers
1 blown; on; off
2 in
3 stand; Tough
4 count; fighting

c 💬 Ask students what you would say to someone who survived being struck by lightning the day before (*Count yourself lucky!*). Put students into pairs. Ask students to take turns to put themselves in each situation and to explain it, e.g. *I've missed my bus.* Their partner then responds, e.g. *Tough luck!*. Tell both students to respond to each situation as there is more than one possible answer. Take feedback as a class.

💡 EXTRA ACTIVITY

Ask students to mark the chance of these things happening in their lifetime from 0 (no chance) to 5 (every chance):

- *they themselves moving and living abroad*
- *electronic money replacing physical money*
- *smoking being made illegal in all restaurants*
- *another language replacing English as an international language*
- *the average retirement age becoming 75 in their country.*

Put students into groups to compare their marks and discuss their opinions.

▶ Photocopiable activities: Wordpower p.250

🔄 LOA REVIEW YOUR PROGRESS

Students look back through the unit, think about what they've studied and decide how well they did. Students work on weak areas by using the appropriate sections of the Workbook, the Photocopiable worksheets and the Personalised online practice.

Teaching plus

Ideas for pre-teaching vocabulary

Before reading and listening tasks, it's often necessary to make sure students understand a few key words. This is called 'pre-teaching'. There are a number of ways to do this. Here are some ideas:

Give a definition: Use a short sentence to explain the meaning of a word. If you wish, use the definitions given in the rubrics or Vocabulary support boxes throughout the Teacher's Notes. You could also use a learner dictionary to find on-level definitions, e.g. *dive – to swim under water, usually with breathing equipment* (from *Cambridge Essential English Dictionary,* Second Edition).

Draw/Show a picture or object: One of the easiest ways to teach students new words is to draw a picture on the board, or show a picture on the interactive whiteboard or on a computer or tablet. Using (or drawing) funny and/or interesting pictures is a good way to ensure students remember the new words, e.g. to teach the word *dive* you could find a picture of a diver with a big shark behind him.

Act it out: It can be useful to show the word by acting it out, rather than giving definitions which may use above-level vocabulary.

Elicit it: Elicitation allows you to check what words students may already know. Don't tell them the word you want to teach. Elicit it by asking questions or saying open-ended sentences, e.g. *What is the activity when we swim under the sea and look at fish?* or *When we swim under water and look at fish, we … ? (dive).*

Gapped sentences: It's useful for students to see the word in a sentence to understand the context. Write a gapped sentence(s) on the board (this can be one from the text), e.g. *Cristina _____ in the Mediterranean Sea every summer. She loves to see the beautiful fish under the water.* (dives). Allow students to guess what word goes in the gap, but don't confirm if they're right or wrong. After they read the text, they can guess again. Then confirm their answer.

Discussion questions: With stronger students you can write discussion questions containing the new words on the board. Then give students one or two example answers to these questions. Students try to guess the meaning. Give more example answers, if necessary. You may then wish to allow students to ask and answer these questions for themselves.

Pre-teaching for listening: You can use any of the above ideas, or others you may have, to teach new words before students listen. It may also be useful to model the pronunciation of the words so students are used to hearing how it sounds. This is particularly useful when a word has an unfamiliar spelling rule. If you don't want to model the word, it can be useful to write the word in IPA on the board (you can find this in all dictionaries).

Extra ideas – how to …

Class survey
Use: to revise tenses, verb patterns, verb collocations, conversational language
Dynamic: whole class
Procedure:
- Write a list of questions which practise the target language. Ideally, each student will have a different question, but if this is difficult, aim to have one question per two students.
- Photocopy the list and cut up into strips to give out. Make sure each student has a question, even if the question is the same as another student's. Alternatively, dictate each question to one (or two) student(s) in turn.
- Ask students a question as an example and elicit a response which uses the target structure. Write the response on the board.
- Set a time limit for the activity, e.g. 10 minutes. Students move around the class and ask their question to as many other students as they can. They write down the responses in their notebooks.
- When the time is up, divide students into smaller groups and ask them to compare their most interesting responses.

Running dictation
Use: to revise vocabulary
Dynamic: whole class
Procedure:
- Choose a short text or a list of sentences/questions which you wish to revise. Around six to ten sentences should be adequate, depending on how confident your students are. Choose a text of the appropriate level for your students and which does not contain unfamiliar words.
- You will need one sheet for each pair of students, plus a few extra sheets. Put the extra sheets on a far wall of the classroom or just outside the classroom door. Mark the halfway point on the text.
- Divide the class into pairs: Student A is a reader and Student B is a writer. A has to go to the text/list and memorise as much as he/she can. Encourage students to remember a few words accurately rather than try to memorise too much. Student A goes back to Student B and dictates what he/she can remember. Student A must walk over to Student B before dictating and not shout the text out! Student A is not allowed to do any writing at this stage. The dictation continues until Student A has reached the halfway point of the text.
- The students swap roles, with Student B dictating and Student A writing.
- As each pair finishes, give them a copy of the text and allow them to check their text against the original. Students should correct their mistakes. Monitor and help students to decide whether any differences are grammatically correct or not.

Grammar auction

Use: to revise a specific grammar area or general grammar
Dynamic: whole class (in teams)
Procedure:

- Prepare 10–15 sentences containing items of grammar from the unit you are currently working on or areas of grammar which you know students find problematic. Some of the sentences should be correct and some incorrect.
- Write the sentences on the board and explain what an *auction* is (when you sell something to the person who offers the most money).
- Put students into small groups and tell them they have £100 and they need to buy the correct sentences. In their groups, students discuss which sentences they think are correct and decide which to buy and how much they are prepared to pay for each. Don't help or allow students to look at their notes or the Student's Book.
- Take the role of auctioneer and sell each sentence to the group which offers the most money. Keep track of how much each group has spent. Remind students that once they have spent all their money they can't buy any more sentences, so they shouldn't spend too much too soon.
- After all the sentences have been sold, go through them one at a time, revealing which are correct and which are incorrect. Ask students to correct the mistakes.
- The winning group is the one which has bought the most correct sentences. If it's a draw, then the group which has got the most money left wins.

Classroom whispers

Use: to revise tenses, verb patterns, verb collocations, pronunciation and listening skills
Dynamic: whole class
Procedure:

- You will need a list of short sentences and/or questions which practise the structures you wish to revise. You will need one sheet per three students in the class.
- Divide students into groups of three. All the Student As go to one part of the classroom, all the Student Bs to another, and Student Cs to another.
- Model the activity by standing with the Student As and showing them the first sentence on the sheet. The Student As then walk to the Student Bs and whisper the sentence they have remembered. Make sure the Student Cs can't hear. The Student Bs then go to the Student Cs and repeat the sentence and the Student Cs write down what they heard. Write the correct sentence on the board. Student Cs compare this with what they have written.
- Start the activity by showing the second item on the list to the Student As. The activity then continues as per your model. After the Student As have had two or three turns, they swap roles with the others in their group. The activity continues like this until they reach the end of the list.
- When the students have finished, give each group of three a copy of the sheet and they compare this against what they have written. The group with the fewest mistakes wins.

Backs to the board

Use: to revise a specific lexical set or general vocabulary
Dynamic: whole class (in teams)
Procedure:

- Put students into small groups of four to five. If possible, mix stronger students with weaker students so no group is noticeably stronger or weaker than another.
- Tell students in each group to sit close together, leaving space between the groups so they can't easily hear one another. Tell one student in each group to sit with their back to the board and the others to sit so that they can see the board.
- Explain that you're going to write a word or phrase on the board and that the students who can see the board have to communicate the meaning to the student who can't. They can use any method to do this, drawing pictures, mime, synonyms, simple explanations, etc. However, use of their own language will mean they are disqualified.
- When the student(s) with their back to the board think they know the word, they put their hand up. Ask the first student to put their hand up to say the word and, if they are correct, award their group a point. If they aren't, the other teams continue. Any student who shouts out the answer is also disqualified.
- The winning group is the one with the most points at the end of the game.

Photocopiable activities overview

GRAMMAR

	Target language	Activity type	Dynamic	Teacher's notes
1A	Adverbs and adverbial phrases	Narrative maze	Groups of four	p.180
1B	The perfect aspect	Find someone who ...	Pairs / whole class	p.180
2A	Comparison	Competitive debates	Pairs / whole class	p.180
2B	Intentions and arrangements	Discussion / group presentation	Groups of four / whole class	p.181
3A	Inversion	Grammar auction	Groups of four	p.181
3B	Future in the past; Narrative tenses	Text completion / Roleplay (solving a crime)	Pairs / whole class	p.181
4A	Noun phrases	Game: sentence chains	Groups of four	p.182
4B	*have / get* passives	Text completion / discussion	Pairs	p.182
5A	Relative clauses	Crossword	Pairs	p.182
5B	Willingness, obligation and necessity	Discussion / roleplay (job interviews)	Pairs	p.183
6A	Simple and continuous verbs	Sentence completion / roleplay	Pairs	p.183
6B	Participle clauses	Rewriting / writing a story	Pairs / groups of four	p.183
7A	Speculation and deduction	Reading / retelling / discussion	Small groups	p.183
7B	Cleft sentences	Reordering statements / discussion	Individually / small groups	p.184
8A	Gerunds and infinitives	Dominoes	Small groups	p.184
8B	Conditionals	Grammar analysis / discussion	Pairs	p.184
9A	Reflexive and reciprocal pronouns	Sentence completion / questionnaire	Individually / pairs	p.184
9B	Ellipsis and substitution	Rewriting / telling / writing a story	Individually / pairs / whole class	p.185
10A	Regret and criticism structures	Text completion / writing criticisms / advice	Individually / small groups	p.185
10B	Passive reporting verbs	Roleplay (media interviews)	Pairs	p.186

VOCABULARY

	Target language	Activity type	Dynamic	Teacher's notes
1A	Language learning	Questionnaire / discussion / advice	Individually / groups	p.186
1B	Describing changes	Describing graphs	Pairs	p.186
2A	Multi-word verbs: Social interaction	Sentence completion / narratives guessing game	Pairs	p.187
2B	Verbs of movement	Writing a story	Pairs	p.187
3A	Wealth and poverty	Text completion / giving advice	Pairs	p.187
3B	Landscape features	Writing for a travel website / discussion	Pairs	p.188
4A	Instinct and reason	Guessing characteristics / discussion	Individually / whole class	p.188
4B	Memory	Matching / questions and answers	Pairs	p.188
5A	Crime and justice	Information gap / discussion	Pairs	p.188
5B	Employment	Find someone who …	Whole class	p.188
6A	Adjectives: Describing arts and culture	Questionnaire / discussion	Pairs	p.189
6B	Emotions	Sentence completion	Pairs	p.189
7A	Compound adjectives	Defining words	Pairs	p.189
7B	Nouns with suffixes: Society and relationships	Discussion / debate	Pairs / groups of four	p.189
8A	Sleep	Odd one out	Groups of three	p.190
8B	Ageing and health	Writing a brochure for a spa	Groups	p.190
9A	Verbs with re-	Sentence completion / questions and answers	Pairs	p.190
9B	Describing buildings	Crossword	Pairs	p.190
10A	Communication verbs	Describing and guessing	Groups of four	p.191
10B	Superstitions, customs and beliefs	Questionnaire	Individually /pairs	p.191

WORDPOWER

	Target language	Activity type	Dynamic	Teacher's notes
Unit 1	Idioms: Body parts	Describing and guessing game	Individually / pairs	p.191
Unit 2	Idioms: Movement	Matching / writing sentences / find someone who …	Individually / whole class	p.191
Unit 3	Idioms: Landscapes	Vocabulary test / text completion / giving advice	Individually / pairs	p.192
Unit 4	*mind*	Find someone who …	Groups / whole class	p.192
Unit 5	Idioms: Crime	Board game	Pairs	p.192
Unit 6	Idioms: Feelings	Describing and guessing game	Groups of three	p.192
Unit 7	*self-*	Matching puzzle	Pairs / groups of three	p.192
Unit 8	*and*	Pelmanism	Groups	p.193
Unit 9	*build*	Matching / discussion	Pairs	p.193
Unit 10	*luck* and *chance*	Sentence completion / discussion	Pairs / groups of four	p.193

PRONUNCIATION

	Target language	Activity type	Dynamic	Teacher's notes
Introduction	Terminology and phonetic symbols	Pelmanism / wordsearch	Pairs	p.193
1B	Sentence stress	Reading out quotations / discussion	Pairs	p.194
1C	Sound and spelling: *ea, ee* and *ie*	Recognising sounds / challenge board	Pairs	p.194
2A	Consonant–vowel linking	Dictation / guessing punchlines	Pairs	p.195
2C	Emphatic stress	Odd one out	Groups of three	p.195
3A	Tone in inversion structures	Pelmanism	Small groups	p.196
3C	Consonant groups across words	Sound maze	Pairs	p.196
4A	Sound and spelling: /ʃəs/, /iəs/, /dʒəs/	Recognising sounds / board game	Small groups	p.196
4C	Homophones in words and connected speech	Aural discrimination	Pairs	p.197
5A	Sound and spelling: *s* and *ss*	Sound maze	Pairs	p.197
5C	Main stress	Ordering / acting out a dialogue	Pairs	p.197
6A	Sentence stress	Roleplay (shortlisting candidates) / discussion	Pairs	p.197
6B	Main and emphatic stress: adverbs and adjectives	Reacting to news	Pairs	p.198
7A	Main stress: compound adjectives	Fortune-telling game	Pairs	p.198
7C	Sound and spelling: *ou* and *ough*	Board game	Groups of four	p.198
8B	Pitch: extra information	Logical puzzle	Groups of four	p.198
8C	Intonation in implied questions	Negotiating game	Pairs	p.199
9A	Sound and spelling: *re-*	Crossword	Pairs	p.199
9C	Sound and spelling: foreign words in English	Information gap	Pairs	p.200
10A	Word groups and main stress	Describing and discussing experiences	Pairs	p.200
10C	Tone in question tags	Roleplay	Pairs	p.200

GRAMMAR

1A Adverbs and adverbial phrases

▶ Photocopiable activity on p.201

You will need one sheet for each group of four students.

Write on the board: *We found the keys.* Ask students to suggest when and where they found the keys and comment on how they felt about it.

Thankfully, we soon found the keys next to the box.

Write these question words on the board and elicit examples of adverbs and adverbial phrases in each category:

how? = very well, angrily, as fast as possible, by chance, gradually, gently

when? = later, the next day, at the break of dawn

where? = there, in the corner, in front of me

how often? = rarely, never, frequently

how likely? = definitely, obviously, without a doubt

comment? = unfortunately, surprisingly, clearly

degree? = a bit, extremely, quite, absolutely

Put students into groups of three or four and give each group a sheet. Set the scene for students. They are hiking alone through the mountains when the weather starts to get worse. Ask them what they would do in this situation. Read the first square together and explain that students must add appropriate adverbials instead of the words in brackets, e.g. (*how?*). Elicit appropriate adverbials:

You are hiking through the mountains in autumn. There's almost certainly going to be a storm.

With weaker groups, you may wish to do the whole activity once as a class, before asking groups to work independently.

In their groups, one student reads out the first square and the group suggest and agree on suitable adverbials. The reader then reads out the options and the group choose what to do next. They continue in this way until they find one of the endings. Monitor and help with any unknown vocabulary. Check students know what a yeti is (*a big creature like a human covered in hair that is believed by some people to live in the Himalayas*).

As feedback, get students to read out some sentences with adverbs and adverbial phrases. As there are different endings, students can play the game several times in the same and different groups.

💡 EXTRA ACTIVITY

Students work alone and use the sheet to write a story. Tell them they can add any additional details they wish. Give students ten to fifteen minutes to do this. Students read their stories out to their groups. At the end, each group votes for their favourite story.

1B The perfect aspect

▶ Photocopiable activity on p.202

You will need one sheet for each student.

Ask some questions in the perfect aspect covering past, present and future, simple and continuous, e.g. *What had you learnt before you started school?*, *Have you ever thought about having your own business?*, *How long will you have been studying English by the end of this course?*, etc.

Put students into pairs and give each student a sheet. Ask students to make the three sets of phrases into questions with the perfect aspect including past, present, future, simple and continuous (sometimes both simple and continuous are possible). Check answers as a class.

Students go round the class and ask each other the questions. They then ask follow-up questions to get more details and write down the answers. Monitor and make sure they are using the perfect aspect correctly in questions and answers. The first student to find a name and answer for all the questions is the winner. You could set a time limit, e.g. 15 minutes, and ask students to ask as many questions as possible to as many people in that time.

As feedback, ask students to report on interesting information they found out about each other using the perfect aspect.

Answers
1 Had you moved
2 Had you started
3 Had you met
4 Had you learned / been learning
5 Had you thought / been thinking
6 Have you won
7 Have you worked or studied / been working or studying
8 Have you travelled / been travelling
9 Have you not had / been having
10 Have you done / been doing
11 Will you have saved / been saving
12 Will you have celebrated / been celebrating
13 Will you have achieved
14 Will you have taken / been taking
15 Will you have prepared or trained / been preparing or training

2A Comparison

▶ Photocopiable activity on p.203

You will need one sheet for each pair of students, cut in half.

Ask students if they would rather have a cat or a fish as a pet. Elicit comparisons using modifying words and expressions: *It's a bit easier to look after a fish. It's a lot more rewarding to have a cat as a pet because they keep you company.* Encourage students to use a range of modifying words and expressions. Encourage students to challenge any statements they think are not true, e.g. *Actually, fish are more difficult to care for, because you need to maintain their tanks.*

Split the class into two teams, A and B. Give each student their part of the sheet, A or B. Explain that each team has opposite statements to justify on their half of the sheet.

Ask students to work in pairs in their teams and think of as many reasons as they can to defend each of the statements on their sheet. Give students three minutes to come up with reasons for statement 1 and ask them to make notes. Point out that they should pretend to agree with the statement even if they have the opposite opinion or no opinion at all. Ask teams to give their reasons in turn. Any pair with a new idea can contribute it. The other team can challenge a reason if it isn't true / it's similar to a reason already given / there's no evidence – the teacher is the judge. The team with the most correct reasons wins a point. Then teams move on to the next statement. The winning team is the team with the most points at the end.

As feedback, ask for students' true opinions about some of the statements.

2B Intentions and arrangements

▶ Photocopiable activity on p.204

You will need one sheet for each group of four students.

Put students into groups of four. Explain the situation: they need to develop a project to benefit the town and present their plan to the town council (i.e. the rest of the class). There are no budget restrictions.

Draw students' attention to the phrases and elicit some possible examples, e.g. *The council is planning to open a new leisure centre. We're about to start discussing what kind of performing arts will be popular.*

Give each group a sheet and tell them to read the projects, and discuss which they think would be most beneficial. Tell students they can think of their own project if they wish.

Give students 15–20 minutes to plan their project and presentation. Remind them to refer to the language at the bottom of the sheet to help them. Monitor and help where necessary. Students should each be prepared to give part of the presentation.

Groups present their plans to the rest of the class. Make sure students are using future forms for intentions where possible. When each group finishes their presentation, other students can ask questions as if they were the town council. You could elicit some possible questions, e.g.: *How is this going to benefit the town exactly?* Then have a class vote for the best project (students can't vote for themselves!).

3A Inversion

▶ Photocopiable activity on p.205

You will need one sheet for each group of four students.

Put students into groups of four and give each group a sheet.

In Activity A, groups 'bet' on whether the inversion language in each sentence is grammatically correct or incorrect, based on how certain they are. They have a limit of $250 to bet in total, and they must bet a minimum of $5 on each sentence. Students correct the sentences they think are incorrect. The teacher then checks the answers with the class. For correct answers and sentences, students win double the money that they bet, but if the answer or sentence is incorrect, they lose their money. The group with the most money at the end wins.

In Activity B the groups write their own sentences with inversion structures and give them to another group to bet $100 with. They should write at least two sentences

with a mistake with inversion. Monitor and make sure the mistakes are with an inversion structure.

Check which sentences are correct so groups can see how much they have won. As feedback, write some of the incorrect sentences on the board for the whole class to correct.

Answers

The following sentences are incorrect in Activity A:

4 Seldom ~~have been I~~ in such a situation. *have I been*
6 ~~Not only once~~ did the idea come into her head. *Not once*
7 ~~Only then John did~~ realise he was in big trouble. *Only then did John*
8 ~~Not we did waste a dollar~~ while travelling around the world. *Not a dollar did we waste*
9 Scarcely had we ~~arrived~~ it was time to leave. *arrived than it / when it*

💡 EXTRA ACTIVITY

For pronunciation practice, drill all ten sentences in Activity A with the fall–rise intonation over the inversion.

3B Future in the past; Narrative tenses

▶ Photocopiable activity on p.206

You will need the top part of one sheet for each pair of students. You will need one set of character cards for each group of up to 15 students, cut up.

Ask students to tell you about a real-life crime story where a famous piece of art was stolen. You may wish to give an example of your own to demonstrate. Ask students to briefly say what happened. Highlight good examples with narrative tenses and future in the past and correct any errors.

Put students into pairs and give them the top part of the sheet. Students read the texts together and choose the best verb forms. Check answers as a class. You may wish to pre-teach the words *widower* (a man whose wife has died and he hasn't remarried) and *late* (a person who is no longer alive). Ask students to discuss in pairs what each person's motive for stealing the picture could be. Ask for feedback on students' ideas as a class. Take a class vote to see who the most popular suspect is.

Tell the class that they are going to find out who took the picture and what he/she did with it. Tell students you will give some of them character cards which they must keep secret. Give the six character cards to six students in the class. (If you have more than 15 students, split the class into groups of eight or more and give out a set of character cards to each group.) The students without character cards are the detectives. Demonstrate the activity by asking a character: *What is your name? Why are you visiting Gray Manor?*, etc. The detectives interview the characters and try to deduce who took the picture. Allow ten minutes before asking the detectives who they think the thief is and why. Then ask the real thief to stand up and explain their reason for taking the picture and what they did with it.

Answers

1 had gone   2 would look   3 would not sell   4 was feeling
5 had been borrowing   6 had already been thrown out
7 was   8 didn't want   9 was staying   10 had recently had
11 had told   12 had left   13 was expecting   14 painted
15 had not been going to give   16 had never liked
17 had insisted   18 had been   19 knew   20 had hated
21 only ever visited   22 had been trying   23 had been
24 would reveal

4A Noun phrases

▶ Photocopiable activity on p.207

You will need one sheet for each group of four students, cut up.

Write on the board: *I didn't have any <u>money</u>*. Ask students, in turn, to add one element at a time to make the noun into a complex noun phrase, e.g.

*I didn't have any **spending money**.*

*I didn't have any **spending money for my holidays**.*

*I didn't have any **spending money for my holidays from my parents**.*

*I didn't have any **spending money for my holidays from my parents which I could use to pay for the damage**.*

Elicit from students different ways of making noun phrases complex, e.g. adding adjectives, prepositional phrases, relative clauses.

Put students into groups and give each group a set of cards. Ask students to put the cards face down on the table. One student takes a card and says the sentence, and then adds to the noun to make it more complex. Another student adds to the noun phrase in the same sentence, and so on. The final student to add to the noun phrase and make a meaningful sentence gets a point. Another student begins again with a new card. Play for 20 minutes and see who has the most points.

As feedback, see what the most interesting sentences were and analyse the noun phrases on the board.

 NO-CUT VARIATION

Students choose sentences to start with and then cross the sentences off.

 EXTRA ACTIVITIES

1 As a group, students write down the final version of the sentences. They then check with the rest of the class to find out who made the longest sentence for each card.

2 Students make cards to add to the game.

4B *have / get* passives

▶ Photocopiable activity on p.208

You will need one sheet for each pair of students, cut up.

Start with a review of *have / get* passives. Tell students: *Someone stole my car.* Elicit: *My car got stolen. I had my car stolen.* Tell students that actually it was someone else's fault: *My husband left the car running outside a shop so it was stolen.* Elicit: *My husband got my car stolen.* Tell students: *I couldn't persuade the police to look for the thief.* Elicit: *I couldn't get the police to look for the thief.*

Put students into AB pairs. Give each student their part of the sheet. Ask them to read about the people and rewrite the parts in italics using *have / get* passives. Tell students that there are sometimes different ways of rephrasing the text. Monitor and help as necessary. For weaker classes, put students into AA pairs and BB pairs first.

In their AB pairs, students tell each other their three stories, ensuring they use the passives.

Ask students to discuss which people they think were unlucky, and which people caused their own problems. As feedback, ask if students know of anyone who has had a similar experience to any of the events in the stories.

Answers

Andy   1 getting sacked / fired / made redundant   2 got his hair cut   3 got his old suit cleaned   4 he had it stolen / it got stolen   5 got his neighbour to lend him her bike   6 got him sweating   7 had him waiting / got him to wait

David   1 got (himself) trapped   2 have/get it fixed   3 got David to tell him   4 had been paying him   5 got the lift working / to work   6 David got introduced by the CEO   7 get fired/ sacked   8 had him repaying the money / got him to repay the money

Gerard   1 he got stopped by a security officer   2 had him open / got him to open   3 having the security officer search his bag   4 had/got the coin valued by an expert   5 got himself arrested   6 had/got him to pay a fine

Serena   1 had her practising / got her to practise   2 she got criticised by her mother   3 got her mother to believe   4 she had her photo taken   5 had Serena staying in

Pam   1 she had had it stolen   2 got her neighbour   3 It got Pam thinking   4 the house might get burgled (by the man)   5 to get the man arrested   6 had Pam waiting   7 to have/get the locks changed

Karmel   1 (she) got thrown off her horse   2 had her leg broken / her leg got broken   3 She got taken to hospital in an ambulance   4 had/got her leg set by the doctors   5 had her lying down   6 to get shouted at (by everyone)   7 got her friends to bring   8 got her other leg broken

---

5A Relative clauses

▶ Photocopiable activity on p.209

You will need one sheet for each pair of students, cut up.

Write these definitions with relative clauses on the board:

A person <u>who</u> steals things. (thief)

The place <u>in which</u> trials take place. (court)

<u>Whatever</u> the judge decides to do with a criminal. (sentence)

Elicit the word that is being defined and elicit the relative clauses in each sentence. Give each student a sheet, A or B. In Activity A, students should work in AA and BB pairs. Ask them to complete the relative clauses in each clue. Monitor and help as necessary. Check each pair's answers.

In Activity B, ask students to work in AB pairs. Students read the clues to each other. Their partner tries to guess the correct word to complete the crossword. If necessary, students can expand the definitions further in order for their partner to guess the answer correctly.

As feedback, ask students to tell you which clues they found the most difficult to guess.

Answers

Student A
1 whose   4 of which   6 by whom   7 who/that
8 by which   9 who/that   10 in which   11 whoever
14 which/that   16 when / at which

Student B
1 in which / where   2 that/which   3 whose   5 who
9 when / in which / during which   12 to whom
13 of which   14 when / in which / during which
15 for whom / to whom / whose

5B Willingness, obligation and necessity

▶ Photocopiable activity on p.210

You will need one sheet for each student.

In Activity A, put students into pairs. Give each student a sheet and ask students to read about the zookeeper. Then ask students what requirements there would be for a person in that role. Elicit some ideas, e.g. *It would be essential to have experience of working with animals. Some kind of qualifications in ecology would be desirable.* Ask: *What would the working conditions and the pay be like?* Elicit ideas, e.g. *working outside.* (You may wish to tell students that the pay for a zookeeper in the UK is around £14,000 per year, which is less than half the national average pay.)

Students discuss all the jobs, and complete the requirements section and the conditions and benefits sections for each job. Monitor and make sure they're using the structures for willingness, obligation and necessity where necessary. Take class feedback on students' ideas.

In Activity B, each student chooses a job to apply for and tells their partner what it is. Then each student works alone to prepare interview questions to ask their partner, using their completed job descriptions from Activity A and the language of willingness, obligation and necessity, e.g. *Would you be willing to live on site? Do you have any objection to working weekends?* Students conduct both interviews and each interviewer decides whether or not their partner is suitable for the job they applied for. Take class feedback on the results of the interviews.

6A Simple and continuous verbs

▶ Photocopiable activity on p.211

You will need one sheet for each student.

Read out some sentences in the simple and continuous, and ask students to say if they are correct or incorrect, e.g.: *That fresh coffee smells lovely.* (correct) *What are you thinking about nuclear energy?* (incorrect, ~~are you thinking~~ do you think) *Do you feel all right at the moment?* (correct) *Your attitude is astonishing me.* (incorrect, ~~is astonishing~~ astonishes)

In Activity A, give each student a copy of the sheet. Ask them to complete the sentences with the best form of the verb in brackets, thinking about the tense and whether the verb should be simple or continuous. Tell students that there may be different correct answers. Check answers as a class and ask students to explain why the verb is simple or continuous.

In Activity B, put students in small groups. Students need to decide on a single situation in which four or more of the sentences might come into conversation. They then choose roles and practise a conversation which uses as many of the sentences as possible. Each group performs their conversation for the class. Give each group a point for every sentence they use correctly and points for creativity so that there is a winner.

Answers
1 was / had been hoping   2 don't suppose   3 were leaving
4 don't recognise   5 have been thinking   6 really depends
7 will have been living / lived   8 impresses; 've achieved
9 is being   10 didn't mean   11 have been seeing / seen
12 regard   13 is / was / has been constantly complaining
14 Are; following   15 was / had been wondering

6B Participle clauses

▶ Photocopiable activity on p.212

You will need one sheet for each pair of students.

Write this sentence on the board and ask students to rewrite it using participle clauses:

We were excited by the plans to donate our old clothes and I started organising the collection. (Excited by the plans to donate our old clothes, I started organising the collection.)

Ask students if second-hand shops are common where they live and if they use or would use them.

Give each student a sheet. In Activity A, tell students to work in pairs and rewrite the story using participle clauses where possible. Monitor and check.

In Activity B, put students into groups of four. Ask them to discuss how the story might end, using the prompts to help them, then write the continuation. Give a word limit of 150 words. Remind students to use participle clauses. Each group reads out their stories to the rest of the class, who can then decide which story is the most interesting.

Suggested answer
Walking down the street one day, I noticed a second-hand shop. Not having much time, I was going to pass by but my eye was caught by a coat in the window display. It seemed strangely familiar. Going up to the window, I looked at it more closely. It was my old winter coat! Not having worn it for years, I had left it hanging with all my other old clothes at the back of my wardrobe. Wanting to find out how the coat, bought with my own money, had got there, I went inside the shop. The shop assistant was cashing up for the day and, suddenly feeling quite angry, I rushed up to her and demanded, 'Give me my coat!' Smiling, the shop assistant said, 'Don't you remember the day you gave it to us? And don't you remember why?' Staring at her, I realised she was right. A long-forgotten memory was surfacing in my mind …

7A Speculation and deduction

▶ Photocopiable activity on p.213

You will need one sheet for each student.

Tell students this puzzle: *A man is lying injured in the middle of a field and there is a bag next to him. What happened?* Elicit explanations using the language of speculation and deduction, e.g. *There could have been something dangerous in the bag.* Give the solution – the man is a parachutist and the bag contains his unopened parachute.

Put students into groups of four, ABCD, and give each student a sheet. Ask students to focus on their own story to start with, reading it and thinking of three explanations for it, using the language of speculation and deduction in the box. Point out that there are no correct answers – these mysteries remain unsolved. Ask students to take it in turns to present their mystery to their group and discuss possible solutions for it. The group should think of as many explanations for what happened as they can. Then compare explanations as a class.

> 💡 **EXTRA ACTIVITY**
>
> Students work in pairs to rewrite the Tamam Shud mystery, changing the following details: the beach location and the country; the words on the paper and their language; the place where the book was found; what the woman said on the phone. Students exchange mysteries with another pair and think of as many explanations as they can, using the language of speculation and deduction in the box.

7B Cleft sentences

▶ Photocopiable activity on p.214

You will need one sheet for each student.

Read out some statements and ask students to make them into different types of cleft sentences:

She needs a good holiday. (What she needs is a good holiday. It's a holiday that she needs.)

I went to England to study. (The reason I went to England was to study. The place I went to study was England.)

Give each student a sheet. In Activity A, ask students to work individually and rearrange the sentences. Students compare answers in pairs, then check answers with the class.

In Activity B, students discuss the statements in small groups, seeing how far their classmates agree with each. Encourage them to use cleft sentences where possible during their discussion, e.g. *It's not computer games that are the problem.*

As feedback, find out which statement most students agreed with and which most disagreed with.

Answers
1 What worries me is the amount of time kids spend on computer games.
2 The reason online education is so popular is simply its convenience.
3 What technology does is replace face-to-face communication.
4 It's only people with too much time to waste who use social-networking sites.
5 The worst thing is that our personal data is all over the Internet.
6 It's these online dating sites that are dangerous.
7 It is just older people who still prefer printed books.
8 What the government shouldn't do is monitor and regulate people's Internet use.

ⓦ EXTRA ACTIVITY

Students rewrite four sentences so that they express their own opinions, e.g. *What worries me is the amount of time kids spend online unsupervised.* Then put students into new groups to discuss the sentences.

ⓦ VARIATION

Copy one sheet for each group of eight students in your class and cut up, so each sentence is separate. Give a sentence to each student and ask them to unscramble it. Next, ask students to mingle, reading out their 'opinions' and seeing how far their classmates agree with them.

8A Gerunds and infinitives

▶ Photocopiable activity on p.215

You will need one sheet for each group of three or four students, cut up.

Explain to students that they are going to play a game of dominoes using gerunds and infinitives. Divide the class into groups of three or four and give a set of dominoes to each group. Each student in the group takes an equal number of dominoes.

One student begins by placing a domino on the table in front of the group. Students then take turns to play by placing down a domino which can complete a sentence. The sentences must make logical sense and be

grammatically correct, e.g. *Wouldn't you rather / speak to her?*, *The best thing is / I've got enough money*, etc.

If the student can't find a correct domino or puts one down that isn't grammatically correct, the other player has another turn. The activity is designed so that most dominoes have several options, but monitor and help as necessary. The game continues until all students have placed their dominoes correctly.

⊘ NO-CUT VARIATION

Students work in groups and take it in turns to make sentences using the sentence halves on the sheet, e.g. *Wouldn't you rather have finished?*, and crossing out the squares that have been used. Students are eliminated from the game when they can't make a correct sentence. The last student left is the winner.

ⓦ EXTRA ACTIVITY

Students work in pairs. Give each pair two dominoes (four sentence halves) and ask them to write a short dialogue containing the sentence halves. Ask a few pairs to role play their dialogues for the class.

8B Conditionals

▶ Photocopiable activity on p.216

You will need one sheet for each pair of students.

Write these sentences on the board and ask students to correct them:

If I would speak French, things would be easier. (~~would speak~~ spoke)

Have you reminded me, it would have helped. (~~Have~~ Had)

Don't go in case you're worried. (~~in case~~ if)

In Activity A, put students into pairs and give each pair a sheet. Ask students to read the conditional questions and decide which type of conditional they are. Check answers as a class.

In Activity B, ask students to choose six questions to ask their partner. Students ask and answer the questions. Monitor and make sure students develop the discussion, not just question and answer, and use correct conditional sentences where possible.

As feedback, get students to discuss some of the answers as a class.

Answers
1 0   2 0   3 mixed (0 and 1)   4 1   5 1   6 2   7 0   8 2
9 2   10 2   11 mixed (2 and 3, otherwise = if it hadn't happened)
12 0   13 3   14 3   15 2   16 2

9A Reflexive and reciprocal pronouns

▶ Photocopiable activity on p.217

You will need one sheet for each student.

Give each student a sheet. In Activity A, ask students to complete the questionnaire with the appropriate pronoun. Ask them to compare answers in pairs. Check answers as a class.

In Activity B, put students into pairs. Students ask each other the questions, record their partners' answers and then read the analysis. As feedback, find out who had mostly As, Bs and Cs.

Answers

1	A	me	B	myself	C	myself
2	A	herself	B	her, her	C	each other / one another
3	A	himself	B	himself	C	him
4	A	yourselves	B	myself	C	them
5	A	ourselves	B	each other / one another	C	myself
6	A	myself	B	myself	C	him
7	A	it	B	itself	C	myself

> ⓦ **EXTRA ACTIVITY**
>
> Put students into pairs. Ask some pairs to write 'Five rules for playing it safe' and the others to write 'Five rules for living life on the edge', using at least three reflexive and reciprocal pronouns. As feedback, elicit one rule from each pair.

9B Ellipsis and substitution

▶ Photocopiable activity on p.218

You will need one sheet for each pair of students, cut in half.

Write on the board: *I never wanted to become a teacher but I became a teacher and I enjoy being a teacher.* Ask students to write the sentence down in a more natural way using ellipsis and substitution. (I never wanted to become a teacher but I did and I enjoy it.)

Put students into AB pairs. In Activity A, give each student their half of the sheet and ask them to read it. Then ask students to work on their own and rewrite their story half, making it more natural using ellipsis and substitution. Monitor and help as necessary. Accept all appropriate versions.

In Activity B, Student A reads their version of the first part of the story to Student B. In Activity C, Student B reads their version of the second part of the story to Student A. In Activity D, give students 15 minutes to work in their AB pairs and make an ending to the story. You could ask them to write an ending or just make notes. If students are struggling for ideas, provide some prompts:

How could the house have disappeared? Are there any natural explanations?

Was the neighbour lying when she said she didn't know the narrator? Could she be involved in the mystery?

Who was the person the narrator met yesterday?

What help did that person need?

How could that person help get the house back?

Ask them to compare their endings with the rest of the class. The class can vote on the most interesting ending. As you monitor this stage, write down examples where students could have used ellipsis and substitution better and write these on the board for whole-class feedback.

Suggested answers

I finished work as usual, put my coat on and left the office. I decided to walk home for a change because it was a sunny day. I turned the corner and was going to go up my drive but didn't because I couldn't. Why not? My house wasn't there! It had just disappeared! I couldn't believe it! There was a gap where it had stood, a completely empty space. My neighbour's house was there and so was her car. Anyway, I decided to take some action; I went to my neighbour, an old lady, and knocked on her front door. She came to the door, opened it and asked, 'Who are you?' I said, 'I am your neighbour. I've lived here for ten years.' She looked at me but didn't seem to recognise me and said, 'I don't know you. Nor do I want to. Now go away.' She slammed the door and left me on the doorstep. It was like a dream, a bad dream, and I wanted to wake up but I couldn't. The bad dream was reality. I thought about phoning the police but didn't because they would probably think I was crazy. (You might think so too.) Just as I was beginning to feel desperate, I noticed something on the floor. It was an envelope and inside was a message: 'Do you want to get your house back? If so, follow these instructions and you will. You need to remember someone you met yesterday, find them and help them more than you did before. That person has / They have the key to your house in more ways than you think.'

10A Regret and criticism structures

▶ Photocopiable activity on p.219

You will need one sheet for each student.

Tell students about a situation in the past where you feel you, or someone else, did something wrong, e.g.:

It was my birthday and I had a really big party in my flat. The neighbours got really angry because they couldn't get to sleep.

Invite students to criticise what you did and didn't do, and give you some advice. Write the key structures they use on the board: *You could have ... , You shouldn't have ... , If they had known ...* , etc. Then share a few of your regrets and write the key structures on the board: *If only I had* (told them about the party in advance); *I wish I had* (invited them); *it would have* (been a great opportunity to get to know them better).

Give each student a sheet. In Activity A, ask them to read the problems and choose the correct verb forms. Check their answers as a class.

In Activity B, put students into small groups. Ask them to criticise the people for what they did or didn't do, and then discuss what advice they would give to each of the people using the language of criticisms and regrets. Tell them to write at least two sentences for each post.

As feedback, find out which group has the best advice.

> ⓦ **EXTRA ACTIVITY**
>
> Students think of their own situation where they regret something they have/haven't done. Other students then criticise and give advice.

Answers

1 would   2 hadn't bought   3 wouldn't have taken   4 should
5 have taken   6 would   7 If only   8 would have liked   9 left
10 spoke   11 tried   12 should have warned   13 lived
14 shouldn't

10B Passive reporting verbs

▶ Photocopiable activity on p.220

You will need one sheet for each pair of students, cut up.

Write these sentences on the board and tell students to transform them into sentences with passive reporting verbs:

A lot of taxpayers' money is wasted. (It is widely believed that a lot of taxpayers' money is wasted.)

Corruption is getting worse. (It is thought that corruption is getting worse.)

Many government ministers abuse their power. (Many government ministers are said to abuse their power.)

Divide the class equally into Deputy Ministers of Culture and journalists and give students the corresponding parts of the sheet for Interview 1. Ask Deputy Ministers to work in pairs and discuss what the possible questions might be. Tell the journalists that they have to be careful about what they say. Ask them to work in pairs and prepare questions with passive reporting verbs.

Put students into new pairs (a Deputy Minister of Culture and a journalist) to conduct the interview. Monitor and check that the journalists are using passive reporting verbs appropriately.

Students swap interviewer and interviewee roles, and repeat the procedure for Interview 2 between a Minister of Culture and a journalist.

As feedback, elicit the sentences with passive reporting verbs used by the journalists and compare with the suggested answers. Discuss whether the journalists have enough reliable information from the two interviews to publish a story.

> **Suggested answers**
> **Interview 1**
> It is said that you were the only candidate allowed to apply for the post.
> The Minister and you are reported to be old school friends and former business partners.
> It is alleged that you left business because you were fired for misuse of company finances.
> 800,000 euros are believed to be unaccounted for in the latest accounts of the Ministry.
> It is rumoured that you bought a new yacht costing an estimated 800,000 euros.
> Staff at the Ministry are understood to have been made to work overtime for no extra pay.
> It is suspected that several staff who complained about this were fired.
> The Ministry is understood to have recently closed down a website which was critical of its work.
>
> **Interview 2**
> It is rumoured that the extension to the Ministry of Culture building cost the taxpayer two million euros.
> Funding for the arts is understood to have been cut.
> It is said that your salary has increased 300% since you came into office.
> Cleaners in the Ministry are reported not to have been paid for three months.
> Your partner is said to work as your secretary on a large salary but is never actually seen at work.
> It is reputed that you received a personal loan to build a swimming pool in your mansion.
> Your son is believed to have received a loan to start a tourism company.
> It is alleged that you have just come back from a six-week holiday in Barbados, paid for by the taxpayers.

VOCABULARY

1A Language learning

▶ Photocopiable activity on p.221

You will need one sheet for each student.

In Activity A, tell students they are going to think about how easy or difficult they find their English studies. Give each student a sheet. Demonstrate by asking a strong student: *Do you find it easy to pick up new English expressions?* and ask the student to give his/her answer a score of 1 (very strongly disagree) to 5 (very strongly agree).

Tell students they have to read each statement and give it a score according to how much they agree with the statement.

Give students five minutes to complete the questionnaire. Monitor and help as necessary.

In Activity B, put students in groups of four or five so they can discuss their answers.

Encourage students to ask for and give advice on how to improve various areas.

> ⓦ **EXTRA ACTIVITY**
> Ask the groups to think of a piece of advice for each of the statements. As feedback, ask the class to decide which is the best piece of advice for each statement. Produce a definitive list of advice for the class. This list can be shared on a class noticeboard or class wiki.

1B Describing changes

▶ Photocopiable activity on p.222

You will need one sheet for each pair of students, cut in half.

Put students into AB pairs. Give each student their part of the sheet. Point out that they each have two graphs: one complete, one blank. Tell students not to show their graphs to each other.

Demonstrate the activity by drawing a simple line graph on the board to represent the following information. Describe it to students: *In January, there were 68 students in the school. There was a barely perceptible change in February, and then there was a rapid rise through March and April. There was a steady upward shift over the summer months before there was a noticeable downward trend until November. After which numbers rose substantially to finish the year on 105.*

Ask students to take turns to describe their graph to their partner, who then draws the graph on their blank graph. Student A starts. Tell students they can give the January and December percentages, but not the percentages of the months in between.

When they have finished, students compare graphs to see how accurate they were.

Suggested answers

Student A

In January, 40% of female students and 20% of male students visited the cinema at least once a month.

There was a steep increase in female students visiting the cinema over the first few months of the year, then another sharp increase in June, before there was a slight downward trend to finish the year on about 60%.

There was a gentle decrease in male students visiting the cinema over the first few months of the year and then there was a rapid rise from June to July. Numbers remained steady until October. There was an equally sharp decrease over the last few months of the year.

Student B

In January, 10% of female students and 20% of male students visited the school website at least once a week.

There was a steady increase in female students visiting the school website until June, when there were very rapid rises until figures peaked in October. The figures remained constant until the end of the year.

There was a gentle increase in male students visiting the school website from March and this continued to rise until peaking at 60% in December.

> **EXTRA ACTIVITY**
>
> Ask students to work individually to draw their own graphs (based on real information or their own ideas). Put students into new pairs and ask them to swap graphs and to write a paragraph describing their partner's graph.

2A Multi-word verbs: Social interaction

 Photocopiable activity on p.223

You will need one sheet for each pair of students.

Put students into pairs. Give each student a sheet. In Activity A, ask students to work in pairs to complete the sentences with the correct forms of the multi-word verbs.

In Activity B, demonstrate the activity by giving an example for one of the situations, e.g. *When my best friend had a baby, she didn't talk about anything else. She would tell me what the baby had done, what noises the baby had made, it was really boring,* to elicit the correct verb (*go on*). Emphasise that you didn't use the verb in your description.

Students then take it in turns to choose a situation from the sheet and describe it to their partner, who guesses the situation and the verb. Encourage them to be as descriptive as possible and tell them to describe all the situations.

For strong classes, ask students to turn over their sheet so that they can't see the situations or the multi-word verbs.

Answers

1 fit in 2 bombarded; with 3 brought out 4 come across
5 hold; back 6 cut; off 7 slip out 8 relate to 9 ran; down
10 went on

> **EXTRA ACTIVITY**
>
> Tell students to write sentences summarising their partners' descriptions of the situations, e.g. *When Pedro had an interview, it was important that he came across well.*

2B Verbs of movement

 Photocopiable activity on p.224

You will need one sheet for each pair of students, cut up.

Tell students they are going to write a short story. Elicit some ideas for what information is important in a story: e.g. the time and place, the main character and the other characters, an event.

Put students into pairs. Give each pair a sheet of paper. Ask students to write one or two opening sentences for their story. Then give a set of cards to each pair of students and ask them to place the cards face down on the table. Students turn over the first card and discuss how to continue the story to include the next verb of movement. Students then write the next part of the story using the verb.

Students pass their story on to the next pair. Students read the story they've received, turn over the next card, and write one or two sentences which include the verb on the card.

Students continue passing the stories on until all the cards have been used. Remind them that the last card means they have to write the conclusion of the story.

> **VARIATION**
>
> For weaker groups, put students into groups of four. Begin the activity as above, but instead of giving a full set of cards, give each group six verbs. Students then work in their groups to write the story, incorporating the six verbs as they wish.

> ⊘ **NO-CUT VARIATION**
>
> Put students into groups. Give each group a sheet and ask them to choose a maximum of six verbs to use in a story. Students then read their story to the class, but do not say the verbs. Other groups have to guess what the missing verbs are.

3A Wealth and poverty

 Photocopiable activity on p.225

You will need one sheet for each pair of students.

Put students into pairs and give each pair a sheet. In Activity A, ask students to work together to complete the article. Point out that sometimes more than one answer is possible.

In Activity B, put students into new pairs and ask them to discuss the questions. As feedback, find out what the most common opinions are.

Answers

1 disposable income 2 hardship 3 impoverished/deprived
4 make ends meet 5 destitute/impoverished 6 live within our means / make ends meet 7 well-off 8 prosperity 9 affluent/ well-off 10 deprived

> **EXTRA ACTIVITY**
>
> Play *Backs to the board* using the vocabulary from lesson 3A and the guidelines from the *Teaching Plus* notes on p.175.

3B Landscape features

▶ Photocopiable activity on p.226

You will need one sheet for each pair of students.

Put students into pairs and give each pair a sheet. Go through the instructions with the class. Point to the first picture of a campsite in the desert and elicit any vocabulary related to deserts (e.g. *arid, huge sand dunes, remote area, untouched wilderness,* etc.). Ask students which of these phrases it would be appropriate to use to sell this destination to prospective customers (*untouched wilderness, remote area*). Ask them why these features might be a good selling point and how they would change the current description to include these phrases.

Students work in pairs to improve the website descriptions for each destination. Remind students to use the vocabulary of landscape features from lesson 3B in order to sell each destination. Give students 15 minutes to complete the task. Monitor and help with any vocabulary as necessary.

Students then swap their descriptions of the holiday destinations with another pair. They read and discuss the other pair's descriptions and choose the most appealing destination, giving reasons for their choice.

As feedback, discuss which destination is the most popular and why.

 EXTRA ACTIVITY

Ask pairs to consider the activities that tourists might be able to do in each of the destinations (e.g. *scuba diving in Thailand*). They then add these activities to the descriptions they've already written, again considering how to best sell the activities as part of the holiday package.

4A Instinct and reason

▶ Photocopiable activity on p.227

You will need one sheet for each student.

Give each student a sheet. Ask students to think about their classmates and complete the sentences according to their hunches about them. Tell students to try to use all their classmates' names. They can complete a sentence with two names if they wish.

Demonstrate the next stage of the activity by writing on the board: *I have a hunch that* [student's name] *is usually a rational thinker.* Then ask him/her: *Are you a rational thinker?* Tick the sentence if your hunch is correct and ask a follow-up question according to how the student answers, e.g.: *Do your friends think you are a rational thinker? When did you last make an irrational decision?*

Ask students to mingle and ask each other questions to find out if their hunches were correct. Encourage students to ask follow-up questions. As feedback, ask if anyone learned anything surprising about their classmates.

4B Memory

▶ Photocopiable activity on p.228

You will need one sheet for each pair of students, cut up.

Put students into pairs and give each pair a sheet. Students work together to match the question halves. Monitor and help as necessary. Check answers as a class.

Tell students to take it in turns to ask and answer the questions.

Monitor and note any interesting answers to go through as feedback.

Answers
1 e   2 h   3 i   4 l   5 g   6 b   7 j   8 k   9 f   10 a
11 c   12 d

 VARIATION

As above, but cut the grid in two. Give the first halves of the questions to Student A, and the second halves to Student B. Students take it in turns to read out a half question and their partner supplies the other half. They then ask and answer the questions.

5A Crime and justice

▶ Photocopiable activity on p.229

You will need one sheet for each pair of students, cut in half.

Divide the class into two groups, A and B. Give each student their part of the sheet. Tell students each group has the same story, but with different information missing. Give each pair a sheet. In Activity A, put students in AA and BB pairs. Ask them to read the story and try to complete as many gaps as they can. When students have finished, tell them to work out the questions they need to ask to check their answers.

In Activity B, put students into AB pairs, telling them not to show their sheets to each other. Students then ask questions to check their answers are correct or complete the gaps.

Students then discuss the text and the questions in their AB pairs.

EXTRA ACTIVITY

Have a class debate. Write on the board:

The punishment should fit the crime.

Prison is just a holiday for criminals.

Criminals are victims too.

Put students into groups of five and ask them to discuss the statements. Ask the groups to come up with as many arguments as they can. Then have a class debate, with you as chair.

5B Employment

▶ Photocopiable activity on p.230

You will need one sheet for every four students, cut up.

Put students into groups of four. Give each group a set of cards: one for each student (Student A, Student B, Student C, Student D).Tell students they each have four questions they need to ask to 'find someone who'. Elicit the type of questions students need to ask (*Would you like/hate … ?* and *Do you think … ?*). Then tell students to mingle and try to complete their cards with students' names. Tell them to ask follow-up questions and make a note of the answers.

6A Adjectives: Describing arts and culture

▶ Photocopiable activity on p.231

You will need one sheet for each pair of students.

Ask a strong student: *What was the last book you read? How would you describe it?* (e.g. *exciting*). Write on the board: *A book you think is exciting* and then write the title of the book the student gave you next to it.

Tell students they are going to work together to write the names/titles of books, people, etc. according to descriptions on the sheet.

Put students into two groups, A and B. Then divide each group into pairs and give each pair a sheet.

In Activity A, students work in their pairs (Pair A or Pair B) to think of their examples. Tell students that they need to be able to explain their choices. Monitor and help as necessary. In Activity B, an A pair works with a B pair to compare and discuss ideas. Students then compare ideas in a new AB pair.

As feedback, ask a strong student *Have you found out about a film you would like to see?* or *What interesting thing did you find out?*

6B Emotions

▶ Photocopiable activity on p.232

You will need one sheet for each pair of students, cut up.

Give each student their part of the sheet. In Activity A, students work alone to complete the sentences so that they are true for them. Monitor carefully to make sure the examples are appropriate for the adjectives.

In Activity B, demonstrate the aim of the activity by saying: *When I was ten, I was absolutely devastated when my pet rabbit died.* Put students into AB pairs. Students then read their sentences to their partner without using the adjectives in italics, and their partner tries to work out the adjective in each sentence.

Students can then change partners and repeat the activity.

As feedback, ask students if they learned anything interesting about their classmates.

7A Compound adjectives

▶ Photocopiable activity on p.233

You will need one sheet for each pair of students, cut up.

Put students into two groups, A and B. Give each student their part of the sheet. Point out that students have a grid made up of words and pictures. Tell them to focus on the words. Ask students to work out how they can describe the words that they have, e.g.: *My friend always forgets things – other people's birthdays, where he has parked his car, appointments – he is very …* to describe *absent-minded. An experience that is a little bit dangerous, but very exciting, is …* to describe *hair-raising.*

Give students time to work out how to explain the words. Monitor and help as necessary.

Put students into AB pairs. Tell them not to let their partners see their sheet. Tell students to take turns to ask for an explanation of the missing words by choosing a picture and giving the code (e.g. A1, A2, etc.) to their partner. Student A starts by giving a code to Student B. Student B gives the explanation, and Student A uses the explanation and the picture to work out the word. Students continue until they have worked out all the words.

7B Nouns with suffixes: Society and relationships

▶ Photocopiable activity on p.234

You will need one sheet for each pair of students.

Tell students they are going to create a new community where they can decide on the qualities people have. Put students into pairs. Give each pair a sheet. In Activity A, ask students to look at the words and elicit a few desirable qualities/behaviours and a few undesirable qualities/behaviours. Make sure students understand the meaning of all the words. Ask students to work in their pairs and agree on three desirable qualities their new community or the people in it should have, as well as three undesirable qualities. Tell students to explain how their community would ensure the principles were maintained. Set a time limit of ten minutes. Monitor and help as necessary.

In Activity B, put students into groups of four. Ask students in each group to explain their lists to their group and to agree on two new lists. Do a class survey at the end to find out the three most desirable and the three most undesirable qualities/behaviours.

In Activity C, ask students to stay in their current groups of four and take turns to talk about the community they're living in at the moment. Ask them which qualities/behaviours they would change if they could and why.

As feedback, find out what most people would want to change.

 EXTRA ACTIVITY

In pairs, students write definitions for four words they didn't use from the words on the sheet. They then swap definitions with another pair and try to guess which words are being described.

8A Sleep

▶ Photocopiable activity on p.235

You will need one sheet for each group of three students, cut up.

Put students into groups of three. Give each group a set of cards: one for each student (Student A, Student B, Student C) and one group card. If there is a group of four, two students could share a card.

Students take it in turns to read a sentence on the group card. They then check the responses on their individual cards (including the student who read the group card) and the student who has the correct response reads it out. You could demonstrate the first item as an example. Monitor and help as necessary.

As feedback, go through the sentences and their correct responses. Then ask students to turn over their cards and read out a sentence from the group card yourself. See if students can remember the answer.

Answers

1 Student A   2 Student C   3 Student C   4 Student B
5 Student B   6 Student A   7 Student B   8 Student C
9 Student C   10 Student A   11 Student B   12 Student B

 EXTRA ACTIVITY

In their groups of three, students discuss the sentences and comment on, or provide advice for, the situations. As feedback, find out what suggestions the class has for staying awake till midnight, if any students suffer from insomnia and if any of them have ever fallen asleep in a meeting or in class.

8B Ageing and health

▶ Photocopiable activity on p.236

You will need one sheet for each group of three or four students.

Tell students they are going to open an anti-ageing clinic and they need to produce a publicity leaflet.

Give each group a sheet and draw students' attention to the pictures. Ask students: *What problems or signs of ageing could an anti-ageing clinic help with? What services and products could it offer?* Elicit students' ideas.

In Activity A, give students time to choose three signs of ageing and add three of their own, and discuss and decide how each will be treated at their clinic. Ask students to then decide on five promises they will make to clients. Monitor and help as necessary.

In Activity B, students work in their groups to create their leaflet. Monitor and help as necessary. If your students have completed lesson 8D, you may wish to review the techniques of promotional writing covered there for use in their leaflet.

 EXTRA ACTIVITY

When students have prepared their leaflets, tell them to research anti-ageing clinics online and compare their promotional material with the leaflets produced by the class.

9A Verbs with *re-*

▶ Photocopiable activity on p.237

You will need one sheet for each pair of students.

Put students into pairs and give each pair a sheet. In Activity A, tell students that they're going to complete the questions with *re-* verbs in the correct form. Use the first question as an example. Elicit the correct verb (*recreated*) from the class. Ask students why they have chosen this verb (*because it means to make something exactly the same as the original*). In their pairs, students complete the questions.

Check answers as a class. Where students have struggled to get the correct answer, elicit the rationale for the correct answer from another pair.

In Activity B, put students into new pairs. Students discuss the questions in A. As feedback, students share interesting answers.

Answers

1 recreated   2 revamp   3 redeveloped   4 restore
5 regain   6 reinstated   7 rejuvenated   8 regenerating
9 renovate

 EXTRA ACTIVITY

In pairs, students choose one of the questions and prepare a short speech to answer it. They should explain their reasons or ideas. When all pairs have given their speech, the class votes for the most interesting answer.

9B Describing buildings

▶ Photocopiable activity on p.238

You will need one sheet for each pair of students, cut up.

Explain that Student As will have a crossword with half the answers given and Student Bs have the same crossword with the other half of the answers given. Put students into AA and BB pairs. Ask them to think of clues for their words. Give an example clue, e.g.: *What do you call an area of a town or city where a lot of buildings have been built for people to live in?* (housing estate). Monitor and help as necessary.

Put students into AB pairs. Students complete their crosswords by taking it in turns to ask for a clue, e.g. *What's 5 across?* and giving clues. Monitor and help as before.

10A Communication verbs

▶ Photocopiable activity on p.239

You will need one complete sheet and one cut-up sheet for each group of four students.

Divide the class into groups of four. Give each group a complete sheet and ask them to explain what each communication verb means and to give examples. Then ask students to briefly think of ideas for each topic. Take feedback as a class to ensure all students understand the communication verbs.

Tell students they are going to take it in turns to talk about a topic, and to illustrate the communication verbs. Give each group a set of topic cards and a set of communication verb cards, and place them face down on the table. All students then take a topic card and a communication verb card, and they all have one minute to prepare notes for their talk.

After the preparation time, one of the students starts talking about the topic in the manner of the communication verb on their card. The group try to guess what the communication verb is. If the group guesses correctly, the student keeps the communication verb card and puts the topic card back at the bottom of the pile. If the group guesses incorrectly, the student puts both cards at the bottom of their piles. Then the next student starts.

Continue until all the topic cards have been used, always ensuring students have one minute to prepare.

10B Superstitions, customs and beliefs

▶ Photocopiable activity on p.240

You will need one sheet for each student.

Give each student a sheet. In Activity A, ask students to write *T* or *F* for the statements in the 'Me' column. In Activity B, ask students to add two more superstitions, customs or beliefs from their own country to the bottom of the table and to write *T* or *F* in the 'Me' column. Monitor students and help with vocabulary as necessary.

In Activity C, students work in pairs and talk about why the statements are true or false for them. Students find out if the superstitions, customs or beliefs from their own country are true or false for their partner and write *T* or *F* for all the statements in the 'My partner' column. Take feedback as a class. Find out if there are any students who are not superstitious at all or if most students are a little superstitious.

WORDPOWER

Unit 1 Idioms: Body parts

▶ Photocopiable activity on p.241

You will need one sheet for each student.

Put students into pairs and give each student a sheet. Individually, they read the prompts and think about what they could write for each one. Demonstrate this by doing the first one as a class and elicit some possible ideas, e.g. *a job, a chance to go to New York*.

Students write one answer in each shape. Tell students to write their answers in any order. Monitor and help as necessary. When students have finished, ask them to swap sheets and try to guess which answer goes with which question.

Students then check their ideas by asking each other about the answers in the shapes. Students explain why they gave the answers they did and give any background information.

(If you want to do the extra activity, you may want to do it before the class feedback as it will give away some of the answers.) As feedback, ask students for the most interesting answers, and if relevant/appropriate ask the student who gave that answer to elaborate.

Unit 2 Idioms: Movement

▶ Photocopiable activity on p.242

You will need one sheet for each student.

In Activity A, each student works individually to match the sentence halves. They then compare in pairs. Check answers as a class.

In Activity B, students tick the sentences that are true for them, and change the other sentences to make them true, e.g. change *go round the world on a yacht* to *swim with dolphins*.

In Activity C, students mingle to find out how many classmates have similar opinions. For stronger groups, encourage them to ask follow-up questions, e.g. *Why do your thoughts drift … ? Do you think you ever will swim with dolphins?*

Answers

1 h   2 c   3 j   4 g   5 f   6 i   7 e   8 b   9 d   10 a

Unit 3 Idioms: Landscapes

▶ Photocopiable activity on p.243

You will need one sheet for each pair of students.

Put students into pairs. In Activity A, tell students to work together to make idioms from unit 3. Remind students that they will need to add extra words for some idioms. Students can refer to SB p.42, if necessary.

In Activity B, tell students they're going to read about a language school that isn't doing well. Students work with their partners to complete the gaps in the text. Monitor and help as necessary, then check answers as a class.

In Activity C, students discuss the problem in pairs and agree on three pieces of advice for Bert.

As feedback, the class decides which three pieces of advice are the best.

Answers
A
1 get the lie of the land   2 get bogged down
3 on a slippery slope   4 swamped   5 an uphill struggle
6 not out of the woods   7 a drop in the ocean
B
1 slippery slope   2 drop in the ocean   3 not out of the woods
4 swamped   5 getting bogged down with   6 uphill struggle
7 got the lie of the land

Unit 4 *mind*

▶ Photocopiable activity on p.244

You will need one sheet for every four students, cut up.

Put students into groups of four. Give each group a set of cards: one for each student (Student A, Student B, Student C, Student D). Tell students they're going to ask their classmates questions to complete the cards. Demonstrate by asking a student: *Maria, has it ever crossed your mind to become a teacher?* If she says *no*, ask *Why not?* Then ask another student, and so on. When a student says *yes*, ask *Why?* Tell students they can ask each classmate only one question (and a follow-up question) at a time. Tell students to rephrase the prompts as questions, and think about follow-up questions. Monitor and help as necessary.

Students then mingle and complete their cards.

When students have finished, put them into ABCD groups to compare answers. Take feedback from the class and ask for examples of interesting answers.

Unit 5 Idioms: Crime

▶ Photocopiable activity on p.245

You will need one copy of the board game on p.272, a dice, counters and one sheet for each pair of students, cut up.

Put students into pairs. Give each pair a copy of the board game, dice, counters and a set of question cards.

Students place the question cards face down in a pile on the table. Students take turns to pick up a card and ask their partner the question. If the answer is satisfactory (i.e. it illustrates the expression on the card), their partner rolls the dice and moves his/her counter forward. If the answer isn't satisfactory, their partner can't move his/her counter.

The first student to reach the final square is the winner. If the end of the board is reached before all the questions have been asked, and if the class is enjoying the activity, ask students to continue playing until all the questions have been asked.

As feedback, ask if anyone was surprised by what they learned about their classmates.

** NO-CUT VARIATION**

Give one sheet to each student folded in half vertically. Ask students to work in pairs. Student A looks at the top half of the sheet, Student B the bottom half. Students interview each other, taking turns to ask the questions. Tell students to ask further follow-up questions of their own. The aim of the activity is to have a conversation, not just get to the end! Students then swap partners for another set of interviews.

Unit 6 Idioms: Feelings

▶ Photocopiable activity on p.246

You will need one sheet for each group of three students, cut up.

Put students into groups of three. Give each group a set of cards. Ask students to shuffle the cards and place them face down in a pile.

Demonstrate the activity. Take a card and say: *Every time I go to catch a bus the display says that it's only two minutes away, but it always takes longer than that. Then, when it arrives, it's always full, so I have to wait even longer. This means that I am often late.* Ask if any of the students can guess which expression you are describing (*something that really gets your back up*).

Tell students they are going to take it in turns to take a card and talk for a minute about what is on the card (for weaker groups make the time 30 seconds). The other students in the group guess which expression from SB p.78 is being described. Students continue until all the cards have been used.

** NO-CUT VARIATION**

You will need one sheet for each pair. Students take it in turns to describe one of the situations for one minute and their partner guesses which expression is being used. Students cross off the cards/expressions as they are used.

Unit 7 *self-*

▶ Photocopiable activity on p.247

You will need one sheet for each pair of students or group of three.

Put students into pairs or groups of three. Give each pair/group a sheet. Tell students they have to work out the names of the different people. Each sentence refers to a characteristic, and also spells one letter of that person's name. Students work together to find the correct sentences/letters and work out what the people's names are.

Do an example. Point to sentence S. Ask: *What kind of person always gives to charity appeals?* (self-sacrificing). Then ask students to find the other two sentences that are about a self-sacrificing person, and to use the letters with the sentences to work out the name on each person's

T-shirt (the letters are an anagram of a three-letter name). Take feedback as a class. Check students know what the names are short forms of (*Stu* – Stuart; *Ann* – Anna; *Bob* – Robert; *Meg* – Megan; *Max* – Maximilian; *Val* – Valerie or Valentine).

Answers
1 STU
2 ANN (A Of course I'll pass the exam!)
3 BOB
4 MEG (M I love fashion and I make my own clothes.)
5 MAX (M I realise I have to work harder at my English studies.;
   A I know what my strengths and weaknesses are.)
6 VAL (A I taught myself to play tennis and could play
   professionally.)

 EXTRA ACTIVITY

In pairs, students write another two sentences for each character to demonstrate the *self-* characteristic. Take feedback as a class.

Unit 8 *and*

 Photocopiable activity on p.248

You will need one sheet for each group of three or four students, cut up.

Put students into groups of three or four. Give each group a rectangular set of cards and a square set of cards. Students spread the cards out face down on the table, keeping the two sets separate. Explain that the cards are two words of an expression with *and*. The rectangular cards are the first words of the expressions and the square cards are the final words of the expressions after the word *and*.

Demonstrate the activity: turn over one rectangular card and one square card and ask the class if they make an expression with *and*. If they do, use the expression in a sentence, e.g. *This classroom is showing signs of wear and tear*, and pick up and keep the cards. If the cards don't make an expression, turn them back over and turn over another pair until you can make an expression.

Students then do the activity: Student A turns over two cards. If the cards match and if Student A can make a correct sentence, then he/she keeps the cards. If the cards don't match, the cards are turned back over and the next student has a go. Monitor and help as necessary.

The winner is the student with the most cards at the end of the activity.

Answers
far and wide, far and away, sick and tired, wear and tear, part and parcel, loud and clear, neat and tidy, short and sweet, safe and sound, bits and pieces

 NO-CUT VARIATION

Give each student a sheet. Students work alone to match the halves of the expressions. Students then compare answers in pairs and work together to make sentences for each expression.

 VARIATION

When two cards make an expression, each student in the group makes a different sentence using the expression. The group decides which is their favourite sentence (the funniest, the most difficult, etc.) and that student keeps the cards.

Unit 9 *build*

 Photocopiable activity on p.249

You will need one sheet for each pair of students.

Demonstrate the activity by writing on the board:

Then: *I couldn't run more than 1 km without stopping.*

Now: *I can run a marathon.*

Ask students: *What have I done?* and elicit an answer with *build*: *You have **built up** your stamina.*

Put students into pairs. Give student a sheet. In Activity A, tell students they have to match the 'then' sentences with the 'now' sentences. Check answers as a class.

In Activity B, students work with their partner to decide what has happened between the 'then' sentence and the 'now' sentence and write a sentence using an expression with *build* for each situation.

Answers
1 f 2 h 3 i 4 c 5 d 6 j 7 g 8 l 9 e 10 b
11 k 12 a

 EXTRA ACTIVITY

Students work in pairs to write their own 'then' and 'now' sentences, which they swap with another pair. They then try to link the sentences using an expression with *build*.

Unit 10 *luck* and *chance*

 Photocopiable activity on p.250

You will need one sheet for each pair of students.

Put students into pairs and give each pair a sheet. Demonstrate Activity A by saying: *I think England have a fighting chance of winning the next World Cup.* Ask students if any of them agree with you.

Write three topics on the board: *Sport, Famous people, Work and study*. Tell students they can use any of these topics (or anything else) when they complete the sentences. Students then work in pairs to complete the sentences. Monitor and help as necessary.

In Activity B, ask each pair to work with another pair to compare their ideas and find out how many they agree with.

As feedback, ask each group of four to read out the more interesting version of each sentence, and see if the rest of the class agree or disagree.

PRONUNCIATION

Introduction Terminology and phonetic symbols

 Photocopiable activity on p.251

You will need one sheet for each pair of students, cut up.

The aim of this sheet is to help students learn some basic pronunciation terminology and reinforce phonetic script.

In Activity A, put students into pairs to play pelmanism. Give each pair the two sets of cards from the top half of the sheet: the cards 1–10 have the terminology, and cards a–j have the definition.

Spread the cards out face down in two separate piles. Students take it in turns to turn over a card from each pile to try to find a match between terminology and definition. If they find a match, they keep the cards. If not, the cards are turned over again. Check answers as a class.

In Activity B, give students the second part of the sheet. Students work individually or in pairs to find the pronunciation terms in the wordsearch. Remind them that words can be horizontal and vertical. Refer students to the Phonetic symbols chart on SB p.191.

Answers

A

1 i 2 a 3 f 4 e 5 h 6 c 7 j 8 d 9 g 10 b

B

i	w	h	ɒ	m	ə	f	əʊ	n	t	h
k	iː	ŋ	s	ə	r	t	aɪ	z	e	ŋ
ɒ	k	v	tʃ	s	ɪ	l	ə	b	ə	l
n	f	aʊ	k	ə	l	s	ə	i	m	aʊ
s	ɔː	ə	ɪ	d	ɪ	f	θ	ɒ	ŋ	ə
ə	m	l	tʃ	r	ʒ	r	ɔː	θ	p	l
n	k	uː	c	ə	ə	b	t	p	w	uː
ə	ɪ	n	t	ə	n	eɪ	ʃ	ə	n	n
n	r	i	l	iː	s	t	r	e	s	i
t	k	w	ɜː	d	g	r	uː	p	n	w

 NO-CUT VARIATION

Students match the terminology to the definitions.

1B Sentence stress

▶ Photocopiable activity on p.252

You will need one sheet for each pair of students, cut in half.

Write on the board: *An invasion of armies can be resisted, but not an idea whose time has come.* Ask students if they know whose quotation this is and which century it was written in (*Victor Hugo, 19th century*). Then ask students what tense the verb phrase in the second clause is in (*present perfect*) and which three syllables/words are stressed in this second clause (*idea*, *time* and *come*). Elicit that auxiliary verbs are usually unstressed and main verbs are usually stressed.

Put students into two groups, A and B, and give each student their sheet, A or B. In Activity A, students work individually and read the quotations and underline the syllables/words which are stressed in the perfect verb phrases. Monitor and check.

Put students into AB pairs. In Activity B, students read the quotations to their partner but do not say whose quotations they are. Their partner needs to listen and say which one was written more than 700 years ago. Monitor and check they are using sentence stress well.

In Activity C students work in their AB pairs and discuss whether they like the idea in each quotation. Monitor and encourage students to give reasons for their feelings.

As feedback, ask students what their favourite quotation is and why.

Answers

1

Student A

a has been <u>made</u>; has been <u>put</u>
b have <u>always</u> <u>been</u>
c have <u>not failed</u>; have <u>just found</u>
d have de<u>ci</u>ded
e has <u>come</u>
f will have been <u>said</u> than <u>done</u>

Student B

a have <u>won</u>; have <u>started</u>
b have <u>loved</u> and <u>lost</u>; never to have <u>loved</u>
c <u>Having</u> been <u>poor</u>
d has already a<u>chieved</u>
e have ac<u>complished</u>; have <u>planned</u> for yourself; you have <u>not</u> planned e<u>nough</u>
f has been <u>done</u>

 EXTRA ACTIVITY

Students find their own favourite quotations (any grammar) and read them out with appropriate sentence stress to the rest of the class.

1C Sound and spelling: *ea, ee* and *ie*

▶ Photocopiable activity on p.253

You will need one sheet for each student and two dice for each pair of students.

In Activity A, ask students: *What is the name of our planet?* (*Earth*), *What adjective means in a good mood?* (*cheerful*) and *What's the word for your brother's or sister's daughter?* (*niece*). Write the answers on the board and elicit the pronunciation of *ea, ee* and *ie* in each word (/ɜː/, /ɪə/ and /iː/).

Give each student a sheet. Students work individually and add the words into the correct sound group according to the pronunciation of the letters *ea, ee* and *ie*. Monitor, check and drill the words. Ask the class for other words to add to the groups.

In Activity B, put students into pairs and give each pair two dice. The first student rolls two dice and adds the two numbers on the dice. The student finds the corresponding six sounds in the table for that number. Their partner must then say words for the six sounds which match that number in order, e.g.: 5 =

/e/	/ɪə/	/ɜː/	/iː/	/e/	/iː/

so the student might say *friend, career, learn, meet, head, Greek*. Students cross out each row of correctly pronounced sounds so they don't do the same row more than once. Monitor and make sure students are pronouncing sounds correctly. As feedback, find out which pair has crossed out most rows of sounds.

Answers

/iː/ meet	/e/ friend	/eɪ/ great	/eə/ bear	/ɪə/ cheerful	/ɜː/ research
cheat referee thief	breathtaking ahead	steak	underwear	deer	Earth

2A Consonant-vowel linking

▶ Photocopiable activity on p.254

You need one sheet for each pair of students, cut in half.

Write these phrases on the board and drill them.

one_and two   a big_idea   the sheep_are

Elicit that when one word ends in a consonant sound and the next word starts with a vowel sound, there is consonant–vowel linking.

Put students into A/B pairs. Give each student their sheet, A or B. Tell them to read the complete text on their own sheet and mark where there is consonant–vowel linking. The first is done as an example. If necessary, elicit another example – one from a Student A and one from a Student B.

Student A dictates text A to Student B so Student B can complete the gaps. Monitor that Student A is reading out the text at a natural speed and linking the consonant–vowel sounds in the marked words. Read out the whole text aloud for students to listen and check. Students then practise reading the whole text aloud, concentrating on the consonant–vowel linking. They then try to guess what the worker says. Take guesses from the whole class and then tell them the worker says: *'That was a big tip for a pizza.'*

Repeat the procedure with Student B reading out Text B to Student A. They then compare ideas about what the old lady says. Take guesses from the whole class and then tell them the old lady says: *'I don't know. Here's your five euros.'*

As feedback, drill some of the consonant–vowel linking from the two texts.

Answers
Student A: Text A
A factory is doing badly and they get_a new managing director to improve_efficiency. The new director comes_in and the first thing she does_is to take_a_walk_around the factory and see what_everyone's doing. Everything seems_all right but there's_a man just leaning_against_a wall and playing with_a mobile phone. 'What_are you doing?' the director asks. 'Nothing,' the man_answers, 'I'm just waiting_around to get paid.' The director is furious_and says, 'Well, here's five hundred euros, get_out_of my factory and don't come back!' The man leaves_immediately and the director turns_around to one_of the workers and says, 'What does that tell you?' The worker replies …

Student B: Text B
A genius walks_into a cafe and says, 'I'm going to prove that_I'm the cleverest person here. Just_ask me a question and I'll_ask you one. If you can't_answer my question, give me five euros. If I can't_answer your question, I'll give you five thousand euros.' An_old lady in a corner says, 'I'll try. Ask_a question.' The genius says, 'What's the capital_of the USA?' The old lady thinks_a bit and_answers, 'No idea at_all, here's your five euros' and gives him the five euros. 'Here's my question: what_animal has five_arms in the day and four arms_at night?' The genius thinks long_and hard, then says, 'That's_a difficult one! I don't know …' and_as he gives the old lady five thousand euros, the genius_asks, 'Well, what's the answer?' The old lady replies … 'I don't know. Here's your five euros.'

> **EXTRA ACTIVITY**
>
> Students choose one of the texts to act out to the class. Students add details and more dialogue. Give students time to practise before they present to the class.

2C Emphatic stress

▶ Photocopiable activity on p.255

You will need one sheet for each group of three students, cut up.

Revise the concept of emphatic stress by writing the first item on the board, changing the stress and asking students to think of and say appropriate explanations:

I think it's going to rain tomorrow. But who knows?

I think it's going to rain tomorrow. That will be good for the garden.

I think it's going to rain tomorrow. We'll be all right today.

Divide the class into groups of three. Give each group a set of cards: one for each student (Student A, Student B, Student C) and one group card. Students take it in turns to take the group card and say the sentence, putting emphatic stress on the underlined word. Then they each read the corresponding replies on their own card and the student who has the correct response reads it out. Monitor and help as necessary.

Check and drill answers with the class.

Answers
1 B   2 A   3 B   4 B   5 C   6 A   7 C   8 B   9 C   10 B
11 C   12 A

> **EXTRA ACTIVITIES**
>
> 1 Check and drill all the sentences on the group card. Then ask students to turn over the group card, and listen to you read out a sentence. See if students can remember the answer or think of another appropriate response.
>
> 2 Students go through the group card and put emphatic stress on other words to make the other follow-up sentences appropriate, e.g. the second item:
>
> *My brother knows French. But his English isn't great.*
>
> *My brother knows French. Not my sister.*

3A Tone in inversion structures

▶ Photocopiable activity on p.256

You will need one sheet for each pair of students, cut up.

Write this statement on the board: *I came back from holiday and went straight to work.* Elicit how to say this using *No sooner*: <u>No sooner had I got back from holiday</u> *than I went to work.*

Ask students to say the sentence and then elicit the intonation in the underlined word group (the adverbial): it rises at the end of the word group, and then falls at the end of the sentence.

Put students into pairs to play pelmanism. Give each pair a set of cards. Students spread the cards out face down in two separate sets: adverbials and endings.

Students take it in turns to take an adverbial and then an ending. If they match, the student reads them aloud with the correct intonation and keeps the pair of cards. If they don't match, the cards are turned over again. The winner is the student who has the most cards at the end of the game.

As feedback, check answers and drill all the sentences with the appropriate intonation.

> **Answers**
> 1 g   2 c   3 j   4 a   5 f   6 i   7 b   8 k   9 e   10 l
> 11 d   12 h

3C Consonant groups across words

▶ Photocopiable activity on p.257

You will need one sheet for each pair of students.

Write these phrases on the board and ask students which has a consonant group across two words (wrapped things):

wrapped things   explore other

In Activity A, put students into pairs and give each pair a copy of the sheet. Ask them to circle the phrases in the maze with consonant groups across two words. Elicit that the /t/ in *wrapped things* is not pronounced clearly because it precedes a consonant in the next word /θ/. In spite of this, there is still a consonant group /pθ/. Elicit that /d/ is not pronounced clearly before consonants either.

In Activity B, students work with their partners and move from *wrapped things* to *deep space* using phrases which have consonant groups pronounced across two words, paying attention to words that end in /t/ and /d/. Demonstrate by asking: *After* wrapped things *would the next phrase be* live broadcast *or* weighed two kg *or what you'd?* (*live broadcast* because the /d/ in *weighed* and the /t/ in *what you'd* are not clearly pronounced before the following words). Monitor and help as necessary. Drill all the phrases with consonant groups across two words when students have finished.

> **Answers**
> wrapped things; live broadcast; long story; thanks to;
> Max Redwood; both kinds; aliens look; wealth creation;
> waste money; science fiction; warning shriek; deep space

> **EXTRA ACTIVITY**
>
> Put students into groups to make a story containing all the phrases with consonant groups pronounced across two words, e.g. Student A: *We* wrapped things *to protect them on the long journey.* Student B: *It was exciting to think everyone would be watching us take off as a* live broadcast. Continue until one student cannot think of a sentence. See which group has the longest and most interesting story.

4A Sound and spelling: /ʃəs/, /iəs/, /dʒəs/

▶ Photocopiable activity on p.258

You will need one copy of the board game on p.272, a dice and counters and one sheet for each group of three students, cut up.

Ask students how they keep up with the news and ask for any interesting stories they have heard about. Write this headline on the board:

_____ *shoppers break into supermarket.* Elicit adjectives to complete the gap. Suggest the word *furious* as an answer. Ask students how the *-ious* ending is pronounced (/iəs/) and what the story could be about.

Put students into groups of three. In Activity A, give each group the top half of the sheet. Students add the words into the correct sound group according to the pronunciation of their suffixes. Monitor, check and drill the words. Ask the class for other words to add to the groups.

In Activity B, give each group a set of cards, a dice and counters and a board game. Explain that they spread out the cards a–n face down on the table and take it in turns to roll the dice. When they land on a numbered square, one of the other students in the group takes a card and reads the newspaper headline and says the sound on the card. The student should answer with a word with the sound on the card to complete the newspaper headline.

Students must give an appropriate answer and pronounce the word correctly. If they do, they move forward two squares. If they don't, they move back two squares. If they land on *Go on four squares*, or *Go back four squares*, they obey the instruction. Monitor and help as necessary, and note problematic words to drill with the class afterwards.

As feedback, elicit answers to Activity B and drill problematic words.

> **Answers**
> **A**
>
> | /ʃəs/ | /iəs/ | /dʒəs/ |
> |---|---|---|
> | suspicious delicious | obvious   various previous   luxurious serious | contagious |
>
> **Suggested answers**
> **B**
>
> a ambitious   b Courageous   c Curious   d outrageous
> e cautious   f delicious   g hilarious   h Gorgeous   i Precious
> j Prestigious   k luxurious   l Simultaneous
> m Spontaneous   n subconscious

> **EXTRA ACTIVITY**
>
> Groups expand news headlines into stories. See which groups can include the most words with *-ous* endings in their story.

4C Homophones in words and connected speech

▶ Photocopiable activity on p.259

You will need one sheet for each pair of students, cut up.

Dictate some homophones and get students to write down the different words, e.g.:

/səʊ/ so, sew

/weðə/ whether, weather

/haʊz/ how's, house (verb)

Put students into AB pairs and give each student their part of the sheet. In Activity A, Student A reads out pairs of sentences with homophones. Student B must listen and tick which word or phrase they hear first. Point out that paying attention to the context is important to help them decide. When Student A has read all the sentences, Student B can check his/her answers. Monitor and check the pronunciation.

In Activity B, students swap roles.

As feedback, drill all the pairs of sentences (1–16).

5A Sound and spelling: s and ss

▶ Photocopiable activity on p.260

You will need one sheet for each pair of students.

Dictate the tongue-twister *She sells sea shells on the sea shore* for students to write down. Identify the sound contrast (/s/ and /ʃ/). Ask students to say these sounds (/z/ *and* /ʒ/) and to give you examples with the letters s and ss (e.g., *dessert, television*). Ask students to practise saying the tongue twister in pairs.

Put students into pairs and give each pair a sheet. In Activity A, students need to move through the maze from *mission* to *necessary* using words which have a /s/ or /ʃ/ sound only. Demonstrate by saying: *After* mission *would the next word be* usual, assault *or* vision? (*assault*). Students work in pairs, taking it in turns to identify and say the next word, until they reach the end of the maze. Monitor and help as necessary.

Check answers and drill all the words with /s/ and /ʃ/ sounds when students have finished.

In Activity B, students repeat the activity in the second maze, but with /z/ and /ʒ/ sounds. Monitor and help as necessary. Check answers and drill all the words with /z/ and /ʒ/ sounds when students have finished.

Answers
A mission; assault; permission; comparison; Russian; essay; assassin; impression; tissue; muscle; (dismiss;) necessary
B evasion; vision; possessive; cousin; reason; dissolve; usually; measure; (occasion); rise; positive; dessert

5C Main stress

▶ Photocopiable activity on p.261

You will need one sheet for each pair of students, cut up.

Write on the board:

He drove really well in the race.

He came close to winning the race.

Ask students which word would have main stress in the second sentence and why (*winning* because it is new information).

Put students into pairs. Give each pair the 14 cut-up strips from the dialogue. Tell them to reorder the sentences and mark the main stress in each sentence. Check answers as a class. Students then practise reading out the dialogue. They swap roles and practise the dialogue again.

Take away the strips and give each pair the gapped dialogue. Tell students to complete the dialogue, remembering the words with the main stress. Monitor and check students are using main stress appropriately.

As feedback, drill all the lines from the dialogue.

Answers
favour; Another; often; enough; off; drove; weeks; twelve/12; your; sports; know; driven; seen; trust; driving

6A Sentence stress

▶ Photocopiable activity on p.262

You will need one sheet for each pair of students, cut up.

Write these sentences on the board without the underlining and ask students to identify the stressed syllables and say them.

We are <u>looking</u> for an <u>editor</u> for a <u>photography</u> <u>magazine</u>.

<u>Promising</u> <u>candidates</u> will be <u>contacted</u> for <u>interview</u>.

Elicit that auxiliary verbs are usually not stressed.

Put students into two groups, A and B. Give each student their part of the sheet. Explain the situation: they are looking for an editor for their photography magazine and are shortlisting candidates based on their CVs and an informal meeting. Student A has met two candidates and Student B has two different candidates. Arrange students into pairs and give them their sheets.

In Activity A, students work individually and underline the stressed words in the sentences.

In Activity B, put students into AB pairs. Students take turns to exchange the information they have by asking and answering questions, and completing the table in note form. Monitor and make sure that students are using sentence stress appropriately.

In Activity C, students discuss in their pairs which, if any, of the four candidates should get an interview.

Take feedback as a class.

Answers
Kylie Rogers: <u>Ky</u>lie is <u>ed</u>iting a <u>fash</u>ion <u>mag</u>azine. She was a <u>free</u>lance <u>ed</u>itor. She's been in<u>volved</u> in <u>pub</u>lishing for <u>five years</u>. She's <u>ho</u>ping to do an M<u>BA</u>. She's <u>cons</u>tantly been <u>pho</u>ning a<u>bout</u> the <u>job</u>!
Ivan Ivanov: <u>I</u>van's <u>hav</u>ing a ca<u>reer</u> <u>break</u>. He <u>was</u> <u>work</u>ing as a <u>cam</u>eraman. He's <u>been</u> in the pro<u>fess</u>ion for <u>seven years</u>. He's been <u>think</u>ing of <u>start</u>ing his own <u>mag</u>azine. He was <u>ask</u>ing about the <u>sal</u>ary.
Amelia Lopez: A<u>me</u>lia is <u>writ</u>ing for a pho<u>tog</u>raphy <u>web</u>site. She <u>was</u> <u>writ</u>ing for <u>IT</u> <u>mag</u>azines. She's <u>worked</u> in <u>pub</u>lishing for <u>six years</u>. She'll be <u>stay</u>ing in <u>pub</u>lishing. She's <u>had</u> her <u>work</u> <u>pub</u>lished in our <u>mag</u>azine.
Claudio Torres: <u>Claud</u>io is <u>work</u>ing for a <u>comp</u>etitor as an <u>ed</u>itor. He's <u>al</u>ways <u>had</u> the <u>same</u> <u>job</u>. <u>Soon</u> he'll have been <u>work</u>ing there for <u>ten years</u>. He's <u>look</u>ing for <u>man</u>agement <u>ex</u>perience. He's <u>be</u>ing <u>in</u>terviewed by <u>other</u> <u>mag</u>azines.

6B Main stress and emphatic stress: adverbs and adjectives

 Photocopiable activity on p.263

You will need one sheet for each pair of students, cut up.

Ask students to tell you about times when they felt *really shocked*, *completely exhausted* and *so surprised*. Write these adverb + adjective combinations on the board and elicit the emphatic stress (a rise in pitch on the adverb and then a high fall on adjective).

Put students into pairs and give each student their part of the sheet, A or B. Give each pair a set of cards and ask them to shuffle them and take half of the cards each.

Student A reads the first sentence from his/her sheet and Student B chooses a card with an appropriate adverb + adjective to give a response, with emphatic stress. Remind students to respond with further reactions, e.g.:

A *We lost 6–0 today.*

B *That's terrible news. I'm <u>absolutely devastated</u>.*

Students then swap roles and continue to work through the sentences and give responses using all their cards, if possible.

> ### EXTRA ACTIVITY
>
> Ask students to write two true sentences and two false sentences about themselves using the adverb + adjective cards. Students read the sentences using appropriate emphatic stress and their partners have to decide whether the sentences are true or false.

7A Main stress: compound adjectives

 Photocopiable activity on p.264

You will need two dice and one sheet for each pair of students, cut up.

Write these compound adjectives on the board:

cold-<u>hearted</u>

<u>heart</u>-warming

Ask students to repeat them and say which word is stressed, the first or second. Elicit the rule that whether the body part is used as a noun or an adjective in the first or second parts, it is usually stressed.

Put students into pairs and give each pair a set of cards. Ask students to match the cards to make 12 compound adjectives. Ask them to mark the stressed word in each one. Drill the words.

Give each pair two dice and the sheet of gapped predictions. Ask them to complete the predictions with a compound adjective from the words on the cards. Students take turns to roll the dice three times and receive three predictions from their partner. Their partner looks at the prediction with the same number as the dice, and reads the prediction, including the correct compound adjective.

Students then get into new pairs and repeat the activity. Monitor and make sure students are putting the stress on the correct word/syllable in the compound adjective.

As feedback, ask students if any of the predictions they heard are likely to come true.

Answers

2 warm/kind-<u>hearted</u>   3 <u>heart</u>broken   4 <u>hair</u>-raising / <u>mind</u>-boggling / <u>heart</u>breaking   5 open-<u>minded</u>   6 narrow-<u>minded</u>   7 light-<u>hearted</u>   8 <u>back</u>-breaking   9 warm/kind-<u>hearted</u>   10 <u>mouth</u>-watering   11 <u>mind</u>-boggling / <u>heart</u>breaking / <u>jaw</u>-dropping   12 half-<u>hearted</u>

> ### VARIATION
>
> When students hear their predictions they react to the prediction and ask more questions, e.g. *That sounds extremely unlikely to me? Will this happen at school?* Their partner tries to convince them of the prediction by adding more details, e.g. *Yes. It will be a close friend of yours.* Alternatively, the student can withdraw the prediction, e.g. *I think the dice may be wrong today.*

7C Sound and spelling: *ou* and *ough*

 Photocopiable activity on p.265

You will need one copy of the board game on p.272, a dice, counters and one sheet, cut up, for each group of four students.

Write the English town *Loughborough* on the board and see which student can come closest to pronouncing it (/lʌfbrə/).

Put students into groups of four. Give each group a set of cards. Ask students to make sure the cards are in the correct order. Tell students to put the cards face down in a pile on the table with card 1 at the top of the pile. They take it in turns to roll the dice and go round the board. When a student lands on a square with no instruction, the student to their right picks up a card and reads the clue to him/her, taking care not to reveal the answer. Remind students that it's important that the cards are used in their numbered order. Tell the class that all the answers are words containing *ou* and *ough*. If students give an incorrect answer, don't know the answer or pronounce the word incorrectly, they miss a turn. If students give a correct answer, pronounced correctly, they move forwards one square. Monitor and help when necessary.

As feedback, drill all the answers.

> ### NO-CUT VARIATION
>
> Divide the class into two teams. Each team takes it in turns to answer the clues you give them. If they answer correctly and with the correct pronunciation, they get a point. If they answer incorrectly, don't know the answer or pronounce the word incorrectly, the rival team gets the opportunity to answer. If they get it right, they get two points. The winning team is the one with the most points.

> ### EXTRA ACTIVITY
>
> Students write a sentence with at least three different *ou* and *ough* sounds and dictate it to other students in a class mingle.

8B Pitch: extra information

 Photocopiable activity on p.266

You will need one sheet for each group of four students, cut up. You will also need to ask one student in each group to draw this 6 × 6 grid.

Cabin	1	2	3	4	5
Name					
Age					
Nationality					
Profession					
Luggage					
Destination (country)					

Explain the situation. The computer booking system of a European cruise company has broken down and passenger details are all mixed up. Luckily, some of the staff remember details about the passengers in the five cabins. They need to share information so they can enter the correct passenger details into the new booking system.

Write these sentences on the board:

Trevor Jones, a doctor, is in the first cabin.

Rachel Lopez, American, is in a cabin next to the doctor.

Ask whether the pitch is higher or lower on the underlined information added (*lower*). Drill the sentences.

Ask students where Trevor Jones is (*cabin 1*) and where Rachel Lopez is (*cabin 2*) and tell them to add this information to their grid.

Put students into groups of four. Give each group a set of cards. Tell students that they must share information to find out about the passengers. Students take it in turns to take a card and read the information using the correct tone for the added information. Groups should work together to complete their grids. The first group to finish is the winner. Set a time limit of 15 minutes. Monitor and help as necessary, making sure that students read, not show, their sentences and use the correct pitch.

As feedback, drill some of the sentences.

NO-CUT VARIATION

Students work in groups and take it in turns to read out a sentence and use the information to complete the grid.

Answers

Cabin	1	2	3	4	5
Name	Trevor Jones	Rachel Lopez	Kurt Müller	Diana Moldovan	Mariana Gonzalo
Age	54	30	26	22	47
Nationality	British	American	German	Romanian	Argentinian
Profession	doctor	engineer	accountant	law student	IT worker
Luggage	1 small suitcase	4 suitcases	1 sports bag	1 rucksack	1 large suitcase
Destination (country)	France	Ukraine	Portugal	Germany	Ireland

EXTRA ACTIVITY

Students pick one of the passengers and write a short paragraph about them and their reason for travelling. Tell them to add information and then read out their paragraphs to the group using the correct tone.

8C Intonation in implied questions

▶ Photocopiable activity on p.267

You will need one sheet for each pair of students, cut up.

Read this statement to students twice, once with question intonation (rising) and once without:

I could give you £30 for it.

Elicit the difference and why people use this intonation in implied questions (to be tactful). Check that students know what a *landlord* and *tenant* are. Put students into AB pairs. Give each student their part of the sheet. Don't give students the points calculation.

In Activity A, tell them that they are landlords and tenants and that they are going to negotiate the terms of the rent. Ask them to choose three statements in the box to use with implied question intonation.

In Activity B, students negotiate the rent using the implied questions they chose in Activity A to agree terms, writing down the final figures in their table. Monitor and help when necessary. Make sure students use question intonation. At the end, give each pair the points calculation so they can see who was successful in the negotiation.

	Landlord	Tenant
Monthly rent	+ 1 point for every euro over 2,200	+ 2 points for every euro under 2,400
Deposit	+ 1 point for every euro over 1,500	+ 2 points for every euro under 1,800
Rental period	– 20 points for every month under 32	– 30 points for every month over 24

Alternatively, if you want students to repeat the negotiation with different partners and roles, ask students to tell you their terms and give them their points, so that the points calculation is kept secret.

EXTRA ACTIVITY

Students could think of a different situation where people need to negotiate, like in a market, and make their conversations using implied questions.

9A Sound and spelling: *re-*

▶ Photocopiable activity on p.268

You will need one sheet for each pair of students, cut up.

All the *re-* words are either from the Student's Book, or are C1 or lower on English Profile. Pre-teach any words you think your students might not know.

In Activity A, put students into AA and BB pairs. Give each student their part of the sheet. They each have half of the same crossword. Students pronounce the words on their half of the crossword, making sure the *re-* is either /iː/ or /ɪ/. Monitor and make sure students are pronouncing the words correctly.

In Activity B, put students into AB pairs. Students then need to complete the crossword, taking turns to ask for and give each other the clues for the missing *re-* words.

Monitor and make sure students are pronouncing the *re-* words correctly.

As feedback, drill all the *re-* words.

Answers

/iː/ recharge, reconsider, recreate, redevelop, reinforce, reinstate, relocate, revamp

/ɪ/ recruit, refresh, regain, regenerate, rejuvenate, remove, replace, restore

9C Sound and spelling: foreign words in English

 Photocopiable activity on p.269

You will need one sheet for each pair of students, cut up.

Ask students what foreign words they know in English and how they are pronounced, e.g. *typhoon* comes from Japanese and is pronounced /taɪˈfuːn/ in English.

In Activity A, put students into AA and BB pairs. Give each student their part of the sheet. Ask them to match the complete words on the map with the definitions. Students then pronounce the words in pairs. Monitor and check.

Put students into AB pairs. Ask them to complete all the words on their maps by taking turns to ask for and give clues. Monitor and drill all the words with the class, paying attention to words in which the consonant sounds might be untypical of English (aficionado /əfɪʃɪəˈnɑːdəʊ/, avant-garde /ævɒŋˈɡɑːd/, cappuccino /kæpʊˈtʃiːnəʊ/, déjà vu /deɪʒɑːˈvuː/, faux pas /fəʊˈpɑː/, rendezvous /ˈrɒndɪvuː/, Schadenfreude /ˈʃɑːdənfrɔɪdə/).

Answers

1 b 2 f 3 d 4 h 5 e 6 i 7 c 8 g 9 a 10 j

> ### 💡 EXTRA ACTIVITY
> Students put the words into sentences, e.g. *I always enjoy a cappuccino in the morning.*

10A Word groups and main stress

 Photocopiable activity on p.270

You will need one sheet for each student.

Dictate to students: *I would <u>much</u> rather have been young in the 1960s.* Ask them to write the sentence down and mark the main stress. Repeat the sentence if necessary. Drill the sentence.

In Activity A, give each student a sheet. Ask students to work individually and mark the main stress in each sentence. Explain that there may be more than one word group in a sentence and the main stress may fall on a different content word in each word group, depending on the speaker's emphasis. Check and drill all the sentences.

Students tick each regret or criticism they have experienced.

In Activity B, put students into pairs and ask students to tell each other about the sentences they have ticked, using main stress appropriately, and explaining the circumstances behind them.

As feedback, drill all the sentences again.

Suggested answers

I would <u>much</u> rather have been told the truth.
If I'd known it would be so <u>dangerous</u>, I would <u>never</u> have tried it.
I ought to have thought more about my <u>family</u> than myself.
It's about time they did more for <u>young</u> people where I <u>live</u>.
I <u>wish</u> I had made a better impression at the interview.
It's time we moved to a <u>bigger</u> flat/house.
I ought <u>not</u> to have <u>bought</u> it but I just couldn't <u>resist</u> it.
I needn't have <u>bothered</u> helping him/her.
I might have become a <u>professional</u> if I had had <u>lessons</u>.
I should have trusted my gut <u>instinct</u>.
If <u>only</u> I had studied harder at school.
I would <u>love</u> to have seen more of the <u>last</u> place I went to on holiday.
I <u>wish</u> he/she would stop telling me all their problems.
I ought to have <u>checked</u> that everything <u>worked</u> properly <u>before</u> I used it.
I would <u>much</u> rather do something I really want to do than work just for the <u>money</u>.

> ### 💡 EXTRA ACTIVITY
> Students create a dialogue using one of the regrets or criticisms as a prompt.

10C Tone in question tags

 Photocopiable activity on p.271

You will need one sheet for each pair of students, cut up.

Ask students if they have ever made new friends online and then met face-to-face. Did that person seem different in real life?

In Activity A, put students into AA and BB pairs. Give each student their part of the sheet. Ask students to read the table and elicit what intonation they need to use in the questions for the facts they are sure about (falling) and what intonation they need to use when they're not sure (rising). Give students time to form the question tags and practise asking them. Monitor and help as necessary.

In Activity B, put students into AB pairs. Students act out the role play by asking and answering each other's questions in Activity A, using the information provided in the table in Activity B. Monitor and check they are using the appropriate intonation.

As feedback, elicit some of the tag questions from students and drill them with the appropriate intonation.

> ### 💡 EXTRA ACTIVITY
> Students role play another meeting between friends who are meeting face-to-face for the first time, making up the details and questions.

1A Grammar
Adverbs and adverbial phrases

1 You are hiking through the mountains (when?). There's (how likely?) going to be a storm. Do you … ?
- carry on walking 8
- take cover in a cave 20

2 You move the rock (how?). (comment?) Behind it there is a polished door. What do you do?
- Put the rock back. 13
- Go inside. 19

3 The figure approaches you (how?). Huge, white and hairy – (comment?) it is the famous yeti! What do you do next?
- Take a selfie of you and the yeti. 6
- Ask the yeti to get you out of there. 21

4 (comment?) Your phone won't work. You're getting (degree?) desperate when you see something or someone (where?). Do you … ?
- go and see what is there 17
- walk on 10

5 There is a wooden chest (where?). You open it (how?). Inside is a pile of gold! You put …
- all the gold in your rucksack and run. 18
- half the gold in your rucksack and run. 11

6 (comment?) Yetis don't like publicity. The yeti smashes the camera (how?) and runs away (where?).
- Go to 10.

7 Two more hikers are stuck in the storm (comment?)! They say they know a safe route (where?). Do you … ?
- follow them 12
- try to get away alone 8

8 You walk through the storm (how?). (comment?) Snow is falling (how?) and the wind is blowing (how?). What do you do?
- Walk quicker! 15
- Take cover in a cave. 20

9 The 'hikers' stop you (how? where?) and take all your money and valuables. They run away and leave you on the mountain.
- Go to 10.

10 Darkness comes (when?) and you are (degree?) lost and (degree?) cold. Mountain Rescue will find you (when?), if you are lucky.
Your journey ends here.

11 (comment?) This is stealing! Are you (degree?) sure?!
- Yes, in fact I'll take more gold. 18
- No, I'll just take a photo of it. 14

12 You walk together. The route seems (degree?) strange and you walk for ages. Suddenly, one of the hikers says, '(how?), We're lost.' You decide to …
- run away from them. 10
- keep with them. 9

13 (comment?) You hear voices coming towards the cave. Someone is shouting something (how?).
- Run away before the people see you. 10
- Wait and see. 7

14 You leave the cave (how?) and (when?) find your way down the mountain. You tell the authorities about the secret room and become famous for discovering it.
Good choice!

15 The storm has become an icy blizzard! It's getting (degree?) dangerous. You …
- telephone for help. 4
- walk even quicker! 10

16 You sleep (how?) and wake up (when?). A huge white and hairy creature – the yeti! – is looking at you (how?). Do you … ?
- apologise and get out of the cave 8
- ask the Yeti to help you get home 21

17 It is (how likely?) a human but he or she is (degree?) huge! You have (how often?) seen someone so big. You …
- shout 'Help!' 3
- run away. 10

18 You leave the cave (how?) and struggle through the storm but you don't get very far with all that weight on your back. (comment?) You have to abandon your rucksack.
- Go to 10.

19 (comment?) You find yourself in a palatial room! There's a vast four-poster bed (where?). What do you do next?
- Lie down and have a sleep. 16
- Look around the room more. 5

20 You clamber (how?) into a nearby cave. There is a large rock (where?) which seems to have been moved (when?). Do you … ?
- roll away the rock 2
- sit and wait for the storm to pass 13

21 The yeti takes you on a secret path (where?). You come out of the mountains (when?).
Well done, you're safe and you can say you met a yeti!

1B Grammar
The perfect aspect

Past

Find someone who, by the time they started school, … ?	Name	Details
1 move flat/house more than once		
2 start to speak two languages		
3 meet their best friend		
4 learn how to read and write at home		
5 think about their future profession		

Present

Find someone who, this year, … ?	Name	Details
6 win a prize or competition		
7 work or study too hard		
8 travel to any really interesting places		
9 not have much good luck		
10 do something for the first time		

Future

Find someone who, by the end of the year, … ?	Name	Details
11 save up enough money for something particular		
12 celebrate an important anniversary		
13 achieve something really worthwhile		
14 take lessons in something new		
15 prepare or train hard for something		

Grammar
Comparison

Team A	Team B
1 Life is better in the countryside.	**1** Life is better in the city.
2 Cars are the best kind of transport, better than motorbikes.	**2** Motorbikes are the best kind of transport, better than cars.
3 It would be easier to write a great book than to direct a popular film.	**3** It would be easier to direct a popular film than to write a great book.
4 Skydiving is a more interesting experience than scuba diving.	**4** Scuba diving is a more interesting activity than skydiving.
5 Tigers are more charismatic animals than elephants.	**5** Elephants are more charismatic animals than tigers.
6 A perfect holiday would be a week in the mountains, not at the beach.	**6** A perfect holiday would be a week by the beach, not a week in the mountains.
7 If time travel were possible, it would be best to go back in time.	**7** If time travel were possible, it would be best to go forward in time.

Comparison with *than*	Comparison with *than*
A big difference: a good/great deal, a lot, considerably, decidedly, far, infinitely, miles (informal), much, significantly, three/four/many times (etc.), way (informal)	**A big difference:** a good/great deal, a lot, considerably, decidedly, far, infinitely, miles (informal), much, significantly, three/four/many times (etc.), way (informal)
A small difference: a bit (informal), a little bit (informal), barely any, fractionally, marginally, slightly	**A small difference:** a bit (informal), a little bit (informal), barely any, fractionally, marginally, slightly
No difference: no, not any	**No difference:** no, not any
Comparison with *as … as …*	**Comparison with *as … as …***
A big difference: not nearly, nothing like, nowhere near, twice / three times (etc.)	**A big difference:** not nearly, nothing like, nowhere near, twice / three times (etc.)
A small difference: almost, nearly, not quite	**A small difference:** almost, nearly, not quite
No difference: equally, just	**No difference:** equally, just

Your town has received a large financial investment and you are able to develop the project of your dreams. Think about the town where you live and choose one of these projects (or one of your own) to develop.

Project A: Improve public transport

Think about:

- What are the current problems?
- What forms of transport will be most efficient/economical/green?
- Does the infrastructure (e.g. roads, pavements, pathways, bridges, train tracks, etc.) need improvement?
- What changes could there be to timetables?
- How will you encourage people to use public transport?
- What problems could there be and how will you solve them?

Project B: Improve the local environment

Think about:

- What are the current problems?
- What practical ways are there of making your town cleaner and healthier?
- What can different kinds of people (e.g. residents, businesses, contractors, etc.) do to help?
- How will you make people aware of environmental issues?
- What problems could there be and how will you solve them?

Project C: Hold a performing arts festival

Think about:

- What kind of performing arts (e.g. dancing, singing, etc.) would work best?
- What other kinds of attractions will there be?
- What else do you need to organise (e.g. security, toilets, etc.)?
- How will you get acts to participate?
- How will you promote the festival?
- What problems could there be and how will you solve them?

We**'re intending to** build …

The council **is planning to** …

We**'ll be** distribut**ing** leaflets **with the intention of** …

We**'re intending to** complete work on …

We**'re aiming to** convince …

We**'re about to** start …

We**'re due to** receive a grant from …

We**'re not about to** let …

A Are these sentences correct? You have $250 to bet. Minimum bet is $5.

	Correct (✓) Incorrect (✗)	Bet $	Winnings $
1 Not only did he pass but he got top marks.			
2 Rarely have I tasted anything as delicious as this.			
3 On no account are bags to be brought into the room.			
4 Seldom have been I in such a situation.			
5 No way could that have happened by chance.			
6 Not only once did the idea come into her head.			
7 Only then John did realise he was in big trouble.			
8 Not we did waste a dollar while travelling around the world.			
9 Scarcely had we arrived it was time to leave.			
10 Under no circumstances, should you borrow money without asking.			
Total amount		$	$

B Write five sentences with inversion to give to another group (at least two sentences should be incorrect). You have $100 to bet on the other group's five sentences. Minimum bet is $5.

	Correct (✓) Incorrect (✗)	Bet $	Winnings $
1			
2			
3			
4			
5			
Total amount		$	$

THE MYSTERY OF THE MISSING PAINTING

On 26th April 1879 a painting was discovered missing from the library of Gray Manor. The house was searched from top to bottom but the painting could not be found. Six people were in the house at the time.

Suspect 1: Dorian Gray

Widower Dorian Gray owned the valuable painting of his late wife, Annabelle, which [1]*went / had gone* missing. He had bought the painting for £500 from Basil Hallwood and insured it for the sum of £2,000. He loved the painting dearly and [2]*would look / was looking* at it daily, as the sole reminder of his wife. He [3]*would not sell / wasn't selling* it, despite many offers from art collectors.

Suspect 2: Charlotte Gray

Charlotte, Dorian's daughter, [4]*was feeling / was to feel* angry with Alan, a poor artist and friend of the family, who [5]*borrowed / had been borrowing* more and more money from her. She recently lied to Alan about leaving university; in fact she [6]*had already been thrown out / had already thrown out*. She [7]*had been / was* ashamed and [8]*didn't want / wasn't wanting* to confide in anyone.

Suspect 3: Alan Campbell

Alan [9]*had stayed / was staying* with Dorian for a few weeks while Charlotte was there. He was deeply in love with Charlotte, but also deeply in debt to her. Alan [10]*had recently had / was recently having* an argument with Charlotte. She [11]*had told / was telling* him that she [12]*had left / left* university and [13]*was expected / was expecting* to be cut off from her father's money.

Suspect 4: Basil Hallwood

Basil was the artist who [14]*painted / was painting* the missing picture. He [15]*had not been going to give / didn't give* the picture to Dorian because he [16]*had never liked / didn't like* it (or the late Annabelle Gray), but Dorian [17]*was insisting / had insisted* on paying for it. Since he sold the painting, he had begun to paint in a new style and the price of his work had increased dramatically.

Suspect 5: Sybil Vane

Sybil [18]*was / had been* a very close friend of Dorian's late wife, Annabelle. She was the only person who [19]*had known / knew* that Annabelle [20]*had hated / hated* the picture painted by Basil. Sybil strongly disliked all the men in the house, and [21]*only ever visited / was only ever visiting* when Charlotte was home from university.

Suspect 6: Lord Henry

Lord Henry, Dorian's best friend and a rich art collector, [22]*tried / had been trying* to buy the picture from Dorian for years. He [23]*was / had been* secretly in love with Dorian's wife. He had confessed his love to Sybil, in a moment of desperation, and lived in fear that she [24]*would reveal / would have revealed* his secret to Dorian and that he would never get the painting.

Dorian Gray – You are innocent

You went to bed at 1:00 am after saying goodnight to the picture.

You walked past Alan's room and saw the room was empty on your way to bed.

You heard Basil in the room next door moving around very late in the night.

Alan Campbell – You are innocent

You went to bed at 9:00 pm after a fight with Charlotte.

You went to Charlotte's room to apologise around 12:30 am.

You saw Lord Henry going downstairs at around 1:30 am.

Charlotte Gray – You are innocent

You went to your room at 9:00 pm after a fight with Alan.

You made up with Alan when he came to your room between 12:30 am and 1:30 am.

You heard someone dragging something through the upstairs hall at about 2:45 am and again at 3:30 am.

Basil Hallwood – You are guilty

You burnt the picture because you felt it damaged your reputation as an artist.

You went downstairs at 3:15 am, took the picture and burnt it in your room.

You must lie about your movements to protect yourself.

Sybil Vane – You are innocent

You went to bed at 11:00 pm but woke up again at 2:00 am.

You got up in the night to get a chair from the library at about 2:45 am, so you could read by the fire in your room. You're sure the painting was still on the wall then.

Lord Henry– You are innocent

You went downstairs at 1:30 am to say goodnight to Annabelle's picture and it was still there. This will reveal you were in love with her, so you must lie.

You heard Charlotte, Alan and Sybil's doors open during the night. You fell asleep at about 3:00 am.

Sally has another **suggestion**.	Let's go to the **shop**.	Take the **knife**.	I found two **dogs**.	It's a famous **poem**.
Have you heard the **news**?	I jumped at the **sound**.	Ask the **assistant**.	Wear your **glasses**.	You have to take an **exam**.
Look at that **car**!	She used to be a **nurse**.	I love this **picture**.	It was a beautiful **day**.	There's plenty of **space**.
It's right in the **centre**.	We walked down the **beach**.	You can't explain the **feeling**.	Graham is the **director**.	I can't find my **hat**.

4B Grammar
have / get passives

Student A

Andy was worried about [1]*losing his job* so he took an interview with another company. He took it very seriously, [2]*went to the hairdressers for a haircut* and even [3]*took his old suit to the cleaner's*. Andy was planning to go to the interview by bike, but unfortunately [4]*someone stole* it while he was getting ready for the interview. He [5]*persuaded his neighbour* to lend him her bike. He had to cycle really fast to the interview which [6]*caused him to start sweating*. At the interview they were running late, and they [7]*made him wait* in reception for hours. In the end, they came out and told him that the position had been withdrawn.

David ignored the 'out of order' sign and [1]*became trapped* in the lift. They didn't [2]*arrange for someone to fix* it for hours. A young man had followed David into the lift, and they just had to wait. They started to talk and the young man [3]*persuaded David to tell him* about his job as a sales rep. David said his company was terrible, especially the salary, but [4]*they paid him* extra money every week because he over-claimed driving expenses. Finally, they [5]*made the lift work* and in the office ten minutes later [6]*the CEO introduced David* to his new sales manager – the man in the lift. David didn't [7]*lose his job* but they [8]*made him repay the money* every month from his salary.

Gerard was coming back from holiday in Greece when [1]*a security officer stopped him* and [2]*made him open* his suitcase. Gerard wasn't worried about [3]*the security officer searching his bag* because he had nothing to hide. Then the security officer took a coin from a pocket and said 'What's this?' Gerald said it was a funny coin he had found. The customs office [4]*phoned an expert who valued the coin* and found it to be a precious antique that couldn't leave the country. Gerard said it was his, because he had found it. He lost his temper and [5]*caused them to arrest him*. In the end, they [6]*made him pay a fine* and they released him without the coin.

Student B

Serena's mother wanted her to be a professional pianist and [1]*made her practise* every day. Serena hated it but every time Serena complained [2]*her mother criticised her* for being lazy. One day there was a big rock concert that Serena really wanted to go to. Serena [3]*persuaded her mother to believe* she was ill. Her mother went out to work, and Serena slipped out of the house and went to the rock concert. Serena really enjoyed it and [4]*someone took a photo of* her with the lead guitarist. Serena's mother saw the photo online and [5]*forced Serena to stay in* every night for the next month.

Pam's handbag went missing while she was out shopping. She wasn't sure if she'd left it somewhere or if [1]*it had been stolen*. She [2]*persuaded her neighbour* to let her in to her house. Then her phone rang. It was a man who said he had found her bag and if Pam wanted it back, she should meet him in 30 minutes. [3]*It made Pam think* that if she went out, [4]*the man might burgle the house* with her own keys. Pam phoned the police instead, because she wanted [5]*to cause them to arrest the man*. However, the police were busy and [6]*made Pam wait* on the line so she phoned a locksmith [7]*to arrange for them to change the locks* on her doors immediately.

Karmel was a keen horse rider but one day [1]*her horse threw her off* and she [2]*broke her leg* quite badly. [3]*An ambulance took her to hospital* and [4]*the doctors set her leg*. It was boring because the doctors [5]*made her lie down* for most of the day – she didn't want [6]*everyone to shout at her* for being difficult. Eventually she went home but she still had to rest. Karmel's friends felt sorry for her. Karmel [7]*persuaded her friends to bring* her horse to her garden. She was overjoyed and so excited. Karmel sat on her horse with some help and immediately fell off and [8]*broke her other leg*.

Grammar
Relative clauses

Student A

A Work in AA pairs. Complete the relative clauses in each clue.

Across

1 A person _____ crime is copying and selling films.

4 A verb, the meaning _____ is to say that someone did something bad or illegal.

6 A person _____ a sentence is passed.

7 A person _____ has lost their freedom.

8 The process _____ a criminal is found guilty or not guilty.

9 Someone _____ is not guilty, is this adjective.

10 A job _____ there are many specialities, for example: prosecutor, solicitor, defence.

11 Money offered to _____ can help the police solve a certain crime.

14 Laws _____ send people to prison for a long time are this adjective.

16 The moment _____ police handcuff a suspect and read them their rights.

B 💬 Work in AB pairs. Take turns to read your clues to your partner and complete the crossword.

Crossword (Student A) filled answers:
1 PIRATE
4 ACCUSE
6 JUDGE
7 PRISONER
8 TRIAL
9 INNOCENT
10 LAWYER
11 REWARD
14 STRICT
16 ARREST

- ✂ - - -

Student B

A Work in BB pairs. Complete the relative clauses in each clue.

Down

1 A place _____ criminals serve their sentences.

2 The feeling _____ you get when you think someone is doing something bad.

3 A person _____ job is to investigate serious crimes.

5 A person _____ commits an illegal act.

9 The period _____ police look into a crime.

12 A person _____ questions are asked about what they saw during a crime.

13 A verb, the meaning _____ allows a person to go free again after being imprisoned.

14 The time _____ prisoners are held on their own is this kind of confinement.

15 A person _____ home is a prison cell.

B 💬 Work in AB pairs. Take turns to read your clues to your partner and complete the crossword.

5B Grammar
Willingness, obligation and necessity

A 💬 Work in pairs. What do you need to do in each of these jobs? Complete the descriptions with your ideas.

Zookeeper	Stunt performer
Responsibilities	**Responsibilities**
• preparing food and feeding one particular type of animal	• liaising with the production team to create stunts
• cleaning out pens and cages and monitoring accommodation conditions	• planning stunts, getting equipment and performing stunts
• checking for signs of distress, disease or injury in animals	• carrying out risk assessments, completing detailed paperwork
• caring for sick animals under the direction of a vet	• adapting your movements to match the actor you replace
• answering visitors' questions and giving talks or lectures	• following strict choreography
• keeping daily records, normally on a computer	• performing on location at shoots worldwide
Requirements	**Requirements**
• *experience of ...*	•
• *qualifications in ...*	•
•	•
•	•
Conditions and benefits	**Conditions and benefits**
•	•
•	•

Police detective	Food scientist
Responsibilities	**Responsibilities**
• Establishing controlled crime scenes and examining these for evidence	• inventing new recipes and modifying foods, for example to create fat-free products
• Interviewing complainants, suspects and witnesses	• investigating ways to keep food fresh, safe and attractive
• Preparing charges or information for court cases and providing testimony as a witness in court	• finding ways of producing food more quickly and cheaply
• Preparing warrants and assisting in raids and arrests	• testing the safety and quality of food
• Maintaining progress reports and files on suspects	• providing accurate nutritional information for food labelling
• Conducting surveillance	
Requirements	**Requirements**
•	•
•	•
•	•
•	•
Conditions and benefits	**Conditions and benefits**
•	•
•	•

B 💬 Interview each other for one of the four positions. Use the phrases in the box to talk about the requirements of the position and willingness to fulfil the requirements.

be under no obligation to ...	have no objection to ...	be supposed/expected/required/obliged to ...
be advisable ...	have nothing against ...	have no choice but to ...
be prepared for ...	have no problem with ...	be happy to ...

6A Grammar
Simple and continuous verbs

A Complete the sentences with the best form of the verb in brackets. (Think about the tense and whether the verb should be simple or continuous.)

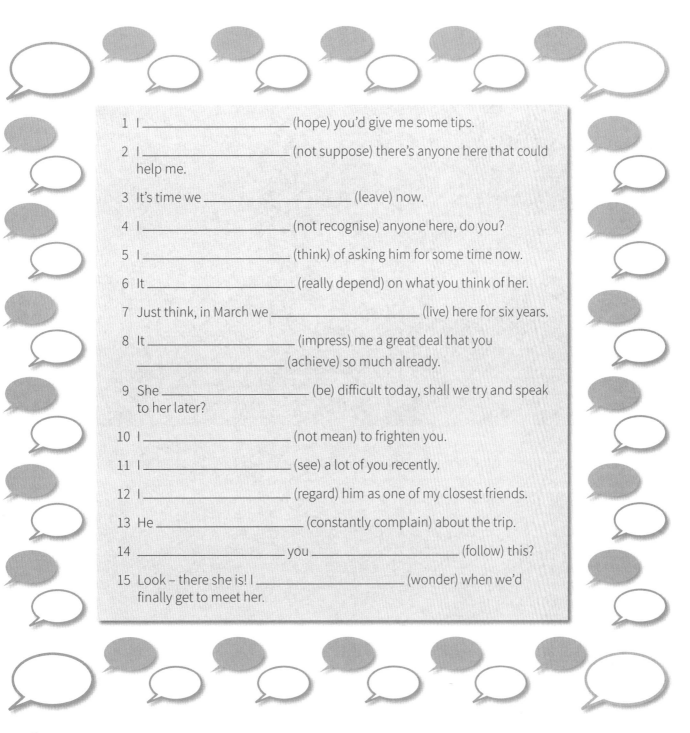

1 I _____ (hope) you'd give me some tips.

2 I _____ (not suppose) there's anyone here that could help me.

3 It's time we _____ (leave) now.

4 I _____ (not recognise) anyone here, do you?

5 I _____ (think) of asking him for some time now.

6 It _____ (really depend) on what you think of her.

7 Just think, in March we _____ (live) here for six years.

8 It _____ (impress) me a great deal that you _____ (achieve) so much already.

9 She _____ (be) difficult today, shall we try and speak to her later?

10 I _____ (not mean) to frighten you.

11 I _____ (see) a lot of you recently.

12 I _____ (regard) him as one of my closest friends.

13 He _____ (constantly complain) about the trip.

14 _____ you _____ (follow) this?

15 Look – there she is! I _____ (wonder) when we'd finally get to meet her.

B Work in groups. Think of a situation in which people might say four or more of the sentences in Activity A. Choose roles and role play a conversation using the sentences.

C Role play your conversation for the class.

6B Grammar
Participle clauses

A 💬 Work in pairs. Rewrite this story using participle clauses.

When I was walking down the street one day, I noticed a second-hand shop. I was going to pass by because I didn't have much time, but my eye was caught by a coat in the window display. It seemed strangely familiar. I went up to the window and I looked at it more closely. It was my old winter coat! I had left it hanging with all my other old clothes at the back of my wardrobe, as I hadn't worn it for years. I went inside the shop because I wanted to find out how the coat, which I had bought with my own money, had got there. The shop assistant was cashing up for the day and, because I suddenly felt quite angry, I rushed up to her and demanded, 'Give me my coat!' The shop assistant smiled and said, 'Don't you remember the day you gave it to us? And don't you remember why?' As I stared at her, I realised she was right. A long-forgotten memory was surfacing in my mind …

B 💬 Work in groups. Discuss these questions and then write a continuation of this story, using participle clauses.

1 How did the narrator know this was his coat? Was there anything special about it?

2 Why did the narrator give it to the shop?

3 Why did the narrator forget about this?

4 Why has no one bought the coat for so long?

5 Does the shop assistant know something important?

6 Will the narrator take the coat back and if so what will happen?

7A Grammar
Speculation and deduction

What do you think was the cause of each of these real-life mysteries? Use the language in the box.

probably   must/could/might/can't (have)   may well (have)   I bet …   I reckon …   There's no way …
There's an outside/slim/good chance that …   It's likely / quite possible / highly unlikely that …

Student A
OURANG MEDAN: THE GHOST SHIP

In 1947, two American ships sailing in waters near Indonesia received an emergency message from a Dutch vessel, the *Ourang Medan*. The message, in Morse code, said that the crew were all dead and ended with the words "I die." When the first American ship reached the *Ourang Medan* they found the deck littered with dead bodies. There were no survivors. The vessel appeared undamaged, but before it was possible to investigate, a fire broke out and the ship exploded and sank. No record has since been found of a ship named the *Ourang Medan*.

Student B
THE DEATH OF BRUCE LEE

Bruce Lee, the most famous martial artist of all time, died at the age of 32. Then based in the USA, Lee had travelled to Hong Kong to promote a film. He had worked the day of his death and, complaining of a headache, went for a nap before dinner. Lee never woke up. Medical reports suggested that Lee had died after a reaction to medication he was taking. However, Lee was famous for his fitness and healthy eating habits, so some people doubt he could have died so suddenly and so young. One conspiracy theory is that Lee was killed or cursed because he had brought the secrets of martial arts to the West. Buried next to Lee is his son, Brandon, who died in 1993 aged 28 … while filming a martial arts movie.

Student C
TAMAM SHUD

In 1948, an unidentified man was found dead on a beach in Australia. Medical reports suggest he had been poisoned, but no poison was found on him. In fact, the man was carrying very little, but investigators did find a secret pocket in his trousers and a small piece of paper with the phrase 'Tamam Shud', which means 'it is finished' in Persian. The paper had been torn from a book in a car found near the beach, and that book contained a phone number and a code. Investigators phoned the number and contacted a woman who said she had given the book to a friend. This friend did indeed have a book of Persian poetry but he was still alive and the book was intact. The code on the piece of paper has never been deciphered.

Student D
NOTHING TO LAUGH ABOUT

One morning in 1962 in a girls' boarding school in Tanzania, three school girls started laughing in class for no obvious reason. They kept on laughing and the laughter spread. Within a few hours they had 95 of the other 195 pupils laughing too, some of them for a few hours and others for over two weeks. The school was forced to close and the girls were all sent home, but that was only the start of the problem. The laughter spread like a disease to the village where many of the girls lived and hundreds of people, mostly schoolchildren or young people, joined in the laughter. Other schools in the area caught the laughter disease until, in the end, 1,000 or so people were affected.

7B Grammar
Cleft sentences

A Put the words in the correct order to make cleft sentences.

1	what worries / the amount / computer games / me is / kids / spend on / of time	_____
2	is so / the reason / its convenience / popular / online education / is simply	_____
3	communication / what / face-to-face / is replace / technology / does	_____
4	who use / it's only / too much time / to waste / people with / social-networking sites	_____
5	● Congratulations! You have won a prize, Sarah!	the Internet / the worst thing / our / is all over / is that / personal data	_____
6	that / it's these / online dating / are dangerous / sites	_____
7	still prefer / is just / who / older people / it / printed books	_____
8	what the / shouldn't / government / is / use / monitor and regulate Internet / people's / do	_____

B 💬 Work in groups. Discuss the statements.

have found them	Wouldn't you rather	listening to all this	We seem to	have been told	I'm tired of
speak to her	There's no point	being left here alone	Let me	even talking about it	I can't imagine
being so negative	I can't stand	spending money on something like this	It's no good	living here any more	I've never approved of
to have disturbed you	I was surprised	to think about	I'm sorry	not to have heard about that	There are too many things
to have it done	It's time	agree with you	I was the first	to start again	She may well
do this again	I was absolutely delighted	being made to do this	Don't make me	to have had the chance to do it	I really hate
have finished	I've got enough money	helping out with this	You'd better	to stay a few weeks	Are you interested in
seeing the results	It's worth	to see her again	The best thing is	asking	I wouldn't like
worrying about it	It's nice	to have to do that	It's not worth	to be appreciated	I'd hate
to have a lovely time	I've made a decision	to be told that	You're sure	to leave my job	I'm not surprised

8B Grammar
Conditionals

A 💬 Work in pairs. Look at questions 1–16 and decide if they are 0, 1, 2, 3 or mixed conditionals.

① When you make plans, do you usually have a back-up plan, in case things don't go your way?

② Should you be lucky enough to have a spare afternoon, do you feel you have to spend your time productively?

③ *Assuming you have a life plan, what will you be doing five years from now?*

④ *Supposing environmental issues are not successfully tackled, how do you think that will affect people in your area in the long term?*

⑤ Assuming humankind succeeds in its mission to create artificial intelligence, do you think there could be any downside to that?

⑥ *So long as it was completely safe, would you like to join an expedition to Mars?*

⑦ What do you do if you are finding it hard to get to sleep?

⑧ *Imagine there was a pill that would let you live to 150, would you take it? Why / Why not?*

⑨ **Supposing I visited your house/flat, what would interest me most?**

⑩ **Supposing you could go back and change one decision you have made in your past, what would it be?**

⑪ *What's the luckiest thing that has ever happened to you? How would your life be different otherwise?*

⑫ *If you want to spoil yourself, what do you do?*

⑬ Had you known what we were going to do in class today, would you still have come?

⑭ What language would you have studied, if you hadn't decided to learn English?

⑮ **What do you think the world would be like if long-distance travel and telecommunications were not possible?**

⑯ If you had to choose only one life goal to achieve in your lifetime, what would it be? Why?

B 💬 Choose six questions to ask your partner. Then answer your partner's questions. Explain each of your answers.

Grammar
Reflexive and reciprocal pronouns

A Complete the questionnaire with the correct pronouns.

ARE YOU A RISK TAKER?

1 You are walking down the street and see a wallet stuffed with money on the pavement. How would you react?
A It would make _____ suspicious – maybe this is some kind of trick with a hidden camera?
B I would help _____ to some of the money, but not all of it.
C I would say to _____ 'This is my lucky day!', take the wallet and run off.

2 A good friend, Ludmila, is in financial trouble and needs to borrow some money from you.
A I wouldn't do anything. Ludmila should sort this out _____.
B I would help _____ by giving _____ a reasonable amount.
C Friends should help _____. I'd give Ludmila all the money I had.

3 Another friend, Carlos, asks you to do a bungee jump with him.
A Carlos can do it by _____; I'm scared of heights.
B If Carlos _____ was prepared to jump first, then I might give it a go.
C Sure, I'd do anything for _____. He's a good friend.

4 An elderly couple at the airport give you a package and ask you to deliver it to their friend at your destination airport.
A I'd say to the couple: 'Take it _____!'
B I'd ask if I could look inside the package _____ before I agreed to anything.
C I'd be glad to help _____.

5 You're at home watching a horror film with some friends. You hear a chilling scream outside the window.
A We'd convince _____ that something terrible had happened and phone the police.
B We'd look at _____ and wait for someone to volunteer to check what was going on outside.
C I'd tell my friends to carry on watching the film and I'd go outside _____.

6 You're walking back home late at night. A man in a car stops and offers you a lift.
A I'd never find _____ in that kind of situation because I never walk alone in the dark.
B I'd say, 'Thanks, but I can get home by _____.'
C I'd thank _____ and get in the car.

7 You get an email saying that you will win $200,000 if you reply with your full contact details.
A I would delete _____ and change my email password.
B Even if the email _____ sounded genuine, I'd email back and ask for further information.
C I would immediately email my details across and feel very pleased with _____ afterwards.

B 💬 Work in pairs. Ask and answer the questions. Record your partner's answers and then read the analysis.

Analysis

Mostly As: You pride yourself on your common-sense approach to life and the only risk in it is not having any fun. Stop playing it safe and live life on the edge now and again. Find a person with 'Mostly Bs' – you have a lot to learn!

Mostly Bs: You've found the perfect balance between being responsible and enjoying your life. Those with 'Mostly As' and 'Mostly Cs' can learn from you!

Mostly Cs: It's surprising that you've survived long enough to answer these questions! You live for the moment and don't spend long enough thinking through the implications of your actions. Stop taking so many risks and find a person with 'Mostly Bs' – you have a lot to learn!

9B Grammar
Ellipsis and substitution

Student A

A Work on your own. Rewrite the first part of a story using ellipsis and substitution to make it shorter and more natural.

The disappearance (Part A)

I finished work as usual, and I put my coat on and I left the office. I decided to walk home for a change because it was a sunny day. I turned the corner and I was going to go up my drive but I didn't go up my drive because I couldn't go up my drive. Why couldn't I go up my drive? My house wasn't there! It had just disappeared! I couldn't believe my house wasn't there! There was a gap where my house had stood, a completely empty space where my house had stood. My neighbour's house was there and her car was also there. I decided to take some action straight away, I went to my neighbour, an old lady, and I knocked on her front door. The old lady came to the door and she opened the door and she asked, 'Who are you?' I said, 'I am your neighbour' and I said, 'I've lived here for ten years.' My neighbour looked at me but she didn't seem to recognise me and she said to me, 'I don't know you and I don't want to know you. Now go away.' She slammed the door and she left me on the doorstep.

B 💬 Work in pairs. Read your version of the first part of the story to Student B.

C Listen to Student B reading you the second part of the story.

D 💬 Think of an ending to the story and compare your idea with the rest of the class.

- ✂

Student B

A Work on your own. Rewrite the second part of a story using ellipsis and substitution to make it shorter and more natural.

The disappearance (Part B)

It was like a dream, it was like a bad dream, and I wanted to wake up but I couldn't wake up. The bad dream was reality. I thought about phoning the police but I didn't phone the police because they would probably think I was crazy. (You might think I am crazy too.) Just as I was beginning to feel desperate, I noticed something on the floor. The thing on the floor was an envelope and inside the envelope was a message: 'Do you want to get your house back? If you want to get your house back, follow these instructions and you will get your house back. You need to remember someone you met yesterday, you need to find the person you met yesterday and help the person you met yesterday more than you helped them before. That person you met yesterday has the key to your house in more ways than you think.'

B Work in pairs. Listen to Student A reading you the first part of the story.

C 💬 Read your version of the second part of the story to Student A.

D 💬 Think of an ending to the story and compare your idea with the rest of the class.

10A Grammar
Regret and criticism structures

A Read these posts on an online problem page and choose the correct verb forms.

Lucia, Florence

I've got a teenage son and all he does, day in, day out, is play computer games. He gets completely absorbed in them and won't do anything else from dusk to dawn. If he was doing something useful with the computer, I [1]*will / would* understand, but all these games are just a waste of his time. I wish I [2]*didn't buy / hadn't bought* him that computer!

_____

_____

Brad, London

I got a great job offer to work in London. I talked it over with my wife and I decided that I should take it, so we moved to the capital. Things were all right at first but then my wife started complaining, and now she says she hates London and wants to move back to where we used to live. I said that I [3]*wouldn't have taken / hadn't taken* the job if I'd known how unhappy she would be. She said she'd kept quiet because she was worried she'd spoil things for me and my career. She [4]*should / would* have told me if she was unsure, but she didn't and now I don't know what to do.

_____

_____

Jin Ho, Seoul

A year ago we won a large cash prize in a lottery. It was the worst thing that has ever happened to us. We ought to [5]*take / have taken* proper financial advice but we wasted a lot of money on a mansion, lost our real friends and met people who were only really interested in our money. I [6]*could / would* much rather be back in my old house than living next to these wealthy neighbours who resent us and where we come from. [7]*If only / Only if* we hadn't won the money!

_____

_____

Callum, Lanzarote

My wife and I retired recently and moved abroad. Personally, I [8]*would have liked / had liked* to have stayed in Scotland but my wife decided it was time we [9]*left / leave* that climate for somewhere warm and sunny instead. The problem is that we do feel quite isolated here especially in the off-season when all the British tourists have gone home. Language is a problem, so it's pretty hard to socialise. I wish I [10]*spoke / had spoken* decent Spanish. Perhaps if we [11]*tried / will try* harder, we would somehow feel more at home.

_____

_____

Stefanie, Frankfurt

My best friend, Anna, has got a new boyfriend, Thomas, who is really bad news for her. Thomas is good-looking enough but he lies to Anna all the time about where he's been and who he's been with. I [12]*should have warned / had to warn* Anna from the start because I know his ex-girlfriend, who basically wishes Thomas [13]*lives / lived* on the other side of the world. I tried to talk to Anna about this the other day but I [14]*couldn't / shouldn't* have bothered because she got all defensive about him.

_____

_____

B 💬 Work in groups. Criticise each person constructively for what they did / didn't do and give them advice.

Interview 1 – Deputy Minister of Culture

A journalist will interview you.

You have prepared some answers to possible questions.

- This is a difficult post and very few people want the responsibility.
- You remember the Minister from school and you did work together somewhere once.
- You decided to leave business and enter politics because of your social conscience.
- The accounts for this year have still not been finalised.
- You have rented a yacht but have no time to use it because of the pressures of work.
- There is a new flexi-time system for staff where they can start late if they finish late.
- Those staff uncomfortable with flexi-time have been transferred to another Ministry.
- The Ministry is trying to promote censorship laws which protect the public from unfair reporting.

Interview 1 – Journalist

You will interview the Deputy Minister of Culture. Ask the Deputy Minister about the stories of corruption and abuse of power, being careful to use passive reporting verbs to keep your sources secret and not make direct accusations.

- The Deputy Minister was the only candidate allowed to apply for the post.
- The Deputy Minister and Minister are old school friends and former business partners.
- The Deputy Minister left business because she/he was fired for misuse of company finances.
- 800,000 euros are unaccounted for in the latest accounts of the Ministry.
- The Deputy Minister bought a new yacht costing an estimated 800,000 euros.
- Staff at the Ministry have been made to work overtime for no extra pay.
- Several staff who complained about this were fired.
- The Ministry recently closed down a website which was critical of its work.

Interview 2 – Minister of Culture

A journalist will interview you.

You have prepared some answers to possible questions.

- The ancient Ministry of Culture building has been renovated (at last!).
- Funding for many arts projects has been frozen in the current economic crisis.
- All government workers have had a salary increase.
- There are problems with a new software system for calculating wages.
- My partner has been very ill recently.
- My health is not great so I've taken up swimming.
- There is a new initiative to fund business projects which promote culture.
- I've just been on a business trip to Barbados.

Interview 2 – Journalist

You will interview the Minister of Culture. Ask the Minister about the stories of corruption and abuse of power, being careful to use passive reporting verbs to keep your sources secret and not make direct accusations.

- An extension to the Ministry of Culture building cost the taxpayer two million euros.
- At the same time funding for the arts has been cut.
- The Minister's salary has increased 300% since coming to office.
- Cleaners in the Ministry have not been paid for three months.
- The Minister's partner works as his secretary on a large salary but is never seen at work.
- The Minister received a personal loan to build a swimming pool in their mansion.
- The Minister's son also received a loan to start a tourism company.
- The Minister has just come back from a six-week holiday in Barbados, at the tax payer's expense.

1A Vocabulary
Language learning

A Circle a number from 1 (very strongly disagree) to 5 (very strongly agree) for each of these statements.

How easy is it to learn English?

1 I find it easy to pick up new English expressions.   1 2 3 4 5

2 I can easily grasp new English grammar.   1 2 3 4 5

3 I expect to attain a good level of English.   1 2 3 4 5

4 I've got accustomed to speaking English in class.   1 2 3 4 5

5 I can hold a conversation in English without difficulty.   1 2 3 4 5

6 I think I have a good ear for language.   1 2 3 4 5

7 I am good at putting what I learn into practice.   1 2 3 4 5

8 I have the motivation to keep at my studies.   1 2 3 4 5

9 I don't usually struggle with English vocabulary.   1 2 3 4 5

10 A lot of interaction in English will stop me getting rusty.   1 2 3 4 5

B Compare your answers in groups. Where you have a low number, try to find someone who has put a high number and ask for advice. Where you have a high number, give advice to classmates who don't have as much confidence as you.

Student A

You have a graph giving information about the percentage of students at The Union Jack English School who visited the cinema at least once a month over a twelve-month period. Describe the graph to your partner. You can give the January and December percentages, but none of the other percentages.

Your partner has information about the percentage of students who visited the school website at least once a week over the same twelve-month period. Draw the graph as Student B describes it to you.

% students who visited the cinema at least once a month

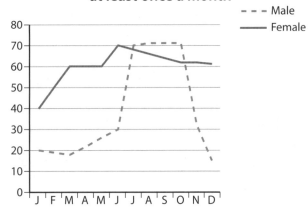

% students who visited the school website at least once a week

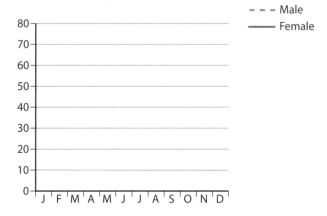

Student B

Your partner has information about the percentage of students at The Union Jack English School who visited the cinema at least once a month over a twelve-month period. Draw the graph as Student A describes it to you.

You have a graph giving information about the percentage of students who visited the school website at least once a week over the same twelve-month period. Describe the graph to your partner. You can give the January and December percentages, but none of the other percentages.

% students who visited the cinema at least once a month

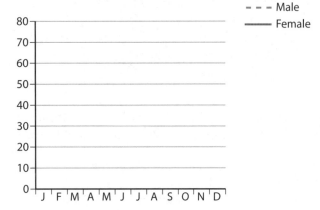

% students who visited the school website at least once a week

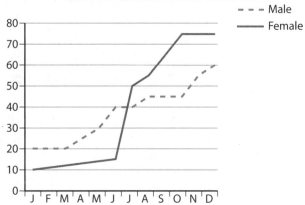

A 🗩 Work in pairs. Complete the sentences with the correct form of the multi-word verbs in the box.

> cut off   hold back   go on   fit in   bring out   slip out
>
> bombard with   run down   relate to   come across

1 ☐ A time when you found it difficult to _____ with a new group of people.

2 ☐ A time when someone _____ you _____ personal questions.

3 ☐ A time when you _____ the best in someone.

4 ☐ A time when it was important for you to _____ well.

5 ☐ A time when you had to _____ yourself _____ from giving your true opinion.

6 ☐ A time when you wanted to _____ yourself _____ from the world.

7 ☐ A time when you let a secret _____ .

8 ☐ A time when you found it easy to _____ new people.

9 ☐ A time when someone _____ a friend _____ and he/she found out.

10 ☐ A time when a close friend _____ about something for several weeks.

B 🗩 Work with your partner. Student A: choose one of the situations in Activity A to describe to your partner, but don't use the multi-word verb. Student B: guess the multi-word verb. If B guesses correctly, put a tick next to the sentence. Then swap roles. Continue the activity and describe all the situations.

soar	roll	crawl
creep	hurtle	plunge
march	limp	rush
zoom	whirl	leap
stagger	stroll	whizz
whoosh	drift	slide

Vocabulary
Wealth and poverty

A 💬 Work in pairs. Complete the article with words and phrases from the box. Sometimes more than one answer is possible.

---

destitute   hardship   make ends meet   prosperity   live within our means

well-off   impoverished   disposable income   affluent   deprived

---

People in this country might feel they are struggling in the current economic climate, but recently published research has shown just how much life has improved in the last fifty years.

As a nation, we are considerably better off than we used to be. In fact, the majority of the population now have more than twice as much [1]_____ as their parents' generation. 50 years ago, a much greater proportion of people faced genuine [2]_____, living in [3]_____ conditions, quite simply unable to [4]_____. Nowadays, far fewer people can be described as [5]_____ and many more of us are able to [6]_____. So despite the feeling of financial decline in the last ten years, most of us are actually quite [7]_____ and over the course of the last half-century the country has been enjoying relative [8]_____.

Is it all positive, though? The truth is that there are still huge differences between rich and poor in our country today, and people in the more [9]_____ neighbourhoods have much better living conditions than those in the more [10]_____ areas in our towns and cities.

B 💬 Discuss the questions in new pairs.

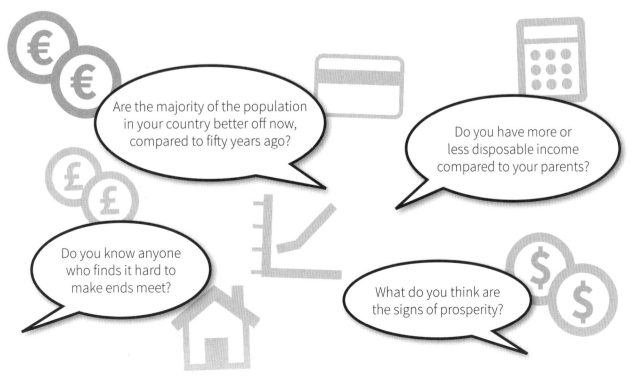

Are the majority of the population in your country better off now, compared to fifty years ago?

Do you have more or less disposable income compared to your parents?

Do you know anyone who finds it hard to make ends meet?

What do you think are the signs of prosperity?

3B Vocabulary
Landscape features

You've just started work as a marketing manager in a failing holiday company. Your first task is to meet with one of your marketing colleagues and improve the information about the holidays on the company website. Look at the pictures and descriptions of holiday destinations on the current website and make them more appealing to prospective customers. Use language from p. 34 and p. 160 of the Student's Book.

Go camping in the middle of a desert that's really far away from people and cities. There's a lot of sand and the ground is full of stones, so it might not be very comfortable.

Stay in a jungle hotel in Costa Rica. The rainforest is humid and hard to get through with some muddy waterholes, but it's still quite nice, even though there are hardly any people.

Visit North England's coastline. It has a lot of grassy areas, some small muddy lakes and hills, but mainly a lot of big rocks facing the sea and sheep.

Relax on Thailand's beaches. The hotel is nice but it is small and simple. There is white sand and lots of palm trees, and the water is beautiful.

4A Vocabulary
Instinct and reason

Complete the sentences with the names of your classmates. Then check if your hunches are correct.

I have a hunch that ...

_____ finds they behave more rationally than other people in an emergency.

_____ isn't money-conscious and often buys things on impulse.

_____ tries to make logical choices in life.

_____ often takes spontaneous decisions.

_____ is very sensitive to other people's feelings.

_____ usually goes with his/her gut instincts.

_____ is never self-conscious in social situations.

_____ would think twice about making new friends online.

_____ thinks over everything that happened during the day when they get home at night.

_____ always weighs up the pros and cons of big decisions by making a list.

_____ is/isn't a very conscientious student.

_____ knows subconsciously when people aren't telling the truth.

_____ is self-confident when meeting new people.

_____ thinks their teacher is a very reasonable person.

_____ thinks being sensible is dull.

4B Vocabulary
Memory

1 What kind of events do you only vaguely	**a** memory of?
2 When you think about holidays,	**b** having a photographic memory?
3 When you cast your mind	**c** a lasting memory of your first teacher?
4 What is your most	**d** people's names?
5 Are any memories	**e** remember from your childhood?
6 What are the pros and cons of	**f** forget painful memories?
7 Do you treasure the	**g** triggered by certain types of weather?
8 What kind of thing	**h** what comes to mind first?
9 Is it possible to make yourself	**i** back, what is your earliest memory?
10 What kind of events do you have a vivid	**j** memory of your first day at school?
11 Do you have a vague memory or	**k** often crosses your mind?
12 Do you often need to refresh your memory of	**l** distant memory?

5A Vocabulary
Crime and justice

Student A

A 💬 Work in AA pairs. Read the story of Sean Brannigan's criminal life. Try to complete the gaps. Student B has the same story, but with different gaps. Decide on questions to ask Student B to check your ideas.

Sean Brannigan had been in trouble with the law all his life. As a teenager, he was always getting into fights, and once the fight was so bad he was convicted of [1]_____ assault. As it was his first offence, he was given community service, but he did not learn his lesson, and even after he was brought [2]_____ with his victim he refused to apologise.

In his early twenties, he was fined £10,000 for credit card [3]_____. On another occasion, he was held in custody on [4]_____ of possession of a controlled substance, but there was not enough [5]_____ to take him to trial.

In his forties, Sean ran a business, and everything was going well until an employee made an allegation of tax [6]_____ against him. He offered the investigating tax inspector £20,000 to forget about it, but he was arrested for bribery and corruption.

Sean's lawyer wanted him to [7]_____ guilty, hoping that he would serve a reduced sentence, but Sean refused. The tax inspector gave [8]_____ in court and Sean was found guilty. Of course, he was not given [9]_____ imprisonment because he hadn't murdered anyone, but he was told he would have to serve the full sentence of ten years in prison. He was also banned from ever [10]_____ a business again.

B 💬 Work in AB pairs. Take turns to ask your partner questions to check your ideas and complete the gaps.

C 💬 Discuss the text in your AB pairs. What should be done with people like Sean? Can they be helped or should they just be punished?

✂

Student B

A 💬 Work in BB pairs. Read the story of Sean Brannigan's criminal life. Try to complete the gaps. Student A has the same story, but with different gaps. Decide on questions to ask Student A to check your ideas.

Sean Brannigan had been in trouble with the law all his life. As a teenager, he was always getting into fights, and once the fight was so bad he was [a]_____ of violent assault. As it was his first offence, he was given [b]_____, but he did not learn his lesson, and even after he was brought face-to-face with his victim he refused to apologise.

In his early twenties, he was [c]_____ £10,000 for credit card fraud. On another occasion, he was held in [d]_____ on suspicion of possession of a [e]_____ substance, but there was not enough evidence to take him to trial.

In his forties, Sean ran a business, and everything was going well until an employee made an [f]_____ of tax evasion against him. He offered the investigating tax inspector £20,000 to forget about it, but he was arrested for bribery and [g]_____.

Sean's lawyer wanted him to plead guilty, hoping that he would [h]_____ a reduced sentence, but Sean refused. The tax inspector gave testimony in court and Sean was [i]_____ guilty. Of course, he was not given life imprisonment because he hadn't murdered anyone, but he was told he would have to serve the [j]_____ sentence of ten years in prison. He was also banned from ever running a business again.

B 💬 Work in AB pairs. Take turns to ask your partner questions to check your ideas and complete the gaps.

C 💬 Discuss the text in your AB pairs. What should be done with people like Sean? Can they be helped or should they just be punished?

5B Vocabulary
Employment

Student A: Find someone who ...

would like to work in the financial sector. _____ Why? _____

thinks the agricultural sector is important in his/her country. _____ Why? _____

would hate to work in the construction sector. _____ Why? _____

thinks that workers in the public sector are overpaid. _____ Why? _____

Student B: Find someone who ...

would like to work in the transport sector. _____ Why? _____

thinks the manufacturing sector is important in his/her country. _____ Why? _____

would hate to work in the energy sector. _____ Why? _____

thinks that people in the retail sector are underpaid. _____ Why? _____

Student C: Find someone who ...

would like to work in the industrial sector. _____ Why? _____

thinks the financial sector is important in his/her country. _____ Why? _____

would hate to work in the manufacturing sector. _____ Why? _____

thinks that people in the transport sector are underpaid. _____ Why? _____

Student D: Find someone who ...

would like to work in the energy sector. _____ Why? _____

thinks the construction sector is important in his/her country. _____ Why? _____

would hate to work in the industrial sector. _____ Why? _____

thinks that people in the agricultural sector are underpaid. _____ Why? _____

Vocabulary
Adjectives: Describing arts and culture

Pair A

A 💬 Work with your partner. Write the name/title of these eight things. Then discuss your ideas with another Pair A.

1 a piece of music you think is very powerful _____
2 a book you think is humorous _____
3 a film you think is flawless _____
4 a building you think is iconic _____
5 a song you think is meaningful _____
6 a sportsperson you think is sensational _____
7 a TV show you think is nonsensical _____
8 a film you think is gritty _____

B 💬 Discuss your ideas with a Pair B.

Pair B

A 💬 Work with your partner. Write the name/title of these eight things. Then discuss your ideas with another Pair B.

1 a building you think is exotic _____
2 a piece of music you think is repetitive _____
3 a song you think is evocative _____
4 a film you think is humorous _____
5 a book you think is very bleak _____
6 an animal you think is playful _____
7 a celebrity whose clothing you think is elaborate _____
8 a writer whose books you think are sensational _____

B 💬 Discuss your ideas with a Pair A.

6B Vocabulary
Emotions

Student A

A Complete the sentences to make them true for you.

1 I would be absolutely *devastated* if _____.
2 I get very *frustrated* when _____.
3 I remember being totally *speechless* when_____.
4 A friend of mine was extremely *jealous* when _____.
5 As a child, I would feel a bit *insecure* when _____.
6 I am a bit *disillusioned* with _____.
7 I would be so *ashamed* if _____.
8 When I was very young, I was absolutely *petrified* of _____.
9 I sometimes get a bit *over-excited* when _____.
10 I always feel *satisfied* when _____.

B 🗨 Work in AB pairs. Read your sentences to Student B, leaving out the words in *italics*. Can your partner work out the adjective you missed out in each sentence?

- ✂

Student B

A Complete the sentences to make them true for you.

1 My friend is absolutely *petrified* of _____.
2 I'm terribly *restless* just before _____.
3 I'm very *protective* of _____.
4 Sometimes I get a bit *insecure* when _____.
5 As a young child, I was absolutely *devastated* when _____.
6 I would be totally *speechless* if _____.
7 I was very *frustrated* recently because _____.
8 I would be so *gleeful* if _____.
9 I must admit I was extremely *jealous* when _____.
10 I remember being so *ashamed* when _____.

B 🗨 Work in AB pairs. Read your sentences to Student A, leaving out the words in *italics*. Can your partner work out the adjective you missed out in each sentence?

7A Vocabulary
Compound adjectives

Student A	A	B	C	D
1	absent-minded		light-headed	
2		glassy-eyed		heart-breaking
3	open-minded		half-hearted	
4		heart-warming		hard-hearted
5	mouth-watering		left-handed	

✂

Student B	A	B	C	D
1		short-sighted		hair-raising
2	mind-boggling		tongue-tied	
3		narrow-minded		warm-hearted
4	back-breaking		clear-headed	
5		jaw-dropping		light-hearted

7B Vocabulary
Nouns with suffixes: Society and relationships

A 💬 Work in pairs. You're going to create a new community where you can decide exactly how people are going to live. Agree on three desirable qualities for your community (or the people in it) and three undesirable qualities. Discuss how you would ensure these principles were maintained in practical terms.

prejudice

closeness

rudeness

materialism

fair distribution of wealth **intimacy**

optimism

tolerance socialism

collaboration

liberalism

exclusion

fairness

isolation **innovation**

loneliness

security

capitalism

selfishness

Desirable qualities: _____ Undesirable qualities: _____

_____ _____

_____ _____

B 💬 Work with another pair. Explain your lists to each other and try to agree two new lists.

C 💬 Work in new pairs. Tell your partner about the community you're living in at the moment. Which qualities or behaviours would you change if you could? Why?

Group card

1 I need to stay awake till midnight – what do I do?

2 Our biology lesson was so boring today!

3 This is the third time you've been late for work this week! What's going on?

4 Wow, you look really tired!

5 It is so hard to get my son out of bed in the morning.

6 Do you find it easy to fall asleep at night?

7 Did you watch the film on Channel 7 last night?

8 I don't think I'll sleep tonight – I'm worried about the exam tomorrow.

9 Have you ever fallen asleep during a meeting?

10 Do you have problems sleeping?

11 The neighbours kept me up all night!

12 Luckily, I heard the burglars before they broke in!

Student A

1 Why don't you have a nap?

2 I know, I nearly fell off to sleep.

3 I'm sorry, I slept over again.

4 I am. I didn't sleep a log last night.

5 Not mine – he's light awake at 6:30.

6 Not really, I toss and turn a lot before I manage to sleep.

7 No, I was deep asleep at that time.

8 Me neither. I usually sleep softly before exams.

9 I nearly fell off to sleep at the meeting yesterday.

10 Yes, I suffer from insomnia.

11 I'm sorry to hear that. I slept like a tree trunk.

12 You must be a weak sleeper.

Student B

1 You could have a log?

2 Absolutely – I nearly tripped off to sleep.

3 I'm sorry, I underslept again.

4 Yes, I didn't sleep a wink last night.

5 Well, my son is wide awake at 6 am!

6 No, I turn and roll quite a bit.

7 No, I was fast asleep.

8 I can't either. I always sleep weakly before exams.

9 Last year, I think I almost got off to sleep at one of our meetings.

10 Yes, I have unsomnia.

11 Poor you! I slept like a log.

12 You must be a light sleeper.

Student C

1 Maybe you should have a wink?

2 I agree. I nearly dropped off to sleep.

3 I'm sorry, I overslept again.

4 I know. I didn't sleep a blink last night.

5 Really? Mine is fast awake at 7 in the morning.

6 No, I roll and move quite a bit.

7 No, I was hard asleep then.

8 Me neither. I always have a restless night before an exam.

9 Yes, I actually drifted off during a finance meeting once.

10 Yes, I suffer from imsomnia.

11 Oh dear, I slept like a board.

12 You must be a low sleeper.

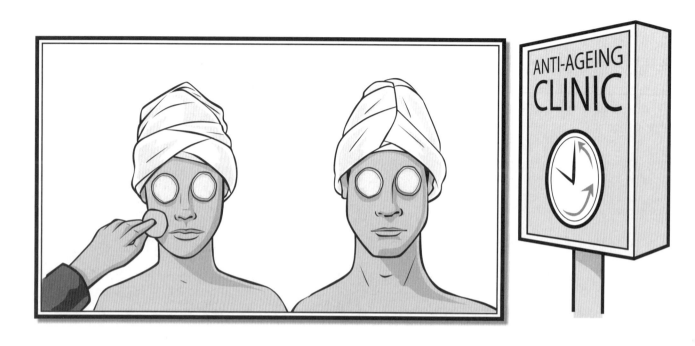

A You are the directors of a new anti-ageing clinic and spa that is going to open soon. You need to produce a publicity leaflet to attract clients. Decide on a name for your clinic and what you will offer to your clients. Choose three signs of ageing from the list and add three of your own, then describe the services or products you will offer. Then decide on five promises you will make to your clients.

Name of clinic _____

Signs of ageing	**Services and products**
dry skin	facials from our expert beauticians to combat skin problems
yellowing teeth and tooth loss	
deteriorating eyesight	
heart trouble	
arthritis	
_____	
_____	
_____	

What do you promise?

_____
_____
_____
_____

B Create your leaflet on a separate sheet of paper or online. Include your prices.

Vocabulary
Verbs beginning *re-*

A 💬 Work in pairs. Complete the questions with the correct form of verbs beginning with *re-*.

1 If a world-famous building was to be rec_ _ _ _ _ _ in your city, which building would you like it to be?

2 If you could rev_ _ _ a shop in your town, which would it be and why?

3 Which part of your town or city would you like to see completely red_ _ _ _ _ _ _ _?

4 Are there any old customs you would like to res_ _ _ _?

5 Is there anything your country has lost which you would like it to reg_ _ _?

6 Are there any old laws you would like to see rei_ _ _ _ _ _ _ in your country?

7 If your street were to be rej_ _ _ _ _ _ _ _ with lots of trendy cafés and boutiques, would you be happy about it?

8 Which city in your country most needs reg_ _ _ _ _ _ _ _ _, in your opinion?

9 How would you ren_ _ _ _ _ your school building / office?

B 💬 Work in pairs. Discuss the questions in A.

9B Vocabulary
Describing buildings

Student A

Student B

💬 Work in groups of four. Each, take one topic card and one communication verb card. You're going to talk about the topic on your card, and you're going to talk in the style of the communication verb. You have one minute to prepare what you're going to say.

Take turns to talk. Continue until one of the other students guesses the communication verb on your card correctly.

Public transport

go into too much detail

Let me tell you about the metro system in my city so that you know how to use it on your visit. It has 195 stations and there are 226.5 km of tracks …

You're going into too much detail!

Topic cards

PUBLIC TRANSPORT	EXERCISE & KEEPING FIT	THE IMPORTANCE OF SLEEP	MEDICAL CARE	HOUSING	RAISING CHILDREN
COMMUNITY ENGAGEMENT	HOBBIES & LEISURE INTERESTS	CLOTHES & FASHION	DIGITAL OR PRINT READING	WORKING CONDITIONS	RESTAURANTS & EATING OUT

Communication verb cards

illustrate a new topic	make throwaway remarks	go into the finer points	attack policies
present a new product	make comments under your breath	go into too much detail	demonstrate a new idea with practical examples
back up arguments	address a conference	move on to a new topic	present results
voice concerns	pay tribute to someone	summarise key ideas	sell an idea

10B Vocabulary
Superstitions, customs and beliefs

A Read the statements. Are they true or false for you? Write *T* or *F* in the table.

B Add two more superstitions, customs or beliefs from your own country to the table. Are they true or false for you? Write *T* or *F*.

C 💬 Work in pairs. Talk about why the statements are true or false for you. Write *T* or *F* in the table for your partner.

	Me	My partner
I always make a wish when I blow out a candle.		
I think the idea that people can be put under a magic spell is a bit dubious.		
I find the idea of good-luck charms quite persuasive.		
I keep my fingers crossed when I need good luck.		
People who touch wood when they think they've tempted fate are a bit gullible.		
I am convinced that breaking mirrors is bad luck.		
I always try things three times – you never know, third time lucky!		
I think the idea that charms can ward off evil spirits is not so far-fetched.		
I believe superstitions about good fortune are based on common sense.		
I'd never live on the thirteenth floor, just to be on the safe side.		

- something you would fight tooth and nail for

- someone who is head and shoulders above other people like them

- a time when you had to bite your tongue

- a time when you lost your head

- a time when you had to stick your neck out

- someone who would be a safe pair of hands to leave the class with

- someone who has a real nose for bargains.

Unit 2 Wordpower
Idioms: Movement

A Match the sentence halves.

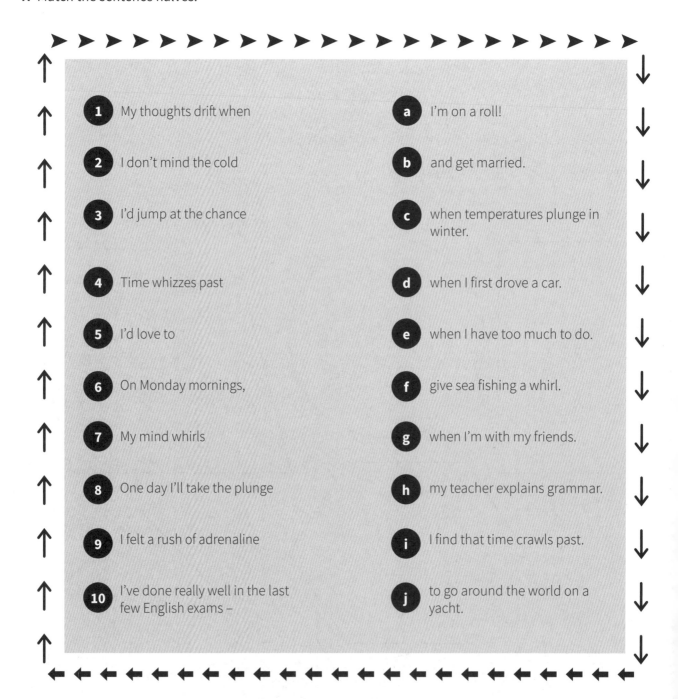

1. My thoughts drift when
2. I don't mind the cold
3. I'd jump at the chance
4. Time whizzes past
5. I'd love to
6. On Monday mornings,
7. My mind whirls
8. One day I'll take the plunge
9. I felt a rush of adrenaline
10. I've done really well in the last few English exams –

a. I'm on a roll!
b. and get married.
c. when temperatures plunge in winter.
d. when I first drove a car.
e. when I have too much to do.
f. give sea fishing a whirl.
g. when I'm with my friends.
h. my teacher explains grammar.
i. I find that time crawls past.
j. to go around the world on a yacht.

B Put a tick next to any sentences that are true for you. Change the other sentences to make them true for you.

C Compare your sentences with the class. How many students have similar answers and sentences?

Unit 3 Wordpower
Idioms: Landscapes

A Work in pairs. Make idioms for the definitions. Use the words in the box and add any extra words you may need.

drop	bogged	slope	get	land	lie	out	not	ocean
get	slippery	struggle	swamped	down	uphill	woods		

1 assess the situation

2 get stuck on a particular point and not make progress

3 a series of events which create worse problems

4 be overwhelmed by too much work

5 a difficult process

6 still having problems

7 not nearly enough

B Work with your partner. Read about Bert and his problems, and complete the text using the correct form of the idioms in Activity A.

Bert, the new owner of The Sunshine Language School, needs your advice. The school has hardly any students and is in debt. If they don't get some money soon, they will be on a
¹_____ to bankruptcy. The school saved a little money by cutting teachers' salaries, but this was just a ²_____ and they are ³_____ yet.

One problem is that Bert has to arrange everything on his own – the timetable, the testing, student enquiries, and so on – so he is often absolutely ⁴_____ with paperwork.

As well as this, he is also ⁵_____ lots of new government rules and regulations.

He knows that it will be an ⁶_____, but once he has ⁷_____, things should start to improve.

C Discuss and agree on three pieces of advice for Bert.

1 _____

2 _____

3 _____

Unit 4 Wordpower
mind

Student A: Find someone who ...

	Name
is never afraid to speak their mind.	_____
thinks they can read their best friend's mind.	_____
always bears the teacher's advice in mind.	_____
feels they can do anything if they put their mind to it.	_____

- ✂

Student B: Find someone who ...

	Name
has had it cross their mind to be a teacher.	_____
has a friend who gives them peace of mind when they are worried.	_____
is always in the right frame of mind for class.	_____
keeps an open mind in political discussions.	_____

- ✂

Student C: Find someone who ...

	Name
has a lot on their mind at the moment.	_____
finds it difficult to put their mind to their homework.	_____
doesn't always speak their mind.	_____
has had it cross their mind to move abroad.	_____

- ✂

Student D: Find someone who ...

	Name
sometimes finds it difficult to get peace of mind.	_____
wasn't in the right frame of mind for class today.	_____
thinks their best friend can sometimes read their mind.	_____
doesn't have a lot on their mind.	_____

When was the last time you gave someone the benefit of the doubt? What happened?	**If a friend's child was up to no good, would you intervene?**	Do you know anyone who often gets away with murder? How do they do it?	*If you caught a flatmate red-handed, eating food you had bought for yourself, what would you do?*
Have you ever got off lightly for doing something wrong? What happened?	*Did your parents have to lay down the law with you when you were young? Why?*	Are there any areas around where you live where you feel you have to look over your shoulder? Why is that?	***Did you have a partner in crime when you were a child? Who?***
When you were a child, what kind of things did you do when you were up to no good?	Have you ever had to lay down the law with someone? Why?	***Are there two people in this class you would describe as partners in crime? Why?***	**What would you do if you thought someone had got off lightly for cheating in a test?**
Did your parents usually give you the benefit of the doubt when you were young?	Have you ever caught anyone red-handed doing something they shouldn't have been doing? What happened?	*Can you think of a time when you got away with murder? What happened?*	***Do you ever find yourself looking over your shoulder even when you've done nothing wrong? When?***

Unit 6 Wordpower
Idioms: Feelings

A time when you couldn't believe your eyes.	A time when you couldn't believe your eyes.	A time when you couldn't believe your eyes.

A time when you were over the moon.	A time when you were over the moon.	A time when you were over the moon.

A time when a friend got on your nerves.	A time when a friend got on your nerves.	A time when a friend got on your nerves.

A time when you had to just grin and bear it.	A time when you had to just grin and bear it.	A time when you had to just grin and bear it.

A time when you were at the end of your tether.	A time when you were at the end of your tether.	A time when you were at the end of your tether.

Something that really gets your back up.	Something that really gets your back up.	Something that really gets your back up.

Match three sentences with each person's characteristic (1–6). Use the three letters next to the sentences to work out each person's name.

O I only meet friends at places that are the most convenient for me.

B I do what's best for myself.

G I pay my own bills and I don't expect help from others.

L I have achieved so many truly amazing things.

N I'm sure I've made the right decisions for my life.

B I always push to the front of the queue in a shop.

V I did really well in the last test and came top in the class.

A Of course I'll pass the exam!

E I grow my own vegetables and make my own bread.

T I'll give up my seat on the bus for an older person.

U I turned down a job because I knew my friend wanted it.

N I expect to get a good job in the future.

A I know what my strengths and weaknesses are.

M I realise I have to work harder at my English studies.

A I taught myself to play tennis and could play professionally.

S I always give to charity appeals.

X I don't always make the best decisions.

M I love fashion and I make my own clothes.

1 **self-sacrificing**   2 **self-confident**   3 **self-centred**   4 **self-sufficient**   5 **self-aware**   6 **self-satisfied**

Unit 8 Wordpower
and

far		
	away	sweet
far		
sick		
	clear	tear
wear		
part		
	parcel	tidy
loud		
neat		
	pieces	tired
short		
safe		
	sound	wide
bits		

Unit 9 Wordpower
build

A Work in pairs. Match the 'then' and 'now' sentences.

Then

Now

Then	Now
1 John couldn't afford to buy a car.	**a** He has a shop in every town.
2 Sally got a manager when she started as a singer.	**b** She now thinks she might well get the job she wants.
3 The Prime Minister couldn't cope with the job.	**c** We've used that to become a multinational, still with great customer service.
4 We were a small company with great customer service.	**d** It is now far more advanced.
5 The car we made was a basic model.	**e** He proposed to her yesterday.
6 We planned to open a new kind of restaurant.	**f** He's buying one today.
7 Coffee used to keep Pat awake at night.	**g** She can drink coffee and still sleep well.
8 Kirsty was cycling down the hill very quickly.	**h** She's a superstar.
9 Matt was too scared to ask Elaine to marry him.	**i** He's having a nervous breakdown.
10 Emma was very nervous before the interview.	**j** We're opening a restaurant that uses only local produce.
11 When the film started it was a bit scary.	**k** Now it is terrifying! I don't know what is going to happen.
12 Jack used to sell sandwiches in the market.	**l** She could go up the other side easily.

B 💬 Decide with your partner what happened between then and now. Use the words in the box and write one sentence for each situation.

build up	build on	build around	build in

1 John built up his savings until he could afford a car.

Unit 10 Wordpower
luck and *chance*

A 💬 Work in pairs. Complete the sentences with your own ideas.

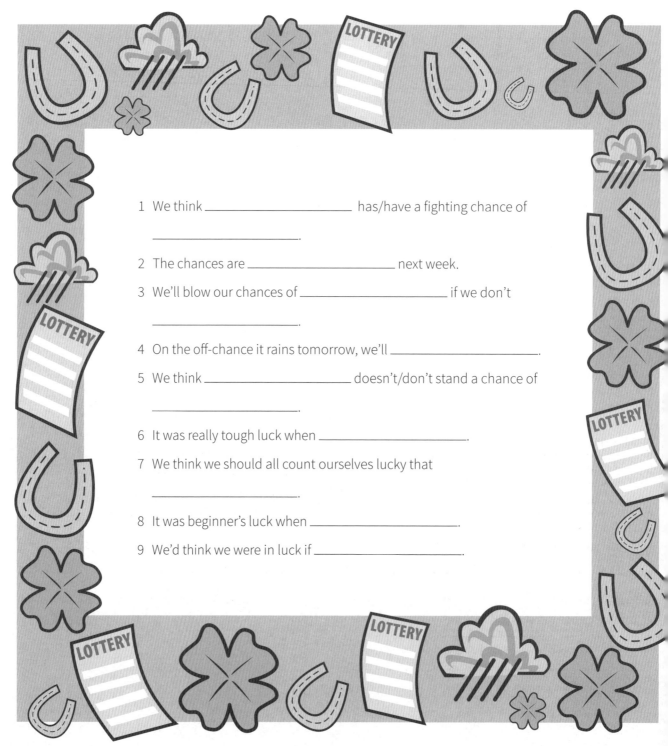

1 We think _____ has/have a fighting chance of
   _____.

2 The chances are _____ next week.

3 We'll blow our chances of _____ if we don't
   _____.

4 On the off-chance it rains tomorrow, we'll _____.

5 We think _____ doesn't/don't stand a chance of
   _____.

6 It was really tough luck when _____.

7 We think we should all count ourselves lucky that
   _____.

8 It was beginner's luck when _____.

9 We'd think we were in luck if _____.

B 💬 Now work with another pair to compare your ideas. How many ideas do you agree with?

1 consonant	a two vowels together, e.g. /əʊ/, /eə/, /aʊ/
2 diphthong	b a sentence or part of a sentence with one main stress, e.g. *Excuse me, where's the hotel?* has two
3 elision	c part of a word or a sentence pronounced louder, longer and at a higher pitch, e.g. *Where's the* **hotel**?
4 homophone	d a sound made without contact between the tongue and the mouth, e.g. /e/, /iː/, /ə/
5 intonation	e words with the same pronunciation but with a different meaning or spelling or both, e.g. /siː/ = *sea, see*
6 stress	f not pronouncing sounds, e.g. /wɒnə/ = *want to*
7 syllable	g a word pronounced with a shorter sound instead of its usual pronunciation, e.g. /fə/ = *for* and /ðət/ = *that*
8 vowel	h a rise or fall in pitch over a word group
9 weak form	i a sound where contact is made between the tongue and mouth, e.g. /b/, /n/, /θ/
10 word group	j a word or part of a word pronounced as one unit, e.g. *television* has four

B Work in pairs. Find the ten pronunciation terms in Activity A in phonetic script. The words can be horizontal or vertical.

i	w	h	ɒ	m	ə	f	əʊ	n	t	h
k	iː	ŋ	s	ə	r	t	aɪ	z	e	ŋ
ɒ	k	v	tʃ	s	ɪ	l	ə	b	ə	l
n	f	aʊ	k	ə	l	s	ə	i	m	aʊ
s	ɔː	ə	ɪ	ɖ	ɪ	f	θ	ɒ	ŋ	ə
ə	m	l	tʃ	r	ʒ	r	ɔː	θ	p	l
n	k	uː	c	ə	ə	b	t	p	w	uː
ə	ɪ	n	t	ə	n	eɪ	ʃ	ə	n	n
n	r	i	l	iː	s	t	r	e	s	i
t	k	w	ɜː	d	g	r	uː	p	n	w

1B Pronunciation
Sentence stress

Student A

A Read the quotations and <u>underline</u> the stressed syllables in the perfect verb phrases in **bold**.

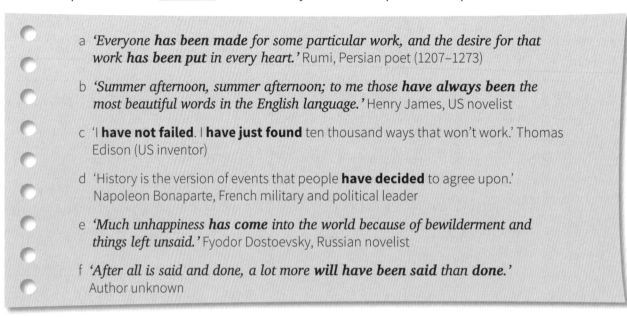

a '*Everyone **has been made** for some particular work, and the desire for that work **has been put** in every heart.*' Rumi, Persian poet (1207–1273)

b '*Summer afternoon, summer afternoon; to me those **have always been** the most beautiful words in the English language.*' Henry James, US novelist

c 'I **have not failed**. I **have just found** ten thousand ways that won't work.' Thomas Edison (US inventor)

d 'History is the version of events that people **have decided** to agree upon.' Napoleon Bonaparte, French military and political leader

e '*Much unhappiness **has come** into the world because of bewilderment and things left unsaid.*' Fyodor Dostoevsky, Russian novelist

f '*After all is said and done, a lot more **will have been said** than **done**.*' Author unknown

B 🗨 Work in AB pairs. Read your quotations to your partner, paying attention to sentence stress. Don't tell your partner who said the quotations. Can they guess which quotation is more than 700 years old?

C 🗨 Discuss each quotation. Do you like it? Why / Why not?

- ✂

Student B

A Read the quotations and <u>underline</u> the stressed syllables in the perfect verb phrases in **bold**.

a '*Tis better to **have loved and lost** than **never to have loved** at all.*' Alfred Lord Tennyson, British poet

b 'With confidence, you **have won** even before you **have started**.' Cicero, Roman politician (106 BC–43 BC)

c '**Having been poor** is no shame, but being ashamed of it, is.' Benjamin Franklin, Founding Father of the US

d '*To understand the heart and mind of a person, look not at what he **has already achieved**, but at what he aspires to.*' Khalil Gibran, Lebanese poet

e 'If you **have accomplished** all that you **have planned for yourself**, you **have not planned enough**.' Edward Hale, US author

f 'One never sees what **has been done**; one can only see what remains to be done.' Marie Curie, French scientist

B 🗨 Work in AB pairs. Read your quotations to your partner, paying attention to sentence stress. Don't tell your partner who said the quotations. Can they guess which quotation is more than 700 years old?

C 🗨 Discuss each quotation. Do you like it? Why / Why not?

1C Pronunciation
Sound and spelling: *ea*, *ee* and *ie*

A Add the words in the box to the correct sound group.

breathtaking   Earth   cheat   referee   steak   ahead   deer   thief   underwear

/iː/ meet	/e/ friend	/eɪ/ great	/eə/ bear	/ɪə/ cheerful	/ɜː/ research
Greek meaning increase niece	meant steadily breakfast	break	pear	hear pierce idea career	learn heard early

B 🗨 Work in pairs. Roll two dice and say the number from 2 to 12. Your partner must say words for the six sounds that match the number in the order the sounds appear, from left to right in the grid.

🎲🎲						
2	/e/	/ɪə/	/ɜː/	/iː/	/ɜː/	/iː/
3	/e/	/ɜː/	/iː/	/ɪə/	/ɜː/	/e/
4	/ɪə/	/eɪ/	/iː/	/e/	/ɜː/	/ɜː/
5	/e/	/ɪə/	/ɜː/	/iː/	/e/	/iː/
6	/ɜː/	/eə/	/iː/	/ɪə/	/ɜː/	/e/
7	/ɜː/	/iː/	/ɪə/	/eɪ/	/ɪə/	/e/
8	/iː/	/ɪə/	/e/	/ɪə/	/ɜː/	/iː/
9	/ɪə/	/ɜː/	/iː/	/e/	/iː/	/e/
10	/iː/	/e/	/ɪə/	/ɜː/	/e/	/eə/
11	/eɪ/	/iː/	/eɪ/	/ɪə/	/ɜː/	/iː/
12	/ɪə/	/iː/	/ɜː/	/ɪə/	/e/	/ɜː/

2A Pronunciation
Consonant–vowel linking

Student A

A Read text A and mark where there is consonant–vowel linking.

Text A

A factory is doing badly and they get a new managing director to improve efficiency. The new director comes in and the first thing she does is to take a walk around the factory and see what everyone's doing. Everything seems all right but there's a man just leaning against a wall and playing with a mobile phone. 'What are you doing?' the director asks. 'Nothing,' the man answers, 'I'm just waiting around to get paid.' The director is furious and says, 'Well, here's 500 euros, get out of my factory and don't come back!' The man leaves immediately and the director turns around to one of the workers and says, 'What does that tell you?' The worker replies…

B 🗨 Work in AB pairs. Read text A to your partner, using consonant–vowel linking. What do you think the worker says?

C Now listen to your partner and complete text B. What do you think the old lady says?

Text B

A genius walks into a cafe and says, '_____. Just ask me a question _____. If you can't answer my question, give me five euros. _____, I'll give you five thousand euros.' _____, '_____.' The genius says, 'What's the capital of the USA?' _____ 'No idea at all, here's your five euros' _____. 'Here's my question: what animal has five arms in the day and four arms at night?' _____, 'That's a difficult one! I don't know…' _____, the genius asks, 'Well, what's the answer?' The old lady replies …

✂ -

Student B

A Read text B and mark where there is consonant–vowel linking.

Text B

A genius walks into a cafe and says, 'I'm going to prove that I'm the cleverest person here. Just ask me a question and I'll ask you one. If you can't answer my question, give me five euros. If I can't answer your question, I'll give you five thousand euros.' An old lady in a corner says, 'I'll try. Ask a question.' The genius says, 'What's the capital of the USA?' The old lady thinks a bit and answers, 'No idea at all, here's your five euros' and gives him the five euros. 'Here's my question: what animal has five arms in the day and four arms at night?' The genius thinks long and hard, then says, 'That's a difficult one! I don't know …' and as he gives the old lady five thousand euros, the genius asks, 'Well, what's the answer?' The old lady replies …

B Work in AB pairs. Listen to your partner and complete text A. What do you think the worker says?

C 🗨 Read text B to your partner, using consonant–vowel linking. What do you think the old lady says?

Text A

_____ and they get a new managing director _____. The new director comes in _____ is to take a walk around the factory _____. Everything seems all right _____ and playing with a mobile phone. _____. 'Nothing,' the man answers, _____ and says, 'Well, here's five hundred euros, _____ and don't come back!' _____ and the director turns around to one of the workers _____. The worker replies …

Group card
1 I <u>think</u> it's going to rain tomorrow.
2 My brother <u>knows</u> French.
3 The match finishes at quarter <u>to</u> seven.
4 My black shoes are <u>still</u> in the box.
5 I <u>borrowed</u> two hundred euros.
6 Is Carlos in <u>hospital</u> again?
7 Why are you criticising the <u>manager</u>?
8 <u>Some</u> of my students got full marks.
9 I <u>was</u> on holiday in Spain.
10 There are <u>29</u> children in the German group.
11 <u>Last</u> summer was too hot for me.
12 <u>Pass</u> me the sugar.

Student A
1 Not today.
2 He doesn't need to learn it.
3 It starts two hours before that.
4 I've no idea where my brown ones are.
5 Not two thousand!
6 He must be really ill.
7 What's the point?
8 That's 100%.
9 It wasn't anything to do with work.
10 They're all under 16.
11 Temperatures were really high every day.
12 Don't throw it!

Student B
1 But I'm not sure.
2 But his English isn't great.
3 Not quarter past seven.
4 I haven't worn them since I bought them.
5 Not three hundred.
6 Or Carla?
7 You should be encouraging her.
8 But only the ones who prepared.
9 Barcelona to be precise.
10 Far more than last year.
11 A lot of people thought it was great.
12 Not the salt.

Student C
1 It will be really wet outside.
2 Not my sister.
3 Not a quarter to eight.
4 I don't have any boots.
5 I'm going to give it back.
6 That's the second time it's happened.
7 Blame the players instead.
8 I've taught them for two years.
9 Ask Simon if you don't believe me.
10 The French class is bigger.
11 This one has been all right.
12 I'm the only one without any.

1 Only on holiday with her friends	a have we seen something like this.
2 Only when I've left	b did she breathe about it again.
3 Not until things had got desperate	c will you realise how much you need me.
4 Never in our lives	d the quality is quite good.
5 Under no circumstances	e we act against our best interests.
6 Barely had he told her what he had done	f should you enter the red zone.
7 Not a single word	g could she finally relax.
8 No sooner had the announcement came	h am I going there.
9 All too often	i when the police arrived.
10 Little did she suspect	j did the bank agree to help.
11 Not only is it cheap,	k than the protests began.
12 No way on earth	l the problems that lay ahead.

Pronunciation
Consonant groups across words

A ◯💬 Work in pairs. Circle the phrases in the maze with consonant groups across two words.

deep space	warning shriek	science fiction	remote area	part time
should get better	a headache again	the heart of	waste money	at Peter's
became a reality	summarise ideas	totally ruin	wealth creation	economic analysis
cheetah in a cage	listen again	cover expenses	aliens look	another journey
famous author	tiny village	one in a million	both kinds	bad personality
explore other	long story	thanks to	Max Redwood	hated the ending
live broadcast	what you'd	hard days	ought to have	disaster fell
wrapped things	weighed two kg	remote part	Westgate Avenue	curious inability

B ◯💬 Work with your partner. Move through the maze from *wrapped things* to *deep space* using all the phrases with clearly pronounced consonant groups across two words. You can only move one square at a time, horizontally, vertically or diagonally.

4A Pronunciation
Sound and spelling: /ʃəs/, /iəs/, /dʒəs/

A Work in groups of three. Add the words in the box to the correct sound group.

contagious   obvious   previous   serious   suspicious   various   delicious   luxurious

/ʃəs/	/iəs/	/dʒəs/
cautious subconscious ambitious precious conscientious	spontaneous hilarious simultaneous curious	gorgeous prestigious courageous outrageous

B

a Are women more _____ than men? /ʃəs/

b _____ granny fights off robbers. /dʒəs/

c _____ cat locked in fridge for 12 hours. /iəs/

d Decision to close archaeological museum is deemed '_____'. /dʒəs/

e England _____ after yesterday's 0–0 draw. /ʃəs/

f Newgrass chocolate is reportedly _____! /ʃəs/

g Prank on celebrity – _____ or just bad taste? /iəs/

h Mr _____ claims looks are not important. /dʒəs/

i _____ jewel found in rubbish bin. /ʃəs/

j _____ university to offer degree in magic. /dʒəs/

k New prisons attacked as '_____'. /iəs/

l _____ snow and heatwave shock scientists. /iəs/

m _____ celebrations break out all over the country. /iəs/

n Social media leads to _____ prejudice. /ʃəs/

4C Pronunciation
Homophones in words and connected speech

Student A

A 🗨 Work in pairs. Read out each pair of sentences to your partner. Your partner will listen and work out which words in **bold** you said first. Then check your partner's answers.

1 a He's got a **great eye** for detail.
  b He's got a **grey tie** on.

2 a She was **caught** stealing.
  b She's in **court** for stealing.

3 a Don't **mime me**, I don't find it funny at all.
  b Don't **mind me**, I won't be long.

4 a How long do I have to **wait** there?
  b Can you **weigh it** over here?

5 a Is that the right **fare**?
  b Is that really **fair**?

6 a Mix the **flour** with some water.
  b Put the **flower** in some water.

7 a **Wait a** minute, please.
  b **Waiter**, please!

8 a They're my **deer**.
  b There, my **dear**.

B Now listen to your partner read pairs of sentences with these words/phrases. Tick (✓) the word/phrase you hear first. Then check your answers with your partner.

9 ☐ seldom ☐ sell them   12 ☐ I can ☐ Hi Ken   15 ☐ father ☐ farther

10 ☐ Police ☐ Please   13 ☐ sent   ☐ cent   16 ☐ Your knot ☐ You're not

11 ☐ guessed ☐ guest   14 ☐ site   ☐ sight

- ✂

Student B

A Work in pairs. Listen to your partner read pairs of sentences with these words/phrases. Tick (✓) the word/ phrase you hear first. Then check your answers with your partner.

1 ☐ grey tie ☐ great eye   4 ☐ wait   ☐ weigh it   7 ☐ Waiter ☐ Wait a

2 ☐ caught   ☐ court   5 ☐ fair   ☐ fare   8 ☐ deer   ☐ dear

3 ☐ mime me ☐ mind me   6 ☐ flower ☐ flour

B 🗨 Read out each pair of sentences to your partner. Your partner will decide which words in **bold** you said first. Then check your partner's answers.

9 a You can **sell them** down the market.
  b You can **seldom** see them.

10 a **Police** – can we help you?
   b **Please**, can you help us?

11 a I **guessed** it too late.
   b Our **guest** is too late.

12 a **Hi Ken**, how are you?
   b **I can**, how about you?

13 a I haven't got a **cent** to pay you.
   b I've been **sent** to pay you.

14 a I know her web**site**.
   b I know her by **sight**.

15 a Get it **farther** away from me.
   b Get her **father** away from me.

16 a **Your knot**, not mine.
   b **You're not** mine.

5A Pronunciation
Sound and spelling: *s* and *ss*

A Work in pairs. Move through the maze from *mission* to *necessary* using words with letters in **bold** pronounced /s/ and /ʃ/ only. You can only move one square at a time, horizontally, vertically or diagonally.

mi**ss**ion	a**ss**ault	explo**s**ion	compari**s**on	phra**s**e	po**s**itive	po**ss**ession	mea**s**ure
u**s**ual	vi**s**ion	permi**ss**ion	deci**s**ion	Ru**ss**ian	conclu**s**ion	revi**s**ion	exi**s**t
a**ss**ault	de**ss**ert	pri**s**on	cou**s**in	rea**s**on	e**ss**ay	trea**s**ure	ea**s**y
impul**s**e	conver**s**ation	choo**s**e	exerci**s**e	a**ss**a**ss**in	televi**s**ion	accu**s**ed	di**s**mi**ss**
wilderne**ss**	rea**s**on	increa**s**e	di**ss**olve	impre**ss**ion	ti**ss**ue	mu**s**cle	nece**ss**ary

B Work with your partner. Move through the maze from *evasion* to *dessert* using words with letters in **bold** pronounced /z/ and /ʒ/ only. You can only move one square at a time, horizontally, vertically or diagonally.

exi**s**t	impul**s**e	wilderne**ss**	increa**s**e	spou**s**e	in**s**tant	man**s**ion	de**ss**ert
pa**ss**ion	mi**ss**ion	cou**s**in	rea**s**on	di**ss**olve	profe**ss**ional	a**ss**istant	po**s**itive
a**ss**istant	po**ss**essive	discu**ss**ion	a**ss**ault	impre**ss**ion	u**s**ually	di**s**mi**ss**	ri**s**e
vi**s**ion	Ru**ss**ian	nece**ss**ary	impul**s**e	compari**s**on	conver**s**ation	mea**s**ure	occa**s**ion
eva**s**ion	mu**s**cle	di**s**mi**ss**	permi**ss**ion	ti**ss**ue	witne**ss**	e**ss**ay	pa**ss**ion

I've seen you drive a sports car.	I know it's a sports car. I've driven a sports car.
I don't trust your driving.	Well, you know my car is off the road?
OK, but could I borrow your car?	Borrow my sports car?!
I don't often ask you favours.	I know you drove it off the road.
You said you wouldn't have your car for 12 weeks.	Don't you trust me?
Er, I've got a favour to ask.	Often enough.
And I won't have it for a few weeks?	Another favour to ask?

A Er, I've got a _____ to ask.

B _____ favour to ask?

A I don't _____ ask you favours.

B Often _____ .

A Well, you know my car is _____ the road?

B I know you _____ it off the road.

A And I won't have it for a few _____ ?

B You said you wouldn't have your car for _____ weeks.

A OK, but could I borrow _____ car?

B Borrow my _____ car?!

A I _____ it's a sports car. I've _____ a sports car.

B I've _____ you drive a sports car.

A Don't you _____ me?

B I don't trust your _____ .

6A Pronunciation
Sentence stress

Student A

A You and your partner are looking for an editor for your photography magazine. You have read the CVs of Kylie Rogers and Amelia Lopez and met them informally. <u>Underline</u> the stressed syllables in the sentences about Kylie and Amelia.

B 💬 Work in AB pairs. Take turns sharing the information you have about the candidates using the appropriate stress.

C 💬 Discuss with your partner which of the four candidates should get an interview.

	Kylie Rogers	**Ivan Ivanov**	**Amelia Lopez**	**Claudio Torres**
Current occupation	Kylie is editing a fashion magazine.		Amelia is writing for a photography website.	
Previous occupation	She was a freelance editor.		She was writing for IT magazines.	
Total experience	She's been involved in publishing for five years.		She's worked in publishing for six years.	
Future plans	She's hoping to do an MBA.		She'll be staying in publishing.	
Other information	She's constantly been phoning about the job!		She's had her work published in our magazine.	

✂ -

Student B

A You and your partner are looking for an editor for your photography magazine. You have read the CVs of Ivan Ivanov and Claudio Torres and met them informally. <u>Underline</u> the stressed syllables in the sentences about Ivan and Claudio.

B 💬 Work in AB pairs. Take turns sharing the information you have about the candidates using the appropriate stress.

C 💬 Discuss with your partner which of the four candidates should get an interview.

	Kylie Rogers	**Ivan Ivanov**	**Amelia Lopez**	**Claudio Torres**
Current occupation		Ivan's having a career break.		Claudio is working for a competitor as an editor.
Previous occupation		He was working as a cameraman.		He's always had the same job.
Total experience		He's been in the profession for seven years.		Soon he'll have been working there for ten years.
Future plans		He's been thinking of starting his own magazine.		He's looking for management experience.
Other information		He was asking about the salary.		He's being interviewed by other magazines.

Student A	Student B
1 My team has been beaten 6–0.	1 I needed 60% to pass the test but I got 59%.
2 I've had to walk all the way home.	2 The postman has delivered a really big parcel.
3 I've just won first prize in a crossword competition.	3 I've been waiting in this queue for two hours.
4 My neighbour has just bought a new sports car.	4 I've just spilled coffee all down my shirt.
5 I've passed the last module – finally! I graduate next month.	5 I've just got a phone bill for 500 euros!
6 I've lost my train ticket and the inspector is coming.	6 I think someone is following me …
7 I was driving through a storm and lightning hit my car.	7 I was cycling and a car passed so close it almost hit me.

absolutely devastated	**extremely jealous**	**so surprised**	**really shocked**
completely exhausted	**very frustrated**	**terribly restless**	**absolutely petrified**
totally speechless	**so ashamed**	**extremely embarrassed**	**really annoyed**

minded	minded	raising	warm
heart	narrow	kind	boggling
hair	hearted	breaking	hearted
broken	open	mouth	watering
back	hearted	mind	jaw
hearted	light	half	dropping

🎲🎲	Prediction
2	Someone very _____ is going to help you with a problem you have.
3	A big plan you have won't work out. You may feel _____ but don't let it get to you – it is all for the best.
4	You're about to have a _____ experience … get ready!
5	You're going to hear some surprising news. You'll need to try to be _____ about the situation if you don't want to hurt anyone's feelings.
6	Someone _____ will disagree with your ideas, but don't let them discourage you.
7	Someone you love is going to make a _____ , throwaway remark about you that you will take too seriously.
8	You'll have to do some _____ work but it'll be worth it.
9	A new person in your life may seem _____ but they want something from you.
10	A _____ prospect is coming up, but be careful not to rush into it. It may look appealing, but it's too good to be true.
11	You'll discover something _____ about someone close to you and it'll change your perception of them forever.
12	Your _____ approach to work/study will start to show in the results you get. Try to be more conscientious or there will be consequences.

1 A preposition meaning during the whole of a period of time.

throughout /uː/ /aʊ/

2 You might do this if you have a cold.

cough /ɒ/

3 A way or direction.

route /uː/

4 How you feel when you want what someone else has got.

jealous /e/

5 *Eat* and *write* are verbs, *peace* and *sector* are … .

nouns /aʊ/

6 Not too much and not too little.

enough /ʌ/

7 It comes between *third* and *fifth*.

fourth /ɔː/

8 When you faint, you aren't … .

conscious /e/

9 A common hot starter in restaurants.

soup /uː/

10 To move a liquid from one container to another.

pour /ɔː/

11 The opposite of *north*.

south /aʊ/

12 The adjective of the answer to 11.

southern /ʌ/

13 Uneven and not smooth.

rough /ʌ/

14 Done in a very careful and detailed way.

thorough /e/

15 A word meaning *but*.

though /aʊ/

16 A shirt for a woman.

blouse /aʊ/

17 A study programme.

course /ɔː/

18 A modal verb meaning *ought to*.

should /ʊ/

19 To make contact with your fingers.

touch /ʌ/

20 Another word for *zero*.

nought /ɔː/

The accountant is going to Porto, that's Portugal, to meet some friends.

Trevor Jones, a doctor, is in the first cabin.

The American lady has a birthday today, she's 30.

The person in the last cabin is from South America, Argentina.

Kurt Müller, from Germany, is in cabin 3.

The Romanian passenger going to Germany is travelling light, just a rucksack.

The passenger in cabin 1 is from Birmingham, the UK.

The person in cabin 4, a young woman, is from Romania.

Mariana Gonzalo, who's 47, is in the last cabin, that's cabin number 5.

The 30-year-old has a lot of luggage, four suitcases.

The 22-year-old Romanian is a student, a law student.

Rachel Lopez, American, is in a cabin next to the doctor.

The accountant doesn't have much with him, one sports bag.

The American is going to Odessa, in Ukraine, for a few days.

The German is quite young, 26 years old, and he's an accountant.

The doctor, age 54, is carrying a small suitcase.

The Argentinian, in cabin 5, is going to Waterford, in Ireland.

Diana Moldovan, a 22-year-old, is in a cabin between Kurt Müller and Mariana Gonzalo.

Mariana Gonzalo works in IT, designing and testing software.

The passenger's ticket, that's the doctor's, is to Nice in France.

The person going to Ireland has brought luggage with them, a large suitcase.

The person with the most luggage, four suitcases, works as an engineer.

Student A: Landlord

A You're a landlord of an office space and you're going to negotiate the terms of the rent with a new tenant. Choose three statements in the box to use with implied question intonation.

It's advertised as _____.   _____ is a really good deal.   _____ is a special offer.

That's not what was advertised.   I could make it _____.   I could take _____ euros off.

I can't give it to you for less than _____.   I'd be prepared to accept _____.

B 🗨 Work in AB pairs. Negotiate the terms of the rent with the tenant using the statements you chose in Activity A with implied question intonation. Try and get the best deal possible. Write down the final figures you agree.

	As advertised	Would accept	Final figure	Points
Monthly rent	2,500 euros	2,200 euros		
Deposit	2,000 euros	1,500 euros		
Rental period	32 months +	18 months		

- ✂

Student B: Tenant

A You need to rent some office space and you're going to negotiate the terms of the rent with the landlord. Choose three statements in the box to use with implied question intonation.

I see it was advertised as _____.   It depends on the price.   That's a bit too much.

I'm not sure I can afford it.   I could manage _____.   _____ would be acceptable.

I'd be prepared to offer _____.   _____ sounds reasonable to me.

B 🗨 Work in AB pairs. Negotiate the terms of the rent with the landlord using the statements you chose in Activity A with implied question intonation. Try and get the best deal possible and use appropriate intonation in the implied questions. Write down the final figures you agree.

	As advertised	Could offer	Final figure	Points
Monthly rent	2,500 euros	2,400 euros		
Deposit	2,000 euros	1,800 euros		
Rental period	32 months +	24 months		

- ✂

	Landlord	Tenant
Monthly rent	+ 1 point for every euro over 2,200	+ 2 points for every euro under 2,400
Deposit	+ 1 point for every euro over 1,500	+ 2 points for every euro under 1,800
Rental period	− 20 points for every month under 32	− 30 points for every month over 24

Student A

A Work in AA pairs. Take turns to say the *re-* /riː/ or /rɪ/ words in your crossword.

B 💬 Work in AB pairs. Take turns to ask for and give your clues. Complete the crossword.

Across

1 The council want to _____ the old port area and turn it into a marina.

2 If you want to _____ yourself, have a swim in the cool lake.

10 If we _____ the east side of the city, people might start to move back there.

12 You can plug in your phone over there if you need to _____ it.

Down

3 It's not easy to _____ employees of the right quality. The HR department has a difficult task.

6 We have decided to _____ with our family to London. We're starting the move in October.

7 I have several arguments to _____ my point.

11 We want to _____ the atmosphere of the 1970s so we bought a big disco ball for the party.

(Student A crossword — filled letters)
- 1 Across: REDEVELOP
- 2 Across: REFRESH
- 10 Across: REGENERATE
- 12 Across: RECHARGE
- 13 Across: RE...E

Student B

A Work in BB pairs. Take turns to say the *re-* /riː/ or /rɪ/ words in your crossword.

B 💬 Work in AB pairs. Take turns to ask for and give your clues. Complete the crossword.

Across

5 It would be impossible to _____ this vase, it's unique.

8 If you want to look younger, this cream will _____ your skin in 14 days.

9 Artists managed to _____ the 18th-century painting almost to its original condition.

13 A month after his unfair dismissal, the company agreed to _____ him in his job.

Down

1 I think you should _____ your decision to quit your job. You're not being very sensible.

4 The pilot couldn't _____ control of the jet so he activated the parachute system.

8 At last they are going to _____ that ugly statue from the park.

10 It's time to _____ the airport and make it more attractive.

(Student B crossword — filled letters)
- 5 Across: REPLACE
- 8 Across: REJUVENATE
- 9 Across: RESTORE
- 13 Across: REINSTATE

9C Pronunciation
Sound and spelling: foreign words in English

Student A

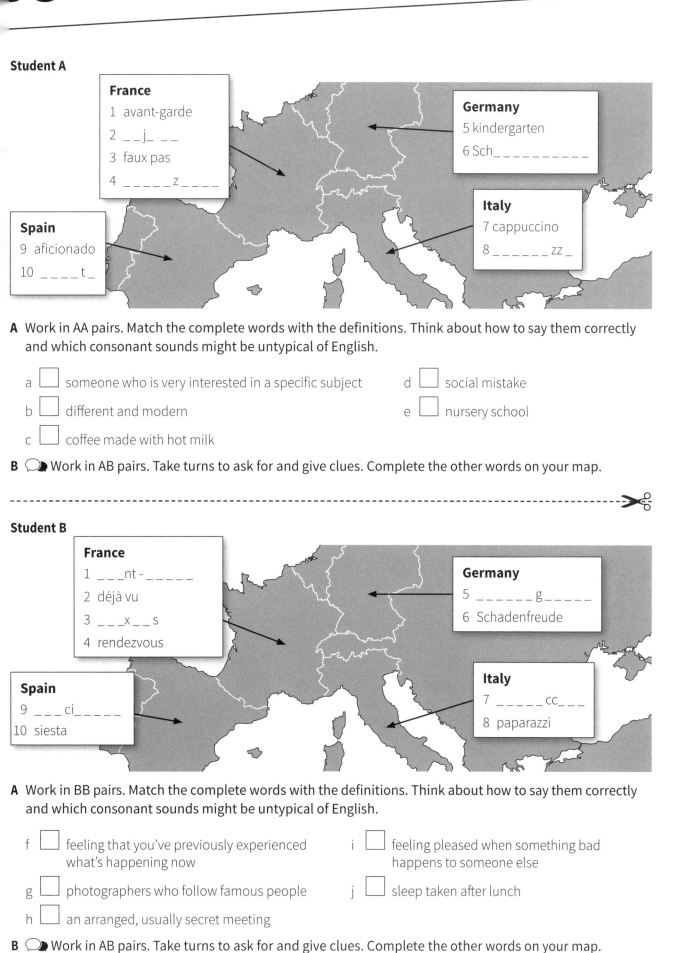

France
1 avant-garde
2 _ _ j_ _ _
3 faux pas
4 _ _ _ _ _ z _ _ _ _

Germany
5 kindergarten
6 Sch_ _ _ _ _ _ _ _ _ _

Spain
9 aficionado
10 _ _ _ _ t _

Italy
7 cappuccino
8 _ _ _ _ _ _ zz _

A Work in AA pairs. Match the complete words with the definitions. Think about how to say them correctly and which consonant sounds might be untypical of English.

a ☐ someone who is very interested in a specific subject
b ☐ different and modern
c ☐ coffee made with hot milk
d ☐ social mistake
e ☐ nursery school

B 💬 Work in AB pairs. Take turns to ask for and give clues. Complete the other words on your map.

- ✂ - - - -

Student B

France
1 _ _ _nt - _ _ _ _ _ _
2 déjà vu
3 _ _ _x _ _ s
4 rendezvous

Germany
5 _ _ _ _ _ _ g_ _ _ _ _
6 Schadenfreude

Spain
9 _ _ _ ci_ _ _ _ _
10 siesta

Italy
7 _ _ _ _ _ cc_ _ _
8 paparazzi

A Work in BB pairs. Match the complete words with the definitions. Think about how to say them correctly and which consonant sounds might be untypical of English.

f ☐ feeling that you've previously experienced what's happening now
g ☐ photographers who follow famous people
h ☐ an arranged, usually secret meeting
i ☐ feeling pleased when something bad happens to someone else
j ☐ sleep taken after lunch

B 💬 Work in AB pairs. Take turns to ask for and give clues. Complete the other words on your map.

10A Pronunciation
Word groups and main stress

A Mark the main stress on these criticisms and regrets. Then tick the criticisms and regrets if you've ever experienced these feelings.

I would much rather have been told the truth.

If I'd known it would be so dangerous, I would never have tried it.

It's about time they did more for young people where I live.

I wish I had made a better impression at the interview.

I ought to have thought more about my family than myself.

It's time we moved to a bigger flat/house.

I might have become a professional if I had had lessons.

I needn't have bothered helping him/her.

I would love to have seen more of the last place I went to on holiday.

I should have trusted my gut instinct.

I ought not to have bought it but I just couldn't resist it.

I wish he/she would stop telling me all their problems.

I would much rather do something I really want to do than work just for the money.

I ought to have checked that everything worked properly before I used it.

If only I had studied harder at school.

B 💬 Work in pairs. Take turns to tell your partner which sentences you ticked and explain the circumstances behind the criticism or regret.

10C Pronunciation
Tone in question tags

Student A

A You've made a new friend online and now you're going to meet them face-to-face. You know some things about him/her already but there are things you're not sure about. Look at the questions you want to ask your friend and prepare tag questions with the appropriate intonation.

Questions to ask	
has always lived in the countryside	?
doesn't feel very comfortable there	✓
job is related to computers	?
would like to work in an office again	✓
plays a lot of computer games	?
watches a lot of cookery programmes	?
is going to run a marathon	✓
will probably improve marathon time	✓

B 💬 Work in AB pairs. You're talking with your friend at a café. Ask them your questions and answer their questions using the information in the table.

Home	small flat in Cambridge, you've lived there for ages you're moving to a house outside town soon
Job	sales manager you do a lot of travelling and don't like that part of the job went to Paris last week
Interests	walking, part of a walking club cycling, prefer off-road
Other	doing a part-time MBA, really useful for work

- ✂ - - -

Student B

A You've made a new friend online and now you're going to meet them face-to-face. You know some things about him/her already but there are things you're not sure about. Look at the questions you want to ask your friend and prepare tag questions with the appropriate intonation.

Questions to ask	
has lived in a flat for a long time	✓
is moving soon	?
enjoys travelling on business	?
went to Paris recently	✓
likes going for walks on their own	?
goes road cycling	?
doing an MBA course	✓
would recommend an MBA course	?

B 💬 Work in AB pairs. You're talking with your friend at a café. Ask them your questions and answer their questions using the information in the table.

Home	used to live in London but renting a cottage in a small village it's a bit remote but you love it
Job	IT specialist started your career in an office now you work from home – great!
Interests	not computer games you like cookery, a big fan of TV cookery programmes
Other	training for a marathon, not sure you'll break your personal record

Board game

Wordpower Unit 5 Idioms: Crime (Teacher's Notes on p.192); **Pronunciation** 4A Sound and spelling: /ʃəs/, /iəs/, /dʒ (Teacher's Notes on p.196) and **Pronunciation** 7C Sound and spelling: *ou* and *ough* (Teacher's Notes on p.198).